320

DEAD FAMOUS

Also by Greg Jenner

A Million Years in a Day: A Curious History of Daily Life,
from Stone Age to Phone Age

DEAD
FAMOUS

*An Unexpected History of Celebrity
from Bronze Age to Silver Screen*

GREG JENNER

WEIDENFELD & NICOLSON

First published in Great Britain in 2020 by Weidenfeld & Nicolson
an imprint of The Orion Publishing Group Ltd
Carmelite House, 50 Victoria Embankment
London EC4Y 0DZ

An Hachette UK Company

1 3 5 7 9 10 8 6 4 2

A CIP catalogue record for this book is
available from the British Library.

ISBN (Hardback) 978 0 2978 6980 1
ISBN (eBook) 978 0 2978 6981 8

Typeset by Input Data Services Ltd, Somerset

Printed and bound in Great Britain by Clays Ltd, Elcograf S.p.A.

MIX
Paper from
responsible sources
FSC® C104740

www.weidenfeldandnicolson.co.uk
www.orionbooks.co.uk

To our darling daughter, Esmé,

Like a superstar diva, you made us wait so long, and arrived in a whirlwind of drama. But it doesn't matter because we'll always be your biggest fans.

With so much love,

Your proud parents xx

Contents

Introduction

On 11 January 2016, I awoke unusually early. Normally I'm an inanimate, bed-hogging lump until at least 9.30 a.m., but this morning was different. After weeks of discussion, and months of preparatory reading, I'd finally been approved to start work on my new book (*this* book!) and I was eager to begin. I bounded downstairs with Tiggerish energy, grabbed my laptop, created a digital folder called 'DEAD FAMOUS', and prepared myself to care deeply about celebrities for the next few years. And then my phone beeped, and everything suddenly stopped. David Bowie was dead.

The announcement pulverised all other news into insignificance. Twitter exploded; my timeline became a torrent of shocked sadness, confusion, heartfelt personal anecdotes, hastily written newspaper obituaries, trite reactions from politicians who thought they should be seen to join in, and an avalanche of fans screaming 'What do you mean he's *dead*?!? His new album came out THREE DAYS AGO!' That last one was the real kicker. *Blackstar* had been released on Bowie's sixty-ninth birthday and was so new that even some diehard fans hadn't heard it yet. Bowie seemed full of life. Indeed, the opening line of *Pitchfork*'s album review still makes me gulp: 'David Bowie has died many deaths, yet he is still with us. He is popular music's ultimate Lazarus . . .' Seventy-two hours later, Bowie's treacherous tumours made a mockery of that headline.

Where other artists might have cherished their rapturous swansong - the farewell performance, the last great interview, the thumbs up from the hospital bed - Bowie allowed fans and critics to judge his final songs on their own merit, without the rosy hue of hagiography. 'What do you reckon, any good?' he seemed to ask us, courageously inviting the critics' claws that would've surely stayed sheathed for a dying man. It was an astonishing exit from a man famed for astonishing exits. In the summer of 1973, he killed off his Ziggy Stardust alter ego live on stage with a farewell rendition of 'Rock'n'Roll Suicide'. Fans were dumbstruck; but so were his bandmates. He'd kept it a secret from everyone. In 2016, Bowie had repeated the trick, stage-managing his own demise so that none of us realised it was even happening. The shock wrong-footed both the public and the media, causing a cascade of mourning that didn't just lament the passing of a hero, but also the scary instability of mortality itself.

On that chilly January morning, I didn't succumb to tears and seismic emotions because I wasn't a huge Bowie aficionado. Not properly, anyway. I loved the hits - 'Life on Mars', 'Space Oddity', 'Heroes', 'Ashes to Ashes' - but I'd missed entire dec-ades of his output. Every time I saw him on TV, or spotted him making ironic movie cameos, I thought: 'Hey, that's David Bowie! He's so interesting, and clever, and cool, I should probably learn everything I can about him', but then I'd get distracted. Neverthe-less, when the news broke, I assumed I knew enough to appreci-ate what the world had just lost. Turns out I was bell-clangingly wrong.

I'd completely underestimated his impact. Bowie was like a moon; beautiful, shadowy, unknowable, ever-changing, and yet with a vast gravity that had pulled the tides of popular culture back and forth; he'd been both pop superstar and avant-garde intellec-tual, weirdo jazz crooner and fist-pumping Glastonbury headliner. He'd starred in iconic movies and made a couple of the greatest rock albums of the twentieth century. And this only started to dawn on me when I switched on the radio and heard my favourite music broadcaster, Lauren Laverne, convert her three-hour BBC show into a Bowie tribute. She didn't just play the hits; Laverne instead invited an audio community to an unplanned funeral, one in which they would be giving the eulogy.

Throughout the programme, fans phoned in requesting rare

songs, and shared how David Bowie's life had contributed to their own. It was a joyous chorus of gratitude: stories of teenage crushes, of exhilarating live gigs, of first kisses, of amusing encounters with the great man himself, of clarifying moments of sexual awareness, of lyrical inspiration in hard times, of fun, of glamour, of art, of rock'n'roll, of life. Bowie's existence had changed these people, and they were profoundly grateful.

But he wasn't just any old singer; people thought he'd possessed exceptional qualities: unerring charisma, prodigious creativity, bewitching beauty, and the endlessly protean ability to transform himself. He was ethereal. Someone on Twitter joked he hadn't died, he'd simply returned to his home planet, as if he were some messianic alien rather than just a gender-fluid musical polymath with a fondness for the saxophone. The newspaper obituaries offered the human flipside. They spoke of his kindness, his taste in books, how uproariously funny he could be, and how quaintly British he was with that sort of modulating mockney accent. The wave of public affection was so deep, I realised that I'd undervalued the emotional power of fame. David Bowie wasn't just a dead celebrity. For many, this was a personal bereavement.

Are you rolling your eyes? Fair enough, for I too was once a cynic. In 1997, when Princess Diana died, I was just about to turn fifteen, and was at the peak of adolescent arrogance. I gazed upon the national weeping and screwed up my face into a curmudgeonly harrumph. 'Sure, it's very sad her kids will grow up without a mum, but why is everyone shrieking in the streets? They've never even met her!' In truth, this was teenage bravado, because I was shocked. On that fateful day, my family was staying with my French grandmother, only a few miles from the crash site, and, when she'd woken us up with the tragic news, we'd simply refused to believe her. 'Princess Diana can't die, don't be ridiculous! Silly old Mamie is going batty!'

Our stubborn denial was a micro-encapsulation of how celebrities function as psychic breeze blocks; they're part of the sturdy foundations upon which we build our identities. Those clickbait

articles lurking at the bottom of the internet are perfect examples
of weaponised celebrity nostalgia: 'Remember that cute kid from
the show you loved in 1998? You won't believe what she looks
like now - CLICK HERE!' These articles get billions of hits from
around the world. We can't help it. Celebrities are our companions
through life - if they're ageing and dying, then so are we.

Britain's Diana-shaped grief spiral was a national howl of many
varied voices - she'd been a unique entity; a celebrity-royal hybrid
who became an avatar for deceased mums, dads, children, pets,
friends, and whatever trauma had been bottled up and buried
deep. She was a lightning rod for personal sadness. But Diana
wasn't just a hollow proxy without her own qualities. Much like
Bowie, she too had shown rare charisma while also being ac-
cessibly normal; she'd been the so-called 'People's Princess'. We
all knew her, we'd watched her wedding day, seen her raise two
children, followed her life in the tabloids, admired her fashion
sense, surveilled her through a spectacular divorce, and speculated
about her new lovers. As Eddie Izzard later noted in a stand-up
routine, her death was akin to your favourite TV show killing off
its lead characters at 3 a.m. on a Monday - 'What?! Has it finished
now? I was watching that!' - Princess Diana was a human box-
set we'd been bingeing on for years. And suddenly she'd been
cancelled.

Celebrity is often decried as superficial vacuity crammed into
glittery trousers; a mind-numbing, money-making sham. And, I'll
hold my hands up, I was probably going to write a snarkier book
until Bowie's death knocked me off-kilter. But in that bubbling
cauldron of grief, I realised just how productive celebrity culture
is: how much it shapes us; how we chart celebrity careers against
our own ambitions; how we devour the gossip with a mix of ironic
detachment and zealous emotional investment; and how useful it
is as a social glue that binds us together in voyeuristic fascination.
Many of us live out our entire lives in the refracted glow of other
people's shimmering stardom. And despite all the huffy bluster,
and all pretensions to immunity, even the staunchest cynic would

lose their cool if Tom Cruise sat down next to them on a plane, offered a handshake, and said, 'Hi, I'm Tom.'

Celebrity is one of the defining phenomena of our age, but this book is about where it came from, rather than its current state. If you've started reading in the hope of learning how to be a super-star, you'll definitely pick up some handy pointers, but it's not a wannabe's blueprint. If you love reading glossy magazines filled with beautiful people, or you squeal in excitement at the lurid adventures of reality TV stars, then you'll find plenty of historical comparisons to snack upon. Indeed, I hope you'll be convinced that the rhythms of twenty-first-century celebrity culture aren't new at all.

However, as the dutiful historian trussed up in my ceremonial tweed jacket (patches on the elbows, natch), I'm also going to try to convince you that the past *was* different. Some of the things mentioned in this book wouldn't apply today, and much of modern celebrity fizzes with an energy that was impossible to produce in the past. But celebrity isn't new. It can't be. I've gazed at the vibrant, verdant foliage and, noticing the huge spread of its canopy, have gone digging for its deep-buried roots. Much like the joke about Hollywood actresses, celebrity can't be as young as it claims to be. No tree grows that big, that fast.

Full disclosure: until a few years ago, I'd never bought a celebrity gossip magazine, didn't watch reality TV, and believed there was only one Kardashian. Then I learned they're a whole K-branded family. And then I learned some Kardashians are also Jenners, which really confuses Kardashian fans who find me on Twitter and assume I must be Kendall Jenner's weird British cousin. I see them pop up in my timeline, I start the clock, and then I start tweeting arcane bits of historical trivia until they unfollow me. My record is fifty seconds. But, of course, I'm not a Kardashian; my bum is a deeply disappointing spectacle.

If I'm not an inveterate celebrity-watcher, how did I end up writing this book? Well, I'd intended to write the first biography of Bill Richmond, who was liberated from American slavery and

became Britain's first black sporting celebrity in the early 1800s.*
That didn't pan out. But I realised I'd been calling Richmond a
celebrity without checking if such a concept had existed in 1811.
As I began to interrogate the notion, I noticed that a whole
field of scholarship had opened up over this exact territory. I'd
accidentally blundered my way into the vanguard of a new historical movement, so I decided to pick up a banner and keep
marching.

Until very recently, sociologists argued that *celebrity* was invented just over 100 years ago, in the flickering glimmer of early
Hollywood. There had been *fame* before, sure, but the democratising technology of cinema transformed that into a new thing: *celebrity*. This is still a commonly held opinion, but a new generation of
historians have pushed the genesis point back way beyond Hollywood; first to Oscar Wilde, then to Dickens, then Byron, then Sarah
Siddons and Jean-Jacques Rousseau, then David Garrick. A few
historians now teeter on the edge of the seventeenth century, and
yet still find those familiar scorch marks where great lives burned
bright. There's even a wonderful ongoing debate about whether
medieval saints might be considered celebrities, while the classicist
Robert Garland has made an intriguing case for their existence in
ancient Rome and Greece. So, celebrity invented in Hollywood?
Pah! No way, mate.

That brings us to the obvious question: when *did* celebrity
begin? I'm a natural coward, fleeing confrontation like a squirrel
flees a Rottweiler, but, after four years of research, I've found
myself convinced that it began in the early 1700s. Having accrued
1.4 million words of notes - by having devoured a mix of primary
sources and a vast trove of scholarship by brilliant historians (without whom this book would've been impossible) - this book is my
synthesis of celebrity's overall trajectory, using cherry-picked case
studies to speak for the wider trends.

---

* As it happens, soon after, an excellent biography, *Richmond Unchained*, was
written by Luke G. Williams.

History books are often straightforward chronologies, but I found that many celebrities adopted multiple, overlapping approaches to career maintenance: working hard to get discovered; doing interviews; being seen at big events; wearing distinctive clothes; controlling their image; utilising/resisting how their bodies were perceived; embarking on romances and feuds with fellow celebrities; attempting bold publicity stunts; trying to influence their coverage in the media; monetising their fame, or stopping others from doing it to them; inviting scandal, or desperately trying to suppress it; giving their fans access to their privacy while attempting to maintain a private life. These tactics cropped up so often that it seemed useful to make them the thematic keystones for each chapter, and you'll see that many of the celebrities pop up in multiple chapters, as proof of how multifaceted celebrity is.

If the book's structure is unorthodox, so is the range. My research scope has been very wide - terrifyingly so - and I was aghast at how much material there was to pick from. With so much ground to cover, and with classical *fame* extending back to the distant Bronze Age, I've drawn a demarcation line at 1950. This is roughly the threshold at which TV and pop music first appeared. Everything beyond this anniversary has been extensively covered by other writers, and you know about Elvis, and The Beatles, and Marilyn Monroe already, don't you? If not, well, there are wonderful books on all of them. My aim is to tell you about the megastars you didn't even know existed.

Of course, it was constantly tempting to compare the shiny starlets of today with those of the past, but - save for a few occasions - I'll mostly let you do that for yourselves, because celebrity culture moves too damn fast. The average pop career lasts just four to six years[1] and predicting longevity is tricky. I once saw a TV documentary forecasting the future presidency of Britney Spears, and though President Trump has since lowered the bar to ankle height, and then repeatedly set it on fire, that documentary naively assumed exponential fame was inevitable for a nubile popstar, forgetting that her appeal was built on youth. Alas, sex appeal often fades like our favourite pair of jeans. I very much doubt Britney will ever get the nuclear codes.

Youth isn't essential to success, but I recommend thinking of celebrity as a form of harmless radioactivity. Celebs radiate awesome biology-altering power. They can't cure cancer, or turn fish into terrifying multi-ocular mutants, but place a devoted fan near their idol and you'll expect to see such symptoms as sweating, increased heart rate, gabbling, stunned silence, shrill screaming, hysterical crying, and uncontrollable lust. But that power wanes; the radioactive half-life kicks in. Though some can go the distance, not least the narrow-hipped, geriatric strut machine that is Mick Jagger, often the passage of time renders the former sex god into little more than an inert fleshbag in fancy togs. While the same fan, now many years older, may still be excited to meet a former hero, the heart palpitations will be gentler and other passers-by will simply shrug and shout: 'Hey, didn't you use to be famous . . .?'

Oh, and one last thing. You may *think* you know what a celebrity is, because I thought I did too. But trying to formally define it was like wrestling an octopus. Every time I grappled with an idea, another seven would curl menacingly around my throat. Authors are meant to be authoritative, unapologetic, and in control of their arguments, but I think it's exciting to admit that a popular phenomenon so fundamental to our culture, and one obsessively consumed by billions, is more slippery than a fresh-caught eel. I'll openly admit that Chapter 3, where I disentangle *celebrity* from *fame* and *renown*, is where I expect to be proven wrong, probably by someone who, shortly afterwards, will find themselves also proven wrong. All considered, I actually find that rather thrilling. The wonderful thing about history is that it's constantly changing.

So, with caveats aside, here's my definition of a celebrity which I'll be using throughout the book:

CELEBRITY (noun): A unique persona made widely known to the public via media coverage, and whose life is publicly consumed as dramatic entertainment, and whose commercial brand is profitable for those who exploit their popularity, and perhaps also for themselves.

Okay, with that lodged in your mind, it's time to begin our rummage through the annals of celebrity history. And I'd like to begin with the extraordinary story of my favourite historical celebrity; a man who, despite being a raging prat and a transatlantic scandal magnet, has somehow seduced me into rooting for him, some two centuries after his chaotic peak. Please allow me to introduce you to Edmund Kean, the unlikeliest of superstars . . .

Chapter 1: Getting Discovered

The long road to fame

With ankles swollen and heels slapping against the unforgiving road, Edmund and Mary Kean trudged out of Birmingham. Ahead of them were 178 miles of purgatorial pathway, stretching all the way to Swansea, and they'd have to cover every inch on foot. It was June 1809 and the summer sun sizzled their skin. Progress was slow. He was encumbered by their few worldly possessions; she by the child growing in her belly. Unlike Joseph of Nazareth, Edmund had failed to rustle up a donkey for his pregnant Mary. But she was in love. Her charismatic new beau was eight years her junior, and he had charm, he had verve, he had . . . well, sod-all money. *Mrs Edmund Kean* - it had a nice ring to it; but, alas, probably a lot nicer than the ring on her finger.

A clever Irish girl with a good education, Mary had crushed her parents' hopes that she would become governess to some precious child of privilege to instead join the theatre, where she'd fallen for a penniless actor. Newly-weds often start married life with the romanticised austerity of second-hand furniture, but this wasn't a newly-wed romance. It was Act 1 of a quiet tragedy. Mary had married an alcoholic screwup, a wandering actor whose boyhood had been scarred by tragedy. Edmund's father had died by suicide, his actress mother - Ann Carey - had succumbed to prostitution to keep the wolf from the door. With absent parents, the boy had been raised on the stage by his aunt, Charlotte Tidswell, and uncle, Moses Kean, who'd administered their backstage parenting in between rehearsals and performances. But, for all their affection, there had been an unfixable crack in his temperament. He was impulsive, unreliable, and prone to doing a runner; he'd often been found sleeping up a tree, like a runaway cat.

Mary had married Edmund when he was in his early twenties, but puberty had misfired – the growth spurt had been more a splutter. He was small, and that had forced him down the path of juggling, tumbling, and cartwheeling. He was a proficient harlequin, and knew his way around a comedy pratfall, but he craved the role of tragedian. He longed to glide around the stage with elegant grace, but leading men were handsome with mellifluous voices and faces like soft-chiselled Roman statues. That wasn't Edmund. He was funny looking – not exactly 'Steve Buscemi funny looking', but squat and dark-haired, somewhat sharp-featured. His voice rasped rather than enraptured. Perhaps his only truly alluring characteristics were the dark, flashing eyes that gazed out with angry energy. There was definitely *something* intriguing about him, but the spectre of failure seemed to haunt his face.

In his youth, there had been a slight brush with fame, when his mother had advertised her scrawny teenager as a boy genius, the London playbills falsely promoting him as 'the celebrated theatrical child, Edmund Carey, not yet eleven years old'. Making the most of his underdeveloped frame was a useful lie, as was the story he'd started telling himself about his lineage. It seems Aunt Charlotte had once embarked on an affair with the illustrious Duke of Norfolk, and her role as surrogate mum seems to have confused an impressionable Edmund into assuming he was their bastard love child. In which case, noble excellence coursed through his veins! He fervently bought into this delusion, which is perhaps why the clowning roles scalded his ego. He was better than that.

The walk to Swansea was the latest failure born of brittle arrogance. It had come after yet another casting snub in Birmingham, whereupon he'd vanished to the nearest tavern to waterboard his sorrows in a gallon of booze, a habit that later drove Mary to the edge of despair. This time, he'd emerged from his epic hangover with a plan. He'd told the theatre manager into which orifice to cram his crappy role, as he'd found a better job in Swansea. What's more, he'd even convinced his new boss to advance his wages, so he could settle his debts. But the cost of boozy oblivion had proved steeper than expected, and every penny of that advance was already owed to the tutting Brummie landlord. Edmund and his pregnant wife had to walk to Swansea on an empty purse, sleeping under the stars like vagrants. At the 100-mile mark, he'd had to write ahead, begging for another advance to cover their meals. To clear his debts, he arrived indebted. It wasn't much of a plan. But Swansea was a fresh start and a new opportunity. At last, could this be the making of him?

In the Hollywood movie that someone should definitely make,* the trek to Swansea will be the moment of revelation, Kean's Damascene delivery from bitter failure. The fevered Welsh audience will scream in acknowledgement of his genius, and then he'll go to London and wear fancy hats and meet the king, and be happy forever. That's how stories work. But the reality of history isn't nearly as formulaic. There was more suffering ahead. In fact, Edmund Kean's life continued to get progressively worse for another five agonising years before it suddenly got miraculously better.

After Swansea petered out, he was back on the road, now with a baby in his arms, dragging his family on tours of Ireland, Scotland, and England, and emerging with very little to show for it. Sometimes they were forced into begging in the streets. In York, it was only the generosity of a stranger that saved the family from starvation, and funded passage back to London. All the while, his pleading letters to London's theatre managers went unanswered, and his performances varied wildly in quality as the alcohol pickled his wits.† Four years of being coupled to this human train wreck

---

* No, but seriously, *please* make this film. And if you do, call me?

† There are many drunk Edmund Kean anecdotes. I'm especially fond of the one where he gets so pissed he forgets buying a yacht – an actual yacht! But perhaps the best is the time Kean failed to show up for a performance, forcing the theatre owner to play King Charles I instead. As the crowd grew restless with the unprepared understudy, a voice yelled out: 'Well done, my boy, well done!' In an act of outrageous farce, Edmund had dragged himself in from the pub, stumbled up the stairs, and had slumped into one of the boxes, apparently with the intention of watching his own play. He was fired. Obviously.

proved exhausting for Mary, who watched her alcoholic beau flail through life while their eldest child, Howard (named in honour of Edmund's apocryphal dad, the Duke of Norfolk), became increasingly poorly. She wrote to a friend: 'I saw nothing but misery before me . . . Little Howard is very delicate, the Measles has weakened him very much. Mr Kean's aunt has been trying to prevent his living with me - Oh! You know not half what I am suffering.'

The Keans were on the road to Hell. But, finally, a dollop of luck smeared itself upon their worried brows. Edmund landed some leading roles on the Exeter regional circuit, and there was the odd occasion when Shakespeare's classics needed a leading man. Drunk or not, he knew those plays inside out. It was on one of his better nights that a certain Dr Drury, Harrow School's retired headmaster, was in the audience. Impressed by the short-statured tragedian with bewitching eyes, Drury sent his recommendation to London's prestigious Drury Lane theatre* - one of the two foremost playhouses in the land - and they dispatched their general manager, Samuel Arnold, to take a look. Arnold agreed. There was definitely *something* intriguing about this simmering misfit.

A contract was written up, and Edmund happily bit their hand off. But then came the snag. Edmund had also just accepted a contract from the lowlier London Olympic Theatre, and the proprietor, Mr Elliston, refused to break it. Edmund had tumbled into the classic joke about two buses coming along at once; he'd boarded the slower one and was now staring longingly out of the rear window as the sleeker bus overtook them. Was his explosion into the big time about to be extinguished beneath a mountain of paperwork? It felt like his rock bottom, to which Fate seemingly said: 'Hand me that pickaxe, I can go deeper.' Within days, their sickly little boy was dead.

Mary and Edmund were devastated. Beset by grief and financial uncertainty, they crashed at Aunt Charlotte's house - penniless and morose - waiting for the two theatres to thrash out a deal. It

---

* The fact they were both named Drury was a weird coincidence.

took weeks of stubborn negotiation; all the while Edmund hung
uselessly around the Drury Lane theatre, prowling the wings like
a malevolent imp haunting a gothic cathedral. He wasn't a popular
guest. One of the actors noted 'the little man with the great capes
is here again',[1] joking that he was swamped by his dramatic fashion
choices, while another actor blanked him entirely. The superstar
actress Sarah Siddons, who we'll meet later in the chapter, cruelly
mocked him. These condescending jibes fuelled his resentment.
He was desperate to enter a place where he clearly wasn't wanted.

Eventually, compensation was arranged, and it was decided that
Edmund's Drury Lane wages would subsidise the Olympic's lost
earnings; his £8 pay packet was cut to £6. It didn't matter. Finally,
after a lifetime of trying, he would play to the most discerning of
audiences, in Britain's premier playhouse, and in his preferred
role as tragedian. This was the dream. There was no higher peak
to climb. At least, that was the idea. In truth, the Drury Lane theatre – though dignified by royal warrant, and one of only three
London theatres officially licensed to stage proper plays – was in
crisis. After burning down in 1809, the lavish rebuild had plunged
the business into debt. Audiences had also drifted away to the
rival Covent Garden Theatre which boasted the refined talents of
John Philip Kemble, brother to Sarah Siddons. Drury Lane was
drowning.

And so, as we begin the task of uncovering how a wandering
failure could become a megastar, here we find the most powerful
fulcrum in Edmund Kean's rise. He was levered out of poverty,
and deposited in the shining hall of celebrity, because of sheer
financial desperation. The contract offer wasn't so much shrewd
talent-spotting by a far-sighted visionary as it was a panicky, chuck-
stuff-at-the-wall punt by the Drury Lane committee members; the
theatrical equivalent of promoting a competent busker to Vegas
headliner. Maybe this intense little man with the strange voice and
burning eyes was their salvation? Bizarrely, it worked. Within a
week, Edmund Kean was the talk of the town. Within a month he
was a bona fide superstar.

I'll be honest, I absolutely love this story. I'm probably meant to be the dispassionate narrator, but Edmund Kean's triumph is so improbable that I still feel the urge to root for him, even though he was a total prick to his family, cheated on his wife, became progressively incapable of remembering his lines, alienated his closest friends, and later caused a literal riot in Boston by being a spoiled diva. Regardless of his extensive flaws, his sudden transformation from abject, itinerant poverty to London's hottest talent is the most thrilling example of that bizarre metamorphosis we call 'getting your big break'; a sequence of events in which opportunity turns a nobody into a somebody, and they smash their way into public consciousness to arrive, shiny and new, as an object of human fascination. As a *celebrity*. It's a brilliant story that hums with romantic power; the sort of fairy tale we love to tell kids about the importance of never giving up.

But perhaps I've let my giddy Kean fandom get the better of me. Does celebrity *really* require transformation from nobody into somebody? Do all celebs start out in obscurity? Well, not necessarily . . .

Fame thrust upon 'em

Edmund Kean owed his career to William Shakespeare, and it's to the famous Stratfordian that scholars of celebrity also owe plenty. There's a celebrated line in *Twelfth Night* that goes: 'Some are born great, some achieve greatness, and some have greatness thrust upon 'em.' It's an oft-quoted observation, and it forms the basis of the sociologist Chris Rojek's typology of modern celebrity.[2] Here's my simplified summary of his categories:

1. *Ascribed celebrity* - people are born already famous (e.g. the child of movie stars).
2. *Achieved celebrity* - fame requiring a 'breakout', earned through talent and effort (e.g. a star athlete).
3. *Attributed celebrity* - reputation externally applied to the

person by the public or the media. It's either positive or negative fame imposed without the celebrity's consent or intent (e.g. a notorious criminal, or a venerated religious figure).

This category trio describes *how* a celebrity debuts into public consciousness. A few celebrities - such as the children of existing stars, or royalty - are made famous by association, and, even as kids, photos of them stomping around in tiny welly boots will shift thousands of gossip magazines. Most celebrities, however, find fame in adulthood: they intentionally *achieve* celebrity through a combination of talent and self-promotion, or they are flung headlong into sudden fame by the media/public arbitrarily *attributing* notoriety to them.

But here's a thought. Could a celebrity tick all three boxes? Well, actually, yes! And my proof, dear reader, is Miley Cyrus. Now, I'll admit that I'm nervous about using a modern reference because, by the time you read this, she may no longer be famous; she might be a yoga teacher, or a digital avatar uploaded to a cloud computing network. Maybe you're a robot too? Hello, future dystopia! I'm veering off topic . . . Let's just agree that Miley Cyrus is a popstar with a pulse. Arguably, she first came to prominence as the child of a celebrity, her dad being the bounteously bemulleted country singer Billy Ray Cyrus. Plus, her godmother is Dolly Parton. This double whammy of illustrious lineage lands her in Category 1: *ascribed celebrity*. She was born famous.

But if she'd been a talentless klutz who couldn't sing, act, dance or memorise her lines, then she never would've made it as a Disney child star, aged eleven, in the smash-hit TV show *Hannah Montana*, which also launched her successful solo music career. Her young audience adored Cyrus's own performing abilities, their fandom wasn't contingent on the foot-stomping catchiness of 'Achy Breaky Heart', so her career is largely owed to hard work and natural talent. That's *achieved* celebrity. However, Billy Ray Cyrus played a main character in the show, as did the very famous

Dolly Parton, so part of the programme's success was its ability to frame Miley Cyrus within an existing celebrity context. Her family connections gave it oomph. Her celebrity was both *ascribed* and *achieved*.

Bearing in mind we're talking about a sweet-smiling Christian teen fronting a Disney show about a sweet-smiling Christian pop-star, Cyrus's fourth solo album, *Bangerz*, was one hell of a departure. Although she'd already embraced a sexier look in the promo for album number three, sporting leather boots and a high-waisted leather leotard, this was largely in keeping with the 'all grown up now' model that transitions famous girls into famous women. But *Bangerz* was a wild escalation that caught everyone off guard. Cyrus didn't just dial up the sexy, she went nuclear, reinventing herself as an off-the-rails, hip-hop-loving hedonist who partied hard, posed nude, wore outrageous costumes, twerked her buttocks into an older man's crotch, simulated masturbation on stage, and bestrode giant inflatable penises. It wasn't so much a sexual awakening as a full-blown radicalisation.

Whereas Britney Spears and Christina Aguilera had also drawn flak in the 90s when they'd first started writhing around in their PVC catsuits and leather chaps, at least their Disney TV days had been long behind them. By contrast, in 2013, America's impressionable kids were still avidly watching repeats of Hannah Montana cheerfully belting out songs about being an 'Ordinary Girl'; all the while Miley Cyrus was on stage pretending to give a blowjob to a dancer in a Bill Clinton mask.* One can only imagine the epic range of swearing heard in the Disney boardroom that week.

Inevitably, Cyrus was vociferously demonised by conservative media outlets for her pernicious immorality and for leading vulnerable youth astray. She was a twenty-first-century Socrates in hotpants; a Socra-*tease*, if you will. Cyrus was perceived as a threat to others. The big debate in liberal, left-leaning discourse was about whether Cyrus was a threat to herself: was she a sex-positive

---

* Yes, that actually happened.

feminist asserting her freedom after years under the Disney yoke? Or a vulnerable victim of some secret, cynical Svengali forcing her onto the torrid path of psychological meltdown and career destruction? Liberation or exploitation – place your bets! Happily, as I write this, Miley Cyrus seems a well-adjusted twenty-seven-year-old with a flourishing music and acting career, suggesting she'd been in control all along. Phew.*

But here's the thing: even if she'd been deliberately provoking outrage with her new image, how the conservative media chose to portray her was their choice, not hers. Regardless of her intention, Miley Cyrus's years of positive fame were stripped away and transformed into negative notoriety. Hannah Montana was dead, and 'Miley' was apparently the demonic succubus who'd possessed her soul. This new identity was reported as a novel phenomenon – some terrible contagion from which kids had to be protected. The scandalised huffing and puffing also introduced her to those who hadn't seen the TV show or heard her earlier albums, including me. The media frenzy made her famous anew, to new audiences, for being something new. To some she was Billy Ray's daughter; to some she was Hannah Montana; and to some she was a terrifying sex terrorist/empowered young woman. She straddled Rojek's three categories of *ascribed*, *achieved* and *attributed* celebrity, and she did it in leopard-print, arseless chaps. Classic Miley.

Rojek's system is useful, but Miley Cyrus reveals how categories of fame can awkwardly overlap. Indeed, so much of celebrity theory leaves scholars scratching their heads and wondering where the edges are; even the idea of *celebrity* itself is maddeningly complex to define, hence I've parked it in Chapter 3, to give you a bit of a run-up before we tackle the hard stuff. I'll pursue *attributed* celebrity in Chapter 2, focusing on people whose status was thrust upon them: either as an exciting, enjoyable novelty or as a live

---

* Okay, shortly after I wrote this sentence, Miley Cyrus announced the breakup of her marriage. But that's not so unusual in Celebrityland, and it appears to be an amicable split.

grenade which detonated white-hot shrapnel into their faces. But, in this chapter, I want to concentrate on those who *achieved* fame deliberately: the wannabes and dreamers who seized their chance when it came, no matter how long they had to wait for it. And so, we return to Edmund Kean - a man whose overnight stardom required years of painful incubation.

Some of the celebs in this book were so bursting with energy that, had I built a time machine to go back and thwart them at their breakthrough moment, they still would've found another way to get famous. But Kean fascinates me because he might just have easily died in a ditch while trudging miserably to his latest short-term gig. Fame never seemed likely, let alone inevitable. In the movie *Sliding Doors*, we see two parallel realities for Gwyneth Paltrow's character: one where she hops onto the train before the doors slam shut, and one where she arrives moments too late. A single moment dramatically alters her destiny. But Kean's story is so unlikely because his fame needed a series of doors to slide open at exactly the right moment. Amazingly, that's what he got.

All the world's a stage

When we last left him, Kean was about to make his London debut after an agonising few months. Torn apart by fresh grief for his dead son, wounded by years of failure, inflated by delusions of nobility, angry at the other actors who mocked him - Edmund Kean took to the stage in January 1814 to play one of Shakespeare's most compelling characters, Shylock, the Jewish moneylender whose complexity dominates *The Merchant of Venice*. From the outset his performance was radical, even the opening line had the small crowd pricking up their ears. January's cold skies had dumped snow on the metropolis and few had tramped through the dirty slush, but those who'd braved the cold were rewarded by a transfixing performance.

Kean howled and roared, then whispered and lamented; his gestures were frenzied and bold, his eyes were crazed. The atmosphere in the theatre was electric, the audience screamed their approval and clapped feverishly. William Oxberry, one of his cast-mates, later recalled with astonishment: 'How the devil so few of them kicked up such a row was marvellous!'[3] With all his lines delivered, the play was still going on when Kean bolted out the back door, skidded wildly through the slushy streets, and burst into Aunt Charlotte's house with the heroic words: 'Mary, you shall ride in your carriage, and Charlie shall go to Eton.' He had done it. At long-bloody-last, success!

You might well ask: if Edmund Kean was such a brilliant actor, why wasn't he *already* famous? Surely great talent always shines through, no? In later life, Kean wondered the same thing, confessing to a Drury Lane committee member, Douglas Kinnaird: 'I have often acted the third act of *Othello*, in the same manner as now calls down such thunders, when the whole house laughed.' Why London suddenly declared his genius when the provinces had shrugged was mysterious. Maybe the fancy new theatre's acoustics better amplified his harsh voice? Perhaps he benefited from the sudden popularity of literary Romanticism and the fashion for aesthetic *feeling*, at that exact moment being dished out by Lord Byron, the devilishly passionate, hot, young sex pirate? Maybe it was just thrilling to see a performer hurl himself at a role with such demented gusto. He was also, presumably, not drop-dead drunk for once.

Whatever the reason, Edmund Kean wowed that audience. But there were just a few hundred playgoers in the theatre, and yet he was famous within the week. How did he conquer all of London so fast? Well, not only was he benefiting from Drury Lane's desperate casting experiment, but he also got lucky with the audience. One of the souls who'd ignored the snowfall was a young journalist named William Hazlitt. Later to become a brilliant essayist and critic, on that night he was just a junior reporter for the *Morning Chronicle* with a deep love of Shakespeare. In fact, Kean had lucked out - there were two journalists in that night - the other wrote for the *Morning Post* - and both critics filed rapturous write-ups of his performance: 'For voice, eye, action, and expression, no actor has come out for many years at all equal to him. The applause, from the first scene to the last, was general, loud and uninterrupted . . .'[4]

From an opening night seen by a measly crowd, the disseminating power of the printing press, and the reputation-making power of the judicious critic, meant thousands were aware of Edmund Kean by the following day. The two reviews were so extraordinary, Londoners immediately had to investigate the cause of the fuss for themselves. The next week, Kean strode out onto the stage before a packed house. Every paper had sent a critic, apart from *The Times*, which staunchly preferred John Philip Kemble's plummy conservatism. The collective verdict was unanimous. Kean was brilliant. To confirm it wasn't a fluke, he soon after gave his legendary performance as Richard III - a tour de force of sociopathic rage, and a role that Kemble had struggled to master. Kean thus bested his established rival, claiming top spot for himself. The accolades poured in.

After years of wandering the desert, of regional theatres and begging in the streets, Edmund Kean had been propelled to exalted stardom in barely a month. Across the capital, his name was uttered in amazement at dinner tables and card tables. Lord Byron couldn't contain his Kean fandom in gushing letters to his friends, while artists debated Kean at the Royal Academy club - was he just the latest fad or a once-in-a-generation talent? With the notable exception of Emperor Napoleon Bonaparte, who was weeks away from being booted off the French throne by British and allied forces, no other person generated such fascination in the spring of 1814. Kean's box office takings soared; crowds queued outside the theatre long before admission time, then elbowed and shoved their way in, desperately scrambling to get the best seats. Kean was a sensation. He was a *star*![5]

A star is born

Star - a word we use so frequently. Big-budget movies cast charismatic stars in the lead roles; TV shows have main stars and guest

stars; supreme athletes are sports stars; gorgeous autotuned singers are popstars; sexual athletes with oversized sexy bits are porn-
stars; and even ordinary members of the public are thrust into the
limelight as reality stars. In our world, stardom simply means pop
culture visibility, coupled with a unique, marketable brand. As long
as they have a *thing* that makes them *'them'*. Such generous usage is
fine, but it suggests everyone famous occupies the same echelon of
cultural importance, and that's not really true.

Let's take the biggest cinema performers: in the 1910s, Hollywood studios first developed the idea of movie stars whose charismatic fame would ensure eager audiences and box office success.
The film critic James Monaco later argued that 'actors play roles,
stars play themselves'.[6] If a friend invites you to see a new film, and
your first instinct is: 'Who's in it?' instead of 'What's it about?', then
that's movie stardom at work. It's the cult of personality over plot.
We knew what we were getting from an Arnold Schwarzenegger
film, regardless of what character he was playing. Stuff exploded,
people got punched, guns were fired, Arnie uttered some iconic,
cheesy quip, and we chomped our popcorn in record time. Movie
stars, then, are meant to be box office heavyweights; guarantors of
commercial success.

More recently, this idea has been splintered into a hierarchy
used to measure the financial power of a celeb. Perched at the pinnacle are the A-listers - previously known as movie stars - who can
reliably turn a profit from a $100m production budget. They're not
A-list if they can't carry a mediocre film to success.* By contrast,
B-listers have plenty of fans and we'd be thrilled to meet one in an
airport, but they're not really a true star. Studios would be gambling by printing their name on the top left of the poster, unless
it's a superhero movie with an established fanbase (such franchises
reliably transform B-listers into A-listers).

Instead, B-listers will play the best friend, or the angry prick

---

* I love Hugh Jackman, but *The Greatest Showman* is cheesier than a fondue
menu.

of a boss, or the cackling villain who gets chucked out of a heli-copter and eaten by a shark while the hero snogs the love inter-est. C-listers, of course, are probably lead actors on a popular TV show. D-listers are TV actors and screen personalities whose face is weirdly familiar, but we don't know what from; they're 'that guy from that thing'. Recently, crueller observers have crowbarred in Z-listers as the 'famous for being famous' also-rans, who squeeze every drop from their fifteen minutes of fame.

This all feels very twentieth century. However, it wasn't the film industry that first invented stardom. One hundred years before Charlie Chaplin was a global sensation, *star* was starting to appear in theatrical advertisements and referred exclusively to actors of truly extraordinary talent. The idea was rooted in the works of earlier writers like Chaucer, Shakespeare, and Molière, who'd in-voked the stars shimmering in the heavens as metaphors for eter-nal beauty. Indeed, Geoffrey Chaucer - writing in the late 1300s - gave us the words *starry* and *stellified* (a gorgeous word meaning a human transformed into a star), but the notion was already an-cient. The Roman poet Ovid tells in his *Metamorphoses* of Jupiter ordering Venus to turn the soul of a murdered Julius Caesar into a 'bright star'.[7] This was lofty poetry based on hardcore astronomy - in 44 BCE, a comet had shone in the sky during a festival dedi-cated to the murdered Caesar, and it became known to Romans as 'Caesar's Comet' or the 'Julian Star'.[8]

Fittingly, the theatre historian Clara Tuite has shown that the first use of *star* in an acting context arose around the time of the Great Comets of 1811 and 1819, which provoked wide coverage of meteorological and astronomical science.[9] And so, in the age of Romanticism - an aesthetic movement underpinned by awestruck wonder at the natural world - celebrities also began to be spoken of as natural phenomena; they were human comets, blazing through the theatre, and to gaze at these meteors was a breathtaking delight. Whereas the Romans made stardom a posthumous transformation, the Romantic era afforded such privilege to the living.

Edmund Kean was a brilliant storm cracking the sky with rolling thunder and, in the words of Samuel Taylor Coleridge, watching him was like watching Shakespeare illuminated by sudden 'flashes of lightning'. Meanwhile, Lady Caroline Lamb recalled meeting her future lover Lord Byron with these words: 'Should I go up to my room and tidy myself before confronting him as I was? No, my curiosity was too great and I rushed in to be introduced to this portent.' Byron the portent – he was no ordinary man, he was some divine omen! A blend of devilish sin and natural genius, his intense fame was rich with both theological and astronomical meaning. That's a proper star!

Start 'em young

Edmund Kean's overnight celebrity was rare and strange, but he'd paid his dues tenfold. On the face of it, we might expect child stars to have dodged such a long apprenticeship, but even they had to mount momentum-building publicity campaigns to break through to mass audiences.

In 1803, an angelic boy captured hearts when he took to the stage and earned himself the nickname 'the Young Roscius', a homage to ancient Rome's finest thespian. Yet the success of this 'heaven-born constellation' – his name was William Henry West Betty, but he was commonly known as 'Master Betty' – lay not just in talent, but also circumstance. Though English-born, he'd grown up in Ireland and in 1803 his world was cast into turmoil by the outbreak of the Irish Rebellion, led by Robert Emmet, against British rule. It was a scary time, and the terrified authorities slammed a curfew into place. The theatres shut down. Society barricaded its doors. Civic life froze. It was in this climate of fear that Betty's father somehow managed to talk up his son's patriotic appeal. Might not a powerful play, with a charming young lead, unite the Unionists and see off the nationalist threat? Well, perhaps.

The theatres were cautiously reopened, but only if little Master Betty was stomping across the stage. Suddenly the eleven-year-old was the focus of intense attention. Was he a good actor? Maybe!

But – as his biographer Jeffrey Kahan points out[10] – it's pretty easy being the number one attraction when you're the *only* attraction. Also, Betty's dad probably bribed a few critics to ensure good reviews, a promotional scam known as puffing. Every little helps. Having successfully charmed loyalists in Belfast and Dublin, they realised young Master Betty was on to a winner.

Next came the Scottish tour, where the boy won over crowds by donning kilt and sporran; the wearing of highland dress had been illegal until 1782, so this potent symbolism thrilled Scottish patriots. With the Celtic leg deemed a success, Betty next travelled south to England, where he found anxious audiences fearing Napoleonic invasion. Betty's arrival into this tinderbox culture provoked a frenzy of excitement as he tuned himself in to the frequency of tub-thumping nationalism. Audiences went berserk for him, leading to scenes of astonishing violence. *Bettymania* had arrived.

But why the extreme reaction? Young William Betty could certainly act, but his sudden and intense fame was more likely earned through a tactically astute promotional campaign in which he appealed to the desires, and mollified the fears, of multiple publics. This child star was a human Rorschach test; people projected ideas onto him. He was small and beautiful and perfect and innocent; a human puppy.[11] Obviously there was a small but noisy contingent of eye-rolling cynics who thought Bettymania was baffling and cringeworthy – the modern obsession of hate-watching popular things is nothing new[12] – but huge numbers of eminent, freethinking people were suckered in by the puffery and the fear of missing out. Even government ministers called a cabinet meeting short to scamper off to watch Master Betty in *Hamlet*.

Inevitably, this intensity was unsustainable. The haters, such as the radical essayist and poet Leigh Hunt, gradually punctured the Bettymania balloon with sustained criticism, and satirists also found a sharp angle when they attacked his boyish femininity, suggesting Betty's Romeo looked and sounded more like a Juliet. Within a couple of years, the bubble had burst; his massive earnings were shredded, and the heat swiftly went out of the fandom.

Though he continued to act, his lack of classical learning - plus the onset of awkward puberty - further disappointed the discerning crowds, and by his late teens he'd quit the stage to study at Cambridge University. News of a comeback, aged twenty, garnered much public curiosity, but the whole thing proved a crushing disappointment. There was no sequel to Bettymania; instead he was instantly written off as a has-been.

In times of uncertainty, there's no finer cure than wheeling in a cute kid. During the Great Depression of the 1930s, the highest-grossing box office star in Hollywood was not Clark Gable, Henry Fonda, Katharine Hepburn, Cary Grant, or Jimmy Stewart, but an adorable six-year-old called Shirley Temple. She was a giggling, grinning, tap-dancing box office powerhouse, and one of the most photographed people on the planet. Talented? Incredibly so. But, most of all, she offered something enormously alluring to a beleaguered public: sheer joy. Temple was a densely packed neutron bomb of sunny optimism, a blonde-ringleted moppet of such prodigious charisma that - as the historian John F. Kasson has shown - she became the torchbearer in Hollywood's mission to lift a broken America out of the Great Depression.[13] Indeed, her first major film, *Stand Up and Cheer!*, features a plot in which President Roosevelt creates a new government quango called the Department of Amusement, its purpose to lift the nation's spirits. The cabinet post goes to a character named Mr Cromwell, but in real life it would have gone to Temple.

Enrolled by her pushy mother in a performing-arts school when she was just two years old, Shirley Temple was immediately talent-spotted and made her screen debut in an array of *Baby Burlesks* that satirised topical news with adorable nappy-clad kids playing the roles of famous adults. Her mum, Gertrude, had seemingly pinned the family's financial hopes on Shirley, and no obstacle could be allowed to get in the way. On the day of her debut, after weeks of unpaid rehearsals, Shirley filmed in the studio for twelve hours straight, despite having been hospitalised the night before with an ear infection and nasty cold. She was barely three years old.

Gertrude had begged for a delay, but, when the producer declined, there was no question of little Shirley going home. Hundreds, if not thousands, of kids would be shoved through this exploitative sausage factory, and dropouts were easily replaced. The show had to go on.

This reckless attitude to child safety permeated the whole enterprise. Despite the cuteness of the eventual films, the shoots were far from frolicsome. To counteract tantrums and misbehaviour, the producers built a soundproof, cramped box in which was stored a large block of ice. This cell was used to punish naughty cast members, with the troublesome toddlers being made to stand in the cold, or even sit directly on the ice, until they'd learned their lesson.[14] Shirley told her mother about it, but a single-minded Gertrude dismissed the idea as childish fantasy. Later, when Shirley was spotted by a studio employee dancing in a cinema lobby and was promptly hired for proper film work, conditions improved.

Now a pint-sized movie star, Temple was cared for on set, but she was still a tiny kid, technically too young even for a game of Hungry Hippos by modern safety standards. To avoid awkward accusations, the studio PR described little Shirley's filmmaking as being no different from ordinary child's play, and Shirley's own words - ghostwritten when she was just seven - said: 'acting is like playing a game of make-believe'.[15] But as an adult she later recalled, 'I went to work *every day* . . . I thought every child worked, because I was born into it.' It was child labour, but in cutesy frocks. Aged only six,* she had already made seven screen outings, and had spent half of her life in the film industry. It's a stark reminder that even infant stars often served an unglamorous apprenticeship.

---

* Some reports aged her down to a mere four years old, to make it seem even more impressive. The head of Fox Studios took a year off her birth certificate (Shirley thought she was only twelve on her thirteenth birthday). It's depressing that even infant actresses have to lie about their age . . .

Waking up famous?

In comparison to Shirley Temple and Master Betty, George Gordon Byron - better known as Lord Byron - was a doddery old man when he burst into the public's imagination as an eroticised literary sensation. He was twenty-four. Some two centuries later, his scandalous reputation remains gloriously intact; this talented, pouty shag merchant with the lustrous hair still looms large in our cultural imagination, gazing out from portraits with the confidence of a man who knows he could seduce your mum, your sister, and your pet dog if he wanted to.

Such is the enduring perfection of the visual brand, it often obscures his poetry (I'd never read a single line until researching this book), but one line that does still seem to do the rounds on the internet is his alleged quote about becoming a celebrity: 'I awoke one morning and found myself famous.' This humble brag was supposedly issued in response to the sudden rush by the public to buy up the first two cantos of his new poem, *Childe Harold's Pilgrimage*, a loosely autobiographical travel romance, based on his post-university travels in Europe, which cast young Byron as the archetype of brooding poetical sexiness. The problem with this story is that it was an exaggeration bordering on myth.

True enough, the book sold out in less than three days, but only from a print run of 500 copies. And only the very wealthy could afford them. After six months, total sales numbered 4,500; this was a smash hit in 1812, and library copies would've increased readership yet further, but it's not as if all of London, a city of nearly a million souls, was reading him.[16] If Byron became the sudden talk of the town, it was mostly the posh nobs who were doing the gabbling. As Mary O'Connell notes,[17] the hidden star in this story was the publisher, John Murray, who played a blinder in marketing Byron as an aristocrat of great dignity, but also as a brooding, moody romantic with a flash of danger running through his heart. While Murray laid the book's marketing groundwork, Byron glided through the fancy drawing rooms of London, wooing his audience in advance.

What's more, we're not even sure Byron ever scribbled that line about waking up famous – it's taken from the biography written by his friend Thomas Moore, who claimed to be quoting from Byron's unpublished memoir, which Moore conveniently burned. What raises suspicion is that Moore was the lead architect of the 'instantaneous fame' idea, later recalling of Byron: 'his fame had not to wait for any of the ordinary gradations, but seemed to spring up, like the palace of a fairy tale, in a night'.[18] Nice line, but is it legit? Moore's desire to cast Byron in the role of sudden superstar was perhaps a promotional tactic designed to make him seem like a natural marvel, and embolden his reputation after a pitiful, premature death suffered in Greek exile.

The way the story usually gets told, we might assume Byron scribbled his first ever poem, bunged it in the post, went to bed, and awoke to find himself covered in frilly knickers chucked through his window by a bevy of impassioned fans. This isn't the case – not least because most women went commando in the early 1800s – but also because this wasn't his first poem, or even his first book. *Childe Harold's Pilgrimage* was his third publication in five years. In fact, his second work, *English Bards and Scotch Reviewers*, was a biting satire of the critical savaging his debut work had received, meaning Byron was already so established that he'd managed to acquire his own legion of haters in his first work, and then publicly diss them in his sequel, all before supposedly waking up famous.[19] In short, there's no doubting Byron's fame was turbocharged by the release of his third work, and he grew to be a publishing phenomenon, but it certainly wasn't overnight success.

Playing the long game

Achieving deliberate celebrity usually took a while and required considerable effort. Patience was often important. Sometimes, however, fame took bloody ages to arrive, and the delay was so prolonged that the eventual success felt like it had hurtled out of left field to the bewilderment of all involved. Edmund Kean is the classic case, but let's enjoy an even stranger one from the world of highbrow modernist literature. In 1933, while little Shirley Temple was trying to dodge the ice-block of doom, a woman named Gertrude Stein became an American literary phenomenon, thanks to her book *The Autobiography of Alice B. Toklas*. Frankly, it's hard to judge who was more surprised by this: Stein herself or anyone who'd read her previous work.

Stein was a sixty-year-old, avant-garde, American expat who was in a closeted lesbian relationship with the aforementioned Alice. She also had a famously impenetrable writing style. Calling her a challenging read is like saying quantum mechanics is 'a bit tricky'. As the founder of an intellectual salon in Paris, where she'd lived since 1903, Stein had hung out with the geniuses of modernism - Picasso, Matisse, Apollinaire, Hemingway, T. S. Eliot, Braque, Pound - and the most evocative stylistic label applied to her writing was 'literary cubism'; it was said by Mabel Dodge, an influential friend with whom she stayed, that 'she is doing with words what Picasso is doing with paint'.[20] But to her critics it was simply incoherent, unpunctuated, pseudo-intellectual drivel. And yet somehow Stein became a bestselling celebrity.

The usual version of the story is that she also awoke famous, or something near enough to that. But - as with the Byron myth - this is pure fable, one comprehensively sledgehammered into fine powder by the scholar Karen Leick.[21] Rather than being a novelty in 1933, Stein had spent two decades being derided and discussed in American publications. In 1914, the *Chicago Daily Tribune* joked that, upon reading her homoerotic poetry compendium *Tender Buttons*, their subeditor 'was not expected to recover', which is a savage joke that makes me laugh every time I read it.

The same paper invited the public to mockingly send in their own attempts at Gertrude gibberish. The humorist Don Marquis adopted her as a running gag in the *New York Evening Sun*, as did a columnist in the *New York Tribune*. *Life* magazine also printed parodic poems in mocking emulation of the Steinian rhythm. If she'd been alive today, Twitter would be awash with nonsensical #SteinPoems and merciless memes. She was a laughing stock. People read out her poems at dinner parties, giggling uproariously at how ridiculously illogical they were. Others were convinced she was a hoaxer, deliberately trolling the literary establishment with literary garbage, just to see which pretentious fools would be suckered by her snob-bait.

But, while American intellectuals debated if her work had any merit, the general public was quietly being primed to think about Gertrude Stein as a famous person. Her friend Carl Van Vechten wrote to her regularly from America, boosting Stein's ego with reports of her influence: 'your name pops up in current journalism with great frequency. You are as famous in America as any histori-cal character – and if you came over I think you might get as great a reception as, say, Jenny Lind [the Swedish opera sensation brought over by P. T. Barnum].'[22] This was hyperbolic flattery at the time, but he ended up being surprisingly close to the mark.

Perhaps what's most surprising about Stein's celebrity isn't that she erupted suddenly from obscurity, like Edmund Kean, but that she was allowed to unshackle herself from two decades of pre-existing notoriety. Stein didn't bounce from obscurity to fame, she redefined her existing reputation by swapping mockery for acclaim. She became something new; Stein was the modernist Miley Cyrus, minus the twerking. This astonishing success was largely achieved through her own change of tack. *The Autobiogra-phy of Alice B. Toklas* was artfully constructed, mostly because Stein wrote it under the guise of her secret lover, making it a playful autobiography of someone else. Determined to be famous, she also softened her style. The sentences became intelligible. In fact, if you forgive the strange punctuation and her fondness for repetition, it's quite the jolly read.

Why Americans flocked to devour this faux memoir of Stein's own Parisian life, replete with anecdotes about Picasso, Matisse, Hemingway etc., is perhaps self-explanatory. She was lifting the lid on some of the best-known cultural figures of the twentieth century, and – in so doing – managed to enrage them. Hemingway labelled the book 'pitiable', Matisse whinged about how his wife was represented, and Stein's own brother, Leo, called it 'a farrago of lies'. None of these outbursts were ideal quotes for the book jacket, but Stein burned her bridges with good reason. She desired fame and money, and for years had been carefully cultivating friendships with influential people in American publishing. Now she had the opportunity to call in her favours.

The other major pillar supporting her campaign was fortunate timing. Just as Edmund Kean probably benefited from Byronic excitement and Romanticism's trendiness, Stein hitched a lift on the coat-tails of fellow modernists James Joyce and Virginia Woolf, both of whom were selling well in the USA. In fact, as Stein's book smashed its way into the bestseller list, Joyce's *Ulysses* was the subject of an obscenity case in a New York courtroom, and the resulting controversy made it an instant bestseller.[23] Both Joyce and Stein soon after graced the cover of *Time* magazine. The *Autobiography* was also marketed brilliantly by her publishers, and the public were strangely thrilled by the Gertrude Stein phenomenon, particularly when she arrived in America to promote her book, oversee an opera she had created, and give a series of lectures on art.

It was a full-on charm offensive by an expatriate whose memories of her homeland differed greatly from the nation she encountered. But what she found delighted her. Stein was mobbed in the street, had her name in lights at Times Square, and became so famous that her earlier poems were referenced in pop culture and product adverts; her philosophical aphorism 'a rose is a rose is a rose' is even quoted in my favourite movie, *Singin' in the Rain*, which came out eighteen years later. This rush of fascination was as exciting to Stein as it was confusing to everyone else. As *Vanity Fair* observed in May 1934: 'we doubt if any one – even Miss Stein herself – ever envisaged a time when a Stein book would, month after month, grace the best seller lists, and a Stein opera [would] run four solid weeks at a Broadway theatre, to re-open three weeks later at popular demand. But this is 1934, and the twin miracles have happened.'

To her credit, Stein oozed charm. A little old lady with an intriguing smile and a ready wit, she was way more charismatic in person than in print; she emitted a sort of Wise Grandma vibe, simultaneously projecting an impressive air of both unpretentiousness and deep cerebral power. As she stepped off the boat in New York, a squadron of journalists launched into an enthusiastic interrogation, but she defused their questions with cheery ease. The long-held notion of Gertrude Stein as perennial nonsense-howitzer, blasting the reader into baffled, cowering submission, instantly shrivelled up and died. *Time* announced her arrival with a wryly captioned photo: 'Expatriate Stein: She was disappointingly intelligible'. It's a lovely gag, and quite revealing. People presumably hoped she'd speak with all the jarring patterns of a malfunctioning robot. By undermining her brand, Stein risked seeming a bit . . . well, dull. But instead her intellect and warmth charmed the nation.

As the scholar Loren Glass points out, 'Stein entered into an already-established authorial star system in which the marketable "personalities" of authors were frequently as important as the quality of their literary production.'[24] There was a massive publicity machine driving the Stein bandwagon in 1933-4, but her personal charisma greased the cogs. She wasn't just a writer; her friend Louis Bromfield dubbed her a 'literary event', while John Malcolm Brinnin later noted her fame was 'shared only by gangsters, baseball players and movie stars'. She's since been dubbed the 'most publicised, least-read writer' of the century. In short, Gertrude Stein's celebrity vastly eclipsed her book sales. And her book sales were pretty damn good.[25] Not bad for a laughing stock accused of being a hoaxer . . .

Practice makes perfect

While I'm having fun popping the balloon labelled 'overnight stardom', Edmund Kean proved it could be done. And we'll see later that heroes, criminals, and those caught up in scandals were also catapulted to notoriety at alarming velocity. But I want to stress how common it was for most celebrities to acquire their fame gradually. This was particularly true if their appeal rested on skill. Without wishing to go all Malcolm 'you need 10,000 hours' Gladwell on you, many historical celebrities were performers whose natural talent proved to be insufficiently explosive ammo to launch them out of the cannon. To detonate a celebrity career, they also needed to log the necessary hours; it wasn't just a lack of opportunities or ability that hampered them, it was earning the vital experience needed to master their craft. Even little Shirley Temple took dance classes.

Let's jump back a century to the 1820s. We might assume the astonishing musical virtuosity of the Hungarian pianist and composer Franz Liszt appeared destined from the outset. As a small boy, Franz was a musical marvel able to play even the most difficult of symphonies from memory or sight-read the most challenging of scores. But Liszt's frenzied adult celebrity wasn't just the inevitable extension of natural genius. He also benefited deeply from a devoted father, Adam, who struggled heroically to get his son the musical education required to maximise his potential. Luckily enough, such was Franz's ability – and his delightful personality – that two of Europe's foremost musicians, Carl Czerny and Antonio Salieri, both offered to teach him for free. This tuition greatly boosted his understanding of composition and creativity, and young Franz was soon ushered into the concert halls of Europe to showcase his gift. But, even though he was immediately hailed as a 'Boy Hercules' in Vienna, Paris, and London, there were several other child geniuses doing the rounds.

The arrival of mass-manufactured pianos had provided a steady flow of rosy-cheeked keyboard prodigies thumping out tricky tunes in the comfort of their own homes. In fact, it wasn't just pianists. In 1824, a boyish Liszt toured Britain to great acclaim, but was upstaged by a three-year-old harpist dubbed the 'Infant Lyra'.[26] Much like Master Betty, she peaked too soon and became nothing more than another minor aristocrat, named Isabella Rudkin, settling for a life of comfortable domesticity at the earliest possible opportunity. A similar fate befell Wolfgang Amadeus Mozart's talented sister, Nannerl Mozart. Though a superb pianist, when she hit eighteen the shutters came down on her musical career - her father, and wider society, demanded she shuffle off into the soft shadows of feminine respectability.

The Mozart family story is particularly interesting because Wolfgang is now so famous, but he too suffered a surprise misfire. More than half a century before Liszt's arrival in Paris, an eight-year-old Wolfgang had come to dynamic, cosmopolitan London - joined by Nannerl and their father, Leopold - to thrill people with the family's incredible musical abilities. Immediately, the siblings secured the coup of performing for the king and queen, and Leopold also made sure to promote his children widely to the public, regularly placing notices in newspapers. Yet, despite all this attention, the Mozarts didn't return home in blazing triumph. So, what went wrong?

Early publicity was positive, but Leopold had succumbed to a sudden, serious illness for several weeks, and - while young Mozart used that time to compose his first ever symphony, which was an achievement of ludicrous precocity - this major interruption hampered their marketing momentum and squeezed the family finances. Upon Leopold's recovery, they'd sought to refill the kitty with a lucrative public concert in February 1765, but ever-fickle Londoners had by now transferred their enthusiasm to another exciting import, the Florentine castrato Giovanni Manzuoli. Celebrity culture is often a story of constant novelty, and he'd hoovered up all the buzz. But there was also a more sinister reason for the underwhelming ticket sales. Historians have since suggested Leopold's exuberant publicity campaign had backfired by alienating the musical community.

While eleven-year-old Nannerl was a wonderful player, Leopold's trump card had always been Wolfgang's improvisational brilliance, declaring in the *Public Advertiser* that his son was 'the greatest Prodigy that Europe or Human Nature has to boast of'.

Yet Wolfgang's extreme youth provoked a barrage of snide accusations from rival musicians; the boy genius must surely be a
fraud, and Leopold a cynical trickster. There was no way a child
could churn out a symphony! Leopold denied the allegations in an
open letter,[27] but it was too late. The media blitzkrieg had burned
through all the goodwill, and now he was the focus of a conspiracy
theory.

Spotting the danger, Leopold invited sceptical scientists and
members of the public to test the boy's abilities for themselves,
choosing to eschew concerts in favour of private demonstrations.
The prominent naturalist Daines Barrington was the most notable of these interrogators, and he was suitably wowed, but his
report wasn't published until six years later, which wasn't much
use to anyone except modern historians.[28] Disappointingly, Wolfgang Amadeus Mozart - now recognised as perhaps the greatest
composer of all time - failed to conquer London. He ended his
time there performing for ordinary punters in a rowdy tavern.
It was quite the tumble from royal recitals, and nothing like the
Bettymania of the next century. Indeed, though the adult Mozart
later enjoyed success composing entertainment for royals,
nobles, and even the new middle classes - particularly popular
were his *opera buffa* works full of saucy jokes about unruly serv-
ants - nevertheless, he only reached full celebrity status after
his death.

Wolfgang, Nannerl, and the Infant Lyra were all exceptional
child prodigies, but only one of them had any major career success;
and even he, a veritable genius, didn't get to be a living celebrity. So
it's no great stretch to imagine how Franz Liszt might've also been
lost to history, particularly when Adam Liszt died unexpectedly
during his son's mid-teens. This tragedy snatched away not just a
loving father, but also his promoter, tour manager, venue booker,
and primary motivator. From the beginning it had been the Adam
and Franz show, but now Franz was bereft; his mother was thousands of miles away in Hungary and the teenager found himself
alone in a foreign city, with a funeral to organise.

Even when she arrived in Paris, after three years apart, Franz became the family's sole breadwinner at the tender age of sixteen, giving piano lessons to pampered tykes of high-born privilege. Adam Liszt's death was destabilising and devastating. Franz went through stages of depression where he couldn't touch a piano. But instead of succumbing to despondency, or surrendering to the usual teenage habit of raiding Mum and Dad's drinks cabinet, Liszt threw himself into music, books, religion, and art. He started hanging out with brilliant creatives. And he started pushing the limits of human endurance.

Master Betty's return to acting, aged twenty, had proved a damp squib. Comebacks weren't always wanted, so Franz Liszt had to do something innovative if he was to claim his celebrity crown and make good on his potential. Having been amazed by the speed of the Italian violin virtuoso, Niccolò Paganini, Liszt resolved to develop his own jaw-dropping, lightning-fast technique on the piano. He began hammering the keys with manic energy, his large hands and long fingers traversing the scales with the sprawling dexterity of hyperactive spiders.

He'd been born a musical savant, but his fame would rest on manual technique patiently perfected in isolation, one finger at a time, hour after hour, day after day, often while reading a book to combat the tedium. Much like the glamorous, long-haired heavy-metal guitarists whom I worshipped as a youth, the most compelling virtuosos are often boring nerds who sat in their room for ten hours a day, practising their scales.* Franz Liszt redefined what was humanly possible for his instrument, and it made him staggeringly famous when he reached his thirties. But *Lisztomania* was a victory won through dogged attrition.[29]

---

* My favourite guitarist is Synyster Gates from Avenged Sevenfold. He's a classically trained harmonic wizard who sports gothic tattoos and dark eyeliner, and looks every inch the rockstar. But his real name is Brian.

The authenticity gimmick

On 29 December 1776, eager audiences piled into London's Drury Lane theatre to watch *The Merchant of Venice*. Advertised in the role of Portia was a 'Young Lady (being her first appearance)' on the London stage, and the crowd was presumably enchanted by her initial appearance. This Welsh rose, named Sarah Siddons, was fresh-faced and attractive; her hair was dark and thick, her eyes expressive; and she possessed a long but elegant nose that somehow suggested a touch of regality lurking in the family genes. Siddons displayed all the physical characteristics of a stage beauty. But then the play started . . .

Despite two years of adult acting experience, and a childhood spent on the stage, this was Siddons's first performance in a big theatre and she crumpled under the pressure. The words wouldn't come out, her voice trailed off, she shuffled stiffly across the boards with guarded hesitancy. She looked exhausted and bewildered. It was hardly surprising; six weeks before she'd gone into labour mid-performance, giving birth to her second child in two years. This poor young woman had then arrived in the capital, barely a month before opening night, sleep-deprived and with a babe on her breast and a toddler tugging at her petticoats, to find herself performing for the famed David Garrick, in the famed London theatre, before a famously demanding crowd. Though newcomers were usually cut a bit of slack, she was totally out of her depth and Siddons was a disastrous debutante.[30] After six months, her contract expired and there was no chance of her being offered a new one. She'd squandered a chance that Edmund Kean - in the same rebuilt theatre, in the same play - would later snatch up with manic vigour.

She began the resuscitation of her career in Birmingham and York, and then arrived in the fashionable city of Bath, whose theatre had been awarded a royal warrant only a decade beforehand. It was a great place to plan a second assault on London; Bath welcomed sophisticated audiences, but the pressure was less strenuous. It didn't take long for Siddons, now choosing to focus on tragic roles over comedy, to build up a head of steam, or for London's theatre scouts to take notice of her renewed momentum. Redemption wasn't swift in coming, and neither would David Garrick be made to eat humble pie – he died before she could unfix his mind – but by 1782 she'd evidently done more than enough to earn her second chance in the metropolis. The comeback was on!

For the second time, Siddons arrived in London with a newborn baby – her fifth child, although only four had survived – but this time Drury Lane was under the tenure of its new manager, Richard Brinsley Sheridan. He'd eagerly been trying to recruit her for a while, and the juicy carrot dangled before Siddons was the lead role in Garrick's adaptation of *Isabella, or, The Fatal Marriage*. This time, she nailed it. Audiences lost their minds in praising her performance. So, why the turnaround?

Obviously, she'd become a more experienced actress, which was vital. But, let's not forget she was also, once again, nursing a small baby, juggling three other kids, and having to deal with her constantly disappointing husband, William, who was, to put it mildly, a bit of a plonker. These burdens surely drained her energies. So, what key variable made the big difference? The secret had been to turn the overwhelming maternal responsibility into an asset. She had a hook: motherhood.

Isabella, or, The Fatal Marriage is a powerful, sentimental play about a widow who remarries, only to discover her dead husband still lives. Like a child entranced by the illuminated panel in a lift, it emphatically prods all the audience's buttons at once, and keeps prodding them until the electrical circuits frazzle – contemporary reviews recounted how the theatre became a den of hysterical shrieking, wailing, sobbing and fainting fits. Men and women lost total control of their emotions, some had to be carried out. It's that sort of play.

But Siddons could claim much of the credit. Six years beforehand, when it had all gone so horribly wrong, her son Henry had been the cheeky toddler tottering around her dressing room. Now, in 1782, as she made her heroic return, he took to the stage alongside her, playing Isabella's child. The crossing of identity boundaries – between Sarah and Isabella, performer and character, real mother and stage mother – dazzled audiences. They were overwhelmed with tears as Sarah cradled her little Henry, the devastated pair lamenting the death of a fictional husband and father. It was a powerhouse performance, but it also felt viscerally grounded in truth. Audiences witnessed a real dynamic between the grieving characters, because the Siddonses were a real family.[31] She was one of the first celebrities to use their children as a PR prop, and it's been a valuable tool ever since.

Courting controversy

Siddons enjoyed an almost flawless career from then on, and was among the least controversial celebrities I've encountered, with her only scandals being muffled grumbling about her tight-fisted miserliness, and allegations of an affair with her married fencing teacher. Others, however, built their name as provocateurs. Implicating oneself in sex scandals has always been an effective but risky strategy for getting noticed. The public love to be scandalised, but we're also hypocrites who'll shun those whose naughty adventures we've so enjoyed gossiping over. Between 1700 and the 1830s, there were numerous high-class courtesans who published accounts of their sexual encounters with the great and good, in so-called 'whore biographies'.[32] But these brazen confessors often struggled with the moral backlash – unfurling one's dirty bedsheets was a quick but uncomfortable path to celebrity, and not one offering reassuring longevity.

Perhaps the most famous was Harriette Wilson, the 'demirep' lover of many elite nobs including the hero of Waterloo, the Duke of Wellington. She was angered that her former conquests hadn't provided long-term financial security, and also that unscrupulous publishers were issuing fake memoirs using her name, so she published a scandalous memoir in 1825 through a pornography publisher. Because it was essentially a moneymaking scheme, she first had him contact her aristocratic exes with blackmailing letters, demanding £200 from each not to include their names in the book. Some coughed up. Wellington famously refused, responding: 'Publish and be damned!'

Wilson and her publisher allegedly raked in a fortune of £10,000 from their cynical plan. The episodic releases were a huge hit; they issued thirty-one editions in the first year alone, and so-called 'Wilson Mania' struck the bookshops, with people battling to buy copies. But they were then hit with libel lawsuits and all sorts of other trouble, including rebuttal memoirs by former friends who attacked Wilson's version of events. In the end, she tried to launch a writing career from the publicity, looking to go legit as a creative artist, but it didn't really take off. As was common for many beauties who aged out of their public allure, Harriette Wilson died in obscure poverty in 1845, just shy of her sixtieth birthday.[33]

Lord Byron's bedroom adventures were of enormous fascination to his fans, who interpreted his poetry as a coded erotic autobiography (which, in fairness, it totally was). His fame was inseparably intertwined with his scandalous sexuality, and it led to his ditching England for a life in European exile, yet he'd already weathered howls of outrage because he was a writer of dazzling skill, but he was also male, and a titled lord, to boot. Yes, he'd had to work for his money, due to his father's ruinous debts, and he'd endured a deeply traumatic childhood, but an adult Byron enjoyed male, noble privilege. Women, however, were not granted such leeway, and the inevitable moralising, or what some now call 'slut-shaming', was always much more of an obstacle, as discovered by the famous beauties Mary Wells and Emma Hamilton, who fell from grace when their wealthy lovers dumped them or died. But this is why Mae West is particularly intriguing.

In the mid-1930s, until Hollywood's moral censors dragged her down, West was the queen of comic innuendo, having made her hugely successful screen debut in *She Done Him Wrong*. Yet this new screen star had been no fresh ingénue plucked straight off the train platform; she was pushing forty when American cinemagoers first clapped eyes on her playful winks and radioactive blonde hair. Indeed, she'd barely scraped a film deal in the first place, such was her provocative reputation – the movie studio's internal censors were yanking their hair out at the news, terrified that they'd be ruined by her controversial brand. They had reason to be nervous.

Raised as a working-class 'Tough Girl' in Brooklyn, West had probably been sexualised at just thirteen,* was a vaudeville performer by fourteen, married at seventeen, and separated by eighteen. She'd dragged herself up on the seedier side of the theatrical scene; rejected by the increasingly wholesome vaudeville circuit, she'd paid her dues in vulgar, sleazy burlesque. After two decades of performing she was thirty-two years old and going nowhere. So, in 1926, she booked a theatre, hired a director, and mounted her own play, in which she would play a Montreal sex worker. The play was called *Sex*, though it may as well have been titled *SeXXX!* The public response was huge. And so was the outrage.

The *Daily Mirror*, one of New York's less subtle tabloids, printed this delightfully unsubtle, all-caps headline: 'SEX AN OFFEN-SIVE PLAY. MONSTROSITY PLUCKED FROM GARBAGE CAN, DESTINED TO SEWER', which was followed by a review describing it as disgusting social contaminant: 'This production is not for the police. It comes rather in the province of our Health Department. It is a sore spot in the midst of our fair city that needs disinfecting.' Even serious critics lost all sense of perspective, damning *Sex* as a repellent, dangerous assault on public decency. It wasn't simply that the play was about sexuality – as West's biographer Marybeth Hamilton noted, other plays had been permitted to tackle this taboo – but it was Mae West's lewd burlesque persona, fused to working-class themes, that upset their sensibilities.

It seems at this stage, in 1926, she hadn't yet developed her ironic comic style. Instead, the horrified critics saw comic realism, a bawdy authenticity that threatened public decency; some

---

* Her first boyfriend, Joe, was nineteen. This would have been statutory rape under New York law.

horrified critics even suggested that she was sexually aroused by the brothel scenes – to them, it was a live-sex show starring a low-class, tough broad straight off the sidewalks. The law agreed. West served eight days in prison for the crime of public indecency. Audiences, of course, love to be titillated and flocked to see it for themselves. Whereas others were destroyed by scandal, sensation was Mae West's springboard to fame. *Sex* wouldn't be her biggest hit, but it was proof of concept. As she later cheekily punned: 'I climbed the ladder of success wrong by wrong.'

Mae West had played a dangerous game, but she was bursting with natural talent and showcased a brand of risqué sauciness that seemed to tickle taboos rather than smash them. She was a provocateur, but one who carried the public with her in support, which was no small feat. And while it's tempting to declare West as leading the vanguard of shocking celebrity culture – a harbinger of bold new attitudes towards women and sexuality – we might also recall an earlier example of the funny, sexy, ballsy, working-class gal who threatened the establishment while amusing the public. West was perhaps following in the footsteps of Nell Gwyn, the seventeenth-century actress-turned-mistress to King Charles II, who we'll meet in a later chapter. If true, it made Mae West not so much a twentieth-century pioneer as an echo of celebrity's very earliest days.

A recipe for success

So can we declare that, having scoured the annals of history, the formula for stardom was as simple as celebrity = talent + graft? Sadly not. How many careers fizzled out on the launchpad, to the point that we don't even know where to look for them? In the case of the Mozart siblings, we see that limitless talent wasn't the only requirement, and that other external pressures applied. Wolfgang and Nannerl were the victims of their father's bad luck and worse health, and found themselves overshadowed by a more established rival who gobbled up the public's attention. Like baby emperor penguins, crammed with their parents into tight winter huddles, many a hopeful starlet was trampled underfoot before they ever grew big enough to withstand the scrum.

With the Mozarts, we also see the peril of overplaying the promotional game. Their father pushed too hard, burned through his supplies of goodwill, and incited a backlash; his claims of infant genius were well founded, but vulnerable to pooh-poohing and organised sabotage because they sounded like the hyperbolic claims of a huckstering hoaxer. As a result, history's greatest composer ended up playing in a pub. As for his sister, her potential celebrity was killed by an even simpler force. Whereas Mae West accelerated her fame by subverting gender expectations - and Sarah Siddons found celebrity by conforming to them - Nannerl Mozart was never allowed to even try flying solo. Her womanhood was a fatal wound.

Over the course of the past three centuries, many people competed in the race for celebrity and crossed the line to see their names charted on the scoreboard. Many more tripped on the hurdles and landed face-first in the dirt. Those who sought fame required endurance, ability, luck, and favourable conditions if they were to succeed. And some people simply weren't allowed to enter the race in the first place. Yet those who gathered at the starting line were willing participants. This wasn't usually the case for those in the *ascribed* and *attributed* categories, for whom fame was something done to them without their intent or consent. Rather than volunteering to join the obstacle race, these victims were instead kidnapped, loaded into a circus cannon, and fired over the finish line in a parabolic arc of terrified screaming, with their limbs flailing and their faces smashing into every hurdle along the way.

But that's a story for a new chapter . . .

Chapter 2: Fame Thrust upon Them

Famous for being famous

Who does this sound like to you? A spoiled little rich girl who turns up to parties wearing the latest fashions, gets paid to be seen with the other beautiful people, and graces the cover of every magazine because she's 'famous for being famous'. She has no talent. She doesn't do anything. She's just a glamorous socialite, with a wealthy daddy, whose only skills are an innovative use of makeup, being spotted by the paparazzi, and dating famous guys.

Hands up if you're thinking Kim Kardashian? And why not – she's very much our *celeb du jour*. Perhaps you've only just woken from a coma, having bumped your head in 2006, and Paris Hilton is your go-to reference? Both are good guesses, but this enraged rant is my summary of how harrumphing cynics felt in the 1930s about a high-society beauty named Brenda Frazier. And yes, I realise you don't get too many sexy Brendas gracing the covers of magazines these days, but this one was properly glam. Brenda Frazier* might've seemed your quintessential D-lister; the omnipresent party girl swishing from event to event with paparazzi lolloping behind. And she was exactly that. But unlike some modern celebs – who seem to stalk fame with a wolf-pack mentality – she had celebrity dumped in her lap without ever really asking for it.

In 1936, the fabulously monikered society columnist Cholly Knickerbocker† declared: 'It may seem a bit early, but I – here and now – predict Brenda Frazier will be one of the belles – if not the

---

* Not to be confused with the goofy but handsome actor Brendan Fraser.
† Real name Maury Henry Biddle Paul; he was definitely right to use a pseudonym.

Belle – of her season.'[1] Two years later, he was proven correct when the seventeen-year-old was declared the standout stunner at the debutante ball held in New York's Ritz-Carlton hotel. This was *the* party in the elite social calendar, the glitzy, champagne-drenched springboard for a new cohort of privileged youth, and Frazier's instant elevation to 'Glamour Girl #1' launched her not just into high society, but into the newsstands, dentists' waiting rooms, and hair salons of America. Immediately, her pale-powdered face was everywhere, offset by her dark curls and distinctive scarlet lipstick. Journalists and photographers chased her around town, feverishly documenting her glamorous existence. Within six months she'd appeared thousands of times in the American press, made the cover of *Life* magazine, graced adverts for products she couldn't or wouldn't use herself (she posed in a car advert despite not being able to drive), and was a byword for prestigious glamour.

By 1939, another influential gossip journo, Walter Winchell, had decided the unparalleled scale of her fame as a 'celebrity debutante' necessitated a whole new word: *celebutante*.[2] Brenda Frazier erupted like a glitter-filled volcano to become an all-pervading American icon of beauty. To the public it probably felt like an overnight success story, but we know Cholly Knickerbocker had pinged her on his radar a couple of years before. In fact, she'd already been a fixture of café society since the age of twelve. Even as a child, Brenda Frazier had been creepily objectified for her looks; though struggling with low self-esteem, others had seen something uniquely beautiful in the schoolgirl. By fourteen she was probably sexually active with adult men,* encouraged by her ruthlessly ambitious mother. It was just one of several factors that shattered her childhood innocence.

Brenda also witnessed her parents' alcoholism, their infidelities, bitter divorce, and custody arguments. Oh, and then there was the death of her first stepfather, the arrival of a new stepfather, the

---

* If so, this would have been statutory rape of a minor under the laws of the time.

death of her biological father, and her mother's grasping efforts
to prematurely access Brenda's vast trust fund, which was locked
until she reached adulthood. And we're not done yet. Her mother
had arranged for Brenda to undergo painful surgery on her Achilles tendons, ostensibly to prevent swelling but mostly to give
her shapelier legs when sporting high heels. Long before Cholly
Knickerbocker decided to elevate her to public scrutiny, Brenda
Frazier had already been living the exhaustingly dramatic life of
a soap opera character. It's no surprise her nickname in the press
was 'poor little rich girl'. Fame only made things worse: unhappy
romances, anorexia, bulimia, depression, pills, alcohol abuse,
multiple suicide attempts, and poor mental health would dog her
for the rest of her life.

Brenda Frazier's arrival into bewildering and painful celebrity
is also a fitting prologue for this chapter. She serves both as handy
historical avatar for the 'famous for being famous' poseurs, and as
a painful reminder of the humanity behind the headlines; the celebrity victim who never desired fame and couldn't adapt when it
crashed down upon her. Her massive celebrity was sudden, superficial, and short-lived (though her name popped up in tabloids for
years to come). She'd possessed no obvious skills, had left formal
education at fifteen, and would openly admit: 'I'm not a celebrity.
I don't deserve all this. I haven't done anything at all. I'm just a
debutante.' So why the big deal?

The media saw the 'poor little rich girl' as ideal headline fodder;
she offered up the moreish gateau of privilege, wealth, and beauty
drizzled with the curdled custard of family discord and bitterly
contested lawsuits. Frazier was fascinating; she was made into a
celebrity because she looked like one, because she was a doe-eyed
trust fund millionaire in a time of economic depression, and because her screwed-up family provided a perfect counterweight for
the perfection of her photogenic face. She didn't have to do anything except be Brenda Frazier. Her celebrity image was forever
beyond her control; it was *attributed* to her, making her what the
film theorist James Monaco has called a *quasar*. In his words: 'it is

not who they are or what they do, but what we *think* they are that fascinates us'.[3]

Becoming a celebrity *sounds* exciting. Scroll through social media and you'll find thousands of young people imitating the perceived aristocracy of media success. Some wannabe digital influencers even pretend to have sponsorship deals because that's what internet fame looks like, and you've gotta fake it till you make it.[4] Several psychology studies have found young people rank 'being famous' at the top of their ambitions.[5] But becoming a celebrity can be a shockingly bizarre, existentially debilitating metamorphosis done to a person with or without their consent. And, when it goes wrong – and it often does – it can devour the soul.* Fame can be fun, or it can be a Faustian pact with the devil. It dumps barrowloads of cash, parties, and private jets at the celebrity's feet, but it also entitles the public and media to savagely interrogate their right to exist in our eyeline. It invites emulation, obsession, and fantasising; but it can also bring demonising, dehumanising, and degrading aggression.

Most celebs, therefore, slide up and down the axis of adoration. One week they're loved, the next week we hate them, but we remain invested in their story because they're frosted mirrors for reflecting who we are, who we think we should be, and who we want to be. Brenda Frazier had fame thrust upon her when she wasn't emotionally ready, and it broke her. She was never hated – at worst, people booed her for her lack of substance – but nor was she beloved either. She was just a famous beautiful woman; a compellingly gorgeous image, attached to a car crash of a family, who was easily replaced when she got married and settled down. Her job was to fill column inches and sell products.

However, some celebrities aren't made this way, they don't get to slide around being loved and loathed depending on who

---

* In the space of just two weeks, while I was editing this book in September 2019, the popstars Justin Bieber, Taylor Swift, Jesy Nelson (Little Mix), Lily Allen, and Paul Cattermole (formerly of S Club 7) all revealed the ways in which being famous had caused them pain, confusion, and financial pressure.

they've insulted or hooked up with that week. Instead, they're moral agents specifically designed as inspiring role models, or as dangerous monsters who threaten public decency. Such binary tropes of hero and villain, exemplar and transgressor, superhuman and barely human, operate on a more extreme level than ordinary celebrity. But, often, these people also had their fame unexpectedly hurled upon them.

Amazing Grace

It was 4.45 a.m., on a cold September morning in 1838, when Grace Darling glimpsed an unfolding tragedy through a telescope. She was on watch duty at the Longstone Lighthouse built proudly upon one of the Farne Islands. Her family's job was to guide the ships passing along the Northumbrian coastline of north-east England. As she stared into the murky dark of a treacherously stormy night, Grace was startled by the shadows of a terrible shipwreck; the SS *Forfarshire,* a paddle steamer carrying sixty passengers and crew, had smashed into the rocks and been ripped asunder. Its bow had become lodged on jagged rocks while the rest of it had sheared off and sunk, sucking most of those aboard down to their cruel deaths. Grace could see no survivors through the gloom. If anyone had escaped, they might be clinging to an outcrop known as Big Harcar Rock, but they'd be a mile out to sea, in a howling gale. Only the dawn light would confirm it, and by then it might be too late.

Grace raced to alert her parents, William Sr and Thomasin. It was just the three of them in the lighthouse; most of her siblings had moved away, and her only remaining brother, William Brooks Darling, was ashore with the herring fleet in North Sunderland. The trio agreed that he and the local fishermen wouldn't dare launch a rescue in such bad weather. If anyone clung to that rock, only the Darlings at Longstone were close enough to save them. The responsibility fell on William Sr's shoulders. He was an experienced oarsman who knew the rocks; but he didn't trust in his own strength. He couldn't do it alone. William agonised over endangering his family, but the choice was taken out of his hands when Grace volunteered to join him. At 7 a.m., the dawn light revealed movement on Big Harcar Rock. Survivors! They had to act. Grace and her father launched their boat and began to row.

Pulling themselves through the ferocious waves and howling gale, the Darlings drew close enough to realise there were too many survivors to fit in the coble. They'd have to make two trips. William leapt onto the rock to assess the situation, leaving his daughter in sole command of their escape; she skilfully bobbed between the jagged edges, riding the surging waves and keeping the boat out of trouble. The Darlings took five people off the rock and left four strong men behind. Back they rowed to the lighthouse, where Thomasin and Grace began caring for their new arrivals. William and two of the survivors got back in the coble and returned for the remaining four. By 9 a.m., two hours after they'd set out, everyone was safely back on dry land. Soon, Grace's brother and his fellow fishermen turned up. They'd valiantly braved five miles of savage stormy waters only to discover the shipwreck had already been evacuated.

Several heroes announced themselves on that cold September morning, but only one would become an instant celebrity. Actually, instant isn't quite right; it took a week for news of Grace Darling's heroism to spread. Initial media focus instead fell on the cause of the shipwreck, with immediate questions being raised about the *SS Forfarshire*'s seaworthiness. An inquest found that its boiler had been poorly maintained, and accusations of criminal negligence were an obvious journalistic scoop. But, within a week, regional newspapers sought a new angle on a complex legal case, and the story of the survivors' escape was the solution. That, in turn, led to the rescue. And that led to Grace.

A journalist named David Kennedy of the *Berwick and Kelso Warder* set the tone for the ensuing deluge of praise, declaring the rescue was 'amongst the noblest instances of purely disinterested and philanthropic exertion on behalf of suffering individuals that ever reflected honour upon humanity'. Kennedy wasn't one for pithy understatement - perhaps he'd been at the cooking sherry? - but his hyperbolic prose kickstarted a public obsession with Grace Darling, and launched a feedback loop as local, regional, national, and international newspapers excitedly reprinted each other's content.

Already the myth was being created. Kennedy erroneously reported that Grace had convinced her reticent father to launch the rescue, and that she'd been awakened by the survivors shouting for help. Neither was true, but they boosted her role in the story. Instead of a brave woman working under her father's guidance, the newspapers invented a proactive heroine booting her cowardly dad up the arse as she sprinted off to fetch her oars. It remained a potent lie; in some later versions, he was airbrushed out entirely, leaving Grace to be depicted rowing solo. But Grace's recasting was also born of her marketability. Most obviously, she defied gender expectations.

As Darling's biographer, Hugh Cunningham, has convincingly argued,[6] the Irish philosopher and politician Edmund Burke had previously set out a framework for thinking about sensory aesthetics. His most crucial point was the power of the sublime and the beautiful.[7] *Beauty* equated to love, comfort, feelings of human intimacy, and also notions of perfection; this was associated with female delicacy. By contrast, the *sublime* generated the sensation of awestruck fear in all its eye-popping, heart-pounding physicality. It was the thrill and panic of being in mortal danger, as if staring over the edge of a cliff. The dreaded zenith of sublime terror was the murderous deep; every marine voyage was a game of chicken played with the Grim Reaper. Only men were allowed to play.

And yet, somehow, a young lighthouse keeper's daughter hadn't flinched as she danced between the fangs of peril's gaping jaws. Women just didn't do that sort of thing! They did needlepoint and were supposedly allergic to the very notion of adventure. Grace Darling was a woman beyond compute. We see such bafflement in the overwrought tribute published in *The Times*: 'Surely, imagination in its loftiest creations never invested the female character with such a degree of fortitude as has been evinced by Miss Grace

Horsley Darling on this occasion. Is there in the whole field of history, or of fiction even, one instance of female heroism to compare for one moment with this?'

It was clearly an overreaction - the ghost of Joan of Arc was probably scribbling her affronted complaint from the afterlife - but such is the casual hyperbole of celebrity coverage, with stars frequently declared the most beautiful, the sexiest, the best, the worst, the most exciting, the most scandalous, the wealthiest; and then, six months later, the pecking order changes and in come a new batch of glorious and villainous creatures. Celebrity culture demands a never-ending carousel of ranked superlatives, and ongoing fetishisation of novelty. Grace Darling was simply the shiny new thing of 1838, one prematurely thrust into the pantheon of historical greats by gasping observers with short memories.

But there was more to her appeal than defiant femininity. Ironically, Grace Darling was herself the perfect storm. Not just a Burke debunker, she was also an ordinary, anonymous member of the lower classes living her life on the faraway edge of northern England. This was a Romantic trope; she seemed both earthy and authentic, and yet somehow representative of a national fantasy. As Hugh Cunningham perceptively notes, Darling seemed to embody a fictional character, Jeanie Deans, created by the celebrated Scottish novelist Sir Walter Scott for one of his most successful novels, *The Heart of Midlothian*. Jeanie is a paragon of virtuous charity, she walks from Scotland to London to exonerate her sister of a crime, and the ordinary, innocent, northern Grace seemed to occupy the same emotional space in Britons' hearts.

Oh, and then there was that name! Is there a more inspiring, elegant name than Grace Darling? It literally means 'Divine Salvation Beloved' - you could dump a million quid in the lap of any advertising agency, give them a year, and they'd still fail to brainstorm anything as catchy. The *Monthly Chronicle* presumably spoke for many when it asked: 'Were two such words ever before combined to form a name? The one expressing the natural quality of the bearer of it, and the other defining what her deeds have made her in the regard of others.' The *Scotsman* was bluntly honest: 'Had Grace Darling been a married woman, dwelling in some poor alley in an ordinary town, and with no rarer or prettier an appellation than Smith, Brown, McTavish, or Higginbottom, a greater deed would, perhaps, have won her less favour.' Her fame glinted with the golden sheen of nominative destiny, as if Dickens – in his most sentimental mood – had created her for the page.

The combination of all these factors was overpowering; her celebrity was a Venn diagram of overlapping wow-factors and it made the public desperate for access to her life. Journalists raced to interview her family; artists scrambled to paint her; sightseers flocked to her family home; strangers wrote her letters begging for locks of her hair; a national fund was raised in her name; her likeness was mass-produced in Staffordshire pottery; drawings of her family were exhibited publicly to huge crowds; a circus promoter asked whether she fancied being exhibited, like some exotic performing beast; and a theatrical impresario offered her thick wodges of cash to play a heavily fictionalised version of herself in a London play. She cautiously declined.

This last request was odd. Was the truth not interesting enough? Apparently not. The first four books published about Darling were works of fiction. It seems people couldn't resist reshaping her into something even more perfect. The fact that she then died tragically young, just four years after the rescue, meant her brand was both frozen in its glorious prime and yet easily divorced from an un-quibbling corpse. Though her family valiantly struggled to correct the record, Grace Darling had already become public property; her heroic hour was a malleable and exploitable legend. She was exactly what people needed her to be. And when she wasn't, they invented her anew.

Partners in Crimea

So delighted were Britons with their plucky heroine, it was only a decade after her death before Victorians rushed to canonise two more maidens of devotion: Florence Nightingale and Mary Seacole. Recently, Seacole has been restored to the history books after having been forgotten in the twentieth century. A fascinating figure, she's become an icon of black history, and the recipient of a well-intentioned campaign to give her equal status to the more privileged Nightingale. This has accidentally led to some modern mythmaking, but both women were already semi-mythic figures in their lifetime, so perhaps it's somewhat fitting?

We'll begin with Nightingale, who was indeed properly live-in-a-country-house, summer-in-Italy posh - I mean, her sister was called Parthenope,* for goodness sake! - but young Florence was a source of constant disappointment to Ma and Pa. They desperately wanted her to swish through high society, in an assortment of fancy frocks, with a respectable husband draped on her arm. She, however, was a talented mathematician who embarked on the quaintest of rebellions by announcing that God had called her to heal the sick. How bloody selfish! Nightingale ditched her suitable boyfriend, picked up some practice abroad, and got her big chance with the outbreak of the Crimean War. In 1854 Britain ganged up with France and Ottoman Turkey in a bid to stop Russian imperial expansion.

It was a perfectly sensible war apart from the fact it was a disaster. The British Army's logistics were horrendously disorganised, and the onset of a cruel winter soon blasted its weary men into chilly desperation. Though Russian bullets and sabres thudded into British flesh, the greatest enemy was disease. Soldiers requiring medical care were shipped off to military hospitals in Turkey, but they might've been safer languishing in their tents. Ward hygiene was appalling. Nobody washed their hands, faeces were smeared on floors and walls, rats scurried around at leisure, bedsheets were infested with lice, and the amputated limbs hacked from screaming soldiers were simply fed to nearby dogs.

---

* Parthenope was the ancient Greek name for Naples, Italy, where she was born. Lucky she wasn't born in Slough, I guess.

For all the running around with guns and swords, it was typhoid, typhus, cholera, and dysentery that did most of the killing. The Crimean War was a full-blown crisis; one made embarrassingly obvious by the presence of W. H. Russell - arguably the world's first war correspondent - whose urgent battlefield updates were speedily whizzed off to *The Times* by the revolutionary telegraph machine. Britain had blithely stumbled into a military catastrophe, only to have the bad luck of broadcasting its humiliating blunder to the world's media. But that same journalist's reports also inspired Seacole and Nightingale to cross the oceans and do their bit, so not all bad, then.

Determined to launch her do-gooding career, the well-connected Florence Nightingale gained authorisation from a family friend - the Secretary of State for War, Sir Sidney Herbert - to lead a team of thirty-eight volunteer nurses to Scutari hospital in Turkey. She arrived in early November 1854, when things were at a low point. More than 4,000 men died that winter, and the obstinate army doctors battled with her over every little thing. They didn't want some opinionated woman meddling in the chain of command. Defiantly, she implemented regular laundry, clean towels, proper cutlery, improved rations, and better ventilation. She also counted the dead and notified their families, which the military had neglected to do. These things helped, but it was the arrival of the Sanitary Commission in March 1855 - which flushed the sewers, removed rotting animal corpses, and rebuilt the hospital foundations - that quite literally stopped the rot and dramatically reduced fatality rates.

In truth, Nightingale's greatest impact came after the war, not during it, because it was there that she fired up her big brain to prove the efficacy of hygiene protocols. The arrival of revolutionary germ theory soon explained why leaving men to wallow in their own shit wasn't too clever. History has thus remembered her as a badass epidemiologist with a penchant for pie chart innovation, but - let's be honest - a flair for eye-catching data visualisation isn't why the Victorians became Florence fans. No, her sudden fame was built during the crisis, and was erected not on scientific rationalism but along religious lines.

She became 'The Lady with the Lamp'; a ministering 'guardian angel' patrolling the wards each night like some docile saint. The first image depicting this vision of Christian heroism was published in *The Illustrated London News* and it had a huge impact as a cultural meme. *Punch* magazine soon joined in, publishing a poem in December 1854 with the lines:

Upon the darkness of the night how often, gliding late and
    lone,
Her little lamp, hope's beacon-light, to eyes with no hope
    else has shone!

As Mark Bostridge has shown in his excellent biography,[8] this visual conjuring alluded to a celebrated recent painting, titled *The Light of the World*, by the Pre-Raphaelite master William Holman Hunt which showed a bearded Christ with lamp in hand, knocking on an old door overgrown with weeds. Florence Nightingale was thus romanticised as a gender-swapped, proxy-Christ in a snug-fitting apron. The glowing light offered hope and comfort, but also spiritual salvation. The truth, of course, was that she needed a lamp to avoid slipping over on the blood-stained floors. But, well, that's somewhat less romantic.

Nightingale's sister became her most enthusiastic champion, and, two years after the Crimean War, Parthenope Nightingale married another Florence devotee in Sir Harry Verney, MP.* Having influential supporters bolstered Florence's influence, but the public was also emotionally invested in her celebrity thanks to the press coverage; during the war, her name cropped up in 200 separate pieces in *The Times* alone. There was also a constant outpouring of imagery in magazines and papers, songs were written about her,

---

* Verney was such an admirer he'd tried to marry Florence first, and was jokingly referred to in Parliament as the 'Member for Florence Nightingale'.

and her name became a potent brand attached to pubs, commercial products, newly launched ships, and even a noted racehorse.

But what about Mary Seacole? She was fifteen years older than Nightingale, but her identity was somewhat more nuanced than the poor, black widow of modern romance. Born Mary Grant, to a free black mother and a white Scottish officer, she was a bi-racial Brit of solid reputation. She'd grown up in the hospitality trade, and became a property-owning businesswoman when she later inherited her mother's hotel in Jamaica, but she'd also learned how to administer herbal remedies to British expats struggling with tropical fevers. She called herself a *doctress*, and caring for others' needs was her thing. After her husband's death, she travelled to Panama, where she attempted to curb an outbreak of cholera. When Russell's reports of the Crimean bungling arrived in Jamaica, she presumably considered herself qualified to join the nursing corps. But Jamaica was a long way from Turkey, and she had a business to run. So, why leave it all behind?

Seacole was ultimately a loyal champion of the Empire. Though legally considered a mixed-race 'mulatta' - she faced overt racism on her travels, particularly in Panama - Seacole felt a strong affinity for Britain's military men (such as her father), and pride in her mixed 'creole' and Scottish heritage. She'd also befriended several of the officers whose regiments had been stationed in Jamaica, and - without her own kids to raise - perhaps felt some maternal instincts towards a few of the fresh-faced youngsters being shipped off to a foreign battlefield. In any case, her autobiography tells us she travelled to London in the hope of joining Nightingale's nursing staff, but was turned down.*

Undaunted, she sailed out to the Crimean front lines to open a general store with her business partner, Thomas Day. She somewhat optimistically titled it the 'British Hotel', which, in fairness,

---

* No official paperwork corroborates this claim, so it's a real bone of contention among historians, but the argument usually offered is that Seacole wasn't selected by the recruiters because of her race. She thought so too, alluding to her 'yellow' complexion as a possible reason.

sounded rather fancy. It actually proved to be less battlefield Ritz, more wobbly snack shack built of driftwood, but any port in a storm. From this rickety establishment she sold useful goods to the soldiers but also to the tourists who enjoyed sitting on the hill with a picnic, watching while men were blown apart and bayoneted in the hazy distance. She also entertained the French, British, and Turkish officers with her own brand of Jamaican cooking and rambunctious humour.

Seacole set up her sutler's shop at Balaklava near the front lines. Nightingale's hospital was far away in Turkey. Separated by such distance, the pair probably never met, but modern retellings seek commonalities between their stories, even going so far as to call Seacole 'a Crimean nurse'. This is a slightly tricky area, and not all historians are comfortable with this label, instead arguing she was primarily an entrepreneur with only a sideline in folk remedies.[9] However, a recently recovered Australian news report from 1857 tells us she did spend the first couple of months volunteering at Balaklava Wharf, refreshing soldiers' bandages and offering them hot tea before they boarded the hospital ships.[10] To me, that's volunteer nursing.

Also, when running her hostel, Seacole certainly cared for whichever soldiers hobbled her way with painful scrapes and dodgy tummies, and even treated a few lightly injured men on the battlefield. Exuding huge warmth, and wielding a variety of poultices and concoctions, she 'nursed' the men in the same way a mum nurses a kid through flu. In return, the grateful soldiers started calling her 'Mother Seacole'. By contrast, Florence Nightingale was not one of life's great huggers, and was more doggedly diligent, ramrod-straight clipboard warrior than guardian angel. But if Seacole did some nursing, it was Nightingale who revolutionised its professional practice and should rightly take more prominence in its history.

Perhaps the most obvious difference between the two women is how they handled fame. Seacole had apparently sold her Jamaican hotel to fund the Crimean adventure and was ruined by the war's unexpected end. Her schlepp back to Britain took many months, but she received the warmest of welcomes. When news of her bankruptcy was reported, her old Crimean acquaintances threw a fundraising party to get her back on her feet, and Seacole's subsequent autobiography[11] - which is an absolute hoot, though a tad unreliable - became a bestseller. She returned to Jamaica, then came back to London, where Queen Victoria offered her financial aid to ensure relative comfort.

Seacole still wanted to be helpful and, in 1857, offered her nursing services to the British Army in India. We don't have any evidence she made the journey, but she was certainly serious about it.[12] In the meantime, she posed for paintings and photos, and sometimes sported mysterious medals that historians squabble over (awarded by whom? The Turks? The French? The British Army? Herself?). Such conspicuous embracing of fame aligns neatly with her identity as aspirational outsider craving acceptance; every name-drop in her memoir clangs like a frying pan tumbling out of a cupboard. She wasn't subtle in her self-promotion, but she was hugely admired, and with good reason. Hooray for Mary Seacole!

Nightingale, meanwhile, despised fame. Her father also found it bizarre, though her sister, Parthenope, was an enthusiastic cheerleader. Florence did all she could to prevent fame's alien tentacles from slithering into her private life, including refusing to pose for any photographs, until Queen Victoria - an avid photography buff - demanded she give the people what they wanted. Nevertheless, Nightingale's heroic reputation kicked open doors that would have stayed bolted, even to a woman of lofty privilege, and she was able to parlay her Crimean kudos into significant influence as a hygiene campaigner. When charitable donations poured in from a grateful public, she funnelled them into the world's first modern nursing school at St Thomas' Hospital in London. Her huge celebrity would serve as barely tolerated means to the noblest of ends.

Thirty-eight nurses volunteered to join Florence Nightingale in the Crimea. Seven fishermen, plus Mr Darling, went to the aid of the SS *Forfarshire*. Mary Seacole had a business partner called

Thomas Day. All of these other people threw themselves into the challenges, yet we don't remember *their* names. The razzle-dazzle process that transforms nobodies into exemplary heroes is a curious one because sometimes it celebrates valour while simultaneously ignoring it in others. None of these forgotten people were any less altruistic than the eventual superstars bathed in limelight, but it was only Darling, Nightingale and Seacole who emitted the right sort of narrative charisma. The media found *them* intrinsically fascinating, and so only *they* were forged into public heroes, while their comrades in risk slunk back into anonymity.

Rage against the machine?

If we re-examine Brenda Frazier's sad rise, or Grace Darling's elevation to heroism, we might easily assume that it's the media which determines celebrity success; the newspapers pluck someone out, bung them on the front page, and hey presto: HERO! Well, yes, that can happen. But I want to hammer a couple of dents into that pristine notion. The relationship between the media, celebrities, and public is full of tension; sometimes it's collaborative, sometimes it's coercive, and sometimes it's combative. As consumers, we're not all blinking, gullible numpties who can be mindlessly injected with propaganda.

This idea of media indoctrination was popular in the 1950s,* and is known as the *Hypodermic (or magic bullet) theory*. It argued that pop culture - and by extension the media - softens our resistance to top-down control, seducing us with a life of empty materialism and fake variety as a way of distracting us from political revolution. The damning phrase often cited was: 'freedom to choose what is always the same'. As much as I love the shouty stylings of Rage Against the Machine, this notion is as simplistic as a toddler's drawing of a horse. It's not totally wrong, just as the kid's drawing

---

* Its most famous advocates were the Marxist intellectuals of the Frankfurt School, such as Theodor Adorno and Max Horkheimer.

probably includes four legs and a head, but the whole thing is strangely distorted.

For example, *Two Step Flow Theory* says: 'Okay, yes, the media *does* have a big effect, but it's filtered indirectly through middlemen and social networks.' We're more easily influenced by our friends, neighbours, family members, and trusted colleagues than by bold fonts on billboards and broadsheets. But our friends must get their ideas from elsewhere - including the mass media - so perhaps it's propaganda as meme culture, with indoctrination being a viral process? Nice idea. But then scholars had another spin of the Big Theory wheel, and began to ask why we engage with media and pop culture in the first place - what do we get out of it? Their answer, *Uses and Gratifications Theory*, hands power back to the consumer and argues that we aren't passive idiots, but rather take pleasure in engaging with news, culture, and entertainment. We aren't victims, we're customers with some agency to choose.

We don't just believe what we're told, not least because sometimes it's fun, or psychologically stimulating, to resist. But also, we're not all the same. From even the most embryonic days of newspaper publishing in the early 1600s, commercial pressures have driven media editors towards satisfying public desires. While many media bodies tried to shift attitudes (and often succeeded), they had to work within the terms of the deal struck with the consumer. Deviate too far, and the customer would simply switch to another product. The powerful architect of late-Victorian journalism, W. T. Stead, argued that newspaper editors were much more in tune with the public than politicians, because every day was essentially a re-election campaign: 'The editor's mandate is renewed day by day, and his electors register their vote by a voluntary payment of the daily pence.'[13]

People choose to consume popular culture, and that means they influence the stuff they're given, just as the stuff they're given influences them. It's a feedback loop. The media undoubtedly affects us, but in much more subtle ways than total indoctrination. On top of that, there's also a deeper complexity. We're irrational fools with warped biases and ideological presets. Psychologists call these *confirmation bias* and *selective exposure*, which are two interlocked concepts that prove how individuals don't just swallow everything they encounter, but instead pick and choose what to absorb, and what to reject, based on whether it reinforces pre-existing ideology.[14] It's this puzzling lack of objectivity that can see us presented with seemingly persuasive information, only to remain irrationally entrenched in our wrongness.*

That same stubbornness also influences how we respond to celebrity culture. Rather than a smooth transmission from mass media to consumer, resulting in a new celebrity being instantly welcomed into the nation's hearts, the creation of historical celebrities often required something closer to bartering, or perhaps even wrestling, until the new star was either accepted or slung back into oblivion. Celebrities rising to reputation wasn't due to their being glitter-sprayed automatons in some Orwellian power game; the public weren't brainwashed sheep bleating in excitable acceptance towards whoever the media decided should be famous. No, the truth is, celebrity is a three-way equation, much like the chemical reaction needed for fire: one can't spark a flame without the triangular relationship of heat, fuel, and oxygen; and one can't produce celebrity without the interaction between a subject, an audience, and a media industry.

But that interaction didn't necessarily have to be positive. The media could choose to trash someone or praise them; the public could embrace the star or reject them; the celebrity could go with the flow, or put up a fight. This trialogue is always needed, but it can be fraught with resistance. Perhaps we see this in the response to the child superstar Master Betty. While most of Britain went crazy for him, smashing up theatres in their quest to bask in his cutesy glory, a small cohort of cynics stubbornly refused to be

---

* Spend a few hours on Twitter during a Saturday afternoon, and you'll see football fans defending their team's players against accusations of cheating or dangerous tackles, only to then make identical charges, for identical transgressions, against another team. See also: Politics.

coerced by the tsunami of praise. Leigh Hunt and various satirists weren't taken in by Bettymania, and, within eighteen months, were smugly saying 'I told you so!' when the bubble burst. But why weren't they charmed by the boy genius when everyone else went bonkers for Betty?

Love 'em or hate 'em

For Hunt, it was painfully personal. He'd been a whizzkid too, first emerging on the literary scene with his schoolboy poetry compilation *Juvenilia*, some of which he'd composed aged just twelve. Hunt was foremost among the defenders of youthful creativity, but, now in his twenties, he seemed to be scared by Betty. Hunt perhaps transposed his own regrets at having been prematurely overhyped onto another younger model.[15] Master Betty's fame was so intense for one so young that the only direction of travel was down. Failure is the only consequence when success is unsustainable, and so it proved for the boy wonder.

But, other satirists had different reasons to prick the balloon. Audiences are complex and rebellious; sometimes it's an act of defiance to go against the crowd, sometimes stuff just isn't to our tastes, and sometimes it's just funny to tip over sacred cows and watch their chunky legs flail pathetically in the air, simply to horrify those who worship them. Much of anti-fandom's appeal seems to come from challenging orthodox opinions. Many of us will hate-watch movies and TV shows for the pleasure of savaging them; that might involve watching some ironically godawful B-movie about Nazi space-sharks, but there's also pleasurable haughtiness to be found in trashing good quality, mainstream stuff that is really popular. Among my friends, *Love Actually* is either a wonderful romantic comedy, or a cinematic crime that needs to be ceremonially eviscerated with bloodthirsty relish. Oddly, both factions will watch it again and again in a ritual of group amusement.[16] In short, Master Betty was the Richard Curtis of the Romantic Era.

If we leap back another century, we find an even more divisive celebrity - indeed, the earliest example in this book. Weirdly, this paradigm-busting maverick wasn't some illustrious actor in fancy shoes, or a romantic poet offering swoon-worthy ballads, but rather a conservative churchman in a ludicrous wig who became a simultaneous hero and villain, depending on how people voted. His name was Doctor Henry Sacheverell, and he was an ambitious Anglican minister who gave a fiery speech from the pulpit of St Paul's Cathedral on 5 November 1709, attacking 'false brethren' in the church. Delivered on the anniversary of Guy Fawkes's plot to blow up King James I and his Parliament, it was immediately perceived as a political broadside against the Whig party by pro-royalist Tories, and thus Sacheverell was thrust into the centre of a political maelstrom. And, in case you're not up on your maelstroms, the eighteenth-century public loved 'em!

Before long, 100,000 copies of his speech had been sold, with estimates suggesting as many as 250,000 people may have encountered the text.[17] London's population was probably no larger than 600,000 people. His next speech was attended by a huge mob, desperate to get into the church. Alarmed at his sudden popularity, Queen Anne's ministers in the Whig government attempted to try him for sedition; but he'd selected his words too carefully, so they instead successfully charged him with High Crimes and Misdemeanours in the House of Lords. The punishment was suspension from his post and the burning of two of his speeches; not exactly the harshest of sentences in a legal system where someone could be hanged for 200 different offences, but, no matter, for it was still perceived as splashing petrol on an already crackling fire.

Sacheverell became a living martyr to the cause; an Anglican hero cheered like a champion boxer as he paraded through the streets, and was commemorated with window illuminations and bonfires across England. The excitement soon turned to violence, and riots broke out in defence of his reputation. Capitalising on his unexpected fame, he began touring the country, escorted on his travels by huge retinues of horse guards; he was wined and dined by the great Tory magnates, cheered by vast crowds in various cities, and wherever he went he preached and hollered against the Whig government in his distinctive style.

Sacheverell was both a criminal and a champion of moral virtue; a patriot and a seditious threat. Moreover, he was a conservative theologian who'd somehow ended up acquiring the glamour of the rockstar rebel, or the dandy highwayman. He didn't just become merely famous, he was transformed into a noisy focal point for identity politics, and then commercialised into a lucrative brand. And it's this last part which made him an early celebrity, in my eyes. As the historian Brian Cowan writes:

> His effigy was reproduced and distributed in paint, print, cloth, wax and sculpture by a rapidly growing commercial art market that seized on the politics of personality and cha-risma as a sales technique . . . The Whig *Observator* exclaimed that 'Sacheverell's picture is now more hugg'd and admir'd than any that we have in the late editions of our Common-Prayer books' . . . Hostile observers such as the Whig cleric William Bisset observed with disgust that 'nine parts in ten of the publick houses, whether taverns, ale-houses, or brandy-shops, are staunch conformists; and most of them have the Doctor's picture in their chief drinking rooms, and some, as I have seen, his sign at their doors'.[18]

Cowan goes on to describe how, at the height of Sacheverell's new fame, penny loaves were inscribed with his name and the year, medals were issued, commemorative plates were struck, ceramic statuettes were made, babies were named in his honour, his chubby face appeared on wax-seals so people could stamp it into their letters, and he stared out from ladies' fans, decks of cards, tobacco pipes, and coat buttons. His name was shouted by rioters, by voters, by enemies and allies alike; he even helped the Tories triumph in the new election, meaning if you think modern celebs telling people how to vote is new, I have news for you - it's literally there on the first page of celebrity's 300-year-old history.

Doctor Henry Sacheverell was an old-school religious figure propelled into an aggressively politicised culture and rendered tradeable commodity. I must stress, celebrity culture was extremely young in 1709, and the next-earliest case studies in this book didn't turn up until the mid-1720s, some fifteen years later. So it's remarkable that Sacheverell was already every inch the modern celebrity. But there's no doubting he was both hugely famous and deeply divisive: a hero to those of his political persuasion; to others a threat. He was a quantum *quasar*, if you will.

Mr Myth goes to Washington

Henry Sacheverell's heroic fame was born of a cause. He was a strong orator and a talented self-promoter, but his power came from widespread engagement. Conservatives needed him, or someone like him, as a talismanic figurehead for their movement. Sixty-five years later, across the Atlantic, there was an even greater need for a figurehead when America was unshackling itself from British rule. The odds were against them. Britain was a military superpower; the American Continental Army was a ragtag bunch of farmers and clerks, equipped with whatever weapons, uniforms, and footwear could be bought, borrowed, or stolen. The only hope of victory was in uniting the Thirteen Colonies behind the cause, drawing in French support, and trusting in the military leadership of a new hero. And that last bit was crucial.

From the moment he was appointed commander of the revolutionary army in 1775, George Washington was the focus of a propaganda campaign designed to transform him into a unifying American symbol. It wasn't just fame that was thrust upon Washington, but the hopes of a nation. As the historian Antoine Lilti describes it: 'Cities and counties were named after him, his portrait was widely distributed through every media channel, newspapers enthusiastically reported his smallest movement as though reporting incredible exploits. Celebrations were organized in honour of "His Excellency," and public parades celebrated his birthday every year . . .'[19]

As with Sacheverell's notoriety and Bettymania's wild excesses, such hero worship didn't go without criticism. Once independence was secured, some feared America's experimental republicanism would be endangered by the seductive idea of another Great Man ruling from on high. Would King George be replaced by another King George? John Adams – who ended up serving as America's second president – feared his own star being overshadowed by the quasi-monarchical razzamatazz of Washington's reverence. The new leader was variously hailed as a master military tactician, a great orator, and a throbbing intellectual genius, but all three were exaggerations. A bustling machine churned out presidential puffery, not so far removed from the cynical propaganda later adopted by the Corsican upstart Napoleon Bonaparte.[20]

What's particularly intriguing is how reluctant Washington seemed to be in his fame. A naturally cautious politician, possessing all the flamboyance of a bowl of porridge, he was so self-effacing that even the idea of writing his own memoirs felt too much like self-congratulation. Despite being America's most famous person, he was modesty incarnate. Indeed, a little too modest? The historian John Ferling has asked if this was a conniving strategy of faux-reticence: was Washington not really the public-spirited, spartan hero but actually a glory-obsessed fame monster? Was his turning down the chance to write an autobiography history's most epic humblebrag?[21]

I'm less cynical. I suspect Washington recognised the importance of his symbolism, but felt awkward squeezing into the superhero's spandex, perhaps because of natural self-consciousness, but also because self-aggrandisement wasn't behaviour befitting a privileged gentleman such as himself. Having won the war, and led America through its wobbly first steps, Washington's reputation was already guaranteed, but his legacy acquired an extra golden sheen when he voluntarily resigned his presidency in 1796. This decision saw his heroic cult supercharged even further by a new association with Cincinnatus, the ancient Roman warrior who took up emergency powers in Rome's darkest hour only to return to his farm when the danger had passed.

Washington hadn't pulled a Caesar, nor done a Napoleon. He wasn't a grubby despot, clinging to power; he'd voluntarily returned the keys to the President's House and wished the next guy good luck. His work was done; he was incorruptible. This meme of moral perfection continued to expand in popular culture until – by 1809 – his childhood had been dramatically rewritten so that, even as a small boy, it was claimed he'd been too honest to lie to his dad about smashing a hatchet into a beloved cherry tree. George Washington had begun adulthood as a loyal British soldier and ended it as an American secular saint, romanticised beyond reality.[22]

This is how celebrity heroes are forged. The person does something exciting, the media takes notice, it greys out others around them – so the star image seems more vibrant by comparison – and then the public and the media collaborate on mythologising this new icon, or rejecting them. Anyone, at any time, was capable of heroic deeds, but to be recognised as heroic meant having others apply the heroising filter. Heroes are always invented, even if the raw material is already there. As the sociologist Gary Alan Fine has argued, such heightened reputations are contracts struck with the public, who agree to think of the hero in a new way. But this also requires the de-personhood of the individual.[23] Heroes must have their flaws and foibles painted over. Their lives are rewritten as hagiographies.*

Meanwhile, villains have their positive character traits warped or obliterated to fit an almost demonic model of public evil: we see this with serial killers where the guy who 'keeps himself to himself' is reconstructed as the 'loner' when the finger of suspicion starts jabbing away. The good guys become perfect role models, the bad guys irredeemable threats to public decency.[24] Complicated people are made into fairy tales; nuance is told to sod off and die!

---

* The term for biographies of Christian saints that turned them into spotless martyrs.

It's a process that's been repeated countless times, perhaps most obviously with military heroes.[25]

Take, for example, Britain's naval titan Horatio Nelson. He rose to fame by kicking Napoleon's arse at the Battle of the Nile, and he celebrated by launching into an open affair with the married Emma Hamilton; it was a romance that couldn't have been more obvious if he'd painted her famously voluptuous breasts on the side of his flagship. Such adultery was usually humiliating, perhaps even career-destroying, but Nelson's shining lustre mostly inoculated him against reputational annihilation. Mistresses were nothing new, but Nelson behaved terribly to his wife, Frances, and that was much less forgivable to some of his senior naval colleagues, who refused to visit Nelson and Emma's shared home. Regardless, the affair was still allowed to play out; satirists eagerly mocked Lord Hamilton for being a blind old cuckold, and increasingly sexualised Emma's image, but the barbs left little injury on the adulterous power couple at the heart of Regency high society. Nelson's heroism defused the explosive anger, leaving only sniggers of innuendo.[26]

But as soon as the French sniper's bullet fatally punctured Nelson's body at the Battle of Trafalgar, the harsh rules of decorum kicked back in. With Lord Hamilton already dead, and her heroic lover's body returning home preserved in a brandy barrel, Emma Hamilton was exposed to a howling gale of moral backlash. Without his protection to shelter her, she was ostracised. Frances Nelson assumed the dignified role of grieving widow, but Emma wasn't permitted to grieve in public. Nelson, having already been a celebrity, became something else in death: the upstanding icon of British masculinity – a naval hero. He had died protecting his country from foreign invasion, and his adventures with other people's wives were hushed up so that only his valour, and not his libido, stood erect atop Nelson's Column in London's Trafalgar Square.

The Nelson brand required whitewashing for the benefit of society. Britain needed its champion; it didn't need Emma Hamilton.[27] As the decades rolled on, his biographers stopped referring to the affair altogether, or decried Emma Hamilton as a terribly judged episode in his life which was best left ignored. She'd risen from working-class sex worker* to diplomat's wife to celebrity beauty to notorious mistress, but now she cycled back to shameful indignity. Indeed, such was her poor reputation that the painter most associated with her numerous portraits, George Romney, was also posthumously dissed by Victorians appalled at his collaborations with her.[28] In the mythologisation process, George Washington was made incapable of lying, and the heroic Horatio Nelson was made incapable of lying with other women. All the while, their real human flaws - one being an unapologetic slave-owner, one a noted philanderer - vanished.

Shooting stars

In 1899, the American opera impresario Oscar Hammerstein opened a new venue in New York called The Victoria Theater. He'd had high hopes, even if he'd saved a few bucks by installing second-hand upholstery, but it didn't go well - all his productions floundered at the box office. By 1904 he'd had to change tack; it now became the successful home of vaudeville acts, and before long his son, Willie Hammerstein, took charge as Oscar went off in search of another challenge. Young Willie, however, didn't share Daddy's highbrow instincts. For him, entertainment wasn't about quality, it was about provoking a reaction. Or, in his own words: 'anything's a good act that will make 'em talk!' And so Willie started booking so-called 'freak acts'.

Among his most memorable bookings were a squadron of salacious tabloid celebrities who'd literally shot to fame: there was Nan Patterson, a dancing girl who'd got off despite shooting her married lover in a taxi; Florence Carman, who'd allegedly gunned down her husband's mistress; and the sensational duo Lillian Graham and Ethel Conrad, who'd shot the millionaire socialite W. E. D.

---

* Probably . . . the evidence isn't conclusive, but most historians think so.

Stokes in the leg while possibly attempting to blackmail him.[29] As the biographer Marybeth Hamilton has noted, quoting a vaudeville insider: 'So great did the vogue for female killers and near-killers become, that "every pawnshop gun sold to a woman practically carried the guarantee of a week's booking".'[30] The most famous of these 'Shooting Stars' was the beautiful Evelyn Nesbit, who didn't wield the pistol herself but was the cause of a murderous feud between her millionaire former lover and her violently unstable trust fund husband. It led to the so-called 'Trial of the Century' that flung Nesbit from the frying pan of horror into the burning fire of legal infamy (we'll cover this horrible story in Chapter 6).[31]

One hundred years ago, the entertainment industry was carving out space for lurid, lucrative celebs whose brand was pure infamy. Who could resist a tap-dancing murderess singing a cutesy ballad about her beloved? Turns out, the musical *Chicago* is basically a documentary, but with jazz hands. Theatre historians have treated this moment as something of an outlier; Willie Hammerstein (father of the brilliant songwriter of Rodgers and Hammerstein fame) was an upstart breed of provocateur willing to boot taste and decency out of the window to instead play to the public's basest instincts. But, in truth, criminals and villains had already been turned into entertainers for at least two centuries, and not always as dark stars whose sinister deeds baffled and transfixed the public. Sometimes they were made into folk heroes, eliciting sympathy from the mob.

If we jump back to the 1720s, following in the wake of Henry Sacheverell's pioneering celebrity, we find two such controversial characters in London and Paris, respectively. England's celebrity bad boy was Jack Sheppard, a young carpenter whose passion for boozing and bonking saw him take up burglary to fund his hedonism. Jack wasn't particularly cunning in evading capture - he had a habit of returning to his favourite haunts like a dog to its own vomit - but he had a magnificent talent for escaping custody. To the astonishment of his jailers, and to the delight of the public, Sheppard managed to break out of prison four times - his final jaunt being an outrageously difficult escape from the secure 'castle' in Newgate Gaol, where he'd been doubly cuffed and had his legs chained to the floor.

Perhaps inevitably, this impish rogue became a working-class hero who 'made such a noise in the town, that it was thought the common people would have gone mad about him, there being not a porter to be had for love nor money, nor getting into an ale-house, for butchers, shoemakers and barbers, all engaged in controversies and wagers about Sheppard'.[32] Meanwhile, street musicians were said to have 'subsisted many days very comfortably upon ballads and letters' that exploited his newfound fame. Sheppard knew it too. His memoir claims he disguised himself as a beggar, just so he could join in gossiping about himself. This is now the sort of amusingly egocentric prank played by undercover celebs on American chat shows, but in the 1720s, when celebrity was barely fifteen years old, this was top-notch innovation in the art of ironic trolling.

Sheppard never expected fame, he was just a petty criminal who didn't want to die, but when celebrity transformed him into a rousing folk hero - an apprentice boy sticking it to the man - he cheerfully played along. The finest artists in the kingdom came to draw him, so he gave them his finest pose. Silk-draped aristocracy visited him in his cells, so he charmed their socks off. Depictions of his daring escapes were circulated in pamphlets, and journalists eagerly puffed him with his explicit permission. He was a media sensation who decided to paddle along with the tide.

Plenty of the journalistic material was anonymous, so scholars furiously debate how much of it came from Daniel Defoe's quill,[33] but there's no doubting the author of *Robinson Crusoe* made great hay from Sheppard's illicit adventures, possibly forging Jack's letter supposedly sent from Australia (it handily namechecked Defoe's newspaper, which seems an all-too-convenient advert). Defoe also probably ghostwrote Sheppard's authorised memoir, which Jack - showing tremendous brand awareness when moments from death - loudly promoted while en route to the noose. Oops! Sorry - spoiler alert. Yes, despite his ingenious flair for breaking chains, Sheppard finally copped it in the winter of 1724.

He'd planned his most audacious escape yet, hoping to be cut down from the gallows, carried away, and revived by his friends, but they were thwarted by the vast, jostling mob of an alleged 200,000 onlookers who'd come to stare at the sensational celebrity they'd heard so much about. Ironically, he was unwittingly killed by his own fans. Jack Sheppard's celebrity burned brighter than an exploding star, and, though he was dead within a year, it continued to glow for decades – even in the nineteenth century, jailbreaks and escapes were described in the press using his name. Having failed to be revived at the gallows, he enjoyed the next best thing: being reanimated as the hero of a nineteenth-century novel by William Harrison Ainsworth.[34] But Sheppard's fictional afterlife was somewhat eclipsed by Ainsworth's other romanticised miscreant.

In the novel *Rookwood*, Dick Turpin is an Essex butcher-turned-highwayman who rides from London to York on his horse, Black Bess. In truth, Turpin made no such ride, and owned no such steed. Nor was he a dashing anti-hero. In fact, he was a savage, pock-marked murderer and thief. We might ask why an early-Victorian novelist would choose to glamorise such a vicious thug, and the answer could be as simple as the fact that Turpin, and men like him, were no longer a threat. Ainsworth's readers in 1834 were starting to take trains, and it would've been an idiotically brave highwayman who stood on the tracks and yelled: 'Stand and deliver!' at an oncoming battering ram of steam and speed.[35] Technological progress had made the world safer: the golden age of piracy was long gone, and the highwayman had been neutralised. Writing about extinct threats was perhaps like shark-diving in the safety of a steel cage. It still got the blood pumping, but the jeopardy was mere simulation. Plus, you know, nostalgia is fun!

I should make it clear that Turpin's reputation during his life had been somewhat glamorised too. In the 1730s, his crimes were reported with outraged alarm, but so was his fashion sense; thanks to the *Whitehall Evening Post* we know he favoured an open-laced hat, while his companion rode with gold lacing.[36] And he performed the role of showman at his execution, bowing dramatically to the rabble and going to his death with a flourish. So, for all the mindless violence, there lurked a celebrity performer in there somewhere. Turpin understood his role, though perhaps – as the historian Vic Gattrell noted – the terror of death, or the desire to throw one last middle-fingered salute to the authorities, might explain the performative bravado with which men like Turpin met the gallows.[37]

Another obvious comparison was Edward Teach – better known as Blackbeard the Pirate – whose ingenious instincts for celebrity branding saw him stuff burning fuses into his thick black beard. This was all part of his performance as deranged slaughterer, and he undoubtedly spilled blood along the way – there's no such thing as pacifist piracy – but he was a cunning tactician who much preferred intimidation over violence; why risk a dangerous sea battle when he could terrify enemy sailors into surrendering without a fight? After a two-year spell rampaging around the Caribbean and making a nuisance of himself with American coastal towns,* he was hunted down in 1718 by the coastguard and, after an exciting battle worthy of a Hollywood popcornfest, had his head sliced off by a British lieutenant. The head was apparently hoisted up on the ship's rigging and then was displayed back on the mainland, with legend telling that someone fetched it down, plated it in silver, and turned his skull into a gruesome tankard used in a Virginia tavern. Blackbeard lived a celebrity and died as one too.

The romantic rascal

Despite all these naughty provocateurs, I previously mentioned two heroic villains: one in London, one in Paris. Jack Sheppard was the first, but now we turn to the infamous 'Cartouche' (real name Louis Dominique Garthausen, although he was also more

---

* He besieged Charleston probably in the hope of acquiring medicinal mercury to treat the crew's venereal disease. It would've been injected up the urethra with a terrifyingly large syringe. If that wasn't bad enough, mercury is dangerously toxic.

famously known as Louis Dominique Bourguignon), whose short life as rambunctious gang-leader was ended when his back was broken on the execution wheel in 1721. His crime? Robbing from the rich to give to the poor. I can hear you gasp excitedly from here: yes, he was a real-life Robin Hood, minus the fannying about in trees and the twanging of longbows. Sadly, his name doesn't scan properly with 'riding through the glen', so we'll just move on.

Cartouche's escapes, crimes, and captures were pored over by an obsessive public; his story was immediately dramatised in two plays, one of which proved so successful the police had to shut it down after thirteen performances. But, as with Turpin, we have to ask: why the appeal? Here was a dude rampaging around Paris, spilling blood, and ignoring the basic tenets of property law. Cartouche was a killer. If they'd met him in a dark alley, Cartouche's fans might have wet their breeches in fear, but, when safely trapped in newspaper ink, he glided across the page like a romantic protagonist in some medieval fantasy. It gave him a fanbase. So why the allure?

Jeffrey Jerome Cohen, in exploring the power of monsters in popular culture, has argued that – for all their chilling subversion – 'the monster also attracts. The same creatures who terrify and interdict can evoke potent escapist fantasies.'[38] These celebrity stories were enticingly mythic, they allowed the public to experience the poetry of a compelling plot. But highwaymen were also a special breed. To explain their heroic appeal, we might invoke E. P. Thompson's idea of *social crime,* meaning an illegal act that feels morally justifiable.[39] Cartouche and Sheppard weren't just threats. To the oppressed members of the lower classes, they were moral bandits, fighting the good fight with necessarily extreme tactics. This was celebrity constructed through heroic defiance.

It's also intriguing to see just how often British newspapers invoked celebrity criminals as satirical mallets with which to thump those in power, launching into 'whataboutery' whenever some petty robber held up a stagecoach by gesticulating wildly not at the pistol-wielding bad guy in the tricorn hat, but at the corruption in government. As Andrea McKenzie notes,[40] the low-status baddies were a problem, sure, and they'd hang for their raucous infringements, but the frequent complaints were that the real abuse was happening in Westminster and Whitehall. The *real* crooks were the politicians.

There were various attempts to downplay the sinister nature of the highwayman, draining his violence of its malice and instead connecting his crime to bigger corruption higher up the food chain. The highwayman was almost noble in his rebellion; an upwardly mobile commoner earning his rakish reputation at the end of a pistol. Violence gave him (or her)* a sort of aristocracy. But the historian Antoine Lilti makes an intriguing alternative suggestion: 'One might hypothesize that Parisian interest in the figure of Cartouche came less from an acceptance of criminality than from a mix of curiosity and empathy which celebrity aroused ... the success of various texts about his life was that they encouraged the feeling that Parisians constituted a public which was interested in the same things at the same time, read the same news, and attended the same plays.'[41]

This feels like an interesting point, so let's develop it a little. In Lilti's words, it's possible public infatuation with Cartouche wasn't them just cheering on rule-breaking resistance, but was also proof of an appetite for shared experiences and a sense of belonging to a community of conversation – this is what the philosopher Jürgen Habermas called 'the public sphere'. Habermas argued that the idea of a general public first arrived in the early 1700s, and was aided by new innovations, like daily newspapers, that allowed people to share information. In his version, the middle-class public now became newly engaged in rational-critical debate about big, important stuff: political news, trade updates, the passage of wars, that sort of thing.

But perhaps Habermas was being a tad highbrow, because, as

---

* We have very little evidence for famous highwaywomen in the 1700s, but they were sometimes written about in folk ballads and fictional pamphlets.

well as affairs of state, we know the public also devoured affairs of love and hate: celebrity sex scandals, petty feuds, love matches, and, of course, the deeds of famous criminals. Those members of the public who excitedly followed Cartouche's crimes weren't necessarily fans, they may simply have found it thrilling to join a citywide, or even nationwide, conversation that bonded them to their fellow citizens. This harmonises nicely with the work of Benedict Anderson, who argued that nations are real political structures built from 'imagined communities';[42] we'll never meet all the people in our country, or even in our nearest town, but we can feel profoundly connected to them through shared symbols such as flags, national anthems, languages, jokes, faiths, foods etc. Americans salute the flag, English people moan about the weather – we all have a thing that fuses strangers into groups.

Rather than everyone cheering Cartouche on, then, perhaps his fame was just the eighteenth-century equivalent of what it's like to be on Twitter when a big scandal breaks. Personally, this is when I get most excited; I always feel compelled to drop what I'm doing and join in, and my heart thumps faster in my chest knowing I'm one of many eager wags desperately trying to fashion a workable pun out of some disgraced transport minister's surname. Often, I don't even care about this person, I may only have heard of them that morning, yet still I gobble up the breaking news and delight in taking part in the conversation. Celebrities help us belong; they glue us together. They're the show ponies that we gather to judge en masse. And criminals have long been fertile topics of communal banter.

But why is that? What's so interesting about criminals?

Ruddy hell!

In 1775, a beautiful courtesan called Margaret Rudd was accused of forging a bond certificate, using a Captain William Adair's name, and then asking Robert Perreau to deliver it for her. Perreau suspected a crime, reported it, and blamed Rudd for the whole thing.

She initially confessed. Then she changed her mind, and retaliated by blaming him and his twin brother, Daniel, for putting her up to it. Were they wealthy fraudsters, and she a vulnerable woman? Or was she the mastermind, and they her rich stooges? The story generated a massive public response, because this was a proper whodunnit played out under the shadow of the gallows. Death awaited any guilty party. The accused and the excited public frantically waged a media war, publishing letters and adverts apportioning blame and chucking around accusations, as if they were proto-Sherlocks with a sharp eye for evidence.

The case has been carefully explored by Donna T. Andrew and Randall McGowen,[43] who show that Rudd was particularly aggressive in her press campaign, complaining that the Perreaus were 'concerting abominable falsehoods, whereby they hope to blacken my character . . . How falsely my enemies represented me . . . how undeservedly I was persecuted and traduced by them.' But who to believe? Many papers played both sides off against each other, finding profit in the friction. Some were partisan, and launched stinging attacks on their preferred culprit. Every element of the suspects' lives was up for grabs; their luxurious clothing and taste in furniture were obsessively reported. The case became a cause célèbre, and the trio were thrust into a strange, unwanted celebrity as the nation debated the quality of their character and capacity for cunning.

The Perreau twins hired a top-notch legal team and mounted a strong defence, which made their guilty verdict all the more shocking. Rudd, however, delivered an emotional masterclass in the witness box, convincing the blind judge, Henry Fielding, of her innocence through the fragility of her voice. The newspapers were split, some calling it a triumph for English law, others a terrible miscarriage of justice. With Rudd now off the hook, she might wisely have slunk off to the shadows, at least until the brouhaha was over; instead, she set about living her best, brashest life as the mistress of the obnoxious rake Lord Lyttelton. She flaunted her escape in everyone's face, wearing her gorgeous frocks around fashionable Bath, and this pissed off pretty much everyone. Soon, the newspapers were almost unanimous in complaining she'd got off on a technicality and that the Perreaus deserved a pardon.

Over the next few months, the rescue campaign escalated. Petitions and letters poured in; people placed bets on a last-minute gesture of clemency, and the press levered every ounce of its influence in trying to save them, reporting with urgent pathos that Robert's wife and kids had personally begged the royal family for a pardon. But the king was unconvinced. When the fateful day came, 40,000 spectators thronged to watch the Perreaus go to the gallows.

There was a standard rubric to public executions; the condemned were supposed to put on a show of contrition, ask for God's forgiveness, and die with as much dignity as an asphyxiating, bladder-emptying human could muster. This ritual of atonement lingered from a godlier age when the criminal's soul was the focus, and spiritual atonement was on offer. However, by the eighteenth century, things had changed. The new popular fascination wasn't with souls wiped clean of sin, but with the sensational details of the crime: the who, what, when, why, and how. These were the explosive ammunition which ignited a new genre of criminal biography that got tongues wagging. The gathered crowd hadn't come for a religious experience, they craved human drama. But faith was still meant to be part of that fatal theatre.

The Perreaus, decked out in their finest clothes, protested their innocence to the very end in moving scenes of mournful farewells. It proved shocking. Where was the heavenly confession? Surely guilty men would renounce their crimes in front of God? Was the real female culprit cavorting in some toff's bed while these two patsies had taken the fall? Executions normally offered up moral absolutism, but it had failed to show up. Instead, their deaths brought only outrageous doubt. The executed twins were now posthumously retitled the 'unfortunate Perreaus', and their fame acquired a tragic hue, while Margaret Rudd – once defended by some as an elegant but mousy scapegoat, lured into a plot by nefarious bigwigs

- now acquired the scorching epithet of 'the infamous Mrs Rudd'.

Their respective stories were turned into plays, poems, and songs, but she bore the brunt, being repeatedly depicted as a conniving hussy who'd married the Devil himself - sadly, nobody thought to title anything *Ruddy Hell!* - and who'd placed her wealth and happiness over the lives of the Perreaus:

> First appeared and to conviction swore,
> Her smallest crime was that of being Whore;
> Adultery she added to her plan,
> Defying equally both God and man;
> In forgery and perjury owned such art,
> She palmed the Gold, while others paid the smart.[44]

As with Miley Cyrus, Rudd's celebrity brand was constructed anew: she'd had two conflicting reputations thrust upon her, the wronged woman and the fatal harlot. Oddly, she seems to have enjoyed both, and did what she could to maximise her celebrity by launching a somewhat unsuccessful writing career; she then seduced the famed celebrity-hunter, and biographer of Dr Samuel Johnson, James Boswell. He was irresistibly attracted to her provocative fame, or what he called 'the universally celebrated . . . feminine sensation' of the winter of 1775-6 and 'the most talked of woman in Great Britain'. But he knew her reputation, noting he was initially as cautious as when opposite a snake 'that fascinates with the eyes'.[45] Boswell knew Mrs Rudd was a man-eating python, but he couldn't resist her allure. As we heard before, the monster also attracts.

Here be monsters

Mrs Rudd had claimed to be a martyr, but was transformed into a demon. Though there was a thrilling sexual frisson attached to her alleged wickedness, which Boswell no doubt enjoyed, she became a controversial celebrity booed in the limelight for years to come, like a pantomime baddie. Her notoriousness was wholly negative, yet it was kinda fun! It seemed to be welcomed, even though it was scandalising. By contrast, Cartouche and Jack Sheppard were edgy and dangerous, they robbed and killed, but they'd exuded a class consciousness that bathed them in the warm light of underdog romance. The public wanted them to get away with it, perhaps because it was exciting to read their exploits, but also because each one of their victories felt like a win for the average Joe; a sharp kick in the shins for the privileged elite.

Criminal heroes also allowed people to vicariously vent their frustrations at a society trapping them in mundane lives. Anthropologists such as Max Gluckman[46] have argued for the existence of 'rituals of rebellion', or so-called 'safety valve' occasions, when rigidly structured societies allow a brief window for booing the priest and chucking rotten fruit at the powerful. These temporary inversions of power, or rather subversions of dignity, briefly allow the shat-upon masses to release their anger, feel better, then go back to normal, allowing the system to carry on unchanged. Later scholars associated this with boisterous carnivals; but might we do it with celebrities? Heroes serve an obvious function - they're meant to inspire and exemplify shared values, acting as beacons for ideal conduct - but, surprisingly, celebrity villains do the same. In the words of David Schmid: 'The famous are simultaneously like us and completely other than us, inhabiting a different order of reality that we both desire and resent.'[47]

Goodies uphold society's ideals, while baddies act as naughty human carnivals that test ethical boundaries. This idea was first proposed by Emile Durkheim, the father of modern sociology, at the turn of the twentieth century. He argued that too much crime is bad, because then you're living in a Mad Max dystopia with heavily tattooed heavy-metal guitarists strapped to the front of weaponised trucks (okay, he didn't say that *exactly*); but, surprisingly, he also said too little crime is bad. What you need, he reckoned, was just the right amount of crime, because crime allows for punishment, and punishment is the process through which society 'heals the wounds in the collective sentiment' and reaffirms shared values.[48]

In Durkheim's ideology, villains have a function. They're the provocateurs who find the limits by crossing them. Celebrity often plays this role; through the provocative deeds of the stars, we're constantly confronting ethical dilemmas about sex, drugs, booze, gender, politics, religion, and the rest. Perhaps the most extreme example is the strangest celebrity villain of them all: the serial killer – the beast who combines shocking *horror* with alluring *mystery* to produce the irresistible fascination of the gothic monster. In the words of the criminologist Scott Bonn, celebrity slaughterers, 'tantalize, terrify, and entertain the public'.[49] Rather than celebrity as monster, they are the monster as celebrity; their cold-eyed savagery becomes a baffling puzzle that we obsess over, looking for clues as to why some people are driven to kill.

This is a rationalist, modern approach to human understanding; it's the realm of forensic psychologists and tense cinematic thrillers. Among us walk those who might be downright evil. But, in the good old days of medieval Catholic theology, it wasn't a small coterie of nasties you had to watch out for, instead Original Sin handily wrote off the entire human race as evil. Humanity started out damned, and then had to spend a lifetime untarnishing itself with an endless ritual of prayer, holy sacraments, good works, and devout faith. Murder was basically inevitable because of Adam and Eve's inquisitiveness; their divine punishment came pre-installed in all of us. It's for this reason that public executions carried that spiritual power of atonement; it wasn't just about the criminal having their soul wiped clean, it was about reminding the crowd of their own potential for sin. Attending a hanging was supposed to be a warning shot, even if the rowdy party atmosphere often suggested anything but.

But then along came the supposed Age of Enlightenment in the 1700s,* when smooth-chinned liberal philosophers stressed

---

* Some historians get quite tetchy over whether this was ever a thing. I'm ringing the doorbell, leaving it on your doorstep, but running away.

humanity's ability to master their passions and adopt a rational mentality. Humans were no longer thought to be innately evil, they were products of their upbringing, and could be taught to be good and wise. If they suddenly lost their cool and killed someone, well, it was probably the 'tempest of the soul' whipping up the waves of emotion, leading to crimes driven by jealousy, passion, and revenge.

This pristine idea was demolished every time some high-functioning member of society decided to poison his wife or set fire to the kids for no apparent reason. The 'why?' of these crimes – what Hercule Poirot might call motive – couldn't be explained by appeals to logic or passion. Some offences defied explanation. Some people were just, well, evil? In such cases, mystery became horror's dance partner in the dark ballet of crime. Humanity's inexplicable capacity for violence became seductively powerful, and this was heightened by a revolution in nineteenth-century journalism that embraced a new tabloid sensationalism obsessed with murder as a genre of titillation.[50]

In the late 1880s, the vile archetype for the modern serial killer stalked London's East End, gruesomely murdering at least five women. He was never caught. Initially the newspapers nicknamed him Leather Apron, or the Whitechapel Murderer, but then a taunting letter – beginning with the greeting 'Dear Boss' – was sent into the Central News Agency. It was ostensibly written by the killer, and he'd signed it 'Jack the Ripper'. When the papers got hold of it, a global legend was born. The horrified public was both scared and morbidly fascinated by this tabloid ruckus, and soon a gaggle of shady sorts quickly monetised the buzz: waxwork museums offered horrific reproductions of the mutilated victims, pavement artists drew their contorted bodies, the bloodstained crime scenes were opened up for paying onlookers, newspapers printed bad-taste jokes,* and penny gaff theatres gave visual tours

---

* Dr Bob Nicholson runs a Twitter account sharing Victorian jokes. You can read them at https://twitter.com/DigiVictorian.

of his rampages, alongside various other famous criminals from history (including Jack Sheppard).[51]

The Ripper became a lucrative gothic industry. He terrified the Victorian public, and yet compelled them to take a step closer, to pay money for access to his crimes, to bask in the brutality of his atrocities, and consume his evil output as a commercial product. 'The monster also attracts.' Today Jack the Ripper is the centre-piece in a London tourist attraction because his sinister brand of transgression still hooks nice, non-murderous people like us, and reels us in, acting as a profound reminder that we live in a society where eviscerating strangers is definitely not okay. Jack the Ripper crossed the line in the most heinous of ways, and some people still find the mystery of his identity incredibly compelling. Personally, I would rather read Hallie Rubenhold's powerful book, *The Five*,[52] which refocused the story on his victims, challenging old myths and reminding us of their stolen humanity.

Blimey! We ended up in a dark place there, didn't we? Sorry about that. But it's important to stress that, though there are obvi-ous differences between the adored and hated - the Grace Darlings and the Mrs Rudds, the George Washingtons and Jack the Rippers - ultimately both heroes and villains were equally shovelled into the steam furnace, to keep society chugging ever forward. It turns out that celebrity and notoriety burn at the same temperature. Serial killers played their public part as much as military generals, while highwaymen and pirates were strangely elevated alongside the more obvious heroines in hospitals and lifeboats.

All of these people had their fame thrust upon them, making them *quasars* who lacked control of their image, but because their reputations were matters of life and death, or crime and trans-gression, it's perhaps tempting to think of them as being different from mere gossip fodder like Brenda Frazier. After all, what did she even do, other than look glamorous and sad? Actually, Frazier may not have battled cholera, won a naval battle, embarked on a crime spree, or slaughtered innocent women, but her existence was sig-nificant in helping to define ideas of beauty, health, gender, youth, aspiration, the importance of marriage, the impact of divorce on children, and whether buying stuff could make you happy.

So even the 'famous for being famous' have a useful role to play. But hang on a second. I keep using *celebrity*, and assuming you know what I mean by it, but it took me eight months of head-scratching before I could settle on a definition, and I've only given you the briefest of summaries in the introduction. Right, then, hold onto your hats, this is where it gets *really* tricky, but *really* interesting . . .

Chapter 3: What the Hell Is a Celebrity, Anyway?

What's in a word?

Celebrity: despite its weird spelling, the word glides off our tongues with ease. Yet its meaning is more slippery than a greased-up pig at a country fair. We know what we think it means, and we cheerfully swap it with other words - stardom, fame, renown, reputation, glory, acclaim, notoriety, VIP, personality - but, while these under-studies do a perfectly serviceable job, in truth they're not pure synonyms. They've all got their own subtle differences. We might assume this is a recent problem, and that our confused celebrity lexicon is the linguistic shrapnel from the messy, glorious explosion of twentieth-century pop culture. Alas, not! The vocabulary of famousness has been frustratingly vague for millennia.

While I'm confident there were celebs in the eighteenth century, nobody was called a *celebrity* until 1849.[1] Originally, the word had meant a solemn ceremony or a major occasion where many people might throng together (such as a coronation or parade); by the mid-1600s, *celebrity* changed to mean 'much talked about' and was loosely applied to people. Yet even in 1751 Dr Samuel Johnson - a man who really knew his way around a dictionary - could only write: 'I did not find myself yet enriched in proportion to my celebrity.'[2] *Celebrity* wasn't yet something he could *be*, it was only something he could *have*. Charmingly, Johnson's dictionary also suggested *celebriousness* as a synonym for personal renown.*

---

* I would gladly welcome it back into our lexicon, if only to enjoy TV shows called things like *Celebriousness Mastermind* and *Celebriousness Tattoo Fixers*. Delightful!

In this chapter, I'm going to advance my own definition of *celebrity*, based on a five-point checklist. Many historical individuals were kindly suggested to me by friends and fellow historians as potential case studies, and a few have ended up in the book, but often they weren't actually celebs. They'd been very well known, for sure, but they fell into other categories, such as fame, renown, royalty, and notorious infamy. These are all similar ideas that confusingly overlap with each other, but they're ultimately distinct concepts, and, to make sense of it all, I've had to rummage through sources ancient and modern to find the discrepancies.

A word of warning, then: we're about to rampage through 3,000 years of history while playing a challenging game of spot the difference. So, if you're feeling a little sleepy-headed, this is a good time for a powernap, coffee break, or intense burst of star-jumps. Whatever works for you. Ready? Okay, let's begin with the most important question of all: 'What the hell *is* a celebrity, anyway?' Well, it depends who you're asking.

Famous for being famous

To my initial astonishment, it turns out there's no single accepted definition of *celebrity* among sociologists and historians. This isn't very helpful. So I'll begin instead with a common response I heard when I mentioned this book to people: 'Celebrities? Bah! Bunch of useless nobodies, most of them just famous for being famous!' This pithy maxim is well embedded in popular culture, and dates back to at least 1967, when the critic and socialist politician Malcolm Muggeridge used it to describe his own antipathy towards being recognised for being on TV.[3] But though he nailed the elegant phrasing, the idea wasn't original. Instead, Muggeridge was smoothing out an earlier quote by the political theorist Daniel J. Boorstin, who defined a celebrity as 'a person who is well-known for his well-knownness'.

Boorstin wrote this in his influential 1962 book *The Image: A Guide to Pseudo-Events in America,*[4] in which he attacked *celebrity* as a diluted, debased corruption of deserved *fame*. You might be wondering what the difference is – after all, we often use *fame* and *celebrity* interchangeably – but *fame* is usually considered to be an ancient idea denoting glorious reputation. In his book on celebrity's history, Fred Inglis summarises *fame* as: '[it] brought honour to the office not the individual, and public recognition was not so much of the man himself as of the significance of his actions for the society'.⁵ *Fame* is a mark of quality.

According to Boorstin, celebrities flunk this test with graceless vulgarity. They make public what's usually private – flaunting their opinions, bodies, and sex lives – but contribute sod all to the betterment of society. For Boorstin, *celebrity* was a hollow and in-substantial 'pseudo-event' manufactured to distract us and sell us mass-produced crap we don't need. 'Famous for being famous' was a damning indictment because it's not *fame* at all; celebs haven't earned their elevation, and the public are gullible idiots for wor-shipping these unworthy frauds.⁶

Here's where I'll sharpen my elbows and charge into the debate, because I passionately disagree. Obviously, it's not a great look arguing with a dead guy, and his book is full of interesting ideas that are well worth your time, but Boorstin's celebrity cynicism presents a false dichotomy. This stuff is way more complex than simply pitting supermodel hottie against Renaissance poet. Firstly, noble repute can exist both inside and outside of *celebrity*. Not all famous people are celebrities, but not all celebrities are passing fads. The Victorian poet Alfred, Lord Tennyson was hailed as a literary 'lion' in his lifetime, not because of his majestic mane (though he did sport luxuriant hair, he was more of a stone-cold fox in his youth*) but because *lionism* was a specific type of intellectual celeb-rity doled out by elite society to a gaggle of serious, chin-stroking brainboxes.⁷ This subset of celebrities were still chased around by excited fans, but their fandom was limited to a privileged class with access to high culture. In particular, lions were the sorts of men (it

---

* Google 'Young Tennyson', the dude had great cheekbones.

was typically men) who were guests of honour at salons hosted by aristocratic women.

Today, the same still applies. Boorstin decried the cluttering crap of lowbrow pop culture which devalues deserved *fame*, but such greatness isn't extinct; there are still brilliantly talented celebrities whose contributions bring joy and cultural enrichment to millions, and whose influence helps redefine gender norms, sexual mores, political ideologies, and the boundaries of good taste. For all the supposedly inane, fake-tanned triffids invading our culture with their stupefying superficiality, and ricocheting between TV reality shows and Instagram adverts for tooth-whitening kits, there are also celebs whose statuses were earned through genuine ability and hard graft, and who contribute to the health of society just as much as some long-dead Austrian composer.

Lowbrow isn't bad culture, it's just different; it's vibrant, immediate, accessible, and fun. There are laudable celebs and regrettable celebs, just as there are sublime operas and ones that make you want to staple your ears shut. So here's my first line in the sand: *celebrity* isn't the antithesis of talent; instead it's to experience a very distinctive, intense type of public reputation. But *how* someone becomes famous doesn't really matter. What's more, it's not mutually exclusive: public figures can enjoy *renown* for their work, or *celebrity*, or hold both simultaneously. Look at David Beckham, Meryl Streep, or Beyoncé. These people are insanely famous, but they've done things far beyond the physical and creative capability of billions of other humans, achieving greatness in their fields, breaking records, and influencing culture as they've gone. And yes, we've also seen them in their underpants.* They're renowned *and* they're celebs.

Celebrity isn't a bastardisation of noble repute. It's not an invasive species that's bumped off the indigenous red squirrels of classical *fame*; nor is it a novel disease metastasising its way through our

---

* Meryl Streep is in her seventies now, but she tastefully disrobed in earlier films.

cultural bloodstream. It's just a hyperactive, dayglo cousin of *fame*; one that lives in the moment. And, no, it's not a recent invention. We've all read despairing articles about modern teens who aspire only to fame: model, actor, rapper, footballer, whatever. 'What a shallow generation!' the commentators shriek. Well, these kids are certainly not the first to aspire to glitzy success. Between 1910 and 1930, tens of thousands of movie fans contracted so-called 'filmitis' – a mocking diagnosis for the viral pandemic of egotistical hopefuls flocking to Hollywood in the expectation of making it big.[8] That was a century ago. But they weren't the first wannabes.

Two hundred and fifty years ago, the infamous Italian seducer, Giacomo Casanova, galloped along the same path. He and his rivals weren't going to wait for glorious *fame* to be posthumously bestowed upon them, they planned to hunt it down, wrestle it to the ground, skin it, and wear it as a hat. Casanova craved the limelight. Ironically, his posthumous *fame* as rampant sex weasel would've surprised him; he wasn't then known as a womaniser.[9] Instead, he aspired to be a famous writer, or astrologer, or preacher, or conversationalist – the eighteenth-century equivalent of model/singer/ actor.

Meanwhile, Casanova also documented the fluctuating reputations of other gossip magnets, including Kitty Fisher, whose fame as London's hottest courtesan was earned in the beds of her wealthy lovers. Her celebrity was heightened in 1759 by her falling from a horse while, as was the custom at the time, wearing no knickers – yes, she enjoyed a tactically brilliant 'wardrobe malfunction' that saw her dominate the gossip sheets for months thereafter – and she asserted her visual iconography by working closely with the portrait artist Joshua Reynolds.

If Casanova was an adventurous fame junkie, Ann Hatton's was perhaps a sadder, more desperate tale of scrambling for fame. She was the sister of Sarah Siddons – who was the leading figure in the illustrious Kemble acting dynasty – but Ann lacked the necessary beauty for a stage career: alas, she was lame and had a squint, and her face was scarred from smallpox. Struggling for money after a failed marriage, she instead published poetry, lectured alongside London's most notorious quack doctor, James Graham, and ran an advert in the papers asking for charitable donations, thereby shaming her famous sister for refusing to offer financial support.

The most dramatic moment in Hatton's life came when she was interrupted in Westminster Abbey trying to drink fatal poison. Given the seriousness of such an act, I'd rather take this as a sign of depressed despair rather than some cynical publicity stunt. But, those of a more cynical bent might comment that she certainly knew how to embellish a story. When a pistol was accidentally discharged near her face, while she was working in a brothel, the papers were told in visceral detail of how she'd lost an eye. This was a wild exaggeration. Both eyes continued to function just fine.

Unable to make much of her career in London, she moved to America in 1793, and found modest success writing an opera and lecturing on human hearts, but she soon returned to Wales, to take up novel-writing under the nom de plume Ann of Swansea. Scholars now take her seriously as an early female writer in her own right,[10] but, throughout her life, Hatton traded on her family's fame; she attempted to sell a tell-all memoir of her celebrity siblings' early years, and, when she returned to acting, she played the roles made famous by Sarah, who responded by paying her sister to stay a hundred miles out of her way, for fear of being publicly embarrassed.*[11]

Daniel Boorstin's book is an energetic polemic, but he was fundamentally wrong. Not only is *celebrity* three centuries old, but the ambition to be famous for the sake of being famous was already thriving in the age of Mozart. Indeed, even in 1786, shortly after Ann Hatton published her first poems, Thomas Busby published a book called *The Age of Genius* which bitterly complained how a new

---

* That last sentence is a real blockbuster. Imagine bribing your sibling to stay outside an exclusion zone because they keep trying to ride on your coat-tails. I bet Christmas was awkward . . .

infestation of shallow celebrities was ruining traditional *fame*.[12] Boorstin was 200 years late to the party. However, in his defence, I can see how he tied himself in knots, because *celebrity* isn't always easily distinguishable from other types of public reputation. What Boorstin was championing wasn't *fame*, but what I prefer to call *renown*.

Let the work speak for itself

I've already mentioned Victorian 'lions' being hunted by enthusiastic fans, but allow me to switch to a celebrated lion-watcher of the modern day. The natural history broadcaster Sir David Attenborough is one of the UK's most recognisable people, inspiring overwhelming affection in millions of television viewers. If he called for armed insurrection in the streets, or demanded we rename Thursdays in his honour, we'd probably see swarms of heavily armed people marching on Downing Street and getting adventurous with their wall calendars. Sir David may well be our most admired, most trusted public figure. But – and this is a BUT with capital letters – I haven't the foggiest idea about his private life. Or if he has kids. Or where he holidays, what car he drives, or how he votes. Attenborough's name carries more weight than a hippo with a slow metabolism, but I don't think he's a *celebrity*. Or, if he is, he's had a very diluted dose.

Could he become a celeb? Sure! I hope Chapter 2 showed it's possible to make the jump, either deliberately or involuntarily. But Sir David Attenborough hasn't undergone this metamorphosis. I've never seen a feature in the *Daily Mail* called 'How to get the Attenborough look!', even though he definitely has a signature look – a natty combo of blue shirt and beige chinos. Attenborough is verging on *celebrity*, he's heroic in a lot of ways, he appears regularly on TV chat shows alongside glamorous actors and comedians, he can get on stage at the Glastonbury music festival and be cheered by 80,000 people, but I don't think he's fully crossed the threshold. Instead, I believe he has *renown*: a public reputation built on admiration for his work, not his personal life. And this is a crucial distinction.

Generally, scholars agree that a *celebrity* is someone well known to a huge number of strangers, thanks to media exposure. However, what differentiates it from *renown*, and the likes of Sir David Attenborough, is the intensity of our voyeuristic curiosity. The scholar Graeme Turner suggests *celebrity* is 'the point at which media interest in their activities is transferred from reporting on their public role ... to investigating the details of their private lives'.[13] Neal Gabler's definition is even pithier; for him celebrity is 'human entertainment'[14] – it's a genre of popular culture in which individuals function as thrilling stories.

Being *renowned* is to be well known for one's work, and some celebrities – the Beyoncés of the world – enjoy both *renown* and *celebrity*, but Attenborough's brand is not a 'life movie'; he's not the story, his TV programmes are. Gabler argues that maintaining narrative momentum is crucial to continued celebrity. These stars are human soap operas we devour with vicarious pleasure, to the point of consuming their adventures as if they were scripted shows, not real people. This is presumably how we can end up screaming obscenities at them on Twitter, or savaging their red carpet fashion choices, or judging them for their bodies when ours really aren't any better. It's not like they're *real* humans, are they?

A human drama

As with planetary gravity, the bigger a celeb becomes, the more likely they are to attract the orbiting moons of drama. But Gabler points out that the bigger the star, the less dramatic they need to be. I'd argue a Hollywood A-lister drunkenly punching a zebra is more compelling than a B-lister punching a zebra, and a Z-lister would probably have to marry the zebra in the middle of Times Square to earn the magazine coverage. Nor is public fascination underpinned by anything as boring as morality or likeability, either.

When a big star fades to career obscurity, it's not necessarily because they're suddenly unsympathetic; maybe their shtick is tired and we've lost interest? Scandal can be dangerous, but it's not always a career-slayer. Sometimes being notorious is just an unexpected second act where the 'life movie' switches genre from bubbly romance to gothic melodrama. O. J. Simpson became vastly more famous during his murder trial than during his stellar football career. Obviously, nobody was offering him TV adverts any more, but he was still mega-famous. I'll keep saying it, and I might even get T-shirts printed: celebrity and notoriety burn at the same temperature.

When the 'famous for being famous' line is hurled like a throwing knife, often the blade is aimed at celebrities whose fame comes through mere association; they're the child of someone famous, or they're friends with a socialite, or they're dating a star. This is nothing new. Alice Roosevelt became a huge celebrity in the early 1900s because her dad was president; people were obsessed with her clothes and her boyfriends, and she was even nicknamed 'Princess Alice'.[15] Sometimes going after these fame-adjacent celebs is valid criticism. But they're often dismissed as 'nobodies', and that fails to recognise that our obsession with celebs stems from something innate in their persona; they're very much *somebodies*.

Obviously, we all know that maintaining a celebrity career requires massive media attention, propelled by the hidden effort of agents, managers, PRs, and stylists. But it's naïve to assume absolutely *anyone* can be transformed into a star, provided they have the right team. We could pluck a random person from obscurity and launch an onslaught of publicity, but, without some intrinsic quality to snag wider curiosity, the public might still shrug in boredom, then wander off to giggle at a cat who looks like Hitler. Plenty of immediately forgotten TV talent show winners discovered this the hard way. It's not enough to just be bathed in limelight. A publicity blitzkrieg can overwhelm the forces of indifference for a while, but true celebrity requires the public's natural curiosity. We have to give a damn.

Various things might enthuse: the public delights in witnessing talent, particularly things of which they're incapable; they also enjoy judging celebrity bodies in a way that simultaneously elevates and dehumanises the star; they enjoy funny people, and bitchy people, and inspirational leaders, and shocking provocateurs; they crave drama in both deed and speech, they want to be thrilled and surprised, to have their hearts swell with sympathy and outrage. 'Make us feel something!' the public screams. But, as we heard in the previous chapter, it's not just the public who decide if someone gets to be famous. Celebrity is the explosion that occurs when we mix a profit-driven media industry, an individual trying to control their reputation, and an audience hungry for titillation. It needs all three elements for the flame to ignite.

Magnetic personalities

Famous people are usually faraway images that reach us through mass media, but sometimes we might bump into a celebrity, or share a lift with them, and the experience can feel a bit weird. Often, fans meeting their heroes go a little giddy, or become speechless; people who've met President Bill Clinton speak of the intense connection he provoked, as if there was nobody else in the room. This indescribable star quality makes celebrities sound almost magical in their allure. But what causes such a hypnotic effect, and what should we call it?

There have been several terms suggested to describe this power. In the early days of Hollywood, it was simply called 'It'. Clara Bow was the superstar actress whose goofy likeability made her immensely popular, and in her 1927 film *It*, in which she plays a shopgirl with effortless charm, a character asserts: 'the possessor of "IT" must be absolutely "un-self-conscious", and must have that magnetic "sex appeal" which is irresistible'. Another character chips in with more suggestions: 'self-confidence and indifference as to whether you are pleasing or not – and something in you that gives the impression that you are not at all cold'. In short, to have

'It' was to be attractive, self-assured, exuding warmth, and yet to be unaware of it.

Given the film's success, Bow - who ticked all the boxes - was soon dubbed the 'It Girl', a phrase we still use for glamorous women who waft through other people's parties, floating on a cloud of champagne privilege. Though she was a playful chameleon, part flirt and part tomboy, Bow's wildness away from the camera got her into hot bother. She had a fondness for gambling and drinking, was an alleged homewrecker, and preferred working-class friends to Hollywood schmoozing. As the classic flapper, her cheeky smile suited the Jazz Age, but the Wall Street Crash of 1929 dampened the national mood. She'd made few allies in Hollywood, and plenty of enemies. She'd also had a couple of breakdowns. By 1933, the biggest star of the 1920s was done with movies. She retired to a ranch, aged just thirty-two.[16]

In the 1930s, out went Clara Bow and in came a new word for a new style of performance: *glamour*. Today it means something exciting and attractive, but originally it was a bewitching enchantment, having derived from the Scottish word *gramarye*, meaning a book containing occult alchemical knowledge.[17] By the twentieth century, that magical patina had mostly been dusted away, and people might have gone on holiday to 'glamorous Rome', where they would've met very few wizards, and definitely no Scottish ones. But subtle traces of the magic remained when Hollywood fan magazines defined *glamour* as a new visual style. It was beauty defined as magnetic, cool, and impassive distance; a stylistically divergent mood from Clara Bow's effervescence. Glamour was mysterious. It was quiet. It was to gaze out, cigarette in hand, and show barely a flicker of emotion. It was a seductive spell, a love potion drunk through the eyes. Greta Garbo was glamour, Marlene Dietrich and Katharine Hepburn too.[18] It wasn't just dressing up in nice togs and bunging on some vibrant red lippy, it was a strategy of attitudinal bewitchment. Celebs had to *be* glam, not just look it.

Hollywood wasn't done there. In 1933, Hilary Lynn proposed 'X'[19] as a sort of algebraic cipher that hinted at the mysterious, scientist-befuddling power of the superstar who could turn mere cinema-going mortals into blubbering, popcorn-devouring fools. From this, we got the 'X-Factor', which in turn gave us the shiny TV talent show of the same name. There was also 'Oomph', an onomatopoeic grunt applied to nubile stars with obvious erotic appeal. Ann Sheridan was voted Hollywood's 'Oomph Girl' in 1939 – it was a label she hated – and a young Marilyn Monroe, then still nice-but-plain Norma Jeane, was declared the most-bountifully *oomphish* (yes, that is apparently a real word) of her high school classmates in 1941.

These were all movie terms, and sociologists have long claimed Hollywood is where *celebrity* was invented. But the most common phrase wheeled out to explain a celebrity's mysterious charm is much older. *Charisma* is an ancient Greek word, most associated with the apostle St Paul – the New Testament's famed Corinthian-botherer – who used it to mean 'grace gifted by God'. However, though it extends back over two millennia, our secular notion of charisma is only a century old, having been laid out by the German sociologist Max Weber in 1922. He described *charisma* as a quasi-magical aura that produces influence over others, and even inspires frenzied loyalty and devotion.

But, before Weber turned up, such mysterious power had pre-viously been dubbed 'human magnetism', thanks to the German physician Franz Mesmer having peddled a dodgy theory that plan-etary magnetism in the solar system affected Earth's natural world, and that people – especially him – could wield it. Mesmer bolstered his fame in the 1700s by performing famously eroticised hypnosis techniques on his patients; indeed, our verb 'to mesmerise' derives from his status as controversial medical celebrity.[20] This supposed power to entrance both individuals and crowds made magnetic people socially important.

In 1841, the eminent British historian Thomas Carlyle wrote an influential book called *On Heroes, Hero-Worship and the Heroic in History*, which argued that great men and women – though mainly men, because Victorian patriarchs gonna patriarch – possessed superior qualities which made them natural leaders, and society should encourage them through public acclaim to achieve great things. From the late 1800s through to the 1920s, America drank deeply of this heady brew, and became intoxicated. Politicians, religious leaders, orchestral conductors, sports stars, and business titans were all hailed for their astonishing connection with crowds.

But it wasn't just a case of natural magnetism seducing the masses; practical techniques could be mastered in the pursuit of such persuasion. Preachers and politicians elicited frenzied responses[21] by adopting the vocal and gestural pyrotechnics first revealed in 1827 by the speech scientist Dr James Rush. He was fascinated by the musicality of syllable length and pitch, and dedicated thousands of hours to shouting and flailing his arms in bizarre ways until he'd found the most effective combination for rousing people to communal ecstasy. It was an impressive commitment to science, but I imagine his neighbours hated him.

So is celebrity charm a natural phenomenon, or just a question of good technique? I'd argue for a bit of both. At the start of this book, we saw the enormous impact of David Bowie's death, so it might surprise you to learn that he'd struggled to become famous in the first place. After five years of musical failures, it took a gimmick song about the moon landing - the eerily beautiful *Space Oddity* - to finally see him break into the charts, but it still took a further three years, and three more albums, before he had another major hit. Throughout the disappointment, Bowie kept readjusting his approach, and part of that experimental empiricism involved learning how to tease fans by always leaving them wanting more, or by bewildering interviewers with wilfully vague answers.[22] Bowie deliberately practised ambiguity as if it were a martial art, realising the emotional distance made people strive all the harder to get to know him. As it turns out, it was an approach not so far removed from Lord Byron's strategy.[23]

But, I really must stress, he also had natural charisma - I mean, just look at him! He was just *so* Bowie! He was innately alluring. Those eyes were tractor beams pulling us in; one ocean blue, one moodily black (caused by a teenage punch to the retina). He may have developed sophisticated techniques of enchantment, but he already oozed charm as if he'd evolved his own charisma gland. Bowie was a rock'n'roll muskrat in immaculate makeup.

It's all about the money, money, money

Uniqueness matters, but celebrity itself isn't just a showcase for dazzling individuality. It's also a brash capitalist system. The historian of celebrity Simon Morgan has pleasingly compressed this idea into a lovely short sentence: 'The celebrity is a known individual who has become a marketable commodity.'[24] In other words, a celebrity is someone who, for whatever reason - whether they're beloved, hated, heroic, beautiful, provocative, weird, or downright dangerous - causes the springing up of their own micro-economy. All told, celebrity culture is a lucrative industry that profits from human novelty, extracting vast sums from selling access to famous lives and bodies. I agree with Morgan, but I think his wording is a tad imprecise. A 'known person' with a marketable brand could include David Attenborough, whose image is used in publicity materials by various environmental charities, but you know where I stand on him.

For all the apparent glamour of celebrity, stars are constantly objectified by both the industry that monetises their fame and the audiences eager to pay for access.[25] The celebrity theorist P. David Marshall sees the rise of star culture in the twentieth century not as a consequence of democratic capitalism, but rather as a fundamental keystone propping up the whole edifice in the first place.[26] For him, celebrity wasn't a noisy, neon consequence of modernity, it helped *cause* modernity.

This might well be true, but it happened much earlier than the early 1900s. For decades, *celebrity*'s origin has been fixed in that pop culture factory that gave us Charlie Chaplin and Greta Garbo. But historians have started rocking up to the party, eagerly clutching their dusty old theatrical bills along with their bottles of Merlot, and they've brought radical thinking to the classic story. Thanks to their archival beavering, we can find that capitalism, culture, and celebrity were already rampantly productive bedfellows in the early 1700s.

The evidence for this ideological ménage-à-trois is strong; and in Western Europe we find plentiful reasons for its arrival. In Britain, the long eighteenth century – or what Brits call the Georgian era (named after the four King Georges who reigned in succession, plus William IV, who obviously didn't get the memo) – witnessed a sea change in politics, as the monarchs lost power and Parliament flexed new muscles. But other things were happening too: there was the lapsing of stringent press regulation, compounded by weak libel laws, which now allowed a hefty dose of free expression.

Up sprang the first daily newspapers in 1702, thanks to increasing literacy, a burgeoning and aspirational middle class, and a reduction in printing costs that made visual media more available. Suddenly it was easier and more profitable to launch into a juicy gossip session. I should caution that newspaper readership wasn't large at this stage, maybe a few thousand copies per title, but it grew through the century as more people were able to feast on that banquet of innuendo.[27] It was an era of press democratisation aided by new technology, changing culture, and the idiosyncrasies of the legal system. Celebrity arrived in Britain thanks to the removal of key obstacles coupled to the development of new opportunities.

A second factor in celebrity's rise was the drab tediousness of the royal courts of London and Paris. Whereas the playboy monarchs of the 1600s, Charles II and Louis XIV, had embraced lavish spectacle, chucking huge resources at ballets, plays, art, and masked balls, both Versailles and Kensington became boring without them. In particular, Louis XVI cared more for the mechanics of clocks and locks than extravagant parties, and George III was particularly fond of reading farming almanacs. This meant that creatives who'd previously orbited the courts in search of patronage and prestige – the aristocrats, artists, actors, fashionistas, and writers – instead muttered their excuses and drifted off to the novel excitements of urban London and Paris. These vibrant, swelling cities became playgrounds to a new, dynamic popular culture rising from below. Meanwhile, King George regaled his family members with the joys of crop rotation.[28]

As Jürgen Habermas argued,[29] a 'public sphere' now emerged; people wanted to engage in public discussion and be heard, and the newspapers responded by serving up hearty portions of gossip and scandal about politicians, actors, writers, and artists - the sorts of people who'd previously drawn little public attention. These were the first true celebrities, and commercial exploitation of this new fascination soon followed. There was money to be made in talking about others; there was money to be made in being talked about. In the words of the historian Stella Tillyard, 'celebrity was born at the moment private life became a tradeable public commodity'.[30]

Before they were famous

Okay, so celebrity culture definitely existed in the early eighteenth century, but might we roll the bandwagon further down the road, back into prior centuries? Well, first we'll have to agree on a definition of celebrity, so here is my checklist:

Celebrity criteria checklist
1. Possess unique personal charisma.
2. Widely known to the public.
3. Brand disseminated by widespread media.
4. Private life consumed as dramatic entertainment by the public.
5. Commercial marketplace based on the celebrity's reputation.

Under these five terms, the hunt for earlier celebrity seems doomed - all those transformations that made the 1700s so conducive to celebrity culture hadn't got up and running in the previous century.

But there are historians making compelling cases for pre-1700s celebrity, so let's hear them out.

Consider, for example, the charming, beautiful, funny, and saucy actress of English Restoration theatre, Nell Gwyn, who, between the 1660s and 1680s, clambered from the lowest rung on the social ladder onto the London stage, and then into King Charles II's bed, where she stayed for many years as his beloved royal mistress. Nell's bold confidence was the key part of her brand, but her breasts were her most famous physical asset. Samuel Pepys called her 'a bold, merry slut' – a slut was an unkempt woman – but there's no doubting her sexual power. Gwyn's amorous adventures with the most powerful man in the country rendered her a national security risk in the eyes of satirists and pamphleteers, but also made her thrillingly titillating. She metamorphosed from commoner to faux-aristocracy, and even returned to the stage after having given birth to the King's bastard, thereby endangering the dignity of the Crown in an era when the previous monarch, Charles I, had lost his head to the executioner's axe. No small thing, that.

As Julia Novak says: 'Gwyn was a celebrity in her own day, treasured and despised, publicly discussed, repeatedly portrayed by court painter John Lely, and frequently written about, especially by Restoration satirists. In an age that witnessed a surge of misogynist satires, the king's mistresses proved a popular target.'[31] Elaine McGirr writes: 'she was a celebrity actress before she was a celebrity mistress',[32] and highlights how artistic representations of Gwyn were individualised and specific. Although overenthusiasm by previous art historians often led to paintings of any busty beauty being falsely labelled as the celebrated actress, authentic portraits by Peter Lely are nevertheless unmistakably distinctive. Her flirtatious gaze is ever-present, while her eyes, lips, and bosom are alluringly full. Gwyn was a charismatic, provocative, socially mobile exception to all of society's norms. Plus, she was really funny. It's no wonder King Charles was besotted with her.

People enjoyed her performances, but they also scrutinised her body and pried into her sex life, perhaps fantasising about how she seduced the Merry Monarch each night in his bedroom. They could also possess her image; indeed, even her nude body. Samuel Pepys was one such customer to hang Peter Cross's portrait of a naked Nell, depicted as a winged Venus holding Cupid's arrow, over his desk at the Admiralty (surely it was NSFW?). All of this certainly sounds like celebrity, doesn't it? It's a really enjoyable argument, and I was almost convinced, but I'm not sure we have enough evidence for widespread coverage in a very early press media.

How widely was the satire read? Were thousands of Londoners hungrily scooping it up, or just a few hundred malcontents at court? Nor do we know how many portrait engravings were sold, and to whom. Only a handful of Peter Cross's Venus engravings survive, and Samuel Pepys was a privileged man, and certainly not representative of ordinary people. Novak and McGirr make a very decent case. Gwyn's fame does feel surprisingly modern; it's almost a prototype for what came later, but I think it falls just short of *celebrity*. Instead, I think it's best described as *fame*, but I'll explain why later on.

And what do we make of Shakespeare's playwriting compatriot Ben Jonson, who, fresh from London theatrical successes, walked from London to Scotland in 1618 and was met by many adoring admirers along the route eager to take him to dinner and bask in his presence?[33] Or what to do with Shakespeare's favourite clown, Will Kemp, who, in 1600, embarked on his 'Nine Day Wonder', in which, as a cash-raising PR stunt, he morris-danced from London to Norwich and then published a pamphlet celebrating his achievement?

These men were popular creatives known to thousands of theatregoers; they were cheered by members of the public who lined the route to say hello; they were perhaps also earning a pretty penny in the process. Is that *celebrity*? Jennifer R. Holl has made an intriguing case for Shakespearean celebrity, arguing that the late-sixteenth-century theatre became a social space for thousands of Londoners where news and opinion were shared. Kemp, and another actor, called Richard Tarleton, were much beloved performers who may well have had devoted fans. But I'm not to-tally convinced that celebrity can exist without printed media, and this was a time when even the most reputable people were only mentioned in a smattering of printed materials.[34]

The same argument applies to any claim to medieval celebrity. In a world of mass illiteracy, prior to Johannes Gutenberg's fifteenth-century printing revolution, how would celebrity images and ideas have spread? We know the powerful Christian Church ran its own communication intranet through which crusades could be adver-tised, but I struggle to see how celebrity culture could have been sustained. And yet ... Medieval Europe was criss-crossed with pilgrimage routes which brought people from all over the conti-nent to the shrines of dead saints, or even the humble abodes of living saints (those 'beatified' by the community as being especially godly). These places soon blossomed into economic powerhouses where eager tourists flocked, like seagulls to a bag of abandoned chips, hoping to witness a miracle.

Hereford Cathedral in western England was one such site, fund-ing the erection of its proud new tower off the lucrative brand of its dead bishop, Thomas de Cantilupe, who was canonised in 1320 thanks to his Lazarene powers of raising the dead. This was quite the neat trick, given that he was also dead. Saint Thomas de Can-tilupe was a posthumous miracle-worker, and his personal brand was therefore potent and widespread. His corpse could do actual magic, and pilgrims travelled to his shrine in pursuit of their own miracle cure – how's that for natural charisma! So were medieval saints *celebrities*? It doesn't tick all five of my boxes, but it's defi-nitely an exciting argument, made most notably by the historian Aviad Kleinberg.[35]

Let's keep reversing our wagon all the way to the Greco-Roman world of some 2,000 years ago. Might there be a stronger case for ancient celebrity in these famously sophisticated cultures, where huge cities brought vast, seething populations into close contact? In his ground-breaking classic on the history of fame, *The Frenzy of Renown*,[36] Leo Braudy extended his range back to Homeric poetry and the golden-maned hero Alexander the Great, arguing that the human urge to be celebrated as unique – a vital prerequisite of celebrity branding – was alive in the Bronze Age, over 3,000 years ago. More recently, Robert Garland makes the same point of the Greek philosopher Socrates, who, when publicly mocked in a theatrical comedy, stood up from his seat to defiantly assert his proud identity before the crowd. He wanted to be known by the mob.

Leo Braudy cautiously notes how ancient *fame* and modern *celebrity* are noticeably different. Garland, however, has written a cheerfully amusing book called *Celebrity in Antiquity*[37], and argues for a proto-stardom* in which cynical 'media tarts', royals, politicians, charioteers, gladiators, and poets fought hard to earn public attention, often driven by an unquenchable thirst for reputation. He describes Emperor Nero as a deranged narcissist who locked audiences in theatres and performed songs not so much *to* them as *at* them, demanding that they applaud his genius. During a tour of Greece in 67 CE Nero demanded the sacred Olympic Games be held in an off-year so that he could compete, but then changed the events to better suit his hobbies. Accordingly, he 'won' every competition he entered, including the chariot race – an impressive feat, given he'd actually crashed. Nero claimed victory anyway, arguing he would've won otherwise. He was very much the Donald Trump of the ancient world.

Nero was one of Rome's most controversial tyrants, but he had plenty of competition in the douchebag stakes. Ruling some 130 years later on, Emperor Commodus became so enraptured by the acclaim given to famous gladiators that he jealously strode into the Colosseum himself, eager to soak up the cheers. Whereas Nero changed the rules or denied the reality of displeasing outcomes, Commodus simply cheated by mutilating defenceless animals, or fighting against human amputees armed only with soft sponges. Commodus aspired to be a triumphant sportsperson, but the crowd saw only a deluded despot slaughtering the harmless and

---

* I know, I know. I really tried to think of a better word . . . I promise.

the armless. This embarrassing behaviour was akin to when Boris Johnson played rugby against children, and smashed into a tiny child with his full adult bulk. Johnson went on to be prime minister, but Commodus was promptly assassinated for his cringeworthy behaviour.

Garland's book is an enjoyable provocation, but it's hard to know if his suggested celebs were hailed by the ordinary people who shared their cities and sewers, or whether we've been duped into thinking of these people as celebrities only because they've been preserved in ancient, elite writings? Were there any popular gladiators who became celebs, for example? We might assume so, given Commodus' jealousy. Also, according to the Roman poet Martial, a charioteer called Scorpus was so widely beloved that he earned huge cash bonuses from senior politicians and was depicted in gold-plated statues. A century later, the gender-fluid teenager Elagabalus - one of Rome's most controversial emperors - fell for a beautiful blond charioteer named Hierocles and 'married' him, elevating this former slave to his equal and even trying to make him heir to the entire empire. This was deemed unacceptable by fellow courtiers and both were also promptly assassinated.[38]

So, Roman gladiators and charioteers could graduate from life in the gutter to hobnobbing with the elite. But ancient nobility fawning at their sweaty feet isn't solid proof of ordinary Romans doing the same. One of my favourite *Monty Python* sketches depicts archaeologists finding the snapped-off toe from a giant animated foot; they take it to the British Museum and, with only a single bone available, reassemble the foot as they think it would've looked. The result is an adorably ungainly pink elephant. Might we similarly misassemble Roman history by putting far too much emphasis on a tiny handful of reports centred on high-status individuals? As G. S. Aldrete notes, 'almost all surviving literary and much of the artistic evidence regarding Roman sport and spectacle was produced by and/or intended for the consumption of a tiny group of elites . . . we lack any accounts whatsoever from the millions of ordinary Romans who constituted the vast majority of spectators'.[39]

Okay, let's look a little later, and further to the east. Constantinople was the seat of power for the Byzantine Empire (the eastern chunk of the Roman Empire which outlived its Western counterpart by a cool 1,000 years), and here the populace was obsessed with chariot-racing. In 520 CE, the frenzied crowd, crammed into the enormous hippodrome, began rioting. Ostensibly, the dispute was between rival fans of the Blue and Green teams, but the rioting mob's demands were simple and singular: they demanded that their hero, Porphyrius, come out of retirement to race once more.

Though born in what's now Libya, he was an honorary son of the city. His name was praised in poems inscribed on the hippodrome's central gallery; his heroic image was visible in bronze statues and stone relief carvings around the city; one of his statues may have stood next to a masterpiece depicting none other than Alexander the Great. Porphyrius was the empire's most famous man, besides the Emperor Justin. His races had been seen not just in Constantinople but also on tour in Antioch, Beirut, and Nicomedia. In 520 CE, he was sixty years old, but the crowd was adamant they would see him race again. It was to be one of ten riots associated with chariot-racing in only a thirty-year period.[40] The mob got their wish.

Porphyrius' career had been exceptional, not least for the fact that he'd escaped the usual mangling which killed so many other drivers. Unlike Hierocles, he'd not gravitated towards the corridors of imperial power to be destroyed by its shadowy jealousies, but nor had he shunned politics either. In 507 CE, Porphyrius had led a violent anti-Semitic attack on the Jewish quarter in Antioch, burning a synagogue before erecting a crucifix in the smouldering embers. Clearly, being a ringleader in an atrocity suggested he was both a horrible arsehole and a charismatic leader, capable of rousing the passions of strangers.

Porphyrius was undoubtedly famous, and perhaps - thanks to all those statues - even recognisable on the street. But, if we recall the five-point checklist, was there a market economy attached to his brand? Did he flog olive oil in cheesy commercials? Was his name painted on the signs of taverns? Did people pay money to read about him, and his sex life? We just don't know. As the famous aphorism goes: 'Absence of evidence is not evidence of absence'; just because we don't have proof of a thing doesn't mean it didn't happen. But nor can we assert it did happen without sufficient proof. Porphyrius was *famous*, but I don't have enough evidence to call him a celebrity.

So, if we're going to get an answer on whether there was ever a Roman celebrity, it's time to bring out the big guns . . .

Hail, Caesar!

Stop what you're doing and grab the nearest person. Got someone? Okay, now ask them to list three famous Romans. I bet you £20 that Julius Caesar makes that list. As Maria Wyke has shown, Caesar is surely history's most famous Roman, and has defended his championship belt for centuries.[41] The reasons are obvious: he was charismatic, clever, and privileged; he was also a ruthless soldier, smashing the Gauls with such ferocity that even fellow Romans accused him of what we'd now call genocide.

Other notable conquests included chilly southern Britain, and the much less chilly Queen Cleopatra, who bore him a child. He ended a civil war in Egypt and started one in Rome. He defeated his mighty frenemy Pompey the Great, squabbled with the celebrated Cicero and Cato, lived in the age of Catullus, and - most famous of all - crossed the Rubicon river with his loyal troops, snatched up supreme political power, and was then murdered by his own friends for corrupting the Roman Republic. Regardless of moral judgements, Caesar really put in the hours. Fair play to him, the guy got stuff done!

Given all that, it's no surprise that he was extensively discussed in ancient chronicles. But it's arguably since his death that his fame has grown, his biography having proved fertile territory for subsequent stories, songs, plays, films, and TV shows that transformed his tumultuous life into compelling narrative drama, often infused with contemporary topicality. For us, Julius Caesar is as much a product of Shakespeare's quill as of ancient history. And such re-tellings have, in turn, exerted their own influence on later events.

Before rising to become France's egomaniacal emperor, Napoleon Bonaparte had been a nerdy Corsican teenager enthralled by the ancient stories of Caesar and Alexander the Great. When he got the chance to invade Egypt in 1798, he not only walked the same sands as his boyhood heroes, but also kickstarted classical Egyptology by bringing a 160-man team of handpicked scientists, artists, and archaeologists to investigate the ancient culture he'd read so much about. It's extraordinary to think that the course of modern history – the Napoleonic Wars, the naval heroics of Admiral Nelson, the discovery and decoding of the Rosetta Stone – was, in some small way, Napoleon writing his own Caesar fan fiction with ink made from the blood of a million men.

In death, Julius Caesar ticks all five of my boxes. He's now a bona fide posthumous celebrity – but what about during his lifetime? Upon crossing the Rubicon river in 49 BCE, Caesar began minting coins depicting his head adorned with the laurel wreath of martial victory. His image was thus widely circulated. Statues were also erected. Soon after, in 46 BCE, he crushed Pompey in battle, and around the same time was granted an unprecedented quadruple triumph for victories against foreign enemies. A triumph was an opulent spectacle to make the Super Bowl half-time show look like a covers band in your local pub; it was an enormous military parade centring on Caesar, dressed conspicuously in purple and gold, showcasing his glory before a huge Roman crowd. From the treasure trove of war loot, he doled out cash to the troops and the plebs, sponsored huge public entertainments, and funded the building of a temple to Venus.[42] In a city of a million souls, his name was surely spoken tens of millions of times – and that's not even counting the other Roman provinces beyond the capital city's walls. It was all going swimmingly.

But soon people noticed Caesar was still sporting his triumphal robes and red boots – the hated footwear of the wonderfully named Tarquinius Superbus, the archaic king who'd been deposed and replaced with the Roman Republic. Caesar was dressing like a monarch, in a political system famed for ditching its monarchs. In January 44 BCE he was honoured with the title of *Dictator Perpetuo* – *Dictator for life* – which, as job titles go, wasn't very subtle.* Before a large crowd, his friend Mark Antony tried to place the crown on his head, but Caesar waved it away to great cheers.

If this staged humility was meant to endear him to most Romans, it looked like cynical populism to his Senatorial enemies. On the Ides of March, they plunged their knives into his body twenty-three times in an attack of such wild ferocity that some accidentally stabbed each other in the melee, adding a frisson of comic farce to political violence. Caesar's toga was drenched with gushing blood until it matched the hue of his hated boots. He died in infamy, but his name would endure eternal.

So was Caesar a celebrity? Well, his image and name were widely spread through coinage, sculpture, legal decrees, and his sponsorship of public events. Of my five-point celebrity criteria checklist, he nailed the widespread renown and probably the charisma too. We might even generously say the coinage counts as a form of media. Millions of people knew who Caesar was. But do we have evidence of people making money from his existence, trading upon a public desire to engage with his persona? Were millions familiar with his international bed-hopping and personal vendettas? I'm not sure we have the necessary evidence. Instead of *celebrity*, what Caesar managed to acquire was the opulent cloak of royal authority – an elevated status often compared to *celebrity*, but *royalty* isn't *celebrity*. Or at least it didn't use to be.

And we'll never be royals

Both royals and celebs carefully manipulate their image to communicate glamour, health, power, authority, prestige, and uniqueness.

---

* He should've plumped for Vice-President of Senatorial Logistics.

They perform their public identities, projecting artfully constructed personas; and the fictions are so dominant, and so pervasive, that a glimpse of either looking slouchy in sweatpants while picking their nose is a potent image for which we'll pay good money. In particular, the celebrity industry deliberately fosters this dichotomy. It elevates the poised, glamorous persona as the apotheosis of allure, so that we're thrilled by the long-range paparazzi snaps of celebs looking tired and frumpy. There's a goldmine to be plundered in building them up to knock them down, and it's a violent game of dodgeball that begins as soon as someone arrives in the public arena, ready or not.

Royalty's image construction is outwardly similar, projecting glamorous excellence. However, unlike celebrity, the traditional royal image could never slip, for the glamour of the royal aesthetic represents much more than just the individual; the monarch is a political idea, it's the nation in fleshy form. In medieval Christian theology, a monarch had two bodies: one mortal and one political. When the silver-haired ruler wheezed their last breath, or took an assassin's dagger to the gut, the cry went up: 'The king is dead. Long live the king!' A monarch was both person and ideological concept, the individual perished but the Crown was immortal. We see this in the portraits issued by England's long-reigning Virgin Queen, Elizabeth I, which froze her regal beauty in the prime of health;[43] all the while her body sagged with age and her teeth blackened through sugar consumption.[44] They're astonishingly sophisticated artworks, pregnant with symbolism about the robust health of the monarchy, but there's little of the real woman in there – I believe the most revealing thing about them is what she chose to hide.

Usually, *royalty* upholds the status quo. *Celebrity*, by contrast, initially appears to be disruptive. It chucks stones through the windows of traditional privilege, then proffers a ladder for low-born scruffs to clamber in through the broken glass. It's a profitable system designed to tickle a fickle public through repetitious novelty; a constant churn that's achieved by shaking the ladder to dislodge those at the top. The rhythms of this brutal turnover are jerkily aggressive compared to the gradual, generational handover of power that royal inheritance provides. But, in truth, celebrity is not actually all that disruptive, because we've already heard how famous provocateurs perform a social function as arbiters of public taste and decency.

So *celebrity* and *royalty* are similar but separate. However, they have sometimes fused together. When Max Weber wrote his masterwork on charismatic power, he created three categories: *charismatic authority* (heroes with dynamic personalities), *traditional authority* (hereditary rulers upheld by custom), and *legal authority* (political office upheld by law). During Weber's lifetime, royalty seemed to be in trouble. Even though ermine robes and shiny gold hats are tremendously dapper, he assumed the concept of monarchy was under threat from exciting celebrities and shouting revolutionaries.[45] As it turned out, some monarchs had already spotted the danger. The most obvious response was a sudden upswing in historicised pomp and ceremony, with the British monarchy suddenly giving it large on military parades and faux-medieval ceremonies to convince unruly subjects of the eternal legacy of the Crown.[46]

But royals didn't just try to drown out celebrity with gaudier, noisier parades; they also embraced its techniques. In the mid-nineteenth century, both Queen Victoria and Kaiser Wilhelm I of Germany welcomed photography as a way of bolstering their fading charisma. The risks were palpable: while increasing access made monarchs reassuringly present in the public's lives, it arguably cheapened royal prestige, with these images being sold side-by-side with those of common actresses, musicians, and even criminals. It was the equivalent of a Hollywood A-lister appearing in a late series of *Celebrity Big Brother*; we'd obviously watch the hell out of that, but we'd lose respect for them when we saw them squabbling over whose turn it was to do the washing-up. But these royals mostly got away with it, not least because they refused to totally commit - Kaiser Wilhelm was willing to pose for photos, but he blanked requests for autographs. Portraiture had a prestigious heritage, autographs did not.[47]

In 1934, the royal wedding of Prince George, Duke of Kent, and the glamorous Princess Marina of Greece was also surprisingly 'modern'. He was thirty-one, she was twenty-seven, and the public treated her more like a celebrity than royalty. She was pretty and fashionable, loved to smoke cigarettes and dance at parties, and the press were thrilled by the romance. As the historian Edward Owens notes: 'More than on any previous occasion, [the wedding] was a royal event driven by publicity, intimacy, and a coterie of courtiers, clerics, and newsmen who were committed to elevating a "family monarchy" as the emotional centre-point of national life.'[48] The Windsors embraced the public curiosity and laid on a wedding low on pomp and circumstance, but high in narrative charm. It was a clever strategy, unfortunately undercut soon after when King Edward VIII abdicated the throne to marry the scandalous American divorcée Wallis Simpson.

Continuing the trend, Britain's current monarchy has re-energised its twenty-first-century brand through the media-savvy tactics of Princes William and Harry, and their wives. Though born into the most rarefied of families, the young Windsors grew up in a youth culture which has profoundly shaped their tastes. Prince Harry likes grime music! He calls people 'mate'! The Duchess of Cambridge wears Topshop! The Windsors have cunningly bolted the accessible aesthetics of celebrity to the structural privilege of ancient royalty, creating a powerful hybrid that shields them from serious media intrusion (the tragic fate of their mother has strengthened their arm in this), yet granting them a movie star glamour that makes them likeable to a younger generation.

The fact that both princes married gorgeous commoners also sells the idea that royalty is no longer a bastion of snobbish exclusion; it's not democratic, but it's becoming more demotic. Even oiks like us have the tiniest chance of marrying into ancient hereditary power. And while such increased accessibility could've devalued the power of traditional pageantry, it turns out the world goes even more doolally for a royal wedding when it involves a celebrity. One third of Brits watched Meghan Markle, an American actress, wed

Prince Harry in 2018, and some estimates put the global audiences at nearly 2 billion.

This strategy has boosted the monarchy's popularity after years of tabloid scandal. Yet they should be cautious. The same tactic eventually failed with Princess Diana – whose celebrified brand dragged the royal family into prolonged crisis before her tragic death reset the machine – and, as I write this, Meghan Markle seems to have inherited Diana's mantle of being the beautiful tabloid punchbag, not least because she's American, a woman of colour, and a former actress, all of which seem to bring out the worst in certain media commentators.

Diana wasn't the first case study in disaster. In the 1780s, Queen Marie-Antoinette, having found the stuffy protocol of Versailles too restrictive, began seeking a life away from her husband's stifling court. She attended the theatre and opera while incognito, but the sort of ludicrously obvious incognito that made everyone go: 'Er . . . isn't that the queen?' Much like Caesar, she had all the subtlety of a foghorn. She also began issuing startlingly intimate and informal portraits of herself wearing what looked to be underwear, but were in fact simple new gowns designed by her fashion guru, Rose Bertin, who capitalised on the Queen's patronage by then selling these gorgeously elegant designs to the public from her Parisian showroom.[49] Yes, even in the 1780s, people could choose to dress like the stars.

Marie-Antoinette was recast from austere queen consort into trendsetting celebrity; but it meant the distance between her and scandalous actresses shortened year on year, until soon her sex life was up for grabs, with rumours of frenzied masturbation, scandalous lesbianism, and extramarital shagathons dominating Parisian gossip. The pornographic satire was incredibly visceral.* When the French Revolution erupted in 1789 – born from a variety of complex socio-economic causes – Marie-Antoinette was beyond

---

* If you're feeling brave, google it – you'll see her alleged lover riding a giant cock as if it's a two-legged horse.

saving. It wasn't just her exorbitant spending on diamond neck-
laces, alienation from the struggling poor, and alleged pro-Austrian
treachery that doomed her. The monarchy's mystique had been
slowly eroded by caustic celebrity drama. The queen had become
no different to any other salacious courtesan.[50] Royalty had lost its
mysterious power. And so she lost her head.

So royalty and celebrity can overlap, which brings us back to the
Julius Caesar question. If he wasn't a celebrity, what was he? Well,
I think he was the same as Nell Gwyn. I think he was *famous*. This
is another word we chuck around with indiscriminate abandon,
leading to its modern definition becoming baggier than a wizard's
sleeve. *Famous* means anyone or anything with a public reputation.
A building can be famous, or a doughnut, or a train crash, or a
cartoon tiger used to sell breakfast cereal. We happily use *fame* and
celebrity as synonyms – I'm sometimes doing it in this book, when
I can't be bothered to think of a better alternative – but distinctions
can be made. The problem is, those distinctions are really elusive.
But it's high time we gave it a go . . .

What's the story, mourning glory?

Probably composed by the poet Homer in the mid-eighth century
BCE, the *Iliad* recounts an episode at the end of the ten-year siege
of Troy, undertaken by a Greek coalition led by the kings Agamemnon, Menelaus, and Odysseus. Their enemy is King Priam of
Troy and his sons Paris and Hector. As you may know, Paris is
the beauteous hunk who's done a runner with Menelaus' stunning
wife, Helen, and so this decade-long conflict is largely the fault
of insanely good chemistry between two stunners. However, the
poem's real protagonist isn't any of these people; instead it's Achilles – the semi-mortal warrior famous to sports physiotherapists
everywhere.*

---

* I tore my Achilles tendon and calf muscle playing football, and my whole leg
went blue. I don't recommend it.

You might only know two things about Achilles: first, that his divine mum, Thetis, has dunked him in the protective waters of the River Styx, thus rendering him totally stab-proof except for the heel where she'd grasped his dangling body. Secondly, that he then gets shot in that heel and snuffs it. Confusingly, neither of these plotlines is found in the *Iliad*; they actually come to us from later sources, including the Roman poet Statius. But we're focusing on Homer's classic because an existential dilemma underpins the poem, and this tension forms the bedrock of Western culture's traditional interpretation of *fame*.

In Homer's version, Achilles is sulking because King Agamemnon has nabbed his beautiful war trophy, Princess Briseis, whom he planned to keep as his sex slave (yes, Achilles is fascinating, but he's also a jerk). Insulted by Agamemnon's 'theft', Homer's pouty anti-hero sulks on the sidelines, like a moody teenager dragged on a family caravanning holiday, while everyone pleads with him to get stuck back into the fighting. But we soon realise Achilles isn't just a petulant brat, he's also brooding over his own mortality. Because of his semi-divine power, he gets to determine his future. It's been revealed to him that he must make the ultimate choice:

For my mother Thetis the goddess of the silver feet tells me
I carry two sorts of destiny toward the day of my death.
  Either,
if I stay here and fight beside the city of the Trojans,
my return home is gone, but my glory shall be everlasting;
but if I return home to the beloved land of my fathers,
the excellence of my glory is gone, but there will be a long
  life
left for me, and my end in death will not come to me
  quickly.

Thetis has laid out two options to her not-quite-immortal son: he can choose a long, boring life of inconsequence by going home; or he can die young at Troy, but shine eternal with radiant glory.

Achilles sensibly prefers the sound of a future retirement doing the proverbial crossword and watering his begonias, and is all set to sling his hook when his explosive rage is triggered by his best friend (and perhaps lover?) being slain by Hector. Incensed, he exacts brutal vengeance on the Trojan prince, defiles Hector's corpse, and refuses to return it to King Priam for burial. This violent deed signs his contract with destiny; no comfy retirement for him, it's to be big-time glory all the way.

Oddly, Homer doesn't actually kill off Achilles in the *Iliad*, so it's left to later reworkings of the poem to dramatise the celebrated moment when Paris - Hector's grieving brother, and the selfish prat who caused all the trouble - shoots the poisoned arrow into the vulnerable span of his ankle. It's one hell of a shot, so fair play to the lad, though the gods have steadied his bow. Frankly, I don't know why Achilles didn't just order a pair of armoured boots; surely a cobbler and a blacksmith could've bodged something together? Anyway, footwear quibbles aside, Achilles' death earns him posthumous *fame*, or what the ancient Greeks called *kleos*. In doing so, he became the archetype for the illustrious hero whose eternal renown compensates for a life cut short. Achilles earns glory. Sounds nice, right?

Intriguingly, Homer's sequel poem, the *Odyssey*, finds Achilles regretting his glorious fate as king of the Underworld; he'd much rather be resurrected as some mud-caked peasant than sit on his eternal, ghostly throne. Achilles has learned a hard lesson that many modern celebs have since discovered: the pressures of fame can make mundane anonymity seem appealing. Despite Homer's surprising ambivalence towards glory, the cultural celebration of heroic death continued in early medieval poems, such as 'The Battle of Maldon' and *The Song of Roland*, both of which celebrate outnumbered warriors choosing to die honourably rather than flee to fight another day. In short, *kleos/glory/fame* - or, whatever you wanna call it - usually came to mean immortality earned by kicking the bucket while swinging a sword. Yet, truth be told, it wasn't solely reserved for the dead.

Our word *fame* derives from Fama, the Roman goddess of rumour-mongering, but she wasn't some benign gossip nattering at the hairdresser's about a friend's dirty weekend with a married man. While the Greek equivalent, Pheme, was a beautiful goddess with long flowing tresses who parped the horn of reputation, the Roman version was starkly different. In his classic foundation myth the *Aeneid* – a parallel text to Homer's Troy story, but one following a Trojan warrior on his journey to Italy – the great writer Virgil describes Fama as a 'dreadful monster' whose body bristles with feathers and wings; and from the tip of each feather are extra eyes, ears, and mouths representing how rumour spreads. Her need for neither sleep nor shelter means she's constantly on the move, travelling great distances overnight, and she grows in scale to match the popularity of her slanders – she might start small, as a new rumour is first nervously uttered, but then she expands until her head is lost in dark storm clouds, and only her torso and feet are visible.[51] In short, Fama is less goddess, more B-movie monster intent on trashing Tokyo.

Until now, we've used *fame/kleos* as Daniel Boorstin would've wanted, meaning a lasting, deserved form of glory. But let's look closer, because Virgil's personification of public recognition is terrifying. Fama's name derived from the Latin verb *fari*, 'to speak', and this reveals one of the inconsistencies of ancient reputation. In Virgil's depiction, Fama was equally the goddess of widespread praise as of career-destroying scandal; the only criterion for her involvement was that a person's name be on people's lips, for reasons good or ill.

Indeed, to make sense of the confusion, the scholar Gianni Guastella draws a distinction between Fama-Rumour and Fama-Glory[52] – the former being short-lived gossip, almost akin to celebrity status, and the latter being that enduring reputation meted out to Achilles and those stupidly brave medieval warriors. So here's where things get annoyingly vague: ancient *fame* could be temporary or permanent, positive or negative. That in itself is rather inconvenient to the *fame* = *glorious renown* idea. But – given that

Mercury, the messenger of divine opinion, was often depicted as a handsome, honest man with winged sandals to propel him at speed - it's pretty revealing that Virgil's courier service for *public* opinion was a chimeric beast which would've made even Godzilla piss himself in fear. That really doesn't sound like a good thing.

Virgil wasn't alone in finding fame unsettling. The great Roman orator Cicero had first earned his reputation with victory in a landmark legal case, and he was still widely admired when Mark Antony's assassins hunted him down, during the bloody repercussions from Caesar's murder, and displayed his severed head and hand on Rome's speaking platform, the *rostra*. Before his brutal end, Cicero had written about *fame*, and in particular this perceptive line addressed to his son: 'If someone from his early years has some claim on fame and distinction, whether bequeathed by his father . . . or by some fluke or chance happening, the eyes of the world are directed upon him. People enquire about his activities and about the sort of life he is living. As if he were caught in a dazzling spotlight, no word, no deed of his can remain hidden.'[53]

This observation might easily apply today to a newly appointed cabinet minister whose old speeches are inspected for problematic opinions. *Fame* invites the invasive gaze and has done so for two millennia. Both Virgil and Cicero seemingly judged public opinion a fickle and dangerous creature, neither reliable enough to trust nor toothless enough to ignore. Virgil was a modest man who, the ancient historian Suetonius tells us, hid from his admirers and blushed when they praised him. But one wonders if such modesty wasn't gawky introversion, but rather a defence mechanism against the perils of over-exposure. His scary depiction of Fama makes public notoriety seem the work of some alarmingly inhuman natural force, akin to being in the path of a tornado or finding oneself stalked by a ravenous predator.

Yet this terror wasn't generated by fickle gods and savage nature, but by human behaviour - gossip, jokes, slander, envious innuendos, heartfelt compliments, and the rest. Another ancient writer, Plutarch, admitted: 'Men in public life are responsible for more than their public words and actions: their dinners, beds, marriages, amusements and interests are all objects of curiosity.' To be famous was to be scrutinised by strangers, and to have one's private life interrogated. *Fame* wasn't only heroic glory, it could be a curse. Particularly when the public didn't always like what they saw.

Infamy, infamy, they've all got it in for me!

Let's rewind back to Homer. In the *Iliad*, Achilles acquires his immortal *kleos* by slaying Hector, but this act of bloodshed also transforms Hector too. Like a Bronze Age Obi-Wan Kenobi, struck down by Darth Vader, he becomes more powerful in death. Though he initially flees from his vengeful enemy, Hector is eventually tricked by the gods into showing courage against a pissed-off, semi-divine killing machine. He gets a sword in the throat for his troubles, but there's no shame in losing to a furious beefcake with molten grief powering his mighty limbs. However, had Homer wanted to vilify Hector as a coward, and tarnish him with disgraceful fame, he could've used a specific Greek word: *duskleês*. But, weirdly, it barely shows up in classical literature. The Greeks seemingly preferred *kleos* as their go-to label for everything, even a bad reputation, despite the headache this produces for modern historians.[54]

You might be assuming the Romans corrected this problem. After all, modern English gives us the thrilling *infamy* as a badge of shameful disgrace, and that sounds properly Roman, doesn't it? Curiously, the answer is 'No!' *Infamy*'s negative meaning only entered English usage circa 1380, during the life of Geoffrey Chaucer. For the Romans, *infamia* wasn't a moral judgement, but a legal term for an outlaw stripped of legal rights, or it was a sociological category for being low status - a slave or gladiator, perhaps.[55] Even at the height of his various controversies - even when accused of genocide - Julius Caesar never lurked under *infamia*'s dark umbrella. He just had bad *fama*. Oh, and before you get your hopes up about *notorious*, don't bother. It's medieval Latin for someone 'of note', whether good or bad.* Our negative meaning, which promises such thrilling transgression, dates back only as far as Shakespeare's day.[56]

In short, then, the ancients were an annoying bunch whose choice of vocabulary is a proper nuisance. Didn't they realise how awkward this all was? Actually, maybe they did. As a way of highlighting the jarring dichotomy between glory and gossip, ancient tradition declared the heroic Alexander the Great to have been born on the exact day on which a heinous crime was committed, meaning glory and infamy would forever be linked. The sinister culprit was Herostratus, and he's given his name to the diagnosis for the deviant thrill experienced by mass murderers when their names appear in rolling news coverage; it's an impulse so dangerous that some psychologists wonder if we shouldn't broadcast reports of terrorist attacks at all, for fear of inspiring the next one.[57] This disturbing desire for fame by any means is dubbed Herostratus Syndrome, after the arsonist who burned down the Temple of Ephesus, one of the 'Seven Wonders of the World', in 356 BCE.

Herostratus was caught and tortured into confessing. He'd wanted to acquire glorious *kleos* and - being low-born, talentless, and poor - figured his best shot was destroying something famously beautiful. Recognising this vainglorious motivation, the authorities punished Herostratus by erasing him from history. He would be made *aklees* (stripped of his *kleos*), so that no one would ever know his name. And yet . . . we do! His crime was so appalling, ancient writers couldn't help themselves. Herostratus lured them into the irresistible outrage which granted his wish and keeps him posthumously alive. He's a real-life Voldemort, a Sauron of history. He whispers to us from the shadows, imploring us to be offended. He has a Wikipedia page and a syndrome named after him. He's the focus of this paragraph. His *kleos* is undeniable. Dammit, the bastard won!

---

* The Notable B.I.G. doesn't really have the same ring to it, does it?

Famous, last words

Ancient *fame* was strangely two-headed. The traditional idea that it was awarded as posthumous glory, by elite juries of subsequent worthies, certainly applies to the heroes of myth and poetry, but it doesn't fully reflect the experiences of real people who found themselves roasted by the burning glare of public fascination. Virgil and Cicero didn't seem to think so, anyway. To be *famous* wasn't just to be painted on a vase, looking buff with your shirt off; *famous* was also to be unique, known to many and rendered vulnerable to the sharp opinions of strangers. It was about rumour. It came from the verb 'to speak'. It got personal. And it applied to the living.

I see *glory* and *fame* as similar but separate ideas, so I'm on board with Gianni Guastella's division of Fama-Rumour and Fama-Glory.[58] Plus, there's my other category, *renown*, to consider. Though that's a public reputation which brings plenty of attention, I believe it can also arrive without the aggressively invasive rumour-mongering, as we've seen in the career of Sir David Attenborough. All told, we have a few things to consider, and there are some murky overlaps, but I believe *celebrity* differs from *fame*, *glory*, and *renown* because they don't rely upon the support of capitalistic mass media; they could all thrive in a pre-modern age, before newspapers, photographs, branded merchandise, and the internet.

Julius Caesar was hugely *famous*, a Greek scientist like Archimedes was *renowned*, Achilles was posthumously *glorious*, but none of them were *celebrities*. If you'll let me coin a slogan: 'All historical celebrities were famous, but not all famous people were celebrities.' Feel free to tattoo it on your forehead. *Glory*, *renown*, *fame*, and *celebrity* are inextricably linked, and it can take a migraine-inducing feat of patience to untangle them, but Daniel Boorstin was wrong to think modern *celebrity* usurped the others. Instead, they've co-existed for centuries, and still do today.

We see this in Casanova's memoirs, which were written in French. As Nicola Vinovrški summarises: 'The adjectives he used most frequently to describe well-known people were *célèbre* and

fameux. On some occasions, the word *fameux* had negative con-
notations and was akin to *notorious*. Most frequently, he used *la
renommée* to indicate fame but also used *célébrité*. *Infâme* . . . was
an insult and it applied to people who were not necessarily well
known. To describe making an impression in public, Casanova
almost always used *briller* [the verb 'to shine']. He described being
well known as being talked about, frequently using the metaphor
of creating noise (*faire du bruit*).'[59] Notice how Casanova replicated
ancient custom by making *fameux* mean both positive and negative
fame? It's no wonder we get so confused with our synonyms for
famousness. We've learned from the best.

You might assume things are much more straightforward with
infamy and *notoriety*, but no! Despite being negatively charged fame
particles, they curiously mirror positive ones. A famous villain will
be widely known, distinctive, and the subject of media coverage
- this might equate to negative *renown* if only their wicked deeds
are widely known, or if they're an absolute tosspot of a politician.
But a famous criminal or hated provocateur might also become the
subject of media gossip about their private life, or even the focus
of a commercial market. Alarmingly, Jack the Ripper - with his
lucrative industry of gothic fright - ticks all five boxes on my celebrity checklist. He's *infamous*, *notorious*, and a *celebrity*. He's also,
much to my horror, *glorious*, I suppose, though not in the positive sense of the word. He's acquired posthumous *kleos* through
committing dramatic, disgusting atrocities. He's the modern
Herostratus.

Where does that leave us? There are obvious overlaps, and the
blurred edges are somewhat maddening, but I do see some important distinctions: those with both positive and negative *glory/
kleos* have a powerful posthumous reputation; those with *renown*
are noted for their achievements, but not their private lives; those
with *fame* suffer the slings and arrows of personal gossip, and perhaps are known for their achievements too, but they lack a commercial economy of their own. But standing separate to them all
is *celebrity*:

CELEBRITY (noun): A unique persona made widely known to the public via media coverage, and whose life is publicly consumed as dramatic entertainment, and whose commercial brand is profitable for those who exploit their popularity, and perhaps also for themselves.

Phew! Do you need a lie-down? I feel like I need a lie-down. Thankfully, things get a lot simpler from here. Now we know what a celebrity is, it's time to find out what they look like. Or, rather, how the celebs of yesteryear manipulated their visual image to maintain their careers.

Chapter 4: Image Is Everything

You are always on my mind

If I suddenly shout 'ELVIS PRESLEY!', does he burst into your conscious, all swivel-hipped and kiss-curled? Can you see him in the white Vegas jumpsuit? What if I bellow 'MARILYN MONROE!'? Is she giggling coquettishly as her white dress flaps up? You can play this fun game for ages, because there are literally thousands of celebs. Obviously, it doesn't work with esoteric Argentinian snooker players, or Belgium's premier radio host, but our brains are a thick catalogue of famous faces. Your ability to recall their images is no accident; like walking, talking paintings by Renaissance masters, celebrities are perfectly formed icons that live in our heads. Even when we're doing other stuff, those images are still up there, biding their time in neurological storage.

But we don't store banal images. You didn't imagine Elvis doing the hoovering, or Marilyn Monroe unblocking a sink. Think of a celebrity and I suspect they're not in jeans and a hoodie. Instead, they ooze professionalised glamour: fine fabrics, expertly coiffured hair, impeccable footwear, maybe a jangling accompaniment of bling. They're possibly on a red carpet, doing those weird poses celebs are trained to do. Maybe it's a fashion shoot in some glossy magazine? Or did you go straight to visualising them in their swimsuit? That's all right, there's no judgement here. Okay, now ask yourself: why *this* person? And why *this* image? You've most likely seen thousands of others in your life, yet this is the one that sprang out like a jack-in-the-box. Why?

Celebrity culture is a bizarre phenomenon that convinces us we have intimate relationships with strangers. We may forget the face of our favourite primary school teacher, or kindly ex-neighbour, or the reassuring doctor, but - somehow - we'll still recognise popstars from twenty years ago, even though they've never taught us maths, or lent us a lawnmower, or given us the all-clear from cancer. Now, more than ever, the celebrity image exists in simultaneous ubiquity. We're bombarded daily by their memorable beauty; even if we seek shelter, their toned bodies still whistle down upon us like incoming mortar fire. Nowhere is safe. They're in adverts, news headlines, the sports we follow, the TV shows we love, in fashion mags, and on billboards. Celebrity has never been more pervasive.

I suppose it's hardly surprising that scholars wrongly decided celebrity is a uniquely twentieth century concept; a visual system must surely be caused by visual arts, and the great visual arts of our age are, of course, movies and telly. But you've read enough of this book to already know celebrity is older than Hollywood. And before celebrity there was *fame*, which had also been visualised for thousands of years on pots, coins, murals, paintings, and so much more. Many of us will have trotted up and down the long galleries in European stately homes, with audioguides burbling away in our ears, as we gaze upon rows of aristocratic portraits. The rich, famous, and powerful have long harnessed imagery to reflect their status and submit their candidacy for glorious posterity.

But in the early eighteenth century the public began to want access to those images too. And then they wanted to own them. Celebrity arrived when the human image became a marketplace, forcing celebrities, and those who would exploit them, to begin a never-ending tussle over who controlled their visual brand. Indeed, we'll talk about image piracy and the perils of copyright in Chapter 7. But first, let's talk paintings.

Picture perfect

Laurence Sterne was a nobody, just some forty-something churchman from Yorkshire; another hopeful with a self-published book that only nine people would ever read. Sure, the people of York found him witty, but he had zero clout on the national stage. But Sterne planned to change that. In late 1759, he self-published the first two volumes of a comedy classic, *The Life and Opinions of Tristram Shandy, Gentleman*, his innovative parody of a celebrity memoir. It was a brilliant, funny, inventive book. And nobody cared. Undaunted, Sterne undertook months of networking, and eventually wangled an endorsement from superstar actor David Garrick. That was all he needed. Sterne became a literary sensation, and hurled himself into his newfound celebrity with the panting eagerness of a spaniel leaping into the ocean on a scorching summer's day. He was soon everywhere; at all the best parties, in all the best dining rooms, and merged his own identity with that of his fictional protagonist, so that Laurence Sterne and Tristram Shandy became one and the same.[1] Charmed, London played along with the fun new game.

Eager to sustain his new reputation, he realised he needed to visualise his brand. People knew the name, but not yet the face. And Sterne really wanted to be known. A couple of decades beforehand, the actor, poet, and playwright Colley Cibber - who'd written one of the earliest celebrity autobiographies - had noted in a letter: 'I wrote more to be Fed than Famous.'[2] Sterne jokingly switched it around, proclaiming: 'I wrote not to be fed, but to be famous.'[3] The joke worked better when you saw him; Sterne was skeletally thin and had the gaunt face to match, suggesting he was indeed unfed. Craving acclaim, he scurried off to the studio of the artist Joshua Reynolds to have his portrait done. It took several sittings, but, once the paint was dry, he immediately thrust it into the hands of an engraver, who produced multiple prints.[4] Sterne didn't care for posthumous glory - the thing most highbrow creatives strived for - he wanted immediate recognition. And he published seven more volumes of *Tristram Shandy* to ensure the fandom never dwindled.

Sterne had chosen his artist wisely. Joshua Reynolds was rapidly earning his own celebrity status by painting other celebrities.

Though a brilliant technician and noted art theorist, he'd also begun as a provincial nobody, and still spoke with a rolling Devonshire accent. Usually, portrait artists stuck to the standard clientele of royals, aristocrats, and worthy intellectuals, but the unsnobbish Reynolds painted whoever held the public's attention, so long as there was money in it. As Sterne pulled into London, Reynolds was already being gossiped about as the painter behind the new portrait of Kitty Fisher - the crotch-flashing, high-price courtesan with a knack for scandalous publicity - whom he'd shown in the guise of Queen Cleopatra dissolving a priceless pearl in a cup of wine.[5] To get this joke requires a detailed knowledge of eighteenth-century gossip and a thorough education in ancient history, so allow me to decode it for you.

London's premier sex worker was said to charge £100 per night for her services, but a rumour had circulated in 1759 that the Duke of York had paid only half. Outraged, she'd allegedly eaten the £50 note in a buttered sandwich as a mark of contempt.[6] Casanova - who claimed he was offered the chance to sleep with her, but turned it down - quibbled, saying it was a £100 note from Sir Richard Atkins that she'd eaten.* Perhaps he was correct, because she was soon nicknamed 'the Hundred Pound Miss'.[7] Reynolds, being the history nerd, spotted potential for a gag. According to the Roman historian Pliny the Elder, the ancient lovers Cleopatra and Mark Antony had embarked on a wager to see who could splash the most cash on a banquet. To win the bet, Egypt's queen had dissolved a priceless earring in vinegar and smugly glugged it down, figuring why buy lavish appetisers when she could just eat the money? By the same logic, billionaires shouldn't sail luxury yachts, they should stick them in a blender and drink them.

Reynolds noticed the similarities between the stories, and turned his provocative muse into a new Cleopatra. With his support, Kitty Fisher was therefore able to cunningly mine her dodgy

---

* Casanova claimed to have been offered the chance to have sex with Kitty for only ten guineas, but he didn't fancy her because she spoke no French!

reputation for irony, delivering the most elegant of middle fingers to her haters. Instead of being cast as an ungrateful harlot too big for her boots, she transformed into a legendarily beautiful monarch with money to burn. Plus, if Cleopatra was out-thinking her lover to win the bet, perhaps Fisher was outwitting her suitors too? Adverts for the engraving reveal she personally owned the copyright; she wanted everyone to know that Kitty Fisher was a queen who always got the last laugh.[8]

Fisher sat for several Reynolds portraits before her untimely death. They met twenty-one times in 1759 alone, but she wasn't his only customer of dubious morality. Though the vast majority of his 2,000 portraits were of privileged people with fancy titles,[9] Reynolds was particularly fond of these sassy, saucy ladies who'd risen from nothing; their portraits seem to me as if they're painted with a little more sympathy than those of his duchesses. Part of that is because they were more playful in their poses, compared to the more conservative toffs, but I get the feeling Reynolds simply enjoyed their company.

Even in older age, with dignity guaranteed by his presidency of the Royal Academy – the institution he'd helped to found – Reynolds continued to paint provocateurs, such as Laetitia 'Mrs Smith' Derby. Much like Nell Gwyn's, Derby's love life had begun in poverty: she'd allegedly dated the celebrity highwayman John 'Sixteen String Jack' Rann; then, when he was executed, she'd hooked up with the Duke of York, before bagging her horse-obsessed lover, Lord Lade (whom she married), only to cheat on him (allegedly) with his close friend, the Prince of Wales. The gossip suggested they bumped uglies in Lord Lade's carriage, which is a gift for headline writers.* Reynolds perhaps risked his good name by working with such scandalous models, but his reputation survived unscathed.

---

* Sadly, they didn't have headlines back then, so I'll have to invent my own: 'Lady Lade Gets Laid in Carriage, Lord Lade Dismayed at Marriage!' It might be a tad long, in fairness.

Celebrity collabs

Reynolds was undoubtedly a barometer of upstart notoriety; his paintbrush both confirmed fame and conferred it upon his sensational sitters. Perhaps the most interesting subject was Mai, a young Polynesian man born on the island of Ra'iātea, but who'd fled to Tahiti when his family had been killed by invaders. Mai – though Brits called him Omai – briefly became a London society darling between 1773 and 1776 after arriving aboard Captain Cook's ship. He was perceived as a 'noble savage', a case study for Jean-Jacques Rousseau's controversial philosophy of *primitivism* that claimed living in a natural state made humans happier than so-called enlightened 'civilisation'. But in Reynolds's portrait, there's no hint of savagery; the artist created a romantic image of a barefoot Mai looking serene in white robes and turban (Reynolds's best stab at Tahitian fashion, presumably).[10]

But Reynolds wasn't the sole image-maker; Mai presumably wanted to be seen this way, and was happy to be erroneously described as a prince. Some racist commentators had called Mai's broad nose ugly, but Reynolds's agile hand renders it beautifully, and his graceful pose suggests noble power. Reynolds and Mai shared the load in bolstering a romantic myth, one that had earlier seen the young visitor meet King George III under the guise of being a royal ambassador, during which he'd bowed, taken the king's hand, and charmed everyone by saying, 'How do, King Tosh!' which was his best attempt at saying 'George'. But Mai wasn't Polynesian royalty, he'd just been a guy who'd jumped on a foreign ship, hoping to convince his new friends to provide weapons with which to retake his family's native island.[11] The Reynolds collaboration did them both a favour.

This was Reynolds to a T. He worked with his models to find the best ideas, trusting in their instincts as much as his own. In her memoir, the superstar actress Sarah Siddons recounts the composition of a Reynolds masterpiece, in 1784, when she posed as the Tragic Muse: 'he took me by the hand, saying "Ascend your undisputed throne, and graciously bestow upon me some grand idea of The Tragik Muse".[12] I walked up the steps and seated myself instantly in the attitude in which She now appears. This idea satisfyed him so well that he, without one moment's hesitation, determined not to alter it.' Another version of the story says she changed position midway; a different witness, Samuel Rogers, remembers she came in, sat down, asked how she should pose, and Reynolds said: 'Just as you are.'[13]

It's slightly disappointing Reynolds wasn't like the classic 1960s snapper, shouting, 'The paintbrush loves you, darling!' as he sprawled on the floor, trying to find the perfect, edgy angle. But what's clear is that Reynolds seemed happy in all of these competing versions to listen to the sitter. Indeed, Siddons claims in her memoirs that he'd wanted to put more colour in her cheeks, but 'I then begged him to pardon my presumption in hoping he would not heighten that tone of complexion so exquisitely accordant with the chilling and deeply co-centred musing of Pale Melancholy. He most graciously complied with my petition.'[14] Whereas Siddons claimed the credit, modern scholars suspect Reynolds actually had a lot of input in choosing her pose, as it harked back to an earlier artistic tradition that he'd carefully studied, but the triumph had clearly been forged from a mutual union of actress and artist working in cahoots.

Such collaborative creativity was later championed by William Hazlitt (the critic who first reviewed Edmund Kean) in his essay 'On Sitting for One's Picture', where he described being painted as akin to playing a fictional persona, or being 'like the creation of another self'. It wasn't just a case of holding a pose and pulling a 'Blue Steel' *Zoolander* pout. For Hazlitt, the relationship between painter and subject was an intimate dialogue, almost as if between two lovers.[15] Celebrities could try to control their images, but often they had to share in the creative process.

While Siddons found a willing collaborator who took instructions, Lord Byron's chosen artists kept failing to deliver the moody expressions he desired. Any image unbefitting his sexy gothic brand was declared in need of chucking on the fire. Byron was acutely aware of his own erotic power, and tried to oversee the production of his iconography, but he quickly lost control when his fame grew and others rushed to depict him as they saw fit, creating a standardised version of his face that became iconic in its wide usage. Indeed, as Tom Mole points out, the stereotypical outline of Byron became a silhouette almost as recognisable as a *Simpsons* character in its simplicity; the poet had great hair, though not quite as bountiful as Marge's blue-tinted bonce.[16]

Byron craved uniqueness.* Conversely, Sarah Siddons's cunning strategy was to mimic someone else. She knew that actresses were viewed with sexualised suspicion, so the Welsh actress forged her famous maternal image by mirroring the most respected maternal icon in the land: Queen Charlotte, who'd given King George III fifteen children. Given her acting success, it wasn't too long before the inevitable invitation to the palace arrived. Siddons was fearful of showing herself up, but she delivered another stellar perfor-mance: 'Her Majesty had express'd herself surprised to find me so collected in so new a position, and that I had conducted myself as if I had been used to a court. At any rate, I had frequently personated Queens.' Siddons had spent a career pretending to possess royal gravitas, so feigning it in a genuine palace proved to be a doddle.[17]

Dress to impress

Siddons's dressing like a queen was smart, but she wasn't the first to try it. Actresses carried the constant burden of innuendo, being simultaneously revered and reviled as beautiful, talented perform-ers who'd allegedly shag their way through a queue of men just

---

* Ironically, the most famous portrait of Byron - the one showing him in Albanian costume of red and gold, with draped turban and neat moustache - was shut away in private without being engraved. Painted by Thomas Phillips in 1813, it's an image of glamour, grandeur and exotic Eastern romance. In posthumous hindsight, we judge it the Byronic apotheosis because it reinforces the fatal romance of his death fighting for Greek independence from the Turks.

to get more fame. And it wasn't only a problem in Britain – the celebrated Tawa'if dancers of India were, from the 1600s onwards, also famously admired and shamed as elegant performers and al-leged high-class prostitutes. According to Schweta Sachdeva, they too used art to communicate their beauty through the printed visual image, and later embraced photography as a promotional strategy to market themselves not just as dancers and lovers, but also poets.[18]

So back in Britain, a strategy of aesthetic bomb defusal was deployed by many of the brightest stars, with the plan often built around emulating the ladies of highest rank. We might expect this to have been batted off with furious outrage by duchesses deter-mined to keep the riff-raff out of their hat shops, but celebrity's glamour seduced every social tier. These ladies were thrilled to be copied, and even loaned their fancy frocks to low-born actresses to be worn on stage, allowing them to boast to their friends that they were acting as stylists to theatrical icons. In return, they sometimes borrowed stage costumes so they could swan around at their own glamorous parties while dressed as Lady Macbeth, or whatever was all the rage that week.[19] Celebrity and aristocracy intermixed in the most intriguing of ways. They found each other mutually fascinating, and almost social equals, despite the gulf in class and education that might separate them.

Even as early as the 1680s, three decades before I believe ce-lebrity began, Elizabeth Barry borrowed the wedding suit and coronation robes from King James II's queen, Mary of Modena. By the 1720s, Ann Oldfield wasn't just sumptuously bedecked when in character but was carried around, offstage, in a lady's sedan chair.[20] Fifty years later, the singer and actress Ann Catley developed a hair-style popular among all ranks, while Frances Abington was hailed as the best-dressed woman of her era, being dubbed the 'priestess of fashion' as if she were some sort of divine intercessor with a direct channel to the god of fine tailoring. To maintain this image, Abington was given a whopping clothing allowance of £500 that funded her Parisian fabric imports. But it paid for itself in ticket sales as people flocked to bask in her elegant beauty; a fashionable image was as much a box office lure as her ability to act.

One of the most distinctive fashionistas of the late 1700s was Prince George's mistress, the controversial actress-turned-poet Mary Robinson - commonly known as 'Perdita', after her most famous character - whose taste in clothes made her a fashion icon, but also put a target on her back. Her outfits were obsessively reported by newspapers, and one commentator noted:

> When she was to be seen daily in St James Street and Pall Mall, even in her chariot this variation was striking. Today she was a paysanne, with her straw hat at the back of her head . . . Yesterday she, perhaps, had been the dressed belle of Hyde Park, trimmed, powdered, patched, painted to the utmost power of rouge and white lead; to morrow, she would be the cravatted Amazon of the riding house: but be what she might the fashionable promenaders swept the ground as she passed.[21]

As Michael Gamer and Terry F. Robinson note: 'Over the next two years Robinson would set trends in everything from hats to phaetons [open-topped carriages], hairstyles to portraiture. That spring she caused a stir with an elaborate "Cataract Muff" [a puffed-up hand-warmer with long fringes of fur] and a sensation with the Chemise de la Reine, a puffed and ruffled muslin dress styled after one worn by Marie Antoinette.' This dress scandalised London because it clung to her body, revealing her womanly curves while all the other ladies wore hooped skirts that fanned outwards, hiding their hips and bum in a structured tent of fine fabric.[22]

Mary Robinson led the fashion vanguard of her day, and her high-profile affair with the Prince of Wales made her an obsessively studied clothes horse, but many subsequent pioneers followed this example. In the early twentieth century, the French Broadway singer Anna Held wore extraordinarily elaborate dresses and hats that led one bewildered reporter to proclaim: 'whereas

some actresses very much underdress, Miss Held very much
overdresses!' For Held, fashion was a public performance and she
lamented: 'I live at the dressmaker's . . . I am being moulded into
clothes, all day long. I get no rest. For three months last summer
I have been fitted, and draped, and assassinated by clothes. And
then you marvel that they fit!'[23] Such a complaint was laced with
irony: she knew full well that fashion was one of the sources of
her power.

Ladies and gentlemen

Actresses didn't always have to wear a dress on stage, however.
Some built careers by wearing rakish male attire, playing what
were known as 'breeches roles' which ignited a frisson of excitement among audiences because tight-fitting togs would reveal the
female form. In the 1740s, the Irish star Peg Woffington was well
known for these male parts, and her close-fitting stockings showed
off a shapely pair of legs. Some eighty years later, in the 1820s, Eliza
Vestris played the same game, inspiring a satirical print depicting
her dressed the same as the men who flock excitedly around her.
But she, of course, is so much sexier.

By subtle contrast, in the 1730s, Charlotte Charke – youngest
daughter of the poet laureate Colley Cibber – played breeches parts,
but has since tantalised historians by responding to widowhood
with the decision to live instead as a man called Charles Brown,
and doing a variety of men's jobs, before remarrying and publishing a memoir in 1755 as Charlotte again. Her cross-dressing was
probably more than just a promotional tactic; this wasn't simply a
case of showing off a cracking pair of calves. Charke's prolonged
gender fluidity, even away from the stage, suggests an authentic
queer identity.[24]

If Eliza Vestris eroticised her act by squeezing into chaps'
breeches, Vesta Tilley managed to do the opposite. Tilley was
one of the transatlantic superstars of early-1900s music hall, and –
having begun as a performing toddler from a working-class family

– became a national treasure before retiring, aged fifty-six, to marry a Tory MP and become Lady de Frece. It was a most dignified retirement that was ushered in by an enormous farewell tour of the UK, in which all ranks of society turned out to see her off, and it's rather astonishing that a working-class drag king would end up as part of the establishment, but Tilley had always avoided sexed-up scandal. Her singing male characters were funny, or arrogant, or romantic, or cheeky, but the act was always respectable and her clothes were beautifully tailored to hide, rather than accentuate, her femininity.

She was so good at being a man, Tilley influenced male fashion, recalling in her autobiography:

> I rushed off the stage to make the change from an Eton boy to a Dude (my changes were all done with lightning rapidity, with the help of two maids) and to my horror I found that my maid had forgotten to put cuff links in the cuffs of my shirt . . . I snatched a bit of black ribbon which my maid was wearing in her hair, and hastily tied the cuffs together with a black ribbon bow. Shortly afterwards a leading firm of gentlemen's hosiers, on Broadway, were exhibiting cuff links in the form of a black ribbon bow, as the very latest fashion in London.

Among her most beloved characters were her singing soldiers, and she became a high-profile army recruiter during the First World War, helping to inspire young lads to sign up and fight. In this regard, Tilley marched parallel to the footsteps of Hannah Snell, who rose to brief fame in the 1750s after having fought in the British Army and Royal Marines while disguised as a man. Snell's subsequent celebrity was based on her popular memoir and stage act, which involved singing in uniform while performing military drills.[25] Intriguingly, she wasn't an awkward embarrassment to the navy, which issued her with full rights and pension, but Snell ditched the trousers once her cover was blown. Unlike Charlotte

Charke, Snell's gender swap was purely practical. She'd only pretended to be a fella because women weren't allowed to fight, and once the game was up she returned to her traditional gender role.

A uniform look

Some celebrities spend their careers chasing the latest fashion trends in a bid to stay relevant. Some lead fashion by the nose, becoming influencing trendsetters for other celebs and the rest of the country. Such a career policy requires constant reinvention, the sort of dazzling makeover Madonna and David Bowie became legendarily good at undergoing, but it's not the only way to get noticed. Rather than constantly draping themselves in new styles, some celebrities fixed their images with a singular, iconic aesthetic that they stuck to like glue.

In the 1860s, Europe acquired a new political star in the bearded shape of General Giuseppe Garibaldi, whose revolutionary republicanism helped Italy unify as a single nation. Now noted for his association with fruity biscuits, Garibaldi oozed magnetic appeal; half a million people allegedly flocked to greet him when he visited London in 1864, and they were drawn to his arresting image as much as his military heroism. The clothes were crucial: he'd spent time in South America, and dressed with a distinctive 'gaucho' vibe, usually being seen in a russet-red shirt, with flowing scarves, natty ponchos, and baggy trousers belted high up the waist. He also rocked a beret, because he was one of those suave European types who could pull them off without looking like an utter berk. His image became so powerful, thousands volunteered to join his redshirts, including Brits with no dog in Italy's fight, and scores of women hurled themselves at him. Garibaldi wore his reputation on his back, and he looked great.[26]

Meanwhile, if you ask an American to draw a picture of Mark Twain, chances are they'll depict him wearing a white suit. This iconic outfit actually came very late in his life. In 1906, Twain – his real name was Samuel Langhorne Clemens – arrived at the

US Library of Congress and took everyone by surprise. He was seventy-one years old and had spent much of his life in sober, dark tailoring. But on this day the nation's most beloved humorist had turned up in a summery three-piece suit stitched from white fabric, accessorised with a white shirt and white tie that matched the fluffy white hair on his head and the bushy grey 'tache drooping over his upper lip. He looked a bit like Colonel Sanders, but it wasn't KFC cosplay, it was a weapon. This was his plan to win the hearts and minds of the American public. Or, at least, those who made the laws.

Twain deployed his new look as a promotional gimmick in a legal case arguing for an extension of copyright beyond the death of the author, to ensure their families were financially supported. As he gave a rousing speech, the stark image of him in creamy white, at the centre of an image in which all other figures wore blacks and greys, made him an instant media sensation. Yet despite it being a temporary tactic, it also proved surprisingly durable – this singular image became the perfect, posthumous version of him that shone for decades, with his white suit showing up in countless adverts and jokes. It was a brilliant stunt that retroactively changed how America would remember its comic master.[27]

Sticking with iconic American dudes with copious facial hair, let's turn to William F. Cody – better known as Buffalo Bill – who rose from military scout to become one of the biggest transatlantic showmen of the nineteenth century, offering a romanticised cowboy experience to eager punters in America and Europe. Even at the very dawn of his career, when he was just a small-time scout taking rich guys out to the Wild West for a spot of touristic hunting, Cody knew how to look the part, as one customer described: 'Dressed in a suit of light buckskin, trimmed along the seams with fringes of the same leather, his costume lighted by the crimson shirt worn under his open coat, a broad sombrero on his head and carrying his rifle lightly in his hand as his horse came forward toward us on an easy gallop, he realized to perfection the bold hunter and gallant sportsman of the plains.'

Though Cody knew he was laying it on thick, noting: 'I determined to put on a little style myself', his fringed buckskin jacket screamed rugged authenticity to gullible city slickers. It was a look he never abandoned. Even when age caught up with him, and those luxurious curls limply retreated from his scalp, Cody donned a wig to ensure the image lived on, while that same jacket never left his back. Just as Queen Elizabeth I had frozen her face in official portraits, Buffalo Bill chose to be an eternal idea painted onto a decaying body, for the reassurance of the paying punters.[28]

Wigging out

From one celebrity who couldn't let the public see his wig, let's explore one whose wig was so famous it was named in his honour. In mid-eighteenth-century London, all roads led to David Garrick – a master of both comedy and tragedy, and a reforming producer who re-energised theatre as popular entertainment and art form. He was also a master of self-promotion. As with our earliest celebrity, Henry Sacheverell, Garrick's face appeared on all manner of unlicensed merchandise and satirical imagery, but he battled to control his visual brand, even when it kept eluding his grasp. During his lifetime, Garrick was the most painted man in Britain, and his image was everywhere, because that's exactly what he wanted.

The most iconic image was Reynolds's depiction of Garrick choosing between the two muses of Tragedy and Comedy. It became a huge hit in London and France, as George Colman's letter from Paris reveals: 'There hang out here on every street, pirated prints of Reynolds's Picture of you . . .'[29] Elsewhere, Garrick was frequently depicted in character; we have many prints of him doing A-grade Shakespearean acting where his famously expressive face (his party trick was suddenly switching expressions on cue, from horror to joy to surprise etc.) is given great prominence. Another trick was a wired-up fright wig that he wore for spooky scenes, such as the ghostly revelation in *Hamlet*. At the right moment, he could extend the wires so his hair seemed to stand up in shocked horror. Who needs CGI? Not Garrick!

In his fifties, when his career began to flag, Garrick obsessively linked his brand to that of Shakespeare, helping to forge the playwright's reputation as England's national poet. He organised a massive Shakespeare jubilee pageant in 1769, with himself at the head, and when artists began celebrating the famous Bard of Stratford with new works of sculpture and painting, it was Garrick who wheedled his way into posing as the playwright's body double.[30] If we're being generous, we might say it was well-intentioned homage, but, in truth, it might also be read as a weird hybrid of intense fandom and reputational bodysnatching; a slightly cringey appropriation of genius by someone convinced they're worthy of it, a bit like when Hollywood actors with too much leverage cast themselves in biopics despite being horribly wrong for the part.*

In 1762, at the height of his fame, Garrick hired the German painter Johan Zoffany and set him up as his live-in artist. The most famous painting born from this odd arrangement depicted Garrick not in character, but in backstage profile, looking off to the right, with his wig removed. His head has been shaved - an afternoon ritual for a habitual wig-wearer - leaving only a dark, ratty tail around the nape of the neck. Theatrical masks and props sit at the bottom of the frame, reminding us of Garrick's extensive credentials, but it's not his usual actorly action shot. Instead, it's an image of startling intimacy. He looks vulnerable and unglamorous; his bulbous head is a little egg-shaped, like those elongated ancient skulls archaeologists sometimes find in Mexico that conspiracy theorists declare to be proof of aliens. It's not exactly Garrick's finest look.

The rumour, when the painting was auctioned in 1819, was that Zoffany had hidden himself in a cupboard to sketch Garrick unawares - in which case, this image would be a prototype for the

---

* I'm looking at you, Kevin Spacey. *Beyond the Sea* was bad, but you've obviously done a lot worse since . . .

long-lens paparazzo squatting behind the bins. But trusting that story is to fall for Garrick's ploy. He was famous for his wigs; he even commissioned a special one with five curls called 'the Garrick cut' which became the must-have hairpiece for the chattering classes. And so the revelatory de-wigging was a brilliant stunt of faux intimacy to make his audience feel they'd got closer to the real man. As Ruth Scobie argues,[31] there was no need for Zoffany to lurk like a creepy stalker; Garrick had hired him for this exact purpose: 'it's a choreographed, layered performance of private life', she points out. This image was a controlled release, a simulation of candid intimacy from a man who famously couldn't help but perform the public role of David Garrick, even in private.

This was both his blessing and his curse. Joshua Reynolds – who painted Garrick four times, and frequently joined him for dinner at their private club – found Garrick to be a talented but insincere luvvie who always had to be the centre of attention. Yes, the face-changing trick was impressive, and Garrick was a funny raconteur, but it was quietly depressing that he just couldn't switch it off in polite company. In the words of James Boswell: '[Garrick] by too great a desire after the reputation of being a wit, the object from whom the whole company are to receive their entertainment, spoils every company he goes into.' Spoils has two meanings there, doesn't it? An overabundance of Garrick was both a treasured treat and a trial of patience. He was too much sometimes.

Returning to his portraits, I think we find this narcissism when we look for it. Eighteenth-century satire was merciless in pricking Garrick's inflated ego. Perhaps the most successful assassin was the one-legged comedian Samuel Foote, whose brutally funny impressions of famous people always landed savage body blows. For Garrick, his angle of attack was downward, because the master actor was rather short.[32] But I think Joshua Reynolds may have launched his own subtle attack too. In a celebrated painting, we see the star and his sumptuously dressed wife, Eva – a famous dancer originally from Austria – seated outside on a bench, while Garrick opens his broad body towards her, his legs manspreading as he leans gently into her personal space. There's a faint smile on his face, and an open book in his hand. As Heather McPherson notes, it looks as if he's just read her some lines and now craves acknowledgement of his genius. But Eva looks blankly forward, her left elbow resting on the bench's armrest, while her diminutive, doll-like hand folds against her heavily rouged left cheek.[33]

Perhaps she's rapt with delight, or wistfully deep in thought; perhaps the romantic lines he's just read her are filling her soul with happiness? Theirs was certainly a very happy marriage. But, to me, her eyes look glazed over; her body is turned away. It could be read as Reynolds depicting a strong, mutually supportive marriage - and some art historians are convinced of exactly that - but I can't help detecting a hint of attention-seeking in Garrick's posture. I wonder if Reynolds was actually landing a sneaky punch.*

Wax on, wax off

Paintings and engravings weren't the only visual media of the first celebrity century. At the highbrow end, Paris's most esteemed sculptor, Jean-Antoine Houdon, drew frequent crowds to his gallery of busts depicting France's greatest cultural and political figures, such as Voltaire and Jean-Jacques Rousseau, along with America's revolutionary heroes. In particular, Benjamin Franklin's huge celebrity in France was powered by his deliberately plain clothes and beaver-fur hat; a cultivated image designed to communicate America's simple, backwoods romanticism to a political class used to towering wigs, velvet frocks, and rich fellas in makeup. Weirdly, it worked. Franklin's distinctive face and balding head popped up all over France, making him one of the earliest transatlantic stars and a surprise septuagenarian sex symbol. All the ladies wanted to touch his furry beaver, and I'll let you finish that joke for yourself . . .

---

* I ran a public poll on Twitter: 90 per cent of the 2,000 respondents agreed that Garrick looks like a tiresome jerk in the painting.

Slightly lower down the prestige table were the wax artists. Though originally an ancient technique, revived during the Renaissance, in the eighteenth century wax modelling became a popular art form. In America, touring exhibitions first arrived in the 1730s but grew in prominence during the 1790s, with over 1,500 models being displayed, including royals, famous actors, and great figures from history.[34] But it was in France that the big cheese of waxworks was doing his thing.

Actually, he was a Swiss cheese. His name was Philippe Curtius, a doctor by training, and he'd emulated the sculptor Houdon by displaying images of French royalty alongside the nation's lofty celebs. But what made him stand out, and allegedly drew 3,000 visitors per day, was the Cavern of the Great Thieves, built in 1782. This was a sensationalist precursor to the sorts of gothic spectacle now encountered at the London Dungeon. It allowed visitors to confront notorious criminals, putting these infamous villains in the same space as France's heroic intellectuals and political leaders.

Curtius's talented assistant was another Swiss immigrant to Paris, a young woman called Marie Grosholtz. When the French Revolution turned into the Terror, and the guillotine began to slice through necks with terrifying regularity, she was rounded up as a royalist sympathiser but was spared execution in return for doing a nasty new job: picking up the freshly guillotined heads and moulding accurate death masks so that the public could gaze into the faces of the traitors and bluebloods. Philippe Curtius died in 1794, as the Revolution reached its bloodthirsty zenith, allowing Marie Grosholtz to inherit his wax collection. She promptly married a civil engineer called François Tussaud and they had three kids, of whom only two boys survived.

The marriage stumbled almost immediately, and, in 1802, she moved to London, never to see her husband again, though her sons would rejoin her. Gradually she mastered the art of running a waxwork attraction, beginning with a touring show under Curtius's name, before finally beginning to reel in the posher clientele by marketing her waxworks as educational. Visiting gawpers were treated to an eighty-page catalogue boasting biographical notes for each famous figure, and in 1828 she struck gold with waxworks of Byron and Walter Scott, placed side by side - a response to public demand for these two giants of literature.

Tussaud's gallery now became a sort of proxy cathedral dedicated to the worship of secular celebrity. As Jason Goldsmith argues, 'Madame Tussaud's functioned as a site of national cultural memory . . . As one visitor observed, "It seemed as if we had been ushered into the presence of the great dead, for the figures were natural as life . . . and really it was difficult to distinguish the wax from the live flesh and blood."'[35] In this cathedral dedicated to dead celebs, it wasn't so much 'Christ is Risen!' as 'Byron still lives!'

In 1835, Tussaud moved her exhibit into a permanent space on Baker Street, and soon after modelled a young Queen Victoria, who'd just taken the throne. It was another coup. Madame Tussaud's waxwork emporium flourished, and she promoted it yet further by cunningly publishing her over-embellished memoirs. Tussaud died in 1850, but London continues to hear her name uttered by panicked tourists who get lost on the Underground. Over 200 years have passed, and we're well used to high-resolution photography that produces flawless replication of the real celebrity body, but waxworks - with their subtle moulding errors, and dead-eyed smiles - remain eerily fascinating.*

Copy and paste

Who was your celebrity idol as a teenager? I followed standard bedroom protocol by plastering my walls with posters. Several stars were worthy of my Blu Tack, but the core trio were Cameron Diaz (a gorgeous, blonde actress with a flair for comedy), Eddie Izzard (a gorgeous, blond comedian with a flair for acting), and Jürgen

---

* Personally, I prefer crap waxworks. At a Niagara Falls fairground, in 2006, I saw one of Angelina Jolie as Lara Croft that literally could've been anyone. It was so brilliantly bad, I enjoyed it more than the famous Falls themselves.

Klinsmann (a gorgeous, blond footballer with a flair for sliding on his belly when he scored). And why this trio? Well, Izzard was my comedy god, Klinsmann my favourite team's heroic goal scorer, and Cameron Diaz a dazzlingly charismatic screen queen with funny bones. But, I'll be honest, they also looked magnificent. This was a holy trinity of human hotties, particularly Cameron Diaz, because I was fourteen and . . . well, that's probably enough information.

In my room, I could gaze at these stars on demand. They lived in frozen captivity, I was a teenage Jabba the Hutt and they were my Han Solos encased in carbonite. But, of course, they didn't really belong to me. I couldn't have dressed Eddie Izzard in a golden bikini, even if I'd wanted to. They chose their own clothes, or their stylists did, and they were busily leading their lives elsewhere: starring in fun movies, performing surreal jokes about Darth Vader in the Death Star canteen, and sliding on their bellies after smashing in thunderous volleys. Alas, what I possessed were mere facsimiles; mass-produced copies that adorned thousands of other bedrooms. These stars were unique, their personalities were uncopiable, and yet their image was infinitely reproducible. Such is the strange paradox of celebrity.

In the eighteenth century, the prestige of the painted portrait was measured in its scale and cost; to be painted was an expensive exercise in self-adoration and future-proofing a legacy. But all that money, and all that painstaking effort, produced a single artwork in a frame. It wasn't very shareable. So, unlike earlier *fame*, the true power of the celebrity image wasn't impelled by the canvas hanging in the gallery, but in its affordable reproductions. Though thousands flocked to see original paintings exhibited in London's Royal Academy, what made Laurence Sterne and David Garrick famous were the engraved duplicates sold in the print shops. These came with no fancy frames, and were much smaller, but they kept their power all the same. The public could possess the famous face. Even as early as 1709, at the very dawn of celebrity, Henry Sacheverell posed for the first of twenty-four engraved portraits.[36]

David Garrick's 1762 portrait by Joshua Reynolds was copied

thirteen different times, ending up as a bestseller in England and France. Antoine Lilti argues an average of seventy-two new celebrity prints were published in Paris every year between 1762 and 1784, rising to 100 new prints by the end of the century. Some engravings were high-quality reproductions, others cheap knock-offs hawked by street vendors.[37] A print run might have been only 1,000 copies, but many more pairs of eyeballs would've glimpsed those images in pubs and parlour rooms when their owners showed them off to their pals. Just as we never met Marilyn Monroe, but we all know her face, many Georgians never saw the original painting or met the real human subject. But it didn't matter – the print proliferated. Celebrities existed in multiple places at once.

While paintings, engravings, and waxworks continued to be cherished, the nineteenth century witnessed the increasing influence of printed imagery. Literacy rates were climbing, so newspaper readerships swelled, but there were also technical advances that simplified production: the switchover to rotary-cylinder printing presses industrialised journalism and book publishing, as did the change from soft copper engraving plates to more durable steel ones. Such mechanisation meant it was cheaper to mass-produce black-and-white images, and the use of pictures lured in new punters who weren't necessarily fully literate.[38] In 1841, *Punch* magazine launched in Britain, and used engraved cartoons to deliver topical gags. The following year, the ground-breaking *Illustrated London News* came into existence, and soon acquired copycats. Visual journalism became increasingly popular, even though the artists had to produce their designs on a wooden block which the engraver then used to print the pages.

Chromolithography – a chemical process for making colourised images – emerged simultaneously, and was vital in fusing the celebrity image with the lucrative advertising industry. Surprisingly, photography initially failed to impact upon journalism or poster design, because printing presses could only splurge out one shade of black ink, whereas replicating photos requires tonal range. It wasn't until the 1870s that the halftone process produced a subtle variety of blacks, greys, and whites by using differently sized ink dots to fool the eye into perceiving colour change. But, even then, photographs didn't grace the pages of most newspapers until the end of the nineteenth century. Artists instead redrew or traced photographs by hand, and then had them engraved.

By the dawn of the twentieth century, magazines were much more widely available. In 1900, there were 3,500 titles on sale in America alone (it would grow to nearly 18,000 by the millennium). By the 1920s, the magazine industry's doom was already being prophesised due to the boom in radio, automobiles, air travel, and cinema – who'd want to read an article when we could be racing along in our new car or listening to our favourite singer? But the opposite happened. The novelty of technological innovation and cultural flourishing only drove consumers to want to know more about the ever-changing world.

And magazine readerships kept growing because prices were falling. In the 1890s, Frank Munsey, one of America's biggest magazine publishers, invented the business model that still dominates the media industry today: sell cheaper than it costs to produce, but make up the revenue with advertising. The more people who buy it, the lower the cover price; the lower the cover price, the more people will buy it. Advertising, celebrity, and consumerism became the closest of bedfellows, and have remained locked in their ménage-à-trois ever since.[39]

I've already mentioned photography's disappointing contribution to news journalism, but don't let that get in the way of appreciating just how significant a watershed it was in celebrity's history. If we rewind to the 1840s, initially, this new technology offered only awkward-but-beautiful daguerreotypes, imprinted on sheets of silvered copper, which were annoyingly hard to replicate. But then came the colloidal process of chemical emulsion; this allowed printing on paper, over and over, so that the celebrity image could be faithfully captured and mass-produced. The public could now study the true nature of famous bodies and faces with forensic fascination, seeking evidence of greatness or criminality in the shape of wrinkled foreheads and eagle-beaked noses. And once they'd seen these stars in such human detail, they wanted to collect them. And I *really* mean that.

Cartomania: gotta collect 'em all!

Long before Pokémon, baseball cards, and football stickers, the Victorians went gaga for *cartomania* – the craze for collecting *cartes de visite*. These were small photographic reproductions on cardboard (6 × 9cm in size) depicting full-length portraits of celebrities, heroic figures, and royals. The range was wide: actors rubbed shoulders with soldiers, bishops, criminals, writers, and courtesans in ways that scandalised commentators who thought it unfit that the worthiest and worst in society should be stuck side by side in shop windows and photo albums. But, then again, hadn't Philippe Curtius done the same with his waxworks?

The reigning queen of the early bestseller charts was, fittingly enough, Queen Victoria, who featured in a royal family special album released in 1860. It sold 60,000 copies and helped to introduce *cartes de visite* to the public. Meanwhile, in France, Napoleon III was the big draw early on, at least until all the glamorous actors and actresses got their act together. Americans, of course, fixated on their own stars, including a presidential candidate, Abraham Lincoln, who didn't yet have his famous beard. Actually, the story of how it arrived is totally adorable.

Lincoln was sent a letter by an eleven-year-old girl called Grace Bedell, in which she'd dissed his weird face and suggested he grow some whiskers if he wanted people's votes. Lincoln did as he was told, and met her in her hometown a few months later, whispering: 'Gracie, look at my whiskers. I have been growing them for you.' It's extraordinary that his iconic look was the result of a hilariously blunt child stylist.* However, though news of Lincoln's new beard

---

* We should reintroduce this into modern politics, if only to see the prime minister treading Westminster's hallowed floor in a Spider-Man onesie.

quickly spread, he didn't immediately pose for an updated portrait, so newspaper artists were initially forced to improvise what they thought his bearded face looked like, making him a sort of e-fit president better suited to a 'Wanted!' poster.[40]

Perhaps America's most interesting photographic exponent was Frederick Douglass, the most snapped American of the century, with 160 different shots having been collected by historians, ten more than Ulysses S. Grant and thirty-four more than Lincoln.[41] Douglass had escaped slavery aged only twenty and, seven years later, made his name as the author of 1845's bestselling memoir *Narrative of the Life of Frederick Douglass, an American Slave*. This established him as the intellectual figurehead of the abolition movement, and he toured Britain and Ireland for two years,[42] before returning home to launch his own illustrated newspaper. But, alongside his career of political activism, he was also a brilliantly perceptive art theorist.

For Douglass, politics and photography went hand in hand; the camera captured truth and gave black people the power to represent themselves with dignity, showing their real faces and bodies without the distorting, racist tropes perpetuated by illustrators and engravers: 'Negroes can never have impartial portraits at the hands of white artists. It seems to us next to impossible for white men to take likenesses of black men, without most grossly exaggerating their distinctive features.'[43] When produced by black creators, or in collaboration with trusted white artists, Douglass noted that this exciting new art form showcased a common humanity shared across the races, and revealed the innate beauty of a person.

Meanwhile, on a personal front, Douglass repeatedly represented himself in photos as a self-promotional tool, offering copies of his likeness to audiences in return for their subscribing to his newspaper, or for attending his lectures. To historians, they're a wonderful collection of images charting his changing face: in the 1840s, his smooth-shaved skin and long, tight curls gave him an imperious beauty, and over the years he grew his facial hair into a neat underbeard hovering around the jawline, then a goatee covering chin to lip, then a full beard. Douglass basically tried all the looks a guy experiments with when shaving (apart from the luxuriant Tom Selleck 'tache). All the while, his long, coiled hair transformed into a glorious silvery mane, making him look every inch the nineteenth-century 'lion'.* But these images weren't vanity portraits, they were a currency of intimacy between a communicator and his public, and his changing face was a sign of an ongoing relationship with his fans.

Photography had a profound effect on celebrity culture. It was a democratisation of the visual arts, but it also produced image specificity; anyone could now know what famous people looked like. Indeed, the celebrity American novelist Harriet Beecher Stowe, while touring the UK, was amazed to be stopped by those who recognised her from *cartes de visite*.[44] Such a thing was a novelty of mind-blowing power 170 years ago, even though celebrity culture was already 150 years old by that point.

Technology caused rapid acceleration in the visual aspect of fame, and Victorians collected these *cartes de visite* with loving meticulousness, with some 300–400 million sold per year in the UK between 1861 and 1867.[45] But they weren't just passively acquired; they also allowed the public to actively create meaning and reshape identities while curating their own collections: people could imagine being friends with the celebrities, or create imaginary relationships between two different celebrities, or interrogate their celebrity bodies, or gossip about famous people's private and professional lives, or cultivate sensations of an imagined national community shared with others just like them.[46]

Celebrity photography helped develop new iterations of fandom, and made Britons feel like Britons, and Americans feel like Americans. It reinforced the notion of Benedict Anderson's 'imagined communities'.† And it wasn't just Joe Public doing it; Queen

---

* If you recall from the earlier chapter, 'lions' were celebrity intellectuals in the nineteenth century.

† See Chapter 2.

Victoria owned thirty-six albums, and even demanded the reluctant Florence Nightingale pose, presumably so she could complete her collection.* What celebs *really* looked like became a growth industry which caused other knock-on effects. There was a surge in photographic studios opening up in Europe and North America, and they soon provided opportunities for ordinary people to pose for photos. *Cartes de visite* thus led the way for the public to not just consume celebrity imagery, but to emulate it; just as Instagram influencers define the 'duck-face' pout of a million teenage selfies, aspirational Victorians adopted famous celebrity poses as they played up to an idealised version of themselves as successful, reputable persons of note.

Cartes were also the subject of endless conversation; they helped foster friendships and family relationships, with the sharing and swapping of albums being a way of bonding through mutual interest in intimate strangers. Women were particularly keen collectors, which made them easy targets for gentle mockery in *Vanity Fair* magazine: 'give a woman a photographic album and she will know no peace, nor give her friends any, until every page is filled with a carte de visite'.[47] These women, it went on to joke, should have signs dangled around their necks saying 'Lady Beggar' because they spent all their time desperately trying to acquire famous faces from anyone they encountered. Cartomania wasn't a private hobby, it bled into people's social lives and assisted in the development of friendships. The scholar Annie Rudd has suggested it was an early form of social media, quoting Oliver Wendell Holmes Sr's observation that *cartes* circulated through American society like physical currency, aping cash's role as a symbol of a universal system.[48] Collecting photos brought nations, strangers, and friends together. Celebrity was a social glue.

---

* As royal abuses of power go, asking for a celebrity's pic wasn't exactly Emperor Nero renaming April after himself, so I think we can forgive her.

I fought the law, and the law won

Oscar Wilde wasn't yet an illustrious writer when he arrived in America in 1882; he only had two works of poetry and one play to his name. But, in London, this twenty-seven-year-old wit had already earned a reputation as a dandy aesthete with a penchant for scathing putdowns, and his carefully crafted taste in fashion - velvet jacket, silk stockings, fancy shoes - was maximised by his long dark hair, parted in the centre, that framed his eerily magnetic face with its generous chin and plump lips. He looked magnificent and also kind of alien; a big, broad-chested androgynous beauty.

So why America? Wilde had been lured across the Atlantic for a gruelling but lucrative ten-month tour, during which he'd lecture on his passion for the Aesthetic Movement, but he would also embark on a bizarre task to publicise a Gilbert and Sullivan comic opera, *Patience*, that satirised the Aesthetic Movement through an effete, poetical character called Bunthorne. It was a really strange gig - he was to be the official, international cheerleader for a comedy that made him look like a total arse.* But the money was great, and Wilde was canny enough to see it might boost his fame rather than tarnish it.[49] As he sat in the New York theatre, the audience looked at him, and then at the mincing fool on the stage, and then back at him. And they were captivated. Who was this guy?

Wilde toured the country, and regional journalists flocked to interview him, inevitably making mention of his physical androgyny and extraordinary, quasi-medieval clothing.[50] Soon his image began popping up all over the American press. He was frequently depicted as a human sunflower, his face surrounded by pretty petals, or more simply shown clutching a lily, because plants symbolised natural beauty in his aesthetic credo. He'd arrived as a patsy

---

* The character was initially based on other famous aesthetes, like Algernon Charles Swinburne and Dante Gabriel Rossetti, but Wilde seemed to fit the bill too.

in a PR stunt, but quickly developed a powerful, and lucrative, iconography of his own.

The most significant development, however, came while in New
York, where he visited the studio of the photographer Napoleon
Sarony, who specialised in celebrity profiles. The resulting images
are now iconic; they range in compositions, with one showing
him standing tall in his quilted smoking jacket, looking away in
thought while leaning against an elaborately decorative wall. But
the most powerful ones see him seated and leaning towards us, his
cheek resting on his hand, a book perched on his knee, while his
big brown eyes gaze down the lens with dreamy insouciance. He's
captivatingly beautiful.

And yet, when Sarony later demanded ownership over the photographs - following copyright infringements by pirates - he took
his case to the US Supreme Court, where the judges not only found
in Sarony's favour, but declared that even Wilde's poses were the
creative property of the photographer, not the model. In contrast
to William Hazlitt, who'd said posing for a portrait was both a creative performance and a two-way dialogue, this ruling judged Oscar
Wilde to be merely a human prop.[51] Wilde had literally lost control
of his image. He was someone else's artwork.

In early 1907, a beautiful young musical actress called Gertie
Millar swished into a British courtroom, wearing her finest dress,
and awaited the beginning of a libel trial. She was joined by her favourite photographer, Mr Foulsham, and her theatrical employer,
Mr Edwardes, both of whom hoped for her triumph. She wasn't in
trouble; this was no celebrity crime scandal, though plenty of eager
journalists packed the courtroom, sensing a juicy story. Instead,
this was a libel case brought by Millar against a Mr Dunn, who'd
produced postcards featuring Gertie's head superimposed onto
someone else's body. He'd mass-produced three postcard designs
which, she claimed, damaged her reputation because fans had assumed she'd posed for them. Indeed, someone had sent her one
and asked her to autograph it. Two of the images were a little bit
risqué, though these days you'd see more flesh on a kids' TV show,

and the third image was just a bit weird - it showed her crawling out of a giant eggshell. You know, as you do . . .

The trial proved a crushing disappointment to Millar, her associates, and other theatrical celebrities. A key line of provocative questioning addressed her stage clothing; Dunn's lawyer argued that, as a Gaiety Girl - a troupe of musical actresses famed for their sex appeal - she was often swanning around, in full view of the public, in revealing attire. Had she ever done a scene in a nightgown? Had her fellow cast members? Two centuries had passed since the dawn of celebrity, but actresses were still perceived as promiscuous harlots.

Millar asserted there was nothing inappropriate about her costumes, and that - even if a costume were a little revealing - there was still a big difference between a fleeting performance seen on stage and a permanent photographic image that could be owned for ever. The judge sympathised but saw no reason to proceed. Sticking Gertie's smiling face on someone else's underdressed body was naughty, sure. But criminal libel? Nah. Actresses were pretty things there to be looked at. Their beauty was public property.

Of course, two things were at stake here for Millar. Actresses were already rumoured to be salacious seductresses, on the hunt for rich husbands, so she was trying to minimise any innuendo that might scupper her chances of landing a distinguished beau (she later ended up as the Countess of Dudley, so no harm done!). But, as ever, there was also the question of money. Millar got paid every time she sat for her photographer, or she could also negotiate a flat fee as an annual retainer, while he got paid each time he sold a postcard design. Their rival, Mr Dunn, was undercutting them both, using her image without paying for it, and selling knock-off postcards to her fans at half the usual price, thereby devaluing the market. This wasn't just a case of her image being appropriated and sexualised against her will; this celebrity was being exploited for profit.[52] After the trial, several other British actresses banded together to push for better copyright protection, but without success.

A slightly different case had been more successfully fought earlier, in 1904, when the stage belle Marie Studholme discovered a dentist called Edward Foley had been using a photo of her grinning cheerfully to advertise his dental practice. The problem, however, was he'd blacked out her two front teeth in the 'before' photo, and then used the original image as the 'after' to promote his dental skills. Studholme's lawyers refused Foley's formal apology and offer of modest compensation; he'd printed up half a million of the offending booklets that suggested Marie Studholme's teeth were fakes. In the end, Foley had to pay a sizeable £50 fine, plus legal costs, pulp all his advertorial booklets, and apologise in a newspaper of Studholme's choice.[53]

Millar and Studholme wouldn't be the last to want awkward photos to disappear. In 1926, a gorgeous, long-legged young dancer called Louise Brooks became the hot new thing in Hollywood. Noted for her raven-black bobbed haircut, which curved sharply into her cheekbones, she was the visual epitome of the liberated 'flapper', and she behaved like it too, enjoying a rampant seventy-two-hour orgy with Charlie Chaplin and another couple that culminated with Chaplin coating his engorged penis in bright red iodine (a supposed cure for venereal disease) and gleefully chasing the screaming girls around the room. Brooks, it seems, was no repressed Wichita girl, and had an adventurous sex life that included bedding Greta Garbo. But such things needed to stay secret if she was to be a big hit in Bible-reading Middle America.

As soon as her film career took off, Brooks set about trying to hide her embarrassing past, ostensibly so she wouldn't frighten off reputable suitors. A few months before Hollywood's big shots came calling, she'd been a glamorous Broadway dancer in Ziegfeld's Follies, and had posed nude for photographers. And I don't mean artfully posing with fabric draped over the naughty bits; we're talking the full monty. As film stardom came knocking, she launched a legal injunction to suppress the evidence. Her reasoning in court was straightforward: 'What do you suppose my husband would say if every time he picks up a newspaper or walks up Broadway he is confronted with a photograph of his wife clad in only a lacy shawl?'

The story was soon picked up across American news outlets, my favourite headline being the wonderfully passive-aggressive slam: 'To Keep a Husband She Hasn't Got, Wichita Girl Sues to Suppress "Artistic Photographs"'. Oh, miaow! But she made other arguments too. Brooks was keen to stress she wasn't ashamed of her former life, and nor was she a hypocrite, but she worried that audiences would be shocked by the gap between the nice young ladies she hoped to play on screen and her previous job, where morality standards differed. The photographer on the receiving end of Brooks's injunction was outraged, and leapt to the defence of the nudity tradition in classical art. He also threatened to reveal which other apparently classy ladies had done similar shoots. But, in the end, he relented. The photos stayed hidden for decades. Louise Brooks landed her husband, albeit only briefly, and went on to be one of the most interesting actresses of the silent-movie era.[54]

Camera-shy

Some celebrities stay famous long after their death, and some burn bright only to be forgotten once tastes change. One of the most successful novelists of the late nineteenth century, whose career flourished from 1886 until her death in 1924, was Marie Corelli - but you've probably never heard of her. Corelli (not her real name) was a big deal for nearly four decades, but her style was deeply melodramatic and her passion for esoteric theology and spiritualism made her quickly fall out of fashion after her death. Amusingly, she was also partly responsible for the bullshit curse of King Tutankhamun, whose tomb was discovered shortly before she died. So she was also a part-time *Scooby-Doo* villain, I suppose.

Success aside, what's particularly interesting about Corelli was her fear of being photographed. Though she wrote thirty books, her life in the spotlight was spent in the shadows. She stubbornly refused to pose, claiming she hated the growing culture of self-promotional puffery rife within publishing. It's true that, long before ghostwritten memoirs were pumped out by C-listers, celebrity had already come to dominate the late-Victorian literary marketplace, with Marysa Demoor arguing Victorian agents and publishers promoted the authors, not the books, as the commercial product.[55] However, Corelli was fibbing when she claimed to be above all that; her books were branded with an ostentatiously monogrammed 'MC' in shimmering gold that hardly screamed modesty. She had a carefully contrived image; she just didn't want it to resemble her face.

One of America's most famous writers of the nineteenth century, Fanny Fern, was also defiant in hiding her appearance. Although she was the highest-paid newspaper columnist in the USA, and a bestselling author with 500,000 sales to her name, Fern (real name Sarah Willis Parton) made physical anonymity an advantageous strategy. She relied upon her writing to communicate what she wanted known, while being able to shrink from the publicity if she wished. Indeed, during a trip to the opera one night, she had a whale of a time watching a couple seated in front of her point off in the distance to a graceful, wealthy beauty dressed in luxurious gown and glittering jewels: 'Well, that is Fanny Fern!' one of them said before proudly noting that he knew her 'intimately', and that it was obvious how all the book royalties had gone straight into furnishing her wardrobe and jewellery stand. The real Fanny, meanwhile, was stifling her giggles in the row behind, trying to stop her outraged friend, sitting next to her, from tapping them on the shoulder and kicking off.[56]

Fanny Fern's anonymity was a power stance. It gave her control. Was Marie Corelli doing the same? Perhaps. But, when she finally did release a promotional photo in 1906, we see a more obvious reason for her reticence. The official portrait was heavily doctored; she'd been made to look younger and slimmer, two decades of wrinkles having vanished along with much of her waistline. Corelli's real body had been that of an average middle-aged woman, but it didn't tally with the identity she wanted to convey.

Her harshest critics snidely mocked her for creating young, angelic heroines who seemed to be thinly veiled ciphers for how she saw herself. It was a claim she vehemently denied, but it was a defence which proved tricky to maintain when even her most ardent fans spotted their beloved author bursting out of every heroine like a xenomorph erupting from John Hurt's belly in *Alien*.

The cruellest voice belonged to Mark Twain, who described their meeting with horrified disgust: 'She is about fifty years old but has no gray hairs; she is fat and shapeless; she has a gross animal face; she dresses for sixteen, and awkwardly and unsuccessfully and pathetically imitates the innocent graces and witcheries of that dearest and sweetest of all ages; and so her exterior matches her interior and harmonizes with it, with the result - as I think - that she is the most offensive sham, inside and out, that misrepresents and satirizes the human race today.'[57] Blimey, Mark, but what do you *really* think?!

Modern scholars have been kinder.[58] Corelli was perhaps trying to cling to her fading youth - the equivalent of the parent going raving with their adult kids, hoping to stave off warnings of mortality through the power of neon glowsticks. Or perhaps it was a carefully considered career choice, one acknowledging that her brand was based on romanticised ideas of noble femininity, and male critics would attack her gendered, ageing body as a way to maul her writing? Ultimately, the photo was released because her fans were desperate to know what she looked like, and it helped the book sales. But perhaps they craved the airbrushed myth just as much as she did? We'll never know, because they never saw the real woman.[59]

Marie Corelli did her best to avoid being seen, and cheated when it came to the crunch. But at least she exerted control over the finished product. Other celebrities had to confront what others saw in them, and it sometimes horrified them. Surely the most dramatic reaction came from the celebrity philosopher and novelist Jean-Jacques Rousseau, whose extraordinary fame lit up Western Europe in the mid-to-late eighteenth century. Rousseau was incredibly famous, being both a brilliant public intellectual and the author of the literary super-smash *Julie, or, The New Heloise*, a novel which pretty much invented Romanticism and made readers weep hysterically. To thousands of strangers, Rousseau was 'ami Jacques' – our friend, Jacques – but, in response to all this public adulation, Rousseau gradually descended into paranoid madness.[60]

When his fame grew, Rousseau found himself almost worshipped as a moral leader. But with every obsessive letter, diary entry, article, poem, engraving, painting, and report dedicated to his genius, his inner identity grew ever more distant from the outside image being depicted by artists and fans. A bizarre public spat with the Scottish philosopher David Hume quickly morphed into his own conspiracy theory of paranoid vanity. Rather than welcoming admiring portraits, he was sure that people were mocking him with their terrible paintings that clearly misrepresented him on purpose! Rousseau wasn't just angry that the paintings of him were crap, he was angry that people of good taste thought they were good. Succumbing to a strange egotistical delusion, he assumed this was some sort of devious conspiracy to destroy him.

As Antoine Lilti writes: 'In 1770 he had a visit from M. and Mme Bret. He learned that Mme Bret owned an engraving of him in his Armenian outfit. "Get out of here," Rousseau said furiously. "I never want to see a woman who can look at this portrait and like it, who can keep this monument to my shame, a portrait made to dishonour me, to vilify me; I would rather die than have dinner with her." A few months later, his friend Mme de La Tour wrote to him that she had hung his engraved portrait done by Ramsay above her writing table, "just like a place of devotion above a shrine, an image of the saint to whom she was most fervently devoted." Furious, he did not answer her for a year.'[61]

Jean-Jacques Rousseau struggled desperately with his celebrity, but it was how others constructed his physical image that sent him spiralling into a suffocating mental gloom. Whereas Garrick, Fisher, Siddons, and Douglass hired the best artists to work under their control, and Marie Corelli embraced early photoshopping,

Rousseau found no way to reconcile himself to the idea of people hanging his image on their walls. His response was to reassert control of his brand not by hiring an artist, but by writing his own confessional autobiography, which he introduced with the seemingly boastful statement: 'I have resolved on an enterprise which has no precedent and which, once complete, will have no imitator. My purpose is to display to my kind a portrait in every way true to nature, and the man I shall portray will be myself.' But his claim to innovation wasn't just arrogance; it would have no precedent and imitator because nobody else could do him justice. Being a writer, he'd have to do so with words, not pictures. There was no sense of him sharing in William Hazlitt's idea of subject and artist in two-way collaboration, of that almost eroticised dialogue between lovers. Only Rousseau could capture the essence of Rousseau.

Jean-Jacques Rousseau's extreme reaction wasn't typical, but it serves as a useful reminder that celebrities are often simultaneously victims of outside observation, and micromanaging architects of their own brand. Being visible to the public was vital to maintaining a celebrity career, and yet it often left stars feeling vulnerable and anxious, occasionally forcing them to hire lawyers to fight their corners or to cheat with technology to ensure the disappointing truth wasn't revealed. But if visual representation wasn't always under their control, then there'd have to be other things they could manipulate instead. And that brings us neatly on to the dark arts of the publicity stunt.

Chapter 5: The Art of Self-Promotion

Cheaters never prosper?

In 1703, London was visited by an extraordinary foreigner. His name was George Psalmanazar, and he hailed from the faraway island of Formosa (Taiwan). He was pale-skinned, blond and blue-eyed, and didn't look particularly Asian, but this was before scientific ideas of race had been fully developed in Europe, so perhaps that mattered less. Regardless, some brows were immediately wrinkled in suspicion. I mean, of course they were . . . However, Psalmanazar was a charmer. He floated through polite society, performing the role of exotic marvel with the gift of the gab. His accomplice in this acceptance was an English vicar named Alexander Innes, who made the necessary introductions and told Psalmanazar's story, which was pure potboiler; he claimed to have been kidnapped by a Jesuit, who'd forced him to convert to Catholicism; then he'd been exchanged across Europe. Finally, he'd ended up in London, and was eager to share his culture with its most learned citizens.

And here's what he had to say for himself: Formosans were pagans, and cannibals who ate children and executed criminals. They ate raw meat. But they also grilled human hearts on a little barbecue. They lived underground, and their chimneys were curved inwards, to keep the sun away from their pale skin. The island was under Japanese control, but the Chinese called it Pak-Ando, while natives preferred Gad-Avia. Oh, and Taiwan was a different island entirely. Their alphabet had twenty characters, written from right to left on the page, and their spoken language was a mishmash of many dialects. They had their own numerals, religion, clothing, foods, architecture, and customs. There were only ten months in the year: Dig, Damen, Analmen, Anioul, Dattibes, Dabes, Anaber, Nechem, Koriam, Turbam. In short, *everything* was different. But Psalmanazar was more than happy to teach missionaries and scholars the secrets to fitting in, should they fancy a visit. He was nothing if not generous with his time.

Fascinated, though sometimes suspicious, London's cultural bigwigs reacted with excitement to this strange man whose stories made no sense, yet were told with fluent conviction. Psalmanazar was quizzed by the leading scientists of the day, who tried to catch him out, but he always had an answer for everything. Within a few months, he'd published a lengthy book detailing what life was like on the island.* It was an instant bestseller.

So, was Psalmanazar a celebrity? I wrestled with whether to call him the earliest celebrity in this book, but he wasn't as well known to the wider public as Henry Sacheverell. So I think he merely had *fame*. But I include him here because he was a fascinating exponent of the art of self-promotion. Absolutely everything he said was utter tosh, and Alexander Innes was in on it too, but, for a while, he was spinning so many plates that he made himself the talk of the town. He cheated his way to fame, despite having been born in France.[1]

In the eighteenth century, celebrity went hand in hand with dodgy notoriety. It was an era dogged by rumours of hoaxes, scams, shams, lies, gimmicks, and PR stunts. As Jack Lynch notes: 'In the decade 1700-09, books ... featuring the words "Authentic, Real, Genuine" in their titles numbered just 38. By the decade of the 1740s, it was 316. By the decade of 1790-99 it had reached 840. Part of the growth is simply that more books were being published, but it remains undeniable that something more specific was happening

---

* It had a ludicrously lengthy title: *An Historical and Geographical Description of Formosa, An Island subject to the Emperor of Japan. Giving an Account of The Religion, Customs, Manners, &c. of the Inhabitants. Together with a Relation of what happen'd to the Author in his Travels; particularly his Conferences with the Jesuits, and others, in several parts of Europe, By George Psalmanazar, a Native of the said Island, now in London.*

- writers were increasingly trying to reassure their readers of the accuracy and trustworthiness of their material. This, we might assume, was in response to a rise in frauds and fakery.'[2]

There are several stories we might poke with our inquisitor's stick, beginning with the bizarre claims of Mary Toft, the English-woman from Surrey who in 1726 tricked doctors into believing she'd given birth to rabbits. Though the hoax was eventually un-masked, the king's own credulous doctor was embarrassed by the scandal and the wider medical profession also emerged with egg on its face.[3] There were also literary fraudsters who caused im-mense confusion because their hoaxes were so well executed. The first was Thomas Chatterton, a precocious teenager who forged medieval poetry, which he attributed to a monk named Thomas Rowley. Chatterton's sophistication positioned him as a candidate for greatness until poverty and despair saw him drink fatal poison aged just seventeen.

Then we have the much-debated James Macpherson, Scotland's first celebrity poet, who claimed in 1760 to have compiled and translated an ancient Gaelic text by the poet Ossian, recounting epic stories of the hero Fingal. The Ossian texts were phenom-enally successful - Napoleon was a fan, and Thomas Jefferson declared Ossian the 'greatest poet that has ever existed' - but was Macpherson just making it up? Dr Samuel Johnson, England's most forthright literary critic at the time, declared him 'a mountebank, a liar, and a fraud'. Others were adamant he was legit. The debate still rumbles on to this day.

William Fakespeare

My favourite literary fraudster was William-Henry Ireland, an unassuming legal clerk desperate to win the affection of his cold-hearted, antiques-collecting dad. Mr Samuel Ireland was a Shakespeare obsessive who bemoaned the lack of documentation detailing the life of the great Bard and wished to own just one document in Shakespeare's hand. William-Henry, whose job it was to riffle through old legal papers, realised he could probably forge one himself. So, in 1794, he did exactly that. His dad was understandably delighted to have it thrust before him, not least when an expert declared it to be authentic. Suddenly father and son had something to talk about! Of course, as is the plot of every great comedy, one lie led to many. Samuel now demanded more Shakespearean ephemera, so his son forged another. And another. And before long he'd 'uncovered' an entire treasure chest full of them, his cover story being that they belonged to an elderly benefactor who wished to remain anonymous.

Thrilled that his ruse was working, and proud that his father thought his efforts worthy of Shakespeare, William-Henry maintained the farce. All the while, his father's house became a hotbed of hubbub, with all sorts of famous faces popping in to take a look at the precious documents. Some scholars smelled a rat. One of the big giveaways was William-Henry's ridiculous attempts at Elizabethan spelling which involved the gratuitous use of more 'E' than a 90s rave. Amusingly, one newspaper mocked the claims by 'discovering' its own dinner invitation supposedly written by Shakespeare: 'Deeree Sirree, Wille youe doee meee theee favvourree too dinnee wythee meee onn Friddaye nextte, attt twoo off theee clockee, too eattee sommee muttonne choppes andd somme poottaattoooeesse.'[4] In case the joke wasn't clear, the letter was addressed to another famous playwright of the 1590s, who was presumably living in an echoey cave: 'Missteerree BEENJAAMMIINNEE JOONNSSOONN'.

Okay, so William-Henry Ireland wasn't going to win any spelling bees, but plenty of people were convinced. His use of old parchment and ink was rather good, and some people were desperate to believe the lie because Shakespeare was England's national poet. Hoping to understand him better, their confirmation bias eclipsed all the ludicrous evidence to the contrary. Invigorated with confidence, William-Henry now went for the big one - he wrote his own play; a Fakespeare, if you will, called *Vortigern and Rowena*. Though it was clumsily amateurish in its lyricism, Richard

Brinsley Sheridan agreed to produce it at the Drury Lane theatre, not least because he needed to pull in punters to pay for a recent refit.

Two days before the first curtain call, the greatest Shakespeare scholar in the land, Edmond Malone, published a book rubbishing Ireland's claims in forensic detail. It didn't matter. Hundreds of people scrambled to get into the already-full theatre. The play went ahead and started fine, because Ireland had basically raided other Shakespeare plays for themes, but gradually the audience collapsed into giggles and boos once the weight of his clumsy writing crashed through the plot like a chimney stack through a rotten roof. When the curtain came down, a fight broke out among the pro-Malone sceptics and the romantic believers still clinging to the hope this was Shakespeare writing on a very bad day. The critical reviews were less equivocal. In fact, they were devastating.

Savaged in the press, William-Henry found himself surprisingly relieved to have failed. He'd exhausted himself as a one-man forgery factory, churning out lies to win his father's affection, but realised he needed to fess up. The authenticity debate raged on for months, while he plucked up the courage to tell his dad, but in the end he couldn't do it face to face, so published a full confession instead.[5] Incredibly, not everyone believed him. Some thought he was just too stupid to have pulled it off; others remained convinced it was Shakespeare's quill that had scribbled every inky scratch.

Amazingly, his own dad was in the latter camp. Samuel Ireland went to his grave adamant that his son was an idiot, and that Shakespeare had written *Vortigern and Rowena*. William-Henry Ireland had generated enormous celebrity from behind a curtain, but not for himself; it had landed on his dad and on a dead Elizabethan poet. It was only with his confession that he now acquired his own weird notoriety: he was either a forger, a grasping charlatan pretending to be a forger, or a legal clerk who'd found some amazing national treasures in a dusty old chest.[6] None of these were respectable options. A writing career followed but he never hit the same heights. How could he? They were Shakespeare's heights, and nobody could compete with the National Bard.

A sucker born every minute

The grand emperor of self-promotional hoaxes would come along later to bestride the nineteenth century like a colossus. P. T. Barnum enjoyed titling himself as the 'Prince of Humbugs'; his entire career was built on a flair for sensational fibs that delighted while they deceived. He was a salesman of impossible drama who romanticised cynicism by arguing that people loved to be hoaxed. Famously, it's claimed he declared 'there's a sucker born every minute', and Hollywood recently made him a plucky underdog in *The Greatest Showman*. But his career was built on dodgy ground, and his first success was undoubtedly his most offensive. In 1835, he paid $1,000 to take ownership of an elderly, enslaved black woman named Joice Heth who, he claimed, was 161 years old and had been George Washington's childhood nurse.

Heth was a brilliant storyteller who convinced with tales of the cute kid who'd grow up to become a national superhero, and she sang beautiful hymns from the distant colonial past. She certainly sounded ancient, and she looked it too. The big question is whether Barnum coached her into mastering her gimmick, or if he merely purchased the finished article - at different times, he claimed both were true, meaning he makes for an infuriatingly unreliable witness. But he was an efficient promoter and squeezed what he could from Heth, regardless of whose idea it was. When the excitement dimmed, and crowds started to wane, he dragged the public back in by posing the possibility that she wasn't even human! Maybe she was an automaton, built from gears and cogs? The only way to know would be to pay to see her again. True enough, the entranced public returned for a closer examination.

But he wasn't done there. Barnum legally owned her body in life and death; the exploitation continued even when she breathed her last. He now charged his audience a third time for the chance to watch a sensationalist autopsy. The doctor performing the procedure instantly scuppered Barnum's titanic myth, noting that Heth wasn't 161 at all. In fact, she was barely in her eighties! It had all been a huge hoax, and yet Barnum was delighted to have been rumbled. The unmasking was part of the magic because the public enjoyed being fooled, and he'd already thrice fleeced them of their cash.

As if to rub salt into the wounds, and prove that he could keep spinning the lie, Barnum's assistant, Levi Lyman, then duped the editor of the *New York Herald*, James Gordon Bennett, into believing that Heth was perfectly healthy and living in Connecticut, and that another old lady had been autopsied instead. When the *Herald* ran this story, it caused huge embarrassment to the newspaper, and Barnum became a personal nemesis to the vengeful Gordon Bennett. Why Barnum did this is unclear; he said it was all Lyman's doing, but he was as trustworthy as a toddler with an open tin of red paint. The *Herald* had debunked the famous 'Moon Hoax of 1835', which had said civilised life had been spotted on the moon, so maybe Barnum wanted to prove the debunkers to be just as gullible as the *New York Sun*, which had run the original story? Perhaps he just loved to troll people?

The Heth hoax was Barnum's passageway to notorious celebrity, but he kept a variety of frauds up his capacious sleeves, before shifting towards respectability. His most notable deceit was in 1842, when a British explorer called Dr Griffin, from the British Lyceum of Natural History, arrived in New York with a remarkable specimen. The newspapers were beside themselves in excitement – it was a mermaid, caught off the Feejee islands! Barnum tried to convince Griffin to loan him the mermaid to be exhibited in his American Museum. Griffin resisted. Frustrated, Barnum visited the offices of major newspapers, sighing that he'd been unable to do a deal, so they may as well have his woodcut illustration of three beautiful, long-haired, topless mermaids which he'd commissioned. It was a shame for the artwork to go to waste. Delighted, and assuming they were all getting an exclusive, the editors agreed.

In July, the newspapers went to press with the alluring image. The public was understandably astounded at the news of sea-dwelling humans, and demanded to see Dr Griffin's mermaid. Under pressure, Griffin agreed to a short exhibition at Concert Hall, provided he could lecture on how he came across the creature. Ticket sales went through the roof. There was a huge appetite, so Barnum now convinced Griffin to extend the run and move it to his own American Museum. But when the public finally got up close to the mermaid, they didn't see a gorgeous, long-haired Ariel, they saw a terrifying fish-monkey chimera; the thing was a monstrous hoax, a stitching together of two unrelated species. And who'd paid for it? Barnum, of course!

As it turned out, Dr Griffin - and the ongoing negotiations that Barnum had been having with the reluctant Brit - were all a total fantasy. The British Lyceum of Natural History didn't exist, and Griffin was actually trusty old Levi Lyman again. The whole 'giving the topless mermaid image to the newspapers' thing had been an ingenious campaign of asymmetrical marketing. Barnum had created a frenzied demand by role-playing as the victim of his own dazzling ploy. The public and the press had been fooled at every stage.[7] Barnum had pulled a Keyser Söze.

Two tons of fun

Cynical hoaxers often put time and effort into their craft, to the point where their celebrity was almost deserved. Indeed, George Psalmanazar ended up befriending Dr Samuel Johnson and having a respectable writing career, despite all the lies. But, for the rest of this chapter, I want to focus on celebrities for whom self-promotion was a tactic for supporting an authentic career. And perhaps the most unusual celebrity in the entire book wasn't even human.

A young female named Clara arrived in Europe in 1741, having been transported from faraway India by the Dutch mariner Captain Douwe Mout Van Der Meer, and the sophistication of her manager's marketing strategy turned her into a bona fide celeb. She toured for seventeen years, like some all-conquering rockstar, and became the unlikeliest of fashion trendsetters when women began accessorising their dresses and wigs to look like her. But, unlike a musician, she possessed no talent - her gimmick was simply being a jaw-droppingly massive specimen of extraordinary rarity. You see, Clara was a celebrity rhino.

She was only the ninth rhino ever to have appeared in Europe, and arrived in Rotterdam just as the only other living specimen had died, making her the sole inheritor of an entire continent's attention span. She was 5,000lb in weight, 12ft in length, had to be transported in a reinforced wagon pulled by a team of oxen, and ate a ridiculous amount of food. Her rider wasn't whisky and blue M&M's, but a daily provision of: 'sixty pounds of hay and twenty pounds of bread, and . . . fourteen buckets of water'. She also had a penchant for beer and tobacco, a taste she'd acquired on her six-month journey to Rotterdam. So definitely a rockstar, then.

Unlike previous rhino imports, Clara had arrived as a calf, meaning she promised the thrilling possibility of continued growth. This was a promotional godsend for Van Der Meer who weighed her semi-regularly, enthralling crowds with before-and-after measurements to prove her maturation. Unlike most stars, she wasn't on a crash diet, but rather a crush diet. Van Der Meer estimated rhinos lived to 100, so hoped for many years of adolescent growth before Clara broke the scales at her adult peak. Beside her gargantuan bulk, her rarity was also thrilling. Rhinos had been considered almost mythical, or were confused with unicorns and biblical creatures, and they were said by ancient writers to be natural enemies of elephants. The females were also thought to be sexually rampant, while their horn was believed to be an aphrodisiac. Meanwhile, the most famous illustration of the species, the 1515 woodcut by Albrecht Dürer (who'd never seen a rhino in person), had literally shown them plated in armour.[8]

Van Der Meer's promotional materials played along with expectations, describing his celebrity client both as a biblical beast - the famed Behemoth mentioned in the Book of Job - and as a hybridised natural wonder formed of body parts similar to other, better-known fauna:

> This wonderful animal is dark-brown, like the elephant it has no hair, except for some hairs at the end of the tail; it has a horn on its nose, with which it can plough the ground much faster than a farmer with a plough; it can walk fast, and swim and dive in the water like a duck; its head is pointed at the front; the ears are like the ears of a donkey, and the eyes are very small compared to the size of the animal, only allowing it to look sideways; the skin looks like as if it is covered with shells, overlapping each other, about two inches thick; the feet are short and thick, just like an elephant, but with three hoofs . . . this animal secrets some potion, which has cured many people from sickness.

Clara the Rhino made no sense, except as the sum of other parts. But that made her unique. And Van Der Meer was a remarkably prescient marketer who understood the power of sending out promotional images in advance, hoping to stir up a city's excitement before they arrived. In this regard, Clara's media strategy pre-empted Hollywood's obsession with blockbuster trailers by 250 years. Van Der Meer also monetised the public's desire to remember the encounter, making posters, paintings, souvenirs, fancy porcelain dinner sets, and medals available to buy. And, when the heavy-duty wagon rolled in through the gates of a new city, Van Der Meer injected spectacle wherever possible, such as arranging for a guard of eight swordsmen to escort Clara into Vienna.[9] She was a big deal. Quite literally.

Romance is dead

Here's a question, then: 'Is self-promotion essential to being famous?' Personally, I'd say no. Some of those in Chapter 2 had fame thrust upon them without doing anything to help it along.

But this was a question already being posed in the late 1700s. In Chapter 3, we noted that classical *fame* had been understood as a lasting glory awarded after death by a jury of worthy critics whose cultivated noses could sniff out unheralded genius.[10] If so, that's a rather snobbish idea; it assumes the public is too stupid to detect the brilliance in front of them because they're distracted by the shiny, superficial, self-promoting activities of celebrities.[11] However, that's pretty much how the Romantic poets thought of it, in the early 1800s.[12]

We see this snobbery in William Hazlitt's proclamation that 'fame is not popularity, the shout of the multitude, the idle buzz of fashion, the venal puff, the soothing flattery of favour or of friendship'.[13] Ignoring for a moment that the 'venal puff' sounds like some poisonous tree frog, this was Hazlitt criticising the sort of shameless self-promotion pursued by wannabe celebs. Instead, he and his peers thought the quality of their work would speak for itself; they'd never sink so low as to self-inflate with 'puffery', embrace manipulative publicity stunts, or get their friends to write fake reviews of their new books. Here, for example, is the satirical poet Robert Montgomery:

How nobly different wrestles he for fame!
He hires no trumpet to prelude his name,
He wants no hand to drag him to the goal,
But reaches it by energy of soul;
And, though some clouds of envy may o'ershroud
His struggling light, nor let it be allow'd,
And stars of vulgar fame may pertly frown
Upon his dim approach to fair renown,
Like the broad sun, he'll brighten into day,
Blaze on the world, and blot them all away![14]

Cor! It's stirring stuff. The Romantics had already played Daniel J. Boorstin's tune some 150 years before he grumpily picked up his fiddle. But don't be seduced by those pretty words, because the Romantics weren't above all that. When Lord Byron died, his former friend Leigh Hunt – who'd been reliant on Byron's support – suddenly accused the dead superstar of having been a manipulative, vain, cruel, and self-interested puffer *par excellence*.[15] Hunt was despised by many conservative critics, who thought him an overly opinionated oik, so it didn't take long for Montgomery to leap into the wrestling ring, and slam his satirical poem *The Puffiad* down on Hunt's head:

> Yet one there was, of Treason's rebel crew,
> Coxcombic, vain, and avaricious too,
> Who froth'd his reptile poison on thy name,
> To fill his pocket, and to puff his fame!

According to Montgomery, Byron wasn't the puffer, Hunt was the puffer! He was surely an impoverished, washed-up hack looking for a big payday by dissing his brilliant friend. It was quite the dramatic beef, one made all the funnier by modern historians having discovered that Montgomery was also a wilful self-puffer. They were all as bad as each other: it was a triumvirate of hypocrisy, with the trio paying lip service to worthy fame while secretly using the promotional tactics of the lowbrow celebs they supposedly despised.

What a bunch of stunts

Subtlety is great and all that, but sometimes the best way for a celebrity to cut through the crowd was to have a gimmick that honked as loudly as a furious goose. For the Barrison Sisters, a Danish-American vaudeville troupe of five genuine sisters who found success in the 1890s, their big joke was singing 'Would you like to see my pussy?' Once the audience was suitably noisy, the saucy ladies would lift their skirts to reveal live kittens stuffed into their knickers. Real classy! Meanwhile, another great performer of the Parisian stage was Joseph Pujol, better known as Le Pétomane, whose remarkable talent was his musical anus (yes, really). Le Pétomane loosely translated to 'Fart maniac', and he could entertain huge crowds, including royalty and celebs, by sucking air into his sphincter then controlling its outward flow. He performed the French national anthem, imitated thunderstorms, and could extinguish candles from a distance of several feet. It's not just the Kardashians whose fame rests on their backsides.[16]

But these were performers whose gimmick was integral to their act. What about celebrities who used promo stunts as extraneous devices to promote their wider careers? If Barnum was the Emperor of Stunts, then the Duke and Duchess were the impresario Florenz Ziegfeld Jr and his wife/client, the singer Anna Held. We might as well start with the biggest lie of all, Held's fictionalised biography. She'd been born a Polish Jew in Warsaw, but had been forced to flee the country as a child during the violent anti-Semitic pogroms. She was then orphaned in London, during her early teens. Such trauma gave rise to later lies like this: 'I was born in Paris. Voilà! That is settled. For they have had me born everywhere else, even in Indiana . . . They have had me from Poland, but that was not I but my mother. And my birth the chroniclers had made to occur in London. But I did not see London until I was twelve years old. It was Paris, Paris, Paris.'

A childhood of such pain surprisingly resulted in a celebrity status of endless glamour and giggly innuendo. She was a saucepot with naughty songs and mesmerising fashion sense. And her promotional stunts played into that brand. The most obvious example was the kissing marathon in which she snogged fellow actor Julius Steger 156 times, until she collapsed 'back in her chair - panting, exhausted-white as the flower that had fallen from her hair - as limp as the roses that were dying in the gaslight'.[17] A journalist looked on, making notes, as did a doctor, who handily explained, using cutting-edge science, that women were more easily overcome by passionate emotions due to their fragile brains.* Florenz

---

* I'm not the one saying this. Please don't send me angry emails.

(known simply as Flo) was also there. Instead of being jealous, he was delighted by the publicity, and later admitted that any day in which their names weren't in the papers was a bad day.

The kiss-a-thon actually happened, but lots of their stories were simply lies fed to the press through backdoor means. The most famous myth was that Anna Held bathed in milk, like Queen Cleopatra. Ziegfeld sensed it was too obvious a claim to just blurt out in an interview, so he hired a freelance press agent, Max Marcin, to convince a dairy farmer to take part in the ruse. The farmer was instructed to sue Ziegfeld for unpaid bills, claiming he'd delivered large quantities of milk for use in Held's intense beauty regime. The story was thus leaked to the press as a legal dispute, giving the appearance of a private scandal that Held wanted to hush up. Ziegfeld then sheepishly admitted it was true, thereby getting his story in the press, but made the tactical mistake of saying he'd refused to pay up because the milk was stale on delivery. Obviously, this pissed off the farmer, who was suddenly being publicly accused of selling dangerously out-of-date dairy produce, so he retaliated by revealing the scam and saying he'd never even heard of Anna Held. Ziegfeld was forced to calm him down with some freebie tickets. He got away with it, and the kerfuffle did its job.

Of course, the risk of constant exaggeration is that people stop trusting you, but Ziegfeld couldn't help himself. When he tripped over and banged his knee, he told the press he'd nearly been killed by falling scenery; when Held fell off her bike, Ziegfeld issued a press release declaring she'd leapt off it to save a former judge from being killed by a team of runaway horses. Another popular story claimed Held had visited a waxwork museum and was so silently entranced by their realism that people thought she was a waxwork too. A man was said to have rushed up to kiss her, not realising she was real. Then there was the dubious tale of her posing for a huge, solid-gold, mega-expensive sculpture to be exhibited in Paris. And nor did Anna's idea of a ladies-only motorcar race between New York and Philadelphia ever take place.

Frankly, with all these burst balloons, Ziegfeld and Held – sod it, I'm calling them ZiegHeld – became something ridiculous. The press and public quickly learned to stop believing any of this stuff, but truth didn't really matter. The coverage continued because it was fun. ZiegHeld became a laughing stock, but a welcome one. Here, for example, is a poem published in a newspaper at the time:

> Where do you buy your hasheesh? What is your brand of
>   dope?
> Will you ever reach the end of your imaginative rope?
> Now tell us, Mr. Ziegfeld, when the date and hour are set
> For Miss Held to jump off Brooklyn Bridge and get no more
>   than wet?[18]

This last line was possibly a reference to Steve Brodie, a young man who'd allegedly survived jumping off the bridge in 1886 and used the stunt to become a famous saloon owner and performer.[19] Rumours circulated that he'd cheated by having a dummy chucked off, then swum out from the shoreline. In which case, his dubious association of getting 'no more than wet', when an earlier daredevil had died in the attempt, was a perfect fit in a poem about Anna Held's unbelievable stunts.

But here's the crucial thing. There's no outrage in this poem; both the writer and reader are having a rollicking good time. ZiegHeld's fantasies may well have been swallowed by some gullible readers, but it seems many people were in on the joke. We also see evidence of Held's joke-magnetism with the story of a cow in Port Chester which managed to break its neck in the crook of a tree. The timing was ideal, as it played into the milk bath meme, and a popular cartoon soon showed a cow hanging itself, leaving a note to say: 'As Anna has soured on me there is nothing left but suicide.' This gag about stale milk went viral, as did the notion that other celebrities took milk baths. None of it was true, but that didn't matter. Until suddenly, it did.[20]

In October 1906, Held, Ziegfeld and their touring company were on their luxury sleeper train bound for a gig in Cleveland when the stateroom inside their private carriage was robbed. They awoke in the morning to discover that all their money and her collection of jewels, accrued over a lifetime of performing - and worth somewhere between $120,000 and $300,000* - had been snatched. Held collapsed into hysterical screams. They went to the local mayor and to the police, but the showman also did his usual thing of notifying the media. Newsmen, however, had been lied to for years. When the king of the ridiculous stunt came knocking, they folded their arms and rolled their eyes. Ziegfeld was the showman who cried wolf.

The finger of blame was prodded in various directions. Held said the police acted too slowly, Ziegfeld blamed the train company for lapsed security, the press blamed the couple for making it up, and various witnesses tried to recall suspicious-looking men getting onto the train. Everyone was guilty, it seemed, and the public didn't know what to make of it all. Some reports whispered the police didn't believe her, other statements said her tears were genuine and Held was utterly destroyed by the theft of her life's savings. Remember, this was a woman whose childhood was one of sustained, traumatic loss; it was probably a deeply distressing scenario.

But, after a while, the insinuations began to target Held and Ziegfeld themselves, as we see in this poem printed in the *Cleveland Press*:

> Tell us, Anna, tell us truly, was it all a little fake?
> Have you, honest, wept so madly? Is your heart about to
>   break?
> Did you really split your corsage with the sobs you loudly
>   sobbed?
> Was it advertising, Anna, when you told us you were
>   robbed?
> It was clever, Anna, clever, even though it wasn't new
> Many other folks have tried it, but the mustard's all to you

---

* $300,000 would roughly equate to $8.5 million today.

In a thousand daily papers on the front page up it bobbed
Was it advertising, Anna, when you told us you were
    robbed?

Apparently, the couple managed to retrieve their jewels a few
months later, in private negotiations with the robbers, who presumably ransomed them at a steep price. As Eve Golden points
out, there are some cynical possibilities here: perhaps it had been a
publicity stunt all along? Perhaps it had been Flo attempting some
outlandish insurance fraud which he then regretted when his wife
broke down in tears? Or perhaps the jewels were genuinely snaf-
fled, but the publicity made them too hot to handle, so the victim
was the only buyer who'd take them? In any case, Anna Held and
Florenz Ziegfeld Jr reclaimed their jewels but lost the public's trust.
Eventually, their own bond of trust severed when he cheated on
her. Theirs was a big celebrity breakup in 1913.[21]

Over-egging the self-promotion can therefore be risky. Once
retired, and newly ennobled as Lady de Frece, Vesta Tilley looked
back on her career in a self-congratulatory memoir that made her
status as national treasure seem inevitable. But when she first embarked on her debut American tour in 1894, and the publicity was
put in someone else's hands, she realised too late that she'd been
overhyped:

> Mr. Pastor's press agent had been busy, and my arrival and
> my doings were given more than the usual publicity; in fact,
> I was astonished to read the many interviews in the local
> papers, as I had persistently refused to see any of the news-
> paper men . . . I was frightened by the staring announcements
> of the first appearance of 'England's Greatest Comedienne',
> and I almost broke down when I met Mr. Pastor . . . I felt that
> my audience had been induced to expect a phenomenal per-
> formance . . . previous English artistes had appeared in New
> York and had failed to realise the exaggerated anticipations
> cultivated by press announcements.[22]

Tilley's press agent had set the bar too high, and suddenly she was at risk of failure before she'd even sung a note. Luckily, she managed to win over the frosty crowds and become a much-loved star.

In the autumn of 1850, P. T. Barnum brought the Swedish singing sensation, Jenny Lind, to the USA for a mammoth, and hugely lucrative, tour. It was to be the making of him as a more respectable promoter, and it was the making of her as an international superstar, but it also was the attempted making of other wannabe celebrities. Ever the headline-hunter, Barnum had the bright idea of auctioning off tickets for opening nights in different cities, and secretly colluded with certain businessmen to artificially bump up the winning price. In New York, a hatmaker named John N. Genin won the auction with a hefty bid of $225, but it proved a bargain investment when he leveraged the resulting notoriety to advertise his 'Jenny Lind riding hat', which soon became a must-have fashion accessory. Barnum had, of course, been in on that deal. But little did he know that, when they got to Boston, someone else would spend nearly three times as much on trying to launch himself as a celebrity.

Ossian Dodge - it's a fantastic name, I'll give him that - was a local musician determined to make the most of *Lindomania*. When Barnum arrived, with his angelic import by his side, Dodge bid a whopping $625 (about two years' salary for an average labourer) to choose his own seat in the auditorium. But he wasn't an eager superfan; this was simply a cynical PR move to squeeze himself into the public consciousness. With victory confirmed, Dodge commissioned a lithographic illustration showing him meeting Barnum and Lind, despite the fact that this hadn't happened. He also took out a large advert inside the official programme, announcing that he'd won the ticket auction with a record bid because he was 'a vocalist and musical composer of much celebrity and worth'. Ossian Dodge was trying to buy his way into celebrity, by riding in the slipstream of another star, and, for a while, it sort of worked.[23]

The electricity of eccentricity

One of the nineteenth century's most famous stars was the French actress Sarah Bernhardt, famed for playing passionate, complicated women; she excelled at dangerous provocateurs - murderers, courtesans, adulteresses. These came naturally to her, for she herself was an expert provocateur with a complicated backstory. She'd been born Henriette-Rosine Bernard, the illegitimate daughter of a high-class Jewish courtesan with some very famous lovers; we're not sure who her dad was, but he was loaded enough to buy her a pricey education under the tutelage of nuns. When he died, the most influential man in her life became her mum's lover, the Duke of Morny, who took her to the theatre for the first time, watched her freak out at the emotional power of live performance, and suggested she become an actress. The second most influential man in her life was the famed novelist Alexandre Dumas, scribbler of *The Three Musketeers*, who coached her in stagecraft and helped her get auditions.[24] It was quite the support network.

Her acting career didn't immediately get off to a flyer, but she was already experimenting with image management when she changed her name from Henriette-Rosine Bernard to the overtly Jewish-sounding Sarah Bernhardt. This embracing of her mother's culture would provoke plenty of criticism in an increasingly anti-Semitic France, but she was defiant that she was both a practising Catholic and a proud Jew. Though things started bumpily, gradually she conquered the French stage, then became a transatlantic megastar. Such was her fame that Brits and Americans flocked to watch her perform in French, even if they couldn't speak it themselves - the sound of her voice and the clarity of her gestures were enough to bring the house down.

Her extraordinary reputation became almost incalculable; Sharon Marcus estimates a million Parisians witnessed her funeral procession in 1923.[25] But her rise to established glory didn't make her a cosy pillar of the establishment. Bernhardt was an unmarried single mother to her son, Maurice, and caused no end of outrage when she introduced herself as 'Mademoiselle' rather than 'Madame'. She also had shocking affairs with high-status men. But that was only half of it. Most notably, Bernhardt rejected the rigid customs of the dignified lady and instead turned herself into a patriotic eccentric: she wore a stuffed bat on her head; she covered herself in shimmering jewels; she filled her house with dangerous pets, including lions, tigers, cheetahs, leopards, monkeys, boa constrictors, and alligators (one of which died when she fed it too much champagne, and the other she shot when it ate her dog).[26]

Big cats were her real passion, and her house guests were frequently terrified by the muscular, sharp-toothed beasts prowling aimlessly around the house, which Bernhardt found hysterically funny.[27] Owning big cats was distinctive, but it wasn't totally original. Half a century beforehand, good old Edmund Kean had also sauntered around London with a pet lion on a leash (most likely an American puma), and the two would often be seen floating down the Thames in a rowing boat.[28] Similarly, Byron was famed for keeping a pet bear at university, his cheeky way of skirting the 'no dogs' rule, and in Venice he filled his house with at least thirty-seven animals, that wandered about the place to the bewilderment of guests.[29]

Such was Bernhardt's promotional genius, her nickname became Sarah Barnum, and the novelist Henry James called her 'the muse of the newspaper', in reference to the mythological daughters of Zeus who inspire human imagination. Bernhardt complained that she was constantly abused by the press, but she toyed with them like one of her pet cheetahs might playfully harass a wounded rabbit. Bernhardt also knew the power of gossip and hired press agents, such as Edward Jarrett, to spread gothic stories of her playing croquet with human skulls - not so far removed from the story of Byron drinking from a human skull - and allegedly keeping the skeleton of a man who'd killed himself when she refused to marry him. But perhaps her biggest PR stunt was issuing a photograph of herself asleep in a coffin.[30]

We're not sure when or why she first bought a coffin, but when her ailing sister came to stay in 1873, Sarah put Regine in her big, comfy bed and chose to kip in the wooden box: 'Three days after this new arrangement began, my manicurist came into the room to do my nails and my sister asked her to enter quietly because I was still sleeping. The woman turned her head, assuming that I was asleep in the armchair. Then, seeing me in my coffin, she rushed away, shrieking wildly. From that moment on, all Paris knew that I slept in my coffin.' Realising this was a publicity opportunity, Bernhardt hired a photographer, clambered into the coffin, picked up a bouquet of flowers, crossed her hands over her chest, and shut her eyes. She looked like the Bride of Dracula. The photograph was a huge bestseller.[31]

While Sarah Bernhardt was just starting out in the thespian trade, another electric eccentric rose to prominence in America. Adah Isaacs Menken was an actress and poet whose fame became so big in the 1860s that she was known simply as 'The Menken'. Her biggest success came from the melodramatic play *Mazeppa*, a burlesque adaptation of a poem by Byron (he pops up a lot, doesn't he?) that saw her do stunt work with live horses, playing a character who is punished for an affair by being stripped naked and strapped to the back of a horse which is then turned loose. It was a massive hit in America and Britain. But Menken was more than just a popular actress. She knocked boots with Alexandre Dumas, who was twice her age and probably three times her size, and also hopped into bed with Algernon Charles Swinburne and the famed tightrope walker Charles Blondin, who'd conquered Niagara Falls with such easy flair that he was able to stop midway and cook an omelette!

Before dying at just thirty-three, Menken racked up four marriages in seven years; plus, there was an unfounded rumour of a marriage to the King of Württemberg.* Her love life was hectic, to

---

* Renée M. Sentilles points out this was probably a myth born of how similar Menken's celebrity status was to that of a slightly earlier dancer, Lola Montez, who was equally self-made and had a notorious affair with King Ludwig of Bavaria.

Left David Garrick getting way too familiar with a bust of Shakespeare. Garrick boosted his own career by boosting the Bard's reputation, but it sometimes came off as a bit desperate (Thomas Gainsborough, 1766).

Above A Staffordshire stoneware effigy of Dr Henry Sacheverell, made in 1745. Sacheverell was a provocative conservative churchman who arguably became the first celebrity in 1709 after delivering a fiery speech. The strength of his fame is obvious in the fact this souvenir was made twenty years after his death.

Left Clara the Rhino, the surprise celebrity of the mid-1700s. She toured Europe for about seventeen years, and is painted here by Pietro Longhi during her 1751 appearance in Venice. She became a fashion icon and inspired fashionable women to wear their hair gathered up at the front as a horn.

Sir Joshua Reynolds's romantic portrait of the Polynesian traveller Mai (known then as Omai) painted in 1776. Mai was neither noble nor an official ambassador, but his two years in England saw him be introduced to the King and dine with notable celebrities, so Reynolds painted him with the elegant grace befitting his new reputation.

An infamous actress and writer, Mary Robinson's 1782 portrait by John Hoppner shows her as Perdita, her most iconic role, from Shakespeare's *The Winter's Tale*. Robinson was renowned for her fashion sense and affair with George, Prince of Wales, both of which made her a daily feature in newspaper gossip.

Below Sarah Siddons's iconic pose as the Tragic Muse. The ghostly pale skin was her idea, but credit for creating the pose is debatable (Sir Joshua Reynolds, 1784).

A STRIKING VIEW of RICHMOND.

Above An etching of Bill Richmond made in 1810, when he began training other fighters, most notably Tom Molineaux. Richmond had been born enslaved on Staten Island, but was freed and brought to England. He took up bareknuckle boxing aged forty-one and achieved notable acclaim for his fine technique and gentlemanly wit.

LOVE and BEAUTY -- SARTJEE the HOTTENTOT VENUS.

Right Sara Baartman, appearing in an 1822 print called 'Love and Beauty - Sartjee the Hottentot Venus'. Baartman was a Khoikhoi woman controversially exhibited as a human marvel in London and Paris due to cruel public fascination with her buttocks and genitals.

Left Edmund Kean's extraordinary rise to stardom in 1814 saved the Drury Lane Theatre from bankruptcy, so George Cruikshank drew him in his most iconic role, that of Richard III, propping the theatre up on his hunchback. The title of 'Theatrical Atlas' was a reference to the ancient Greek titan Atlas supporting the world on his shoulders.

Above A typically arresting portrait of Frederick Douglass, the American abolitionist, orator, writer, art theorist, and statesman. The image was taken *c.*1862 by John White Hurn and is one of 160 images we have of the most-photographed American of the nineteenth century.

Left A caricature of W.G. Grace, drawn in 1873 when he was still a young, handsome man of twenty-five. Already the iconic beard is in place. His 1872 tour of North America, plus a brilliant season of batting and bowling, led to him touring Australia in 1873-4, which thrust him onto the pinnacle of international sporting celebrity.

William Cody, better known as 'Buffalo Bill', photographed here by Napoleon Sarony, c.1880. Cody was hyper-aware of the need to look the part, and wore his fringed buckskin clothes almost as a uniform. When his hair fell out, he wore a wig. The wildman of the Wild West couldn't be allowed to get old.

Sarah Bernhardt, the French superstar of the stage, painted here in 1879 by Jules Bastien-Lepage. Despite being an unmarried, Jewish single mother, Bernhardt embraced controversy to become a powerful cultural icon known as 'the Divine Sarah'. Her US and UK tours were hugely profitable, even though she delivered her lines in French.

An iconic image of Oscar Wilde taken by the renowned photographer Napoleon Sarony in 1882, during Wilde's US tour. The image not only helped make Wilde's reputation as an androgenous beauty, but became the focus of a historic copyright lawsuit in the US Supreme Court.

The musical comedian Vesta Tilley, photographed by Barnes, Brown & Bell in the late 1890s. Her range of male characters was extensive, from soldiers to monocle-wearing gents, but this was her at her cheeky-chappie best. She was from a working-class family but ended up retiring as a national treasure, married to a knighted Tory MP, and living in Monaco as Lady de Frece.

Left Anna Held, the famously overdressed singer with the misbehaving eyes. Though Polish-born, she claimed she was French from birth and became a publicity-hungry Broadway star, and the wife of the infamous impresario Florenz Ziegfeld. The photo was taken by Aimé Dupont in 1900.

Right The tragic model Evelyn Nesbit, photographed between 1901-2. Spotted as a teenage girl, Nesbit became the iconic face of the decade in America, but suffered horrific sexual violence at the hands of two men whose mutual hatred led to murder and the 'Trial of the Century'.

Left The French dancer Cléo de Mérode, photographed by Nadar in 1905. Initially famed for her beauty and cascading curls, the public and media became bizarrely obsessed with her ears. Her tour of the US proved anticlimactic when she failed to deliver the erotic charge expected by New Yorkers.

Gertrude Stein, one of the least likely celebrities of the twentieth century, who became a bestselling author in 1933-4 despite enduring years of savage mockery aimed at her inpenetrable modernist style. Her return to America, after three decades in Paris, caused national excitement.

A promo still of Rita Hayworth, as the eponymous lead in the 1946 movie *Gilda*. Her iconic red hair and lipstick were born of an image makeover undertaken in 1937 to transform her from Hispanic dancer Margarita Cansino into a Hollywood bombshell.

say the least, but she was always finding new ways to make herself the story. Indeed, 'The Menken' was a fictional character of her own drafting, one that she kept resetting to suit the moment: she claimed to have been a child genius able to master several languages; told stories of wild, unlikely adventures on the Texas/ Mexico border; said she was born in both France and New Orleans; asserted different racial and religious backgrounds for her parents; and used at least eight names, including Ada, Adah, Adelaide, Marie Rachel and Dolores. 'The Menken' was an accomplished shape-shifter who still defies all attempts to decode her.[32]

Kiss and tell

Until *Mazeppa* made her hot property, Menken was most notorious for the bizarre manner in which she'd announced herself to the nation. In January 1860, America's most beloved boxer, John C. Heenan, boarded a steamer to go and fight the British champion. The *New York Tribune* decided to add a touch of human interest to pep up the story, noting that Heenan's wife, the actress and poet Adah Isaacs Menken, 'was exceedingly anxious to accompany her husband in his professional trip across the water, but he objected to it for various reasons'. Three days later, another paper made a small correction: Oops! No, that couldn't be right, Heenan wasn't married. Menken immediately wrote to the pedantic editor, a man named Wilkes, asserting this correction was wrong. She was definitely Heenan's wife!

Understandably, the story picked up national traction. Was he married or not?! America's plucky pugilist was heading off to take on the old British enemy, and suddenly there was a scandal attached to his good character. It was rich territory for the press. Menken's assertion produced a range of responses: for starters, the idea of a romance between a poet and a pugilist was intriguing, but reactions tended to be split down the middle depending on what word they used to describe her; those who called her a 'poetess' were supportive, those who saw her as an 'actress' were suspicious of her motives. She was a talented writer and a cheeky game-player, so she brilliantly played both sides off against each other, writing her defence in whichever style best suited her. Menken was pretty convincing. But then a bombshell landed: it was a furious broadside in the press from the husband she'd failed to mention, Alexander Isaacs Menken:

> Allow me to inform you, my dear sir, that you were perfectly correct when you stated to your correspondent that John C. Heenan was not married to this individual - at least, not legally married, unless it be lawful in your State for a woman to have two husbands at one and the same time . . . On the third day of April, 1856, in the town of Livingston, in the County of Polk, and the State of Texas, I had the misfortune to be married, by a Justice of the peace, to this adventuress, since which time I have never been divorced from her; on the contrary, have lived with her up to last July . . . I would say, in this connection, that I have instituted proceedings in the proper courts which will rid me of this incubus and disgrace, and that this public exposé of private matters has not been sought by me . . .
>
> Very respectfully,
> A. I. Menken

How could she be Mrs Heenan if she was Mrs Menken? Adah Isaacs Menken was being accused of bigamy, or, at least, being a cynical fantasist - both were hugely damaging accusations. She retaliated by saying the marriage to Alexander Isaacs had never been legal, and he was a terrible drunk, a con artist, and 'a viper' who'd paralysed an innocent woman with his venomous fangs. All she wanted was to be rid of him and to stop being attacked in the press for the crimes of irresponsible men. She begged for the nation's compassion, for she was pregnant by Heenan and just wanted the public to understand her sad predicament.

At this stage, the battle was already a fantastic soap opera, but then a new character burst out of the wings. A woman calling herself Josephine Heenan now declared that *she* was the boxer's rightful spouse, and that Adah Menken was basically stalking her husband. What a plot twist! Heenan had gone from having no wives to two, while Menken had done the same for husbands. It was like a Mexican *telenovela* played out in newspaper ink. Adah, meanwhile, was still signing her letters as Mrs John C. Heenan, and refused to back down. Things got even uglier when John Heenan's ship docked in Liverpool, and the boxer issued his own rebuttal, saying he certainly wasn't married to Adah Menken. The truth, as far as we can tell, is that the pair had indeed shared a house for a few months, and had shared some sort of betrothal ceremony together, or so said several witnesses, and that Heenan had seemingly knocked her up, buggered off on tour, and then refused to acknowledge his baby.

Adah Menken's complaint was valid. Tragically, Adah's baby didn't live long, and the fatherhood issue became moot. But the bizarre scandal undoubtedly helped launch her career. By contrast, John C. Heenan gradually transformed from American sporting hero to washed-up has-been. When he realised he'd ballsed things up, he tried to woo her back, but Adah was having none of it. She didn't need him any more. She was the star, not him. Menken's love life was played out as an international human drama, and her nimble ability to weather the storms and turn each affair into a promotional platform makes her a marvellous case study in the power of the kiss and tell. But there were many others whose dating lives boosted their fame.

In early Hollywood, numerous romances between stars were sold to the public as necessary promotion, or simply as a way to neutralise scandal: some were authentic love matches, such as the fizzing, jubilant affection that Clark Gable and Carole Lombard shared. Others were more strategic, being useful matchmaking projects organised by studio Svengalis, or 'lavender marriages' for closet homosexuals - Rock Hudson was forced to marry his secretary, Phyllis Gates, in 1955 to help stifle the gossip mags who'd zeroed in on his male lovers. And in 1939 the bisexual Barbara

Stanwyck was practically shoved down the aisle by the studio boss, Louis B. Mayer, after rumours spread that she was living in sin with Robert Taylor, who was also rumoured to have bedded men and women.[33]

In 1927, as sound technology was coming into cinema, one of the biggest names was paired up with a rising star, and their chemistry was immediately electrifying. The film was a romantic tragedy called *Flesh and the Devil*, and the duo were John Gilbert and Greta Garbo. The public reaction to their whirlwind affair wasn't entirely positive, however, because there was something odd about their combination – Gilbert was a heart-on-the-sleeve romantic, noted for playing swooning lovers, while Garbo was the 'Swedish Venus' famed for her icy remoteness and melancholic gaze.

There was also a bigger problem. Gilbert was still married, and had a kid, yet here he was snogging his young co-star. Fan opinion splintered into several camps: some thought the romance was merely a temporary Hollywood stunt designed to promote the movie; some thought Garbo was the illicit seductress twisting Gilbert around her little finger; others chastised Gilbert for his egotistical skirt-chasing when he had family responsibilities; the cooler heads argued it was nobody's business what actors got up to in their private lives; and some were delighted that two stars had found happiness together.

While 'ZiegHeld' is my own silly invention, Gilbert and Garbo were one of the earliest celebrity pairings to have their own portmanteau couple name: Gilbo.* But the fan who coined it didn't mean it as a compliment, calling their affair 'Gilbo Garbage'.[34] In the end, the relationship didn't work out; Garbo broke his heart by refusing his offer of marriage, and Gilbert famously struggled to maintain his career in the era of talking pictures. Often in this book, it was the famous women who suffered public backlash more than their male partners, but not for Gilbo. His stardom gradually collapsed,

---

* An earlier one was 'Cléopold', the satirical portmanteau for the alleged affair between Cléo de Mérode and King Leopold II of Belgium.

while Garbo's involvement in the affair served as a launchpad to much greater fame.

Another glamorous power couple who didn't get a happy ending were F. Scott Fitzgerald and his wife, Zelda. In the 1920s, they were the beautiful faces of glitzy flapperdom, with his novel *The Great Gatsby* symbolising the thrills and excesses of the Jazz Age. Until the Great Depression ended their reign, they were the voice of the zeitgeist; journalists scrambled to pose questions and Scott would invariably say provocative things about the radical new trends in sex and relationships, then Zelda would back him up by arguing young women should party hard because it made them more stable mothers in later life. As Sarah Churchwell notes, they were almost symbiotic in their public profile, being a double act of highbrow glamour, he the privileged genius, she his sparky muse. He may have been the more successful writer in the marriage, but her contribution was a powerful dynamo driving much of his fame.

And we know they were strategic self-promoters because they collected scrapbooks filled with their press clippings and photographs, with four being dedicated to Fitz and one to Zelda. Ultimately, however, the glamour was short-lived. Their glorious, golden lives were tarnished by alcoholism, mental breakdowns, money worries, and early deaths.[35] Their suffering as vulnerable people harmed their careers, as is so often the case with celebrity, but it's probably also true that they'd been too reliant on their youth and the temporary charms of the zeitgeist. Some stars can adapt to changing times, but not Scott and Zelda.

Bad romance

So far, I've looked at people from the past 150 years, but romantic gossip was a huge part of eighteenth-century celebrity too. It wasn't always positive, however. Despite being a castrato, and so in possession of zero testicles, the Italian singer Farinelli was still implicated in endless sexualised rumour and was accused of 'ruining families' and 'cuckolding half the nation'.[36] Even if most of these stories were nonsense, his foreign glamour gave him an exotic, dangerous potency in the broadsheets and, so it was claimed, between the bedsheets.

Better evidence is available for Edmund Kean's torrid affair with his wife's friend, Charlotte Cox. They tried to keep it secret by using pseudonyms in their love letters – his nickname for her was 'little breeches' – but sometimes Charlotte forgot to code her letters and he'd berate her horribly, calling her 'an impudent little bitch'. Kean's wife, Mary, was devastated; she knew about the drunken nights in brothels, the dressing-room sex romps between scenes, and the week-long boozy benders, but this was an affair with a friend and equal. It was both a betrayal and a threat to her social status. Kean promised not to do it again. He was lying. He also lied to his cuckolded friend, Mr Cox, to whom he dramatically pledged his undying loyalty before enthusiastically returning to banging Cox's wife.

In the end, the adulterers resumed their illicit romps until an acrimonious breakup saw Kean hire two sex workers to yell obscenities through Charlotte Cox's window. Remarkably, at that exact moment, Charlotte – who had moved on with her life – was mid-romp with her husband's employee. Now furious at Kean for his outrageous behaviour, and determined to leave Mr Cox for her new, younger man, Charlotte went nuclear and left all Kean's old love letters in a bundle for her husband to find. Mr Cox read them, loaded a pistol, and stomped off to kill Kean, bursting into a big event which the actor was hosting. Luckily, the pistol was wrestled away from him before Edmund became Deadmund.

Thwarted in his quest for macho vengeance, Cox instead sued the superstar actor for 'criminal conversation' – the legal term for adultery – and demanded a massive £2,000 in damages. He got £800, which was still a mighty blow. It was an enormous scandal, and the satirists had a blast faking excerpts from Kean's love letters to add to the real ones. The Cox Affair was so humiliating, he fled to America for his second tour, but they too were outraged at his sleaziness, while Bostonians already bore a murderous grudge. Edmund Kean: what a guy![37]

A couple of decades before the Kean controversy, London had thrilled to the shock marriage of Mary Wells. She was a talented impressionist noted both for her uncanny mockery of celebrities and for her bizarre behaviour. It was widely believed that Wells was mad, and each failed relationship only added to the notion. The shock wedding was to a Moorish Jew called Joseph Haim Sumbel whom she met in prison. Born in 1762, she was in her mid-thirties when they met, and it wasn't the most auspicious of places to pick up a new husband, so it's perhaps no surprise that he turned out to be a total bastard.

To be fair, he wasn't the typical prison lowlife; Sumbel was a diplomat at the court of George III who'd been banged up for refusing to explain how he came across some jewels. She, meanwhile, was in the slammer for debt. A mysterious foreigner with dodgy diamonds and a penniless, eccentric beauty? It was a perfect match for gossipers. Given his rank, he'd been allowed to drape his prison cell in pink satin, and Wells was suitably wooed by his charms. Sumbel proposed, she converted to Judaism, and they got married under Jewish custom, seeing as she was technically still married to her teenage sweetheart, Ezra Wells, who'd run off with her bridesmaid many years before.

The Sumbel union was extensively covered by the press, with great attention given to their exotic wedding clothes; but satirists also made sly digs at Sumbel being circumcised and accused Wells of being rampantly sex-obsessed. The newly-weds barely survived a year before it turned sour. Sumbel turned out to be a jealous, abusive husband who locked away her jewellery and ripped an earring through her lobe in a violent rage. She accused him of attempted murder. He accused her of fraud. These accusations were traded in the press, until, as she noted in her later memoirs: 'I now found, for the first time in my life, the difference betwixt celebrity and notoriety.' Sumbel eventually left the country, and Mary kept his surname to use on the cover of that autobiography, in which she discussed her various romantic disasters. The book sold well and helped pay the bills while her daughters grew up.

Just how lousy was Mary Wells's taste in men, you might ask? Well, I've not even mentioned Captain Edward Topham, a handsome soldier whom she met in the 1780s. They had three kids and co-founded a newspaper, but she was unable to marry him due to Ezra Wells having done that cowardly runner. Ultimately, Topham proved to be an adulterous scoundrel who gaslighted her by calling her mad. To be blunt, he wasn't the only one - Frances Burney and Sarah Siddons both thought Mary Wells to be unstable, and even George III called her mad when he was in the midst of being treated for his own mental illness. I suppose it takes one to know one. Wells acknowledged she wasn't in the best of mental health, but blamed Topham, saying the discovery of his affair, when she'd just given birth, gave her 'milk fever'. I suppose we might call it post-partum depression today. She was a victim of bad men. But, in the end, it gave her something to write about.[38]

Feud for thought

Mary Wells had the uncanny knack, or perhaps the unfortunate curse, of turning high-profile romances into media flame-wars. The Sumbel marriage was a particularly nasty grudge match. But feuding with other famous people is a long-established promotional technique that dates back to the very beginnings of celebrity culture. This performative enmity gave fans a rival star to hate (as we'll hear in a later chapter), and produced a media narrative that made celebrity gossip exciting to consume. If you cast your mind back to the definitions in Chapter 3, we noted that celebrity is 'human entertainment', and what could be more fun than gladiatorial combat conducted, not in the blood-soaked arena of the Colosseum, but in the pages of the daily newspapers? Or perhaps in a theatre. Actually, maybe 'fun' isn't the word.

In 1773, the very elderly Charles Macklin took to the stage in *Macbeth* at Covent Garden theatre, only to be hissed by fellow actor Samuel Reddish, who'd clearly taken a disliking to him. As Paul Goring notes: 'a duel between the two actors was narrowly averted but Reddish's supporters staged a riot at a performance of *The Merchant of Venice* where they demanded that Macklin be discharged. Macklin sued the rioters and won, but chose to take his winnings in £100 of theatre tickets rather than the £600 of damages.'[39] This is an intriguing story, with violence at its core, but the upshot wasn't nearly as bloody as what happened some eight decades later.

On 7 May 1849, in New York, things got much more heated between the snooty English actor William Charles Macready and the patriotic American star Edwin Forrest. The pair had been transatlantic rivals for years, and theirs was a clash of cultures: old world versus new, aristocracy versus plucky self-improvement, Britain versus America. Macready had been snobbish in criticising Forrest's fans as a vulgar mob, and Forrest had defended his countrymen, being the first great American actor to have performed in Britain. Both men performed *Macbeth* that night, in two different theatres, but Forrest was cheered while Macready was booed off the stage in a hail of rotten food and broken chairs.

Macready was convinced by several notable figures not to let the bullies win, so he returned to the stage on 10 May. He just about got through the performance at the Astor Place Opera House, but found a huge mob gathered to oppose him outside. Macready versus Forrest wasn't just a petty squabble between two luvvies, it had turned into a class war. The fact that Macready had been invited back by New York's elite, after such a noisy protest stating he wasn't wanted, felt like aristocratic oppression of ordinary New Yorkers. The crowd grew violent, then feral, and the police opened fire, killing twenty-two people, and wounding at least 120 more. It was a horrible atrocity that lived long in the city's memory, but it had all begun with two celebrities beefing.[40]

There were many other celebrity feuds that sold papers, but thankfully didn't result in deaths. Of course, Edmund Kean had his fair share. As Jeffrey Kahan points out,[41] he would sit in the front row and sneer at any actor who'd previously snubbed him; he refused to share a stage with Charles Kemble (same reason); he loathed young Master Betty, who'd twice stolen a role from him;

he destroyed his young imitator, Junius Brutus Booth, by organising for his drinking buddies, The Wolves Club, to boo him; he fired anyone who stole his limelight and surrounded himself with terrible actors so he'd shine brightest; he got actresses fired if they were too tall or too beautiful; he rejected 500 play submissions because other actors would've had fine speeches to rival his own; he even deliberately acted badly to sink plays written by his friends, just to prove his power.*

As for rivals of equal stature, the monstrously egotistical star went head-to-head with William Charles Macready to see who could deliver the perfect *Richard III* and *Coriolanus* in the same month. When his theatre manager, Mr Elliston, hired a hot new talent, Charles Mayne Young, Kean was aghast that the handsome Young was given top billing while he was away on tour. Kean feared being replaced, and pointed out that the Drury Lane theatre committee owed him loyalty because his miraculous rise had saved the theatre during its financial woes. Indeed, a satirical cartoon of 1814, titled *The Theatrical Atlas*, had shown him in costume as Richard III, with sword in hand and hunched back, standing atop a book of Shakespeare and with the Drury Lane theatre balanced on his back.[42] He made such a fuss that Young quit in exhausted frustration. So victory for Kean? Nope! Elliston hired his other rival, Macready, instead.

But the most appalling feud in Kean's dramatic career was with his own son. When the youngster mentioned wanting to follow Edmund onto the stage, he shouted: 'I'll cut his throat ... the name of Kean shall die with me.' In the end, they were eventually reconciled and acted together before his alcohol-induced death in 1833, but he'd never been a supportive dad or husband.[43] Nor was he a reliable friend. Drinking buddies aside, Kean had a knack for letting people down.

In the 1930s, Gertrude Stein also managed to alienate a former friend in Ernest Hemingway when she published her bestselling

---

* My Kean fandom is deeply problematic. He was clearly such a toxic person.

pseudo memoir, *The Autobiography of Alice B. Toklas*. By writing about him, including making an unnecessarily cruel insult, she caused what *Time* magazine called 'one of the most persistent literary squabbles of the generation'. Hemingway was furious that she was claiming to have discovered him when he thought it the other way around. He kept making snide allusions to their broken relationship, writing an unpublished satire called *The Autobiography of Alice B. Hemingway* and spitting out the words: 'Once a woman has opened a salon it is certain that she will write her memoirs. If you go to the salon you will be in the memoirs; that is, you will be if your name ever becomes known enough so that its use, or abuse, will help the sale of the woman's book . . .'[44]

Love lost between old friends was a particularly brutal type of celebrity feud because they knew each other's weaknesses, or where the bodies were buried. For Sarah Bernhardt, her unexpected nemesis was her former bestie Marie Colombier, a less successful actress who used her pen much like an assassin wields a knife. She was a devastatingly caustic writer, whose *Life and Memoirs of Sarah Barnum* – remember that Barnum was Bernhardt's nickname due to her mastery of publicity? – was a scabrous roman-à-clef.*

Colombier was rude and deeply anti-Semitic, and went straight for the jugular. She alleged Bernhardt was greedy and self-obsessed, and had continued the family business by pimping out her own sisters as teenage escorts; she said Sarah was sex-crazed but physically incapable of having an orgasm. Colombier also alluded to Bernhardt's son not being the bastard child of a prince, but the result of various brothel sessions with random punters: 'When you sit down on a bundle of thorns, you can't tell which one of them is pricking you.'[45]

It was an explosive attack on one of the world's most famous women, written by a trusted former confidante. By the time the book came out, Maurice was an adult and Sarah was dating the

---

* A novel in which fictional characters represent real people, but you need the key to decode it.

playwright Jean Richepin, who was a pretty sturdy fella. This is important to know, because all three of them stormed Marie Colombier's apartment to claim their vengeance. Maurice challenged Colombier's boyfriend to a duel (he'd co-written the book, so deserved his comeuppance), while Sarah charged into the room flailing a leather whip which she used to slash her former friend's face. The avenging trio then trashed the place. Needless to say, the story spread like wildfire across France and America, with the *Police Gazette* carrying a cartoon of a black-clad Sarah, with whip raised behind her head, about to furiously strike Marie Colombier while the men look on.[46] It was one hell of a falling-out.

Read all about it!

Feuding between celebrities was often reported in the gossip columns, but what happened when the feuding celebs were themselves gossip columnists? From the 1930s until the mid-1960s, the powerhouses of Hollywood rumour were a pair of women whose combined audience totalled an astonishing 75 million people, but their hatred for each other was almost as much fun as the scandals they dug up.[47] Born only four years apart, and both having experienced life as single mothers, they had plenty in common, but ended up trading blows in the world's largest entertainment industry.

In the 1920s, Louella Parsons was a tenacious journalist with a relentless knack for self-advancement; she'd climbed the ladder at a couple of papers before charming the newspaper tycoon William Randolph Hearst (later the inspiration for *Citizen Kane),* and befriending his mistress, Marion Davies. They responded by making her a movie columnist, initially in New York, then in LA. Hedda Hopper, meanwhile, was an actress with a half-decent film career under her belt. The pair began as collaborators; Hedda passed on gossip from movie sets, and Louella gave Hedda decent write-ups in the papers. It was the perfect mutual arrangement for the rising journalist and rising starlet.

But Hedda Hopper's career faltered badly in the 1930s, and, when the money ran out, she was offered a surprise step into gossip journalism, taking advantage of her network of industry contacts. Though she was a poor writer, and had to dictate her columns, she had a bloodhound's nose for sensation and a ruthless streak that saw her being catapulted onto Parsons's turf in 1938, writing for a rival LA paper. Louella didn't feel like sharing.

As far as we can tell, Hedda Hopper found their friction an amusing marketing tool; for Parsons it was a personal grudge match. Indeed, Hedda Hopper – who became famous for her outrageous spending on big hats – had a talent for pissing people off, and alienated plenty more when, in 1944, she helped instigate the anti-communist witch-hunt against people like Charlie Chaplin and the screenwriter Dalton Trumbo, whom she declared politically and morally un-American. Both women had favourite stars whose careers they championed, so their turf war often involved attacking the other's pet A-lister, with Hopper trying to destroy Chaplin and Parsons outing Ingrid Bergman's affair and scandalous pregnancy. Intriguingly, they sheathed their daggers when it came to the showbiz careers of their own respective children, but that was the only concession.

Both were feared, but Hopper was certainly the more hated in the industry; she called herself 'the bitch of the world' while others called her 'the gargoyle of gossip'. When she accused Joseph Cotton of having an affair, he walked up to her at a lavish do and pulled her chair out just as she was sitting, sending her collapsing to the floor. When news of this spread, he was inundated with gifts of champagne from those grateful for his valiant service. But, despite the fear and loathing, Hedda Hopper continued to work until her death in 1966, and Parsons only retired in 1965. The furious rivals had battled it out for three decades, witnessing the death of the Hollywood studio system and the arrival of the TV celebrity.[48] They'd ruled the gossip industry like nobody before or since; two capricious Greek goddesses presiding over the fates of a thousand little ships, and often sending forth a rampaging sea monster to drown a beloved crew, just to spite their divine rival.

Hopper and Parsons were arguably the zenith of gossip journalism. But where had this genre of muckraking come from? Throughout this book, the power of the press keeps popping up like a whack-a-mole sideshow game. If you recall, celebrity emerged in the 1700s – at least in Britain – because of a confluence of factors: the arrival of the public sphere, an aspirational middle class, a really boring king, the end of aggressive press regulation, and the weakness of libel laws. All of this helped birth Britain's first daily newspaper in 1702, which gave people something to read. But what would they read *about*? Within a couple of decades, celebrities had cottoned on to the possibilities, and by the 1750s David Garrick was always finding ways to get his self-aggrandising puff pieces into the papers, not least because he owned shares in at least four of them.[49]

Newspapers in the mid-1700s weren't yet sold in huge quantities, and were largely bought by a privileged class of wig-wearing men about town. Perhaps only 100,000 copies were sold in London every week, in a city of about 750,000 people,[50] but they were probably read aloud in taverns and gin shops, and might've been passed on to less privileged readers, including women and lower-status men. So news might've reached a quarter of the city's population, and readership grew throughout the century. This wasn't yet 'mass media', but the public were being well served. Garrick certainly saw the importance of being written about, or else he wouldn't have bothered. And he *really* bothered. Crucially, however, the press was a double-edged sword. Despite his best efforts to sneak puffery into every printed crevice, Garrick – like so many others – was frequently smeared with scandalous gossip and satirical jokes.

Being famous inevitably draws a hail of arrows, and superstars like Garrick were easy to hit, not least when famous satirical impressionists like Samuel Foote had so much fun pricking his pomposity. While France's press was more closely regulated,[51] Britain's eighteenth-century media culture was a playground of ceaseless gossip. Perhaps London's most notorious title was *Town and Country Magazine*, which reported scandalous affairs among the aristocracy and celebrity class by illustrating lovers' heads side by side in so-called 'Tête-à-têtes'.

As Stella Tillyard notes: 'Almost anything could be written about almost anyone and newspapers needed to take only the most cursory of precautions when they discussed the actions or opinions of individuals . . . By the 1750s public figures were casually referred to in the press by the initials of their names or titles, while the king was simply called "a certain great personage" . . . If these short cuts were used, no slander or gossip was unprintable, no accusation needed to be justified.' The most common practice was for a celebrity's name to lose its middle letters, so Garrick became G_____k, which fooled absolutely nobody. And to make the sordid allusions cymbal-crashingly obvious, editors often placed a second story about the target on the same page, just to be safe.[52]

Though the London press got its jabs in early, by the 1800s it had done the classic English thing of apologising, popping on its top hat, and asserting a stolid sense of decorum. So from where does the legendarily obnoxious tabloid culture of the modern British press originate? The answer is from across the pond.[53] Pioneering American editors like James Gordon Bennett Sr, founder of the *New York Herald* – and his son James Gordon Bennett Jr – invested resources in rumour-mongering, and these recurring pieces became widely emulated across the American media landscape. Gossip columns returned to Britain as early as the 1850s, but remained rather genteel. It wasn't until the 1880s that Brits were exposed to the blaring horn of 'New Journalism' that prioritised sensation, and filled pages with a hearty dollop of crime, sport, and celebrity coverage.

This imported culture was understandably controversial, because it turned the dial way up, but its chief exponents in Britain – W. T. Stead, the *Daily Mail*'s founder Alfred Harmsworth, and the magazine publisher George Newnes[54] – captured huge readerships by pitching their titles to women, lower-middle-class men, and even kids, none of whom had been much catered to before. The passage of mandatory education laws in the UK meant the population was increasingly literate, and - as we heard in the previous chapter - printing technology was both more efficient and cheaper to run, so there was now an explosion in public consumption of newspapers. This was the dawn of a truly 'mass media'.

While all that was shaking out in Blighty, one of the most notable developments in the American press was the invention of the celebrity interview. Stars weren't just being gossiped about, they were now being quizzed in the comfort of their homes. One of the key architects was the publisher Joseph Pulitzer, today famed for the journalism prize given in his honour, who began the trend of promoting coverage of glamorous celebrities at the expense of politicians and captains of industry.*

When he dispatched his inquisitive scribes, he wanted them to capture the famous interviewees at their authentic best, instructing his staff on the 'importance of giving a striking, vivid pen sketch of the subject: also a vivid picture of the domestic environment, his wife, his children, his animal pets, etc. Those are the things that will bring him more closely home to the average reader.' Such interviews weren't designed to catch the star out, the 'gotcha' didn't exist yet. But Pulitzer wasn't opposed to some sneaky tactics, and hired female journalists, dubbed 'Sob Sisters', to elicit emotional human interest stories, sometimes extracted from the wives and mothers of prominent men.

In the UK, the idea of celebrity interviews caught on. *The World* had a long-running series called 'Celebrities at Home', written by a talented interviewer called Edmund Yates, while the popular *The Strand Magazine* - in which Arthur Conan Doyle launched Sherlock Holmes[55] - called their feature 'Illustrated Interviews', and *The Idler* plumped for a highbrow pun with 'Lions in Their Dens'. As with Pulitzer's policy, these weren't explosive booby-traps designed to

---

* The sociologist Leo Lowenthal, in his 1943 article 'Biographies in Popular Magazines', showed that American magazines between 1900 and 1940 increasingly covered glamorous performers over more 'serious' figures from the world of finance, industry, politics, and the highbrow arts.

make the star look stupid. W. T. Stead often allowed the celebrity to vet pieces before publication,[56] and the style was often safely formulaic, with the celebrity beginning stand-offish but gradually warming up when the flattering wit of their interrogator made them feel special.

In the case of the famously cagey poet laureate, Alfred, Lord Tennyson, a journalist might have softened him up by lamenting how terrible it was that the bearded superstar was stripped of his privacy and hounded by fans. There was an ironic hypocrisy when the man doing the sad, sympathetic head-nodding had inveigled his way into Tennyson's home with the express intention of sharing everything he witnessed with half a million strangers. But it was okay, because *this* journalist's readers were, of course, a much classier type of fan, and not like the riff-raff who pursued famous people![57]

Laying my snark aside, these interviews were doubly powerful because they made the reader feel welcomed in the celebrity's private space; the journalist often described the train journey, the countryside, the garden path, the front door, the way they were greeted, and the dimensions of the house, before then launching into the conversation. It was a neat trick. The journey elements made the readers feel like they were there too, giving the conversation extra emotional weight. The celebrity was turned into a generous host, and therefore a potential friend. It was a classic setup to further the bond of *parasocial* intimacy.[58]

So celebrity gossip journalism had begun in the 1700s with sudden, shocking aggression; it was the journalistic equivalent of opening a jar filled with angry hornets in the midst of a private members' club; everyone was likely to be stung at some point, but those with the richest food and sweetest wine were most under attack. But by the 1890s the gossip industry was much more docile, sometimes even sycophantic, in its treatment of the great and good; celebrities often worked in cahoots with the mass media. If we work backwards, how, then, did we end up with the hated Hedda Hopper?

Knives out

The 1920s were a hugely influential moment in American culture that brought cinematic talkies, jazz, flapper girls, literary modernism, prohibition, gangsters, and post-war energy. In US journalism, the most notable muckraker was Walter Winchell, a former vaudeville hoofer who rose to prominence covering Broadway for a sleazy tabloid in the 1920s before moving into the political world and becoming increasingly conservative by the 1950s. Winchell was a vindictive man whose gossip columns were spiteful grenades packed with explosive innuendo. He aimed to embarrass, and was willing to destroy careers for a great headline. He wrote with a distinctive slang-ridden style, and loved to tease the reader with distinctive phrasemaking and shocking revelations. If we want to chase the roots of aggressive gossiping, and locate Louella Parsons's inspiration, we probably have to put Winchell at the top of the tree.[59]

Joining him in this combative style was a man we've already met, Cholly Knickerbocker - real name Maury Paul, though he liked to call himself 'Mr Bitch'. Whereas Winchell targeted the theatrical world and the smoky backrooms of national politics, Maury Paul's targets were high-society gentlemen and debutantes, the swaggering, fur-clad youth of café society, such as Brenda Frazier - the 'poor little rich girl' - whom he launched to prominence when she was only a teen. Paul was an aggressive rumour-monger who knew when to publish the juicy goods, but also when to leverage his advantage for a better scoop elsewhere. He also had a habit of calling celebs by their nicknames, as if he was friends with them, giving him an identity as frank-talking member of the in-crowd rather than a vulture hovering around the edges, waiting for a wounded animal to drop.[60]

This 'part of the gang' style wasn't solely an American trait, and it simultaneously popped up with wild brio on the other side of the Atlantic. In the mid-1920s, the UK's most famous party animals were the so-called 'Bright Young Things', a group of hedonistic, posh brats who reacted to the generational slaughter of the trenches[61] by getting drunk, racing their cars into oncoming traffic, and throwing fancy dress parties of deliberately irresponsible provocation. Intriguingly, several of them acted as their own gossip columnists, making sure to provide the papers with extravagant details of all the dangerous, naughty stuff they'd got up to the night before.

The UK press plastered their pages with faux-outraged coverage, rightly guessing that the public thrilled to the activities of young, beautiful people with more money than sense. This public thirst for novel scandal invited even more BYT members, and wannabe hangers-on, to play the game. Among the most notable embedded reporters were the celebrity photographer Cecil Beaton - who later became a knight of the realm and an Oscar-winning costume designer - and the future communist politician, clergyman, and maybe spy, Tom Driberg, who wrote for the *Daily Express.*[62]

But perhaps the best-known member of the 'Bright Young Things' was Evelyn Waugh, whose savage, satirical novel of 1930, *Vile Bodies*, captured their antics in rather less jolly style. After all the sex, drugs, drinking, and romantic flailing, the protagonist - who has taken up the job of gossip columnist to earn enough money to marry his fiancée, who then dumps him - eventually finds himself emotionally drained, and stuck in the middle of another battlefield, fighting another ghastly war. *Vile Bodies* is ultimately a downbeat commentary on the supposed highs of being a celebrity gossip columnist. It's a shocking, funny, depressing novel, but - as titles go - it's a bit misleading. There are no vile bodies anywhere to be seen. In fact, bodies are strangely thin on the ground, seeing as much of the dialogue is phone chatter. Thankfully, if it's bodies you want, you're in luck! Where we're going next just happens to be full of them.

Since celebrity's birth, there have always been famous people whose bodies were objectified and scrutinised. Sometimes the uniqueness of physical attributes was the source of a person's fame

- whether it was their eyes, ears, lips, face, buttocks, or hair - and sometimes it was mere bonus supplement; an extra thing to appreciate on top of some wider talent. But, regardless of the cause, the outcome has always been energetic, sometimes even obsessive, debate.

Chapter 6: Bodies of Opinion

The little sphinx

Florence Evelyn Nesbit was first discovered while staring longingly into a shop window. Daydreaming over the birthday dress she wished she could afford, she glimpsed a second face reflected in the glass. An old woman was gazing at her with fascination. Evelyn was dressed in an oversized cloth coat, rolled up at the sleeves, and her muffler was tatty. Her skin was alabaster pale, her brown eyes wide, and her dark hair spiralling in ringlets over her shoulders. She looked like a porcelain doll who'd sprung to life and dressed itself in hand-me-downs. It was an entrancing image. Finally, the old woman spoke: 'Would you like to pose for a portrait?' She was the first of many Americans to be captivated by an era-defining face.

The year was 1898 and Nesbit was barely fourteen years old. Her mother had dressed her in full-length skirts and sent her to work in a shop, hoping the disguise would dodge child labour laws and help bring money in after the death of Florence's father. She was a girl masquerading as a woman, and that would also come to define her celebrity career. After posing for various artists in Philadelphia as the 'rare young Pittsburgh beauty' with the 'strange and fascinating face', Nesbit and her mother moved to New York in late 1900, where she was immediately hired as a professional muse to various artists and photographers, and then became a chorus girl on Broadway. Young Florence now confusingly adopted her mum's name, becoming Evelyn Nesbit.

Mrs Nesbit was a fiercely cautious chaperone, yet the modern eye still detects hints of inappropriate exploitation at work. The elderly artist James Carroll Beckwith helped her career along when he recommended Evelyn to his fellow painters, but his 1901 half-length portrait is startling to modern eyes, because it depicts partial nudity as she removes her dress. It feels voyeuristic, a sexualised image of a teen slowly disrobing. She's barely sixteen. It's undoubtedly the most inappropriate image in her portfolio, but it's not the only one to make us grimace.

Evelyn Nesbit's straddling of pubescent naivety and womanhood was of great appeal to artists because it made her strangely protean. The young model could look much older or younger than her actual years. There's a photo of her at fifteen, taken in Philadelphia, where she might pass for thirty. She has thick eyebrows and reddened lips; her hair is gathered up on her head, and she stares defiantly down the lens with steely arrogance, as if she's the author of a radical feminist novel. And yet, the next year, in 1901, the very same girl posed side-on, with a huge flower held in place by a headband, staring away with sad, innocent eyes as if her beloved kitten had just died; it's an image of such innocent power that it inspired the novelist Lucy Maud Montgomery to write *Anne of Green Gables*, about an eleven-year-old orphan girl mistakenly sent to live on a farm.[1]

Despite her Scots-Irish heritage and pale skin, her dark, slightly kinked curls also allowed Nesbit to be marketed as exotically foreign. Much like the Kardashians, she made her race an alluring question rather than a certainty. On Broadway she played 'a Spanish maiden' and Vashti the gypsy girl; one of her many newspaper nicknames was 'The Little Sphinx'. She was frequently photographed in Turkish costume or representing the beauties of the ancient world: Nefertiti, Cleopatra, Helen of Troy, Sibyl, Psyche, a Homeric Siren, or the goddess Venus. Perhaps the most scandalously famous image was of Nesbit wrapped in a Japanese kimono, snoozing on a polar bear rug. It screamed *oriental** eroticism and became key evidence in the so-called 'Trial of the Century', which we'll get to shortly.

---

* An outdated word we don't use now, but such was the language of the time.

In most American states, the legal age of sexual consent ranged between ten and twelve years old, but the late-nineteenth-century 'social purity movement' argued for sixteen.[2] It means that, even by the standards of the day, Evelyn Nesbit was considered a vulnerable child by many. And yet she became a living fantasy; many women desired her looks, while many men simply desired her. Irving S. Cobb described Nesbit as 'the most exquisitely lovely human being I ever looked at . . . the slim quick grace of a fawn, a head that sat on her flawless throat as a lily on its stem, eyes that were the colour of blue-brown pansies and the size of half-dollars; a mouth made of rumpled rose petals'. It's the language of artistic beauty, yes, but also of physical attraction. It's unsettlingly creepy.

Here, I must warn you. The next stage in her story is marked by sexual violence, and it is truly upsetting. In 1901, Evelyn Nesbit was groomed by a wealthy architect three times her age. Stanford White was a married socialite with a plush penthouse, and he pursued Nesbit, and charmed her mother, over a number of dates. One night, he got Evelyn drunk then raped her while she was unconscious. Despite the traumatic assault, they continued sharing a bed for months thereafter. Eventually, Evelyn began to date other men, but was railroaded into an abusive relationship with a virginity-obsessed heir to a railroad fortune, Harry Kendall Thaw. He had a long history of violent instability, regularly injected cocaine, and drew sadistic sexual pleasure from savagely whipping women.

Thaw was also already locked in a feud with Stanford White - whom he accused of trying to freeze him out from high-society parties - before Evelyn disclosed the rape. Now aware of how she'd been assaulted, Thaw convinced Evelyn to join him on a European tour. The bizarre itinerary involved dragging her to historical sites associated with famous Catholic virgins, including Joan of Arc. Obsessed with the fact that Evelyn's virginity had been stolen by the man he despised, Thaw took out his rage on his vulnerable young partner - he locked Evelyn in an Austrian castle and spent a fortnight torturing and sexually assaulting her. It was an utterly horrific experience, but Evelyn was terrified of falling back into poverty, and had lost touch with her newly remarried mother, so perhaps felt her only option was to marry her abuser.

Thaw wasn't fully content. He still seethed, perceiving White's rape of Evelyn as a despoilment of his wife, and thus an insult to him. In June 1906, while they all watched a show in the rooftop theatre of Madison Square Garden, Thaw pulled out a pistol, screamed: 'You ruined my wife!', and shot White three times in the head. The resulting 'Trial of the Century' was actually two trials, and saw the family spend a vast sum of money on lawyers and doctors to ensure Thaw got away with murder, citing temporary insanity as his defence. Evelyn Nesbit testified on his behalf, having been promised financial security by Thaw's mother. Evelyn Nesbit's celebrity had initially been based on her ambiguous beauty, but the trial shifted the public's fascination with her to more melodramatic themes of sexuality, crime, and deviance.

But let's leave the horror behind and return to what made her so famous in the first place – her beauty. Nesbit's oval face was structurally gorgeous, with a soft chin and a sloping hint of cheekbones. If she'd walked into a Hollywood clinic today, a cosmetic surgeon might puff out their cheeks and scratch their head before suggesting a minor tweak to her slightly snubbed nose, although it was famously perfect in profile. Indeed, such was her beauty, she modelled as a 'Gibson Girl' – a series of hugely influential pen-and-ink drawings by Charles Dana Gibson depicting the ideal upper-middle-class woman – and she was dubbed the 'modern Helen [of Troy]' by a noted columnist. But rather than launching a thousand ships, her face propelled products into the marketplace. In the words of her biographer, Paula Uruburu,[3] Evelyn's 'evocative and soon familiar face launched any number of advertising campaigns as canny entrepreneurs began to capitalize on her uncanny ability to appeal to both sexes and appear chaste and alluring at the same time'.

Nesbit wasn't just a pretty face. Her delicate body also came to usurp the buxom, busty women of the 'Gay Nineties' from their fashion throne. As she later wrote in her memoirs: 'I was smaller,

slenderer; a type artists and, as I learned later, older, more experienced men admired. I had discovered in the studios that artists
cared little for the big-breasted, heavy-hipped, corseted figure,
preferring to paint the freer, more sinuous, uncorseted one with
natural, unspoiled lines.'⁴ Once artists proposed that her slighter
frame be the new paragon of loveliness, popular culture followed
suit. Gorgeous glamour was no longer about voluptuousness, or
the performative fertility of wide hips and narrow waists. By the
early 1900s, when Evelyn ruled the fashion pages from her precar-
ious roost, it was adolescent *jeunesse* that came to dominate. The
ideal woman was barely a woman at all.

In the eye of the beholder

Every year, without fail, I stumble across an article about perfect
human beauty, and I always end up reading it, if only in the desperate hope that skinny, weasel-faced men will finally come into
vogue, and I can saunter through London with the confidence of
a musclebound Adonis. Still waiting on that, sadly. These articles
aren't your standard profiles of shirtless Hollywood dreamboats,
or sun-kissed supermodels. Instead, I'm referring to a genre of celebrity journalism that photoshops various body parts into a com-
posite image of ultimate beauty. They're usually the result of some
PR agency having quizzed the public about which bits of famous
people they really fancy, or are jealous of, and the result is the
journo equivalent of that 1980s movie *Weird Science*, in which two
horny teens design a perfect girlfriend on the computer, and then
she magically comes to life in a sort of nerdy, hormonal *Pygmalion*
tribute, but with bonus lingerie modelling.

Invariably, this stitching together of stunning bits of flesh gets
annually updated as new beauties replace ageing stars. In a 2014
Marie Claire article,⁵ British women declared the ideal woman to be
an amalgam of Cara Delevingne, Jennifer Aniston, Kate Middleton,
Gwyneth Paltrow, Emma Watson, and Elle Macpherson, suggesting that aspirational beauty is apparently the preserve of thin,

white, enabled people who shop at Whole Foods. While we might assume popular beauty is the privilege of twenty-something youth, the readers of *Marie Claire* selected three celebrities in their forties or fifties, presumably because they were drawn to women of their own age who might serve as role models. But if the same voters were polled again, some ten years later, would a sixty-something still play a part in the human Megazord of hotness?* Perhaps not.

Throughout history, celebrity bodies have been examined as public spectacles, and the ageing process has been part of that experience. Modern celebrities, however, refuse to age like the rest of us. The stunning beauties in *Marie Claire*'s Frankenstein look ten years younger than the age on their passports. The modern star can draw upon an arsenal of clock-stopping cheats, including special diets, detoxes, plastic surgery, Botox, plumpers, expensive moisturisers, personal trainers, and extreme yoga sessions. Defying gravity and resisting the ageing process is pretty much their full-time job; plus, they're often ridiculously beautiful to begin with. Meanwhile, we ordinary people frantically scramble from one exhausting work or family obligation to another, just trying to avoid getting yoghurt stains on our crotch. Celebrities are our aspirational trendsetters, the people we are meant to emulate, and we spend a fortune on products, treatments, clothes, and faddy cookbooks in a doomed effort to look like them, forgetting that the game is rigged against us.

But these are modern times. The superstars of yesteryear were much more easily ravaged by Mother Nature's prolonged campaign, and aged much like everyone else, though they weren't above a cheeky bit of Victorian photoshop to hide it. Making her London debut already having birthed two sprogs, Sarah Siddons began her acting career as a beautiful, curvaceous woman, but gained weight after multiple pregnancies. Though much beloved as the nation's theatrical matriarch, satirical cartoons ruthlessly rendered her with

---

* That's a *Power Rangers* reference, by the way – this chapter's pop culture references are definitely coming from the bin marked 'millennial nostalgia'.

plump limbs and a triple chin.[6] She was still greatly distinguished as an artist, but there's no doubting some commenters lamented her changing body and spluttered in disgust when she played young characters. The same applied to Emma Hamilton, famed mistress of Lord Nelson, whose curvaceousness became increasingly exaggerated in satirical cartoons as she gained post-pregnancy weight. What once was bountifully sexy became laughably monstrous.[7]

By contrast, France's Sarah Bernhardt was deemed to be much too thin. One joke went: 'When she gets in the bath, the level of the water goes down!'[8] Bernhardt's body also stoked further interest in later life, when she elected to have her right leg amputated at the knee in 1915, following decades of terrible pain. Unable to wear a prosthetic or walk with crutches, she took to being carried in a litter, which suited her queenly image rather well, and she continued stage work from a wheelchair. Tellingly, the severed leg became a celebrity relic; a sort of secular equivalent to saintly bones, as if it were still imbued with her original talent. Dubious stories recount an American showman offering $100,000 to display it to the eager public, to which she's alleged to have cheekily replied: 'If it's my right leg you want, see the doctors; if it's the left leg, see my manager in New York.'*

Was her lopped-off limb really worth so much? Maybe, but it wasn't the leg's uniqueness that made it special. It was, after all, just a leg. A Bernhardt arm or foot might've been just as lucrative. The only reason people gave a hoot was because these body parts were attached to her, and she was a cultural phenomenon. Her physicality became interesting because she was famous, whereas Evelyn Nesbit became famous *because* of her physicality.

Regardless of why we care, celebrity bodies fascinate us, they allow us to not just ogle those we fancy but also hunt for clues about the private individual hidden behind the flashbulb persona.

---

* Personally, if I were a dodgy showman, I would've waited until she was dead, mummified her organs, bunged her heart in an ornamental jar, and then used the catchy slogan: 'Come see Bernhardt's Urn-Heart!' I missed my calling in PR.

Celebrity bodies also dazzle us with their unique differences, the things that draw the eye or seem uncommonly alluring. Plus, sometimes there's that equalising moment when biology betrays the glitzy megastar and the sneaky paparazzo shot captures their sweat patches and acne. Celebrity bodies are often soaring Himalayan peaks to gaze up at in staggered awe, but sometimes we love to attack them as embarrassing eyesores, if only to make ourselves feel better about our own wobbly bits.

Sarah Bernhardt's Franco-Polish compatriot was the lavishly dressed Anna Held. She was all about winking innuendo, and her biggest song was called 'Won't You Come and Play With Me?', which was delivered with faux innocence in an outrageous Gallic accent, while she cavorted suggestively across the stage. Held was also proud of her eighteen-inch waist and showed it off in photos (curiously, she didn't get the same skinny jokes as Bernhardt), yet her biggest physical asset was her huge brown eyes.[9] From early on, she'd noticed that people were particularly entranced by them; they were the wide, oval peepers you'd see on a Disney princess. Quickly she began to use them as gimmicks in her act, rolling them flirtatiously as a new weapon of comedic entrancement.

It soon became obvious that she needed to champion her best asset in song too. The classic ditty that lodged in the public consciousness was titled 'I Just Can't Make My Eyes Behave'. Here's the chorus:

> For I just can't make my eyes behave
> Two bad brown eyes I am their slave,
> My lips may say run away from me
> But my eyes say come and play with me,
> And you won't blame poor little me,
> I'm sure, 'cuz I just can't make my eyes behave.

Notice how the lyrics refer back to her earlier catchphrase, 'Come and play with me'. That's proper brand synergy, there. Classy stuff.

Ear-resistible beauty

Meanwhile, another French stunner was gracing the stages of London, Paris, and New York, though this one didn't sing. Cléo de Mérode was a classically trained ballerina whose elegant poses were often eclipsed by her photogenic face. Indeed, she wasn't even the best dancer in her company, let alone France, but her beauty mesmerised audiences and saw her catapulted to celebrity status when eminent photographers, such as Gaspard-Félix Tournachon (who worked under the much cooler name of Nadar), came knocking. Mérode's most distinctive physical trait was her hair; Nadar and other photographers captured her staring down the lens with a cascade of dark curls fanning out messily across her shoulders and then being pinned higher up by an elaborate Renaissance-looking hairband, or 'bandeau'. She was part Lady Guinevere, part Mona Lisa, and 100 per cent enchanting.

As Mérode's biographer, Michael D. Garval, recounts,[10] she swiftly became a trendsetter. And not just for humans, either. One source innocently describes how, 'A wife who catches the "fad" does her hair, her daughters' [hair], and her poodle's [fur] in this way.'[11] Much more alarming was the doctor who reported: 'the craze for wearing the hair à la Mérode . . . was the cause of [a] tragic mania, for the ladies who followed the prevailing mode were able to supplant others in the affections of their lovers, and this led to a wave of crime which horrified all Paris'.[12] The result, apparently, was jealous women destroying their rivals' beauty by throwing acid in their faces. It's not often you see a paragraph that starts with poodle hairstyles and ends with such appalling violence. Such is the bizarre drama of celebrity.

Within a few months of Mérode's ascent, in 1896, she courted scandal by allegedly appearing nude in a play, and then posing for Alexandre Falguière, whose nude sculpture of her, *La Danseuse*, caused quite a palaver by showing absolutely everything. Here was an instantly recognisable celebrity posing *sans* togs - not even a drape of fabric to cover her modesty - and it sexualised her brand with a jolt. Rumours circulated that Cléo de Mérode was the mistress of King Leopold II of Belgium – their celebrity couple name at the time was the truly excellent portmanteau, Cléopold – and it was a gossip story that refused to die. There had to be fire where there was smoke, no? Anyway, you're probably thinking you know the Cléo de Mérode appeal: lovely hair, naked statue, sex scandal ... But, the body part most associated with Mérode wasn't her tumbling hair. It was what was hidden beneath.

For a short period, Mérode possessed the world's most fascinating ears. People were obsessed by them; what did they look like? Did she not have any? Were they tiny? Were they massive? Were they deformed? Why did she always hide them under her hair? Was she saving them for a future husband? Or for her regal lover, Leopold?! In Garval's words: 'On both sides of the Atlantic, the press bandied about specious claims and deceiving pictures, in an orgy of misinformation, misrepresentation, and innuendo. Some prints and postcards sexualized her ears, transforming them into female genitalia ... Contradictory depictions cast her as charming ingenue or frightful degenerate.'[13] Her ears became the site of bizarre, eroticised, dangerous conspiracy theories.

How did a ballet dancer's ears become such a strange obsession? As several scholars have noted, stardom's arresting power often lurks in the tantalising gap between what's made public and what's kept private; fans feel intimately connected to celebs, so things that are deliberately withheld become all-consuming obsessions. Such gaps in the knowledge can deeply frustrate the admirer, it's like reading a whodunnit only to discover the final chapter is missing. Hiding such information can be hugely powerful as a promotional tactic. It didn't matter that literally every inch of her naked body was apparently visible, what mattered was the shape of Mérode's ears ... OH, HER EARS! WHY DID SHE TAUNT EVERYONE SO!

The more she hid them, the more people stared. And she noticed. Mérode began playing a cunning promotional game, maintaining her innocence and never confirming any of the sexy scandals. Perhaps it was another actress who'd posed nude for the sculpture? Perhaps she'd worn a flesh-coloured body stocking in that play? Perhaps she'd only once met Leopold in a theatre, and it was a mere passing greeting? She let the stories linger, allowing the flames of intrigue to crackle before occasionally damping them down to preserve her modesty. Despite allegations of harlotry and royal romps, her bestselling photos continued to advertise romanticised, Renaissance beauty; her image was pure while her reputation was salacious. There was a weird disconnect in her brand. And so people fixated on unlocking the mystery by examining what she chose to hide.

When Mérode arrived in New York in the autumn of 1897, the newspapers went potty. Several interviews were published, excitedly revealing dogged efforts to answer the vital question:

> A *World* representative pleaded with her for a glimpse of her ear. She laughed and made two or three little passes of her hand as if to lift the bandeaux, then coquettishly said it was ridiculous, and the bandeaux remained in place. More pleading and then the bandeaux were raised just a trifle and a wee bit of rose-tinted flesh was seen nestling in the golden-brown tresses. It was a lobe at least, that much can be testified to. Further pleadings were useless. With a pretty frown, Cleo changed the subject.[14]

As if to ram home the power of their exclusive (n)ear-miss, the paper published an artist's impression of the moment her tiny lobe made its brief appearance. They must have been delighted. Aha! A tangible sliver of intel on her most cloistered secret. Alas, they soon found themselves scooped by the *New York Journal*'s full-ear portrait (yes, really!), done by the paper's resident artist, who'd seen it up close: 'she shows one ear "white and pink, delicate as a shell, and close to the head" which the artist sketched, before she noted that "her ear is not concealed always for she has all sorts of headdresses on stage." She then exposed her other ear saying "I have refused to show my ears to others who have made the same request, because it seems a very inconsequential request . . . "'

For whatever reason, Cléo de Mérode had at last surrendered her powerful secret. And it proved to be no great revelation at all – it was just an ear, like any other! Such a disappointing revelation was to her cost. Mérode's innate appeal to American audiences was her paradoxical duality: she represented both European sophistication and French sexual liberalism. Thigh-rubbing New Yorkers flocked to watch her perform, hoping for the alluring charade of high art masking erotic kink. But Mérode's dancing didn't match her reputation. Audiences were visibly deflated to witness an elegant ballerina doing pliés when they'd presumably hoped for the can-can. Without her eroticised ears, and the mystery of her authentic self, she was just a pretty lady shuffling around a stage in soft shoes.

The newspapers weren't kind: 'Cléo de Mérode's coming to New York was awaited by all the chappies anxiously. She came. The telegrams announced that her reception was a frost. The explanation comes now. Her style of dancing is pronounced chaste. The chappies look upon it as a swindle.'[15] The *Los Angeles Times* was equally damning: 'Poor little Cleo! . . . She was applauded . . . out of pure sympathy. As she stood on one side of the stage in a helpless attitude . . . she looked the martyr . . . a victim of her own notoriety. The spectacle was a pathetic one. It is difficult to understand why Cléo de Mérode was ever brought here, and why all this fuss was made.'[16] Just as Vesta Tilley had worried she'd been overhyped on her debut US tour, Mérode had set the bar too high. A backlash was inevitable.

The hair apparent

In Chapter 4 we saw that sometimes stars painted their own image, and sometimes the public grabbed its own canvas to produce something much more lurid. Mérode had offered her hair as the story, only for everyone to obsess over her ears instead. Oscar Wilde's physical androgyny also provoked curiosity: his lofty height and broad chest corresponded to male archetypes, but his lisping speech, long dark hair, beguiling face, lips as 'full and as bright as a girl's', 'extremely beautiful' eyes, and skin 'so clear and beautiful that the maidens may well grow green with envy' all hinted at scandalous effeminacy.[17] His body emitted confusing signals. On the one hand, he seemed a hip-swivelling babe magnet, celebrated in a popular song, 'Oscar Dear!', that told of his forwardness with the ladies. Everywhere he went, flowers were sent to him by adoring female fans. And yet his beauty was a signpost to crowds of messenger boys who gathered around him too. His fandom was erotically charged at both the heterosexual and homosexual poles.[18]

Hair kickstarted Mérode's career, and it played a vital role in the rise of the Hollywood goddess Veronica Lake too. The famous stunner with the husky voice and cold blue eyes was a natural beauty; her razor-sharp cheekbones sloped vertiginously down like alpine ski slopes. But it wasn't enough just to be pretty, Hollywood PR gave a bit of a push too. The most obvious tweak was her name. She'd originally been Constance Ockelman – a name best suited to your grandma's friend from the bridge club – and then she changed it to Constance Keane – your grandma's hairdresser – until the producer Arthur Hornblow Jr (another great name!) stared into her magnetic eyes and noted they were 'calm and clear like a blue lake'.[19]

And thus Veronica Lake was invented. But the gimmick with the most impact was her peek-a-boo hair, which arrived entirely by accident. During filming on her breakout 1941 movie, *I Wanted Wings*, her elbow slipped on the table while she was playing a sloppy drunk; the jerky motion caused her fine-stranded hair to tumble over the right side of her face, shading it like a softly billowing curtain. The camera instantly fell in love. Just as Cléo de Mérode posed a question by hiding her ears, Veronica Lake's veiled eye suggested a seductive secret.

Lake spent much of her career partially hidden behind that famous blonde mane, with the hairstyle becoming so iconic it acquired multiple nicknames: the Peeping Pompadour, the Detour Coiffure, the Strip-Tease Hair-Do, and the Peek-a-boo Bang, all of which sound like brilliant titles for thrillers in which Lake seduces the private detective investigating her hubby's suspicious death. The studio publicity gurus soon realised Lake's hair was the focus of her erotic power, and they leaned in hard. In November 1941, just weeks before Japan attacked Pearl Harbor, *Life* magazine published a bizarrely detailed article declaring that her head boasted 150,000 hairs of 0.024 inches in cross-section; and her tresses were 17 inches long in the front, and 24 at the back, falling 8 inches below her shoulders. She shampooed twice each day, then again using hair oil, then rinsed in vinegar before setting and styling it into its famously pendulous waves.[20]

With such detailed instructions delivered into their laps, women scrambled to imitate the Lake look. Soon, however, many of her fans were called to do their patriotic duty in factories, as the American war machine clattered noisily into life, but it was something of a health and safety nightmare having ladies working with explosives and rivet-guns while hair dangled across their eyes. Presumably alerted to the risk, Lake did her bit for the war effort by putting her hair up, and appearing in public safety films, so her mimicking fans wouldn't have their ears ripped off by chuntering machines.[21] Nevertheless, for much of the 1940s Lake's career was intimately tied to mesmerising coiffure. Though a talented actress – I love her performance in *Sullivan's Travels* – she excelled at blonde vamp with an air of dangerous mystery; her peek-a-boo haircut was a cinematic threat that often delivered on its promise.

'Men go to bed with Gilda, but wake up with me'

Lake had phenomenal tresses, but the silver screen's greatest hair toss surely belonged to another. In the 1946 hit movie *Gilda*, there's a scene where the casino boss, Ballin, walks his new business associate, Johnny, into a bedroom and asks: 'Gilda, are you decent?'

The camera cuts to an empty frame; then, suddenly, it's filled from below by an astonishing beauty, flipping her lustrous curls back over her head, before launching an atomic smile. Her eyes sparkle. She speaks only one word: 'Me?' Her voice is resonant, rich and deep. The camera cuts back to a dumbstruck Johnny. Gilda sees him and instinctually pulls a thin bra strap up over her shoulder. Her radiant smile hardens into a powerful, fierce expression; then she unleashes a deliciously saucy line: 'Sure, I'm *decent.*' The tension in that line is palpable. Turns out, Gilda and Johnny used to be lovers, but Ballin doesn't know . . .

This is how the Hollywood goddess Rita Hayworth makes her entrance into the film, with four short words and a parabolic arc of gorgeous curls, and it's one of the hottest moments in the entire history of cinema.* Seriously, google it. Rita Hayworth had the looks to stop both traffic and hearts. She was the pin-up on the walls of army barracks, and the literal bombshell beauty painted onto the atomic weapon dropped on Bikini Atoll in 1946. She defined glamour for a decade.

And yet that image was so carefully manufactured that she spent a lifetime lamenting the yawning chasm between her movie star persona and her private reality. She would frequently sigh: 'Men go to bed with Gilda, but wake up with me.'[22] Rita was nothing like the sizzling seductress on the big screen: she was a 'shy siren', a quiet, kind, diligent professional with a tragic backstory. The journalist Leonard Michaels accidentally misquoted her pithy line about Gilda and instead made it about her: 'A man goes to bed with Rita Hayworth and wakes up with me.' It was a misfire that accidentally hit the bull's-eye; as it turns out, Rita Hayworth was just as much a fiction as Gilda.

Until 1937, she'd been someone else: Margarita Carmen Cansino, daughter of a Spanish dancer named Eduardo Cansino and an Irish-American vaudeville showgirl, Volga Hayworth. With such

---

* This scene is also a key part of *The Shawshank Redemption* movie. A screening in the prison inspires Andy Dufresne to acquire a Rita Hayworth poster.

parentage, it's no surprise that Margarita possessed natural talent. She became her father's dance partner very young, and troubling evidence suggests Eduardo made her perform as his 'wife' when she was only twelve.[23] The 'Dancing Cansinos' performed with moderate success in LA and Mexico, and, barely out of her teens, Margarita quickstepped into the movies in 1935, but could only land background parts or dancing roles. She wanted to act, but studio executives saw no star potential. In Hollywood, Margarita was the wrong type of pretty. She was too curvy, too dusky. To be blunt, she looked too Mexican. So how did she end up as the red-headed pin-up girl?

In 1937, aged just eighteen, she married a much older businessman, Edward Judson, who hatched a plan to rebrand his new wife:

> This modern Pygmalion took his Galatea in hand and transformed her . . . He used the same business principles to sell Rita that he employed to sell automobiles and oil contracts. He mapped out each step of his wife's campaign just as he would map out a sales campaign . . . Step No. 1 will be self-improvement. Step No. 2 will be self-display. Step No. 3 will be making a name for yourself. Step No. 4 will be getting the right roles and keeping you smack before the public so that you'll be 'hot' at the box office.[24]

Steps 1 and 2 in the stardom blueprint were radical. Margarita Cansino became Rita Hayworth - taking her mother's maiden name - but it was no Superman transformation in a convenient phone booth; she didn't just remove her spectacles like the hot nerd in a high-school romcom. Instead, Hayworth underwent a gruelling physical metamorphosis.

Hollywood was one of the earliest adopters of cosmetic surgery, and plenty of performers were coercively reshaped into more marketable beauties, either to launch a career or to halt the ageing process. Gloria Swanson was told to get a nose job (she refused, though she later had lots of work done), Marilyn Monroe had her nose and chin fixed, Joan Crawford and Greta Garbo had their teeth straightened, Marlene Dietrich had her wisdom teeth yanked out so her cheekbones sharpened and her mouth sunk into a pout, and an ageing Mary Pickford had a facelift that allegedly hampered her ability to smile. And it wasn't just the women; Rudolph Valentino had his ears pinned to ensure his screen success, and Dean Martin had his nose reshaped.[25]

Margarita's dark hair was dyed to Gilda's famous copper, paying homage to her mother's Irish heritage; she dieted hard so that her legs seemed to lengthen as her waist shrank; her voice was strengthened with frequent diction and singing lessons; and, most painful of all, she endured at least two years of painful electrolysis to lift her hairline, extending her forehead so that her Bambi-wide eyes had more real estate to dominate. Finally, she donned the mask of the glamour icon, including her trademark scarlet lips and nails. She didn't bleach her skin, as is sometimes reported, but Hayworth did - in subtler ways - realign her ethnicity from Latina to white. It was an erasure of her Hispanic identity in search of a more widely accepted, North European beauty.

And yet none of this was a secret. In her surprising analysis, Adrienne L. McLean shows[26] that Hayworth and Judson publicly discussed the rebrand, and continued to mention it years later: 'I had to be sold to the public just like a breakfast cereal or a real estate development or something new in ladies' wear.' Hayworth not only failed to cover the tracks, she erected neon flashing signposts pointing to the cover-up. Yes, her name and body were dramatically whitewashed, but in February 1940 - in her first major appearance for a national magazine - she smiled out from the cover of *Look* with a garland of red flowers in her tousled black hair, accessorised with red lipstick and red strapless dress, and clutched in her hands, as if midway through an energetic rhumba, were two large red maracas. Yup, that's right, big ol' Spanish maracas! She might as well have been photographed drinking sangria with Picasso while riding a bull and eating paella.

That was the cover image. Yet the four-page photoset inside the magazine revealed the new, red-headed Rita. The cover girl and the interviewee were seemingly different people; when she landed dancing roles with Fred Astaire, the fan magazines were quick to point out that her father was a noted Latin dancer. This became the intriguing promotional strategy of 'brand Rita Hayworth'. She would simultaneously be both Rita and Margarita; white and Latina; exotic and American; her father's abused daughter and her husband's project. Her ethnic identity would become contested territory, depending on the role she needed to play that week. And, throughout it all, she'd be projected on massive screens as the epitome of sexual confidence, and having her body transformed into the site of a million erotic fantasies, while the real woman struggled with romantic heartbreak and battered self-esteem.

A fearless heroine

As Hayworth sashayed towards the hair dye in a successful effort to code as white European, meanwhile, thousands of miles away, a white actress was playing popular Indian characters. Oh, and she wasn't sashaying – she was somersaulting with a whip in her hand. Born in Australia to Scottish and Greek parents, but raised in Bombay (now Mumbai), Mary Ann Evans was a voluptuous stuntwoman with flowing blonde locks, sparkling blue eyes, and pale skin. She looked like a Valkyrie ready to swoop down on some mythological Viking battlefield, and yet this powerful beauty became a box office sensation in Indian nationalist cinema, where she thrived as the fantastically named Fearless Nadia.

While Rita Hayworth was totally convincing as a newly blossomed Celtic rose, Nadia's race was much more detectable. In fact, she barely bothered with a makeover. She was clearly whiter than Donald Trump's untanned buttocks, but that didn't seem to be a problem. Though Neepa Majumdar's research has shown her skin was sometimes darkened in early posters, on camera she refused to wear a dark wig, pointing out that nobody would be fooled. She was right. Her white, Western beauty was a draw, not a hindrance, even though she played proudly Asian characters.

India's vibrant film industry had launched early in the century, importing technical staff from Germany to ensure high production standards, and it had developed its own roster of screen talent – the Jewish-Indian silent film actress Sulochana (real name Ruby Myers), Leela Chitnis (first to do a soap advert!), and the stunning Devika Rani, who married the big-shot producer Himanshu Rai – but none were true movie stars because it wasn't until the mid-1940s that actors like Ashok Kumar reached a new height of film celebrity to match Hollywood's studio system.

But that's not to say Indian moviegoers didn't know what cinematic celebrity was; they knew thanks to imported Hollywood films featuring superstars like Douglas Fairbanks, whose off-screen romances were of equal interest to his action-crammed stunt films. It was his success that inspired an Indian genre of inspirational stunt movies, and, in 1935, Fearless Nadia made her lead debut in *Hunterwali* as one such all-action heroine. It was a monster hit. She played a princess who becomes a masked vigilante, taking on the bad guys and fighting social oppression while jumping over carriages and cracking her whip; she was basically a cross between Wonder Woman and Indiana Jones, with the body of an Olympic hammer-thrower. It was quite the combo – and it worked.

Despite looking white European, she was immediately seized upon by audiences as a potent nationalist symbol in a time of resistance to British colonialism. Her catchphrase, 'Hey-y-y-y!', echoed through the streets, as proud Indians giddily responded to her feisty brand of justifiable rebellion, and branded merchandise was sold in shops. A white woman thus became an unexpected icon of Indian defiance against white colonialism. And the surprises don't end there.

During her successful career, her gender identity was also playfully mixed; she wore traditional saris, donned makeup, and sported jewellery, and yet she also played roles normally reserved for men, spending her movies running around with weapon in hand, riding horses and punching bad guys atop moving trains, all the while showing off her sturdy thighs and toned arms in an array of high-cropped shorts and rolled-up sleeves. She was Clark Gable and Katharine Hepburn combined; a kickass beefcake with a steely moral character, both Robin Hood and the feisty *virangana* heroines of traditional Indian folklore. Nadia was a fascinating blend of competing ideas: white, Indian, male, female, beautiful, rugged, strong, and sensitive. Plus, she kicked like a mule.[27]

Fearless Nadia and Rita Hayworth entered the movie biz in the same year, and became compelling visual symbols. But, for all their success, neither got to keep her true identity. Rita never really managed to be Margarita, despite her constant allusions to the makeover, and - in an Indian film industry that hadn't yet adopted the star system - Mary Ann Evans's personal backstory formed no part of Fearless Nadia's brand, and nor did her private romances. Both women found fame as glamorous ciphers; for Hayworth it was a painful victory, for Evans it was a largely anonymous one. They became beauty icons, their bodies studied by millions of people who gazed up at massive projections and perhaps fantasised about what it would be like to kiss them, or be them; but their true selves remained hidden. Their bodies were elaborate fiction.

Foreign bodies

From celebrities heralded for their alluring bodies, we'll move on to those whose physicality made them objects of cruel interrogation. As with Evelyn Nesbit, I'm afraid these stories are upsetting, and focus on racial exploitation and bodily trauma.

Born in the Dutch Cape of South Africa, sometime in the 1770s, Sara Baartman (also known as Saartjie, a Dutch nickname for a servant girl, and later baptised as Sarah) was a Khoikhoi woman, with light-brown skin, whose real birthname is lost to us.[28] Indeed, so much of her identity is the product of colonial ideas imposed upon her. Her early life has proven very elusive, though Clifton

Crais and Pamela Scully have had a valiant crack at unmasking it. Even with all the missing evidence, the story weighs heavy with sorrow. She lost both parents very young, mourned at least three infant children, and may have been coerced into sex work. We know that she moved to Cape Town after a failed romance, where-upon she entered into lowly domestic service and breastfed her master's child. She wasn't enslaved, but it was a life of undignified servility.

Baartman enters historical record with more certainty in 1810, when she apparently agreed – though did she understand the deal? – to travel to London with a free black master, Hendrik Cesars, and the ringleader of the operation, Dr Alexander Dunlop, a white British surgeon with pound signs flashing in his eyes. The plan was exploitatively lucrative. Baartman would be displayed as a scientific curiosity under the stage name of the 'Hottentot Venus', a label fusing the Roman love goddess with a racist term for the Khoikhoi people. There were already many thousands of black people walking Britain's streets, including the celebrity boxer Bill Richmond, so her skin tone wasn't rare enough to sustain a ce-lebrity career on its own. Indeed, Britain had already met at least three 'Hottentot women' who'd earned notoriety for converting to Christianity. Dunlop and Cesars knew they needed a novel angle. And they found a nastily effective gimmick.

Scientists* of the time were just beginning to develop new ideas of race, and were particularly keen on affixing theories of bodily abnormality to women of Khoikhoi heritage; they were renowned for having buttocks and thighs that were enlarged with fatty deposits, causing the bottom to project outwards at a 90-degree angle. These men of science also claimed Khoikhoi women had elongated vulvas, known as a 'Khoikhoi apron', which hung down around four inches between the legs. It's horrible, but Baartman's

---

* *Scientist* wasn't actually coined as a word until 1834, but 'Natural Philosophers' or 'Cultivators of Science' seem a bit clunky in a sentence. Please forgive my elegant anachronism.

promotional materials would describe this as being like the loose skin of a turkey's neck. Baartman was an intelligent and charming woman who, to drum up business in a bustling metropolis, was to be exhibited as a living curiosity - an example of the Khoikhoi's 'otherness'.

Baartman arrived in London in 1810 and quickly became a celebrity, though certainly without the glamour we might usually associate with the term. Within eighteen months, people could watch a Christmas pantomime about her, or play card games with her image printed on the deck, or see her advertised in newspapers, or hear her name sung in ballads and poems, or read about her in magazines. She may even have inspired Jane Austen to write a West Indian character called Miss Lambe in her unfinished novel, *Sanditon*.[29]

Baartman performed in Piccadilly to inquisitive crowds which responded to adverts, in such papers as the *Morning Herald,* that promised: 'Public will have an opportunity of judging how far she exceeds any description given by historians of that tribe of the human race. She is inhabited in the dress of her country, with all the rude ornaments usually worn by those people. She has been seen by the principal literati in this Metropolis, who were all greatly astonished, as well as highly gratified, with the sight of so wonderful a specimen of the human race.'

Baartman's large buttocks made her an easy target for satire, though she wasn't always the sole target of the joke. Coincidentally, the government at the time was nicknamed the 'Broad-Bottom Ministry', giving a perfect opportunity for satirists to show politicians like William Wyndham Grenville standing next to her, with his exaggerated metaphorical derriere mirroring her famed curves.[30] Another cartoon showed her weighed down with gold trinkets, as a saucy Duke of Clarence - the future King William IV - begs her to marry him. At first glance, we might assume the rich prince has bestowed gold and jewels on her as part of his wooing strategy. Not so. He'd recently dumped the famous Irish actress Dorothy Jordan - after two decades of love had produced ten children - to find a rich wife who could clear his massive debts.* The image doesn't show him chucking money at Baartman; it shows him begging for some of hers. It's a surprise inversion of the 'gold-digger' trope.

Besides kicking unpopular royals while they were down, this joke reveals that celebrities were assumed to be as rich as princes. Celebrity and aristocracy jostled for the same space. The sad truth, of course, was Baartman wasn't rich at all. Though they resided in a very fancy house in St James's, and she performed in Piccadilly's grand Egyptian Hall, what cash she earned during her four-year London residency was most likely going to her managers. The joke was unfounded. Indeed, it was doubly wrong because she had no sexual entanglement with the bankrupt duke either. Her appearance in this cartoon might simply have been a coded way to attack him for an alleged affair with another black woman called Wowski, with whom he'd supposedly bunked up on his ship home from Jamaica. Baartman was merely a new stick with which to beat an old target.

How did she feel about such associations? Was she ever an active participant, or was she a tragic victim of Cesars and Dunlop's machinations? We know it was her name, not theirs, listed as the copyright owner on her most famous posters; was this her asserting creative control? Perhaps. But maybe it was just Dunlop creating the illusion of independence to avoid legal scrutiny. We do see some evidence of Sara's agency: she steadfastly refused to be naked during her performances, and never allowed examination of

---

* Jordan was devastated, in every sense. Though the royal family offered a pension, in return for her acting retirement, she had to return to the trade to clear her daughter's debts, run up by an unruly husband. The pension was cancelled and Dorothy Jordan, the great Irish beauty, faded into obscure poverty. In a sad coincidence, she, Sara Baartman, and Emma Hamilton all died impoverished, in 1815, in French exile. Celebrity claimed many victims, particularly those famed for their bodies. But it was particularly dangerous for beautiful women to attach security to rich men, because beauty fades and men can be fickle.

her private parts; she retained what modesty she could by wearing a tight body stocking and jewellery. Though her performances involved audiences callously prodding her buttocks with sharp fingers and pointy parasols, she didn't just stand there, inert and terrified, but performed music and dance, playing the harp and engaging with the crowds as best she could. She certainly tried to be judged as a skilled musician and dancer, even if the audience only cared about her physique.

Despite her best efforts, audiences were often cruel. In 1810, the famous actors John Kemble and Charles Mathews angrily disrupted a viewing of Baartman after the crowd rushed to grope her. She was greatly appreciative of their compassion; perhaps it took fellow celebrities to recognise the horror of an invasive crowd? More likely, they simply saw the grim reality of the situation.[31] Mathews and Kemble certainly seem to have witnessed something seedier than the usual theatre mob hectoring a beautiful actress. Soon after, Baartman found even more determined champions leaping to her aid.

In 1807, the government in the United Kingdom had banned the slave trade, and it was anti-slavery campaigners, noticing her obvious discomfort, who tried to prove she was being held in enforced captivity by Hendrik Cesars and Dr Dunlop. But the legal inquiry, conducted partially in Dutch to help her give evidence, heard from Baartman's own mouth that she wanted to be in England, was earning a salary, and had entered voluntarily into a six-year deal. The contract was produced as evidence. Historians understandably question this controversial testimony, with some warning that Dunlop may have loomed intimidatingly in the interview room, directing her answers. Frustratingly, these few words are literally all we have of her first-hand thoughts, and they may not have been her thoughts at all. Either way, the case collapsed. Sara Baartman was judged to be a celebrity, not an enslaved person being held illegally.

Eventually, after an underwhelming tour around Ireland and the UK, during which she was baptised as Sarah with an 'h', their business arrangement fell apart. In 1814, Baartman was brought to Paris by a new manager, Henry Taylor, where she repeated the act and finally agreed to be painted partially nude for medical scientists, but she remained determined to shield her genitals from these men. Paris initially welcomed their newly imported novelty, but they had their own stuff going on – most notably, the dramatic fall, exile, and sudden return of the egomaniacal Emperor Napoleon. 'The Hottentot Venus' couldn't compete with the Battle of Waterloo. Taylor handed Sara on to a new master, Monsieur Réaux, but she soon fell ill. Death came fast, and robbed her of the ability to defend herself from scientific inspection. The vicious obsession with her body was about to enter a new chapter.

France's leading anatomist, Georges Cuvier, had met Sara Baartman in person, finding her charming and intelligent company, but he now eagerly seized the chance to slice her open. Her brain was removed and weighed, her limbs were severed and defleshed, her organs were extracted, and her vulva – the focus of so much speculation – was cut off and sealed in a jar. Despite having chatted with a multi-lingual woman, who danced and sang and strummed the harp, Cuvier declared the 'Hottentot Venus' to be 'ape-like'; he said she had a skull and ears more like that of an orang-utan than a woman.

Cuvier was one of the most influential scholars of the nineteenth century, and his imprinting of scientific racism onto Baartman's celebrity body contributed to a legacy of white supremacy that lingered long into the twentieth century. She'd been brought to Europe as an example of a specific people, the Khoikhoi, but Cuvier used her body as supposed 'proof' of his racist theory that all people of African heritage were savage, oversexualised, abnormally shaped, and intellectually inferior. Her body had been objectified in life, but in death it was used as a weapon to objectify billions of others. Many years had to pass, and much had to change, before a campaign was launched to rebury Sara Baartman's bones in her native South Africa. In 2002, she finally returned home and was laid to rest.

The missing link

In 1883, London played host to a new attraction at the Westminster Aquarium. Krao Farini was a young girl from Laos, then in the Kingdom of Siam, whose face and body were quilted with thick, dark hair. Within eighteen months, Joseph Merrick, known as the 'Elephant Man', also went on display. There were many others on the performing circuit, living with a variety of medical conditions, and quite a few who were simply pretending to have unusual bodies. It's often been argued that the former were victims exploited by hucksters. Indeed, the astonishing box office success of Hollywood's *The Greatest Showman* was greeted in some quarters with baffled outrage at the romanticised portrayal of P. T. Barnum, who's depicted as a tap-dancing, jazz-hands dreamer with woke credentials.

Historians of disability and race have long examined Barnum and his ilk, but not all scholars fully subscribe to the exploitation narrative. Both Robert Bogdan[32] and Nadja Durbach have argued that some 'freaks' (the word meant 'marvel' in the nineteenth century; our modern understanding is more loaded) willingly chose to perform, figuring they'd earn what they could from their unavoidable situation, and asserting some creative control in their marketing, costuming, and performance styles. It's a sensitive debate, and - as with Sara Baartman - we often lack personal testimony to reassure us that there wasn't hidden coercion.[33]

So, how do we feel about Krao? Her story begins in rather extraordinary fashion. The Great Farini (real name William Leonard Hunt) had once been a Canadian tightrope walker, famed for crossing the Niagara Falls, but after moving to London he'd started managing his own acts, and often they were foreign people. In the hunt for more human novelties, he'd dispatched the explorer Carl Bock and the anthropologist Dr George Shelly to the jungles of Thailand, and - long story short, though it's a particularly long, confusing story - they acquired Krao and her father. When her dad died of cholera, the Siamese king prevented the orphan girl from leaving the country unless Farini was willing to adopt her as his child. He was. She travelled to Britain as Krao Farini, where her life changed dramatically.

Krao wasn't an ordinary child, but nor was she marketed as just another 'freak'. Farini had a cunning plan: she was to be advertised as Darwin's 'Missing Link', the mid-point in human evolution between primates and modern people. To convey this primitivist fantasy, Farini said Krao was of a species of ape-people who lived in trees, controlled fire, had an extra row of teeth, as well as pouches in their mouths for storing food, were covered in fur, had extra ribs and vertebrae, lacked nose and ear cartilage, and were hypermobile. Krao wasn't a human 'freak', because 'freaks' were exceptions, and Krao was supposedly normal for her species. It was essentially a zoo exhibit. That was Farini's puffed-up fiction, but of course she'd not been typical back home. Most Siamese kids didn't have extensive body hair (*hypertrichosis*).

The 'Missing Link' wheeze wasn't even original. Barnum had got there earlier in the 1860s promoting an African American man called Zip the Pinhead whom he'd dressed up in a monkey suit. Krao's fur was real, but she was still a fraud. Darwin had just died the year before, and Farini was jumping on the evolution bandwagon, weaponising it for entertainment. Had Darwin lived, he would've surely pointed out the specious bullshit in the showman's press releases; after all, Krao was evidently a bright young girl who was quickly learning to speak German and English, and thus very much *not* a tree-leaping, poo-flinging simian. With Darwin dead, other scientists and journalists battled to make this abundantly clear, but Farini's promotional tap dance was just too nimble. That's the thing about tightrope walkers – they're hard to knock off balance.

As she reached her pre-teens, Krao Farini's image was prematurely sexualised in illustrations long before it was appropriate. Her buttocks and thighs were drawn with exaggerated curves, and French posters showed her climbing a tree in just a pair of very tight shorts. As Nadja Durbach notes,[34] sexologists at the time associated hairiness with sexual maturity, and so her hirsute body, plus her long flowing hair that grazed her ankles, emitted an erotic charge. This was boosted by Krao being depicted in promotional imagery reclining languorously on her side, like a courtesan in a boudoir. But Krao was barely twelve. She was an orphaned girl removed from her home, a human-trafficking victim who was eroticised and exoticised by her new father for profit. Farini may have thought himself as a loving and decent parent, and Krao was given nice clothes and a good education, but I don't think I'm alone in finding this story really troubling.

The tragic death of a huge star

In 1809, a man named Daniel Lambert succumbed to sudden heart failure while staying in an inn. Such a thing must have happened fairly regularly, but there was nothing regular about Lambert. So what was his thing - Acting? Writing? Interpretive dance? Dazzling bagpipe virtuosity? Alas not, his celebrity shtick was being the 'heaviest man that ever lived', or at least heaviest in Britain, because he weighed 739lb, or 335kg, or 53 stone, which is quite a lot. In fact, it's more than the combined weight of the Spice Girls. Lambert's extraordinary body required extraordinary tailoring, and it was said that his decision to exhibit himself for three years, first in London's Piccadilly and then on tour, was largely to pay his clothing bill, with each suit costing him a princely £20.

Lambert became a familiar face, and body, in both paintings and satirical prints, his vast girth being used as cartoonish stand-in for John Bull - England's stout icon of barrel-chested masculinity - to contrast with Napoleon Bonaparte, the hated foreign bogeyman often depicted as being cartoonishly thin.[35] Stood side by side, or with the Englishman gorging on a massive plate of roast beef, Lambert represented an exaggerated, tub-thumping analogy for Britain's huge military power next to the weedy Frenchman. He became a mascot for defying the threat of enemy invasion; his body was a metaphor not for gluttony and laziness but robust health and relentless appetite. His fatness was a political virtue. By comparison, Prince George – the hated, debauched Regent who'd also gained weight – was mocked as 'the Prince of Whales'.

Lambert's celebrity only arrived during the last three years of his life. For long before that he'd simply been a much-admired jailer in Leicester. Nevertheless, the brevity of his fame, which should've been extinguished upon his death in 1809, aged just thirty-nine, didn't hamper the quality of the legends that arose after his coffin was lowered into the ground by twenty burly men. He was said to have been an averagely proportioned, agile, sporty teenager. Even in his thirties, when the weight had started to dramatically increase, it was claimed he could kick his leg seven feet in the air, a feat beyond most can-can dancers of the Moulin Rouge; he'd allegedly wrestled an escaped bear in order to protect a nearby dog; he'd also apparently saved some drowning kids by using his body as a buoyant life-raft; he'd run back into a burning inferno to save people from death.

Hardly any of this is believable, of course, but it gave him a mythic power counteracting the classic trope of lazy, immobile corpulence that was hurled at Prince George. It was claimed he apparently didn't eat much, drank mostly water, and was believed to be in fine health, which was true until it very much wasn't. More accurate, perhaps, are claims that he was amusing company, meaning that paying audiences got more than just an eyeful of bulging flesh in return for their shiny shilling. As Joyce L. Huff argues, part of the reason he appealed to the public was the reassurance that it was okay to objectify him because he was exceptional: Lambert was talented, professional, superhuman in strength, and totally fine with being gawped at because he was capable of meeting his interrogator as a social equal, and disarming their invasive gaze with a spot of witty banter.[36] He was a cheerfully heroic celebrity whose body was fascinating but whose mind was just as pleasing to the public.

In death, his fame continued. The phrase 'Daniel Lambert' became a euphemism for something huge, as in, 'This prizewinning turnip is a real Daniel Lambert!' His body was cast in wax and the facsimiles shipped off as far as America; his clothes were auctioned, and copies created as tributes to be exhibited in pubs and meeting halls, and his almost square coffin and specially rein-forced carriage were put on display. Later on, Victorians became increasingly fascinated with statistics, and weighing scales were fashionable from the early 1800s, so Lambert's huge body retained its intrigue beyond his lifespan.

Like Clara the Rhino, Sara Baartman, and Krao Farini, his extreme difference helped to make sense of the average. When P. T. Barnum's touring company arrived in London in 1846, he highlighted the tiny size of his child star, General Tom Thumb – a talented mimic born with dwarfism, at that point standing only 70cm (27½ inches) in height – by inviting him to walk through one of Lambert's shirt-sleeves as if it were a fabric tunnel. The tiny boy navigating the massive man's clothes provided a sort of Goldilocks logic to standard humanity. Tom Thumb was too small, Daniel Lambert was too big, and everyone else was just right.

The perfect man

In the early 2000s, personal trainers began noticing a common request from their male customers – they wanted to look like Brad Pitt in *Fight Club*: lean, toned, smooth, and with abs you could grate Cheddar on.[37] In the years since, Hollywood has bemuscled its iconic screen heroes even further, with Hugh Jackman's Wolver-ine character having gone from dude-in-decent-shape (2000) to a rippling, chest-expanded beefcake with throbbing veins (2015). We might argue such body fetishism began in the 1980s, when Arnold Schwarzenegger's bulging torso launched him to superstardom as Conan the Barbarian, but Arnie wasn't so original. In fact, he'd taken his inspiration from the previous century.

In the 1890s, Friedrich Wilhelm Müller, a Prussian immigrant to Britain, became the possessor of the perfect body. His magnificent physique had more ridges, bumps, and lumps than an Ordnance Survey map of the Yorkshire Dales, and he found tremendous fame as a strongman under the new name of Eugen Sandow (having changed it to dodge military service back home). In a career-making early performance, he challenged two famous strongmen, in front of an excited crowd, but did so by arriving at the venue dressed in a formal suit with a dainty monocle perched over one eye. He looked like a moustachioed Fred Astaire, if the twinkle-toed dancer had been injected with Captain America's super-serum. The crowd jeered this upper-class twit, only for Sandow to respond by literally ripping off his clothes to reveal a Herculean torso of rippling definition. The mockery turned to gasps of awe. A star was born.

Over the next few years, Sandow's act became increasingly sophisticated. His trademark speciality was supporting a board on his back onto which a literal tonne of assorted stuff was piled up, including having a horse and rider walk across him. But my personal favourite was Sandow strapping on a grand piano and then having eight musicians playing on top of it while he went for a saunter across the stage. You just don't see that sort of thing on telly these days. His power was astonishing, but he was crucially different from other strongmen, such as 'Goliath', who were huge man-mountains of wobbly flesh.

Fatness in the twenty-first century is increasingly the site of proud reclamation by the 'body confidence' movement, but - despite such appeals to basic kindness - when celebs gain weight, the ritual shaming in glossy gossip mags and viral memes is still brutal.

But being fat in the late 1800s wasn't always considered a bad thing. Indeed, it was commonly a sign of wealth and health. People could buy books like 1878's *How to Be Plump, or, Talks on Physiological Feeding* that began with the question: 'How shall I get fleshy?'[38] The famous American railroad tycoon 'Diamond' Jim Brady was a notorious glutton, described by the restaurateur George Rector as 'the best 25 customers I ever had!'[39] I can't even fathom the calorie count on his daily binges, but it's safe to say he wasn't on the 5:2 diet, unless it means eat five feasts per day, plus two more for luck. To be large like Diamond Jim was aspirational.

But Sandow changed that. He didn't have an ounce of fat on him, and was much more compact than the trundling strongman Goliath. Instead, he was a master technician who could move with graceful agility and execute perfect somersaults while holding massive weights in each hand; an expert athlete obsessed with good technique and precise muscular control. An American anatomist at Harvard University was fascinated by Sandow's ability to flex individual abs on command, as if they were piano keys being played by an invisible ghost. What's more, Sandow's skeletal structure was found to be totally average. He wasn't a natural colossus in his bones: his beefcake bod was simply a product of the relentless pumping of iron; indeed, he's now known as the father of the bodybuilding industry, hence Arnie Schwarzenegger's fandom. Such dedication to bodily perfection transformed Sandow into something far beyond a simple circus entertainer. He became a prophet of physical purity, and the timing was fortuitous.

I've already mentioned racial ideas several times in this chapter, from the obvious scientific racism affixed to Sara Baartman and Krao Farini, to the ambiguous racial fluidity of Evelyn Nesbit, Fearless Nadia, and Rita Hayworth. But the 1890s were a strange time of cultural crisis in the Western world. New technology – most notably the whizztastic speed of the telegraph machine – had hugely increased the pace of modern life, and psychologists were busily diagnosing patients with a novel nervous disease called *neurasthenia* (nicknamed *Americanitis*) that supposedly made strong, virile men weak and depressed. There was apparently too much information, travelling too fast, and people's brains couldn't handle it.

But, it wasn't just these clattering gadgets that had people harrumphing in outraged alarm. There was also the threatening arrival of dandy aesthetes behaving like women – most famously, Oscar Wilde was jailed in 1895 after a harsh amendment to the law, nicknamed the Blackmailer's Charter, made it easier to prosecute homosexuals despite minimal evidence – while the so-called 'New

Woman' was increasingly behaving like a fella, sporting 'rational dress' (trousers) and jumping onto newly invented bicycles to race around the town, *sans* chaperone. This was a crisis of masculinity, but it would also cause a crisis of race.

In 1893, a German doctor called Max Nordau wrote a bestselling eugenics book called *Degeneration* about how such cultural depravity was also leading to the erosion of white racial superiority. The British Empire's forces had recently been humiliated in the First Boer War of 1880–81 in South Africa and his readers may well have sensed such defeat was proof of decay in the supposed master race.[40] Leaping into this maelstrom of racist angst – propelled by powerful calves built like a quad bike's shock absorbers – sprang Sandow, the Prussian hero offering his flawless body as an inspiring symbol to his adopted nation. He invited every man and woman to improve their physique, and, in so doing, improve the quality of British racial stock. Actually, it wasn't just Britain. Sandow also toured India, Australia, New Zealand, and various other places to great success, and taught the All Blacks rugby team how to lift weights, meaning we can probably blame him for Jonah Lomu pulverising England's defence in the 1995 World Cup semi-final.[41]

Sandow quickly began to market a variety of products and services to the general public, inspiring them to buy into his system of self-improvement. He was the 'Body Coach' of his day, the forerunner to celebrities doing fitness DVDs and the Instagram lifters selling their secrets to getting thighs like tree trunks. Ever the immigrant patriot, Sandow also offered to train British Army recruits during the Second Boer War, and again during the First World War – though by 1914 his fame was in freefall, not least because Prussians were now the hated Hun. But it was towards the general public that he targeted most of his products: fitness equipment, six how-to-get-buff books, a branded magazine, jewellery, nutritional supplements, a short-lived cocoa drink, and more. He began to be known simply by his surname. Sandow became a one-man brand.

One of his biographers, David Waller, sums it up rather nicely:

Kings and crowned princes beat a path to the door of his fitness salon in St James's. Tens of thousands who could not afford his personalised attention subscribed to his mail-order fitness courses. Scientists and artists studied him, deeming him not merely strong, but the perfect specimen of male beauty. Before Sandow, nobody believed that a human body could copy the perfection of classical art. Artists clamoured to paint him, sculptors to model him. The Natural History Museum took a plaster cast of his body as representing the ideal form of Caucasian manhood, the remnants of which still lurk somewhere in their basement. On an early visit to the US, Thomas Edison filmed him* - it was one of the first ever moving pictures - and postcard images of his near-naked body were circulated by the thousand.[42]

Eugen Sandow was jaw-droppingly ripped, incredibly strong, and a massive hit with the ladies. On his American tour, under the watchful eye of his cunning promoter, Florenz Ziegfeld - the man responsible for Anna Held's milk-bath myth - rich society ladies paid a $300 charitable donation to enter his dressing room and squeeze his biceps, while an earlier report in a British newspaper further reveals the sexual power of this Prussian titan: 'semi-delirium seized the delighted damsels and dames. Those at the back of the room leapt on the chairs: parakeet-like ejaculations, irrepressible, resounded right and left; tiny palms beat till gloves burst at their wearer's energy. And when Sandow, clad a little in black and white, made the mountainous muscles of his arm wobble! Oh ladies!'[43] Part of his marketing genius was in relocating his fame away from live physical performance towards a sexualised photographic image that could be widely shared; how he looked in his tiny pants became part of the appeal, and his strength was complemented by the eye-catching aesthetics of his titanic frame.

---

* By the way, those Edison films are on the internet, if you want to watch Sandow flex (because of course you do . . .).

So Sandow was as sexy as he was freakishly strong. But he wasn't a freak of nature. He was literally a self-made man, and his huge popular appeal came from the promise that perfection was attainable by anyone, provided they did the right training. Rather than an *essentialist* celebrity – one held aloft as innately unique, as was the case with Krao or Daniel Lambert – Sandow's body was a carefully promoted product; to the ladies as eroticised fantasy hunk, and to the blokes as model of macho self-improvement.

Daniel Lambert was a patriotic symbol, but ordinary people didn't aspire towards his hugeness. He was a much-admired oddity, not a lifestyle guru. But by the early 1900s, ideal body image was moving away from plump curvaceousness: Evelyn Nesbit's slender shape challenged the feminine silhouette of big breasts and bums, just as Sandow's washboard stomach made inroads against wobbly tums. By the 1920s, the new superman of bodybuilding was the musclebound Charles Atlas, while fat celebrities, such as the silent-movie comedian Roscoe 'Fatty' Arbuckle, were harshly judged as greedy, gorging gluttons; no longer healthy, wealthy men of stout stature, but infantilised man-babies who couldn't control their urges.

Indeed, despite his being a beloved entertainer, nobody leapt to Arbuckle's defence when he was accused of raping and murdering the actress Virginia Rappe in 1921, perhaps because it seemed inevitable that a man of such obvious appetite would be unable to stop himself. Though he was acquitted, his career was destroyed. He'd hated being known as Fatty Arbuckle; he found it demeaning, but the studio PR had forced him to stick it out. As he was fond of saying, even in the glory days of his film stardom, 'Nobody loves a fat man.'[44] The celebrity body was changing with the times, and bodybuilding's rise saw Arbuckle's plumpness fall out of fashion.

With Eugen Sandow we have a celebrity who wasn't just admired; he actually invited public emulation. He put the *abs* in abnormal, but he differed from other celebs by trying to *redefine* normal; his fame was built on the inherent contradiction of promoting uniqueness to the masses, which, if successful, would've rendered him boringly average. Here we find a constant tension in celebrity culture: the ideological war between effort versus talent, and training versus good genes. Celebs are supposed to be better than us, their bodies innately different, more beautiful, and more powerful. But, though his racialised ideas of body fascism are now deeply offensive - he literally put the *Eugen* in eugenics - Sandow's urging that people should better themselves has become a key credo of our aspirational age. We live in a world in which celebrity endorsements promise us the chance to look, or dress, or smell as good as the stars, so long as we purchase their transformative miracle products. Celebrity has become a global marketing industry.

But how did that come about? Well, luckily, that's what the next chapter's all about . . .

Chapter 7: Show Me the Money!

Moneyball

When I was thirteen years old, a footballer called Alan Shearer was sold to Newcastle United for a world record fee of £15m, and, to be frank, my brain basically melted. I was so astounded, I gave a presentation about it in my English class at school. Fifteen million. For one footballer! But, in 2017, a new world record fee was set. Neymar is a Brazilian wing wizard with magical feet and a hilarious flair for the melodramatic. When fouled, he doesn't so much fall over as spiral across the turf like someone's stuffed him in a sleeping bag and rolled him down a mountain. But on the few occasions when he's upright, he's scintillatingly brilliant. So Paris Saint-Germain raided their piggy bank and handed Barcelona £198m to own this mercurial genius. Yes, that's right, ONE HUNDRED AND NINETY-EIGHT MILLION POUNDS.

Extraordinarily, that was the cheapest part of the transfer. There were also agent fees, and bonuses, and legal fees to cover. PSG had to acquire his image rights, so they could use him in their global branding. Oh, and they had to pay his wages: a cool £775,000 per week, or £41m per year. With bonuses, it's more like £56m. All in all, that transfer cost PSG nearly half a billion quid. Neymar, meanwhile, pocketed both his wages and another £14m from personal sponsorship deals with Nike, Beats by Dre, Gillette, McDonald's, and more. Basically, he was earning my entire annual salary in the time it takes him to pick up one of his socks.

So why is he worth so much? Part of the appeal is Neymar's mammoth global celebrity. He's intensely revered in his native Brazil, and lives the glamorous celebrity lifestyle: fast cars, gorgeous girlfriends, luxury-casual clothing, diamond earrings, and a variety of iconic haircuts, including a dazzlingly ill-conceived hypermullet. He's the glamorous face of globalised football. PSG didn't just acquire an elite player: Neymar is his own micro-economy.

Only two decades have passed since Alan Shearer melted my brain, but now football has entered a new gold-encrusted paradigm of financial muscularity. The sport's becoming more popular in America and Asia, but the enormous escalation in transfer fees and wages isn't just driven by new audiences, but by longstanding fans paying more for the privilege of being fans. They'll fork out £60 for a replica shirt, and the same again every time they enter the stadium. More crucially, they'll find another £50 every month for the sports packages that deliver beautiful, slow-mo, pausable HD TV. Neymar's celebrity helps drive the economics of the game; but the game's economics have also propelled his celebrity. We pay so much to watch because he's famous, and he's famous because we pay so much to watch.

Modern sport is utterly removed from its amateurish, historical roots, but if we go back far enough, there might just be a couple of case studies that dwarf Neymar's vast earnings. In the mid-second century, a Roman charioteer called Gaius Appuleius Diocles competed in 4,357 races and won 34 per cent of them. This was a phenomenal achievement in a twenty-four-year career because most charioteers were lucky to survive even a couple of years without being mangled beneath wheels, pulverised by galloping hooves, or crushed against a wall. Life as a Roman soldier was a walk in the park compared to chariot-racing.

Diocles hoovered up a mind-boggling 35,863,120 sesterces in prize money during his career. If he'd saved it up in a piggy bank, then splurged it all at once, he would've been able to fund the entire Roman Empire's military for about three months. There's no way to compare ancient economies to our own, and modern warfare is incomparably expensive, but, if you want to play a fun game, Peter Struck points out that covering the US military's wage bill for three months would now set you back $15bn.[1] If we're happy to speculate like this, then Diocles' ancient earnings make Neymar's fortune look like a child's pocket money.

Much like the Brazilian footballer, who's regularly eclipsed by Lionel Messi's genius, Diocles wasn't necessarily the best; Pompeius Musclosus, who raced for the rival Blue team, won more victories. But Diocles seemingly wasn't driven by glory alone; he prioritised races with the biggest prize money.[2] In such a terrifyingly dangerous sport, who could blame him for choosing to gamble on only the most lucrative events?

Of course, I'm cheating a bit here, because I've previously argued celebrity didn't exist in ancient Rome, and I'm not backtracking on that just for Diocles, either. But he's still an intriguing case study in the economics of fame. Here was an athlete whose value was spectacular because he was a public spectacle. Romans paid to watch him compete, and their entry tickets funded his winnings. The more he won, the more he earned, and the more people wanted to watch him; his success fuelled a narrative of obsessive fandom. It made his rivals hate him all the more, and so made their victories all the sweeter. But at the heart of it all was cold, hard cash.

It's money I want to focus on in this chapter, because the history of celebrity produces surprises when it comes to cashflow. I began with football, my favourite sport, but its enormous financial power is a very recent development. In 1979, Britain's highest-paid footballer, Peter Shilton, was earning only ten times the national average wage. Indeed, sport wasn't a reliable way to become a well-paid celebrity until maybe four decades ago, and there were far fewer sporting celebs in past centuries than there were from the worlds of music, theatre, writing, politics, and war. That said, if we riffle through the annals of history, we do glimpse a few in the early 1800s.

My favourite is the man who first inspired this book, the American bare-knuckle boxer Bill Richmond, who was liberated from slavery during the US Revolutionary War. He was brought to Britain by the progressive aristocrat Hugh Percy, Duke of Northumberland, who paid for him to be educated and apprenticed as a craftsman, after which Richmond should've lived a boring life of married mundanity in Yorkshire. Instead, he took up prizefighting at the age of forty, when most fighters were considering retirement.

Richmond was probably Britain's first black sporting celebrity, and he was widely admired, though his ironic, paradoxical nicknames, 'the Black Terror' and 'the Lilywhite', reveal how race dominated his reputation. But if black people at the time were often portrayed as savage simpletons – or, as physical outliers like Sara Baartman – Richmond challenged such stereotypes with his cultured wit and gentlemanly manners. He was widely hailed as a top bloke. He befriended aristocrats and royals, hung out with Byron and Hazlitt, sparred for the visiting Tsar of Russia, was bodyguard at the coronation of George IV, and was celebrated by sportswriters as a smart fighter and technically innovative trainer. But it didn't make him rich.

Richmond was comfortable for a while. In classic fashion, he bought a London pub that became the informal home of the boxing community, so all the bare-knuckle fighters orbited around him like bruised moons, but he couldn't afford to keep it for long, and, when I came to research his life for an intended biography, I found his later years dominated by cashflow problems, gambling debts, and failed businesses. Richmond died in 1829, and his good name earned him a brief obituary in *The Times*, but his impoverished wife, Mary, was slung straight into the workhouse.[3] Bill Richmond's celebrity had been built on his speed and dexterity: he'd literally danced rings around much bigger men,* and he'd fought into his early sixties, but bodies always fail. When his bones began to creak, there wasn't enough in the kitty to fall back on.

Jump forward a few decades, and the situation was changing a little. Boxing success also foisted celebrity status upon the American prizefighter John L. Sullivan, emphatically nicknamed 'the

---

* Richmond's reputation for innovative footwork – he bobbed and weaved like no other fighter – has led T. J. Desch-Obi to ask if he'd grown up practising an Angolan form of battle dance, similar to Brazilian capoeira, which made him a master of swift evasion.

Boston Strong Boy', which makes him sound like a plucky toddler wearing his dad's shorts. He rose to become the Heavyweight Champion of the World in both gloved and bare-knuckle boxing in the 1880s–90s, and was among the earliest sporting celebrities in America, not least because his fight with Jake Kilrain was perhaps the first to receive nationwide coverage. However, his journalistic allure wasn't just built on pugilistic achievements, or notions of boyish charm; Sullivan had a volcanic temper, an epic drinking problem, and womanising tendencies, and his weight fluctuated wildly. A police officer arrested him for punching a horse.[4] I mean, who does that?!

Sullivan was a violent, chaotic man who guaranteed a story, regardless of whether a bout was scheduled. He fitted the bill for 'troubled sports icon'. But he worked his fame to the max, touring the nation across eight months and making over 200 personal appearances on his 'knockout tour' in which he challenged local audiences to face him in the ring – any man still standing after four rounds would claim a cash prize. Some were stupid enough to try.[5] Seeing the end of his fighting career coming, he used his sporting celebrity to launch other careers as sports journalist, public speaker, and even actor, making him the anti-Stallone: a boxer famed for acting rather than vice versa. He died of the effects of alcoholism aged fifty-nine, despite having kicked the habit, but he'd clung to the limelight enough to pay the bills. He wasn't rich, but he wasn't poor like Bill Richmond.

Meanwhile, between his 1865 debut and his death in 1915, Britain's premier athlete was the cricketing titan, W. G. Grace, owner of sport's most iconic beard. In his twenties he'd been a swift-footed sprinter with the body of a CrossFit-obsessed hipster, but he'd swelled in middle age to resemble a bat-swinging Brian Blessed. Luckily, speed wasn't the essence of his game; thwacking balls was his metier, and he was magnificent at it, meaning he carried on being a cricketing master long after he stopped being able to touch his toes. But there was a strange shadow looming over his career.

English sport was class-obsessed, and Grace was a middle-class 'gentleman amateur' who played for expenses only, as opposed to the working-class 'professionals' who drew a wage from their team. For most of his career, he worked as a suburban doctor and wasn't really meant to be a superstar cricketer, and certainly wasn't meant to earn so much from it. But his iconic physique and ball-smashing brilliance offered up countless opportunities for enrichment, particularly through lucrative international tours, so he stretched the definition of amateur until it audibly twanged. He was more a *shamateur*; a lot of money probably passed under the table, making it hard for biographers to track Grace's income.

We know his celebrity had a quantifiable value. Ticket prices doubled when he played, and there are stories that occasionally he'd refuse to be judged 'out' by the match official because 'the people came to see me bat, not you umpire'. Perhaps the most obvious sources of income for the historian to seize upon were public benefits arranged in his honour. In 1895, the *Daily Telegraph* collected £5,000 for Grace in an exercise of national gratitude which also, conveniently, boosted the paper's circulation. Indeed, several other celebs piggybacked on his fame by scribbling letters to the editor announcing their donations in gratuitously performative style, looking to be seen as generous.[6]

This system of public benefits might seem odd; normally it's the sort of thing we do for fallen heroes in times of hardship - the boxing community held a collection for Bill Richmond's wife when she was widowed[7] - but, in prior centuries, it wasn't just offered as a farewell pension for a declining favourite, but instead exploited audience fervour at the height of a star's appeal. And we find it most commonly in the world of theatre and opera. So, let's ditch sport and skip off to the nearest auditorium for some highbrow culture.

Because they're worth it

In 1734, London welcomed a thrilling new import. He was the great Italian castrato, Farinelli, who was blessed with a truly astonishing voice: the power of a man's lungs, yet the pitch of a soaring soprano. The trick, as the name suggests, was pre-puberty castration. To sound angelic, boys aged eight to ten were dunked in a hot bath then had their testicular ducts, and sometimes the testicles, sliced away by a surgeon. It was illegal and dangerous, but some reports claimed 4,000 Italian boys endured the agony every year. If true, hundreds possibly died.[8] Those who survived to adulthood never went through puberty's testosterone tsunami, meaning they grew into distinctively feminised bodies.

Farinelli had all the hallmark traits: he was tall, baby-faced, long-limbed, and gently curvaceous, possessed no Adam's apple, and could hit a high C6 note with incredible volume.* If you spliced Freddie Mercury, Justin Bieber, and Christina Aguilera together, and made them belt out some Handel, you might get somewhere close.† But, on top of his unusual physicality, which was a draw in its own right, Farinelli was also a sublime technician with unworldly breath control. Castratos were the finest singers of the age, and he was the best of them. So, you can imagine the kerfuffle when Farinelli first showed up in London, at the height of his powers.

But it's not the opening performances I want to regale you with. Instead, here's a newspaper puff piece from the following year:

'Tis expected that Signor Farinello [sic] will have the greatest Appearance on Saturday that has been known. We hear that a Contrivance will be made to accommodate 2000 People. His Royal Highness the Prince of Wales has been pleas'd to give him 200 Guineas, the Spanish Ambassador 100, the Emperor's Ambassador 50, his Grace the Duke of Leeds 50, the

---

* We've no clue how Farinelli sounded, but YouTube hosts the vocal pyrotechnics of the last living castrato, Alessandro Moreschi, recorded in 1904. His voice sounds like nothing you've heard before, and there's considerable debate over how good he was. Farinelli was probably much better, but we'll never know how.

† Or maybe you'd produce a horrifying chimera; to be honest, I'm not really clued up on how genetics works.

Countess of Portmore 50, Lord Burlington 50, his Grace the
Duke of Richmond 50, the Hon. Col Paget 30, Lady Rich 20,
and most of the other Nobility 50, 30, or 20 Guineas each; so
that 'tis believ'd his Benefit will be worth to him upwards of
2000 [pounds].[9]

The opera house was rammed with awestruck admirers, though
it was probably only 940 people, the theatre's safe maximum
capacity, not the vaunted 2,000. But you can see from the quote
that this was no ordinary gig; the greatest lords and ladies in the
land were each donating huge sums, and the public were asked to
do the same. Most would've already basked in his brilliance the
year before, so the generosity wasn't the frenzied hysteria of mere
novelty. Instead, this was a benefit night – a contractual rider that
bookended Farinelli's seasonal obligations.

Once all the scheduled performances of plays or operas had
been laid on, Farinelli emulated the big-name stars of the age by
demanding a gig where all the profits went straight into his pocket,
or were split with the theatre manager. The other performers were
expected to give their time as a favour, or in return for a modest
fee. Farinelli was both star performer and needy charity. Imagine
a comedian introducing a variety bill with the line: 'Tonight's performances are all for a good cause: I want a new Ferrari.' It's an
odd idea, though the stars did have to cover the production costs
themselves, so there was some risk involved.

But benefits weren't just lucrative. They were popularity ba-
rometers, a way of inviting the public to prove their love through
crowdfunding. It was a pre-internet model of patronage, three
centuries before fan-funded Kickstarters; it boosted the star's
salary and confirmed career trajectories. A sparsely attended benefit was a deafening bong on the bells of doom because it meant
bored audiences might not show up to the waning star's next play.
Understandably, then, performers needed benefits to go well; they
called in all their favours and cranked up the full wattage of their
charisma to maximise bums on seats. Such vital self-promotion

required cunning strategies. Several noted actresses of the mid-1700s sold benefit tickets directly from their homes, surrendering a tantalising glimpse of their private life in return for fan loyalty. It wasn't so different to modern celebs taking a fat cheque off *Hello!* magazine to show us around their fancy new kitchen.

As the theatre historian Felicity Nussbaum notes: 'From the 1720s to the 1760s, three Drury Lane actresses – Catherine Clive, Susannah Cibber, and Hannah Pritchard – earned from one-third to one-half of their annual incomes on benefit nights, and each cultivated a devoted following. The most celebrated stars could bargain for acting in their drama of choice, and each of these actresses further improved the theatre's receipts by cleverly asking David Garrick to co-star with them.'[10] Benefits were hugely profitable, but it was easy to misjudge it.

Some thespians were accused of ignoring their ordinary fans because they were so desperate to woo the posher patrons in the comfy boxes. It was one thing to be grateful, but a star couldn't be seen to neglect the people in the cheap seats. All fans expected to be appreciated. The other risk was particularly felt by female performers, who lived under constant scrutiny of their bodies and sexual morals. It's no surprise the classy matriarch of late-eighteenth-century theatre, Sarah Siddons, neutralised this threat by selling benefit tickets from the theatre box office, rather than opening herself up to scandalous rumours of men visiting her home.[11]

The golden wage of piracy

Charles Dickens was at war. In 1837, his debut novel, *The Pickwick Papers*, had propelled him to enormous literary stardom, but Dickens's amusing book had been immediately seized upon by pirates; not the peg-legged, parrot-owning buccaneers of the high seas, but aggressive publishers and theatre producers who laughed in the face of copyright law. Dickens, then known by his pen name, 'Boz', was having none of it. He knew that, since

1710's ground-breaking Statute of Queen Anne, authors and their publishers had owned their creative work. He held the copyright, and he could defend it. Or, at least, that was the theory. In reality, the law was widely flouted by plagiarists and it was uselessly mute on the question of stage adaptations. Over the next five years, Dickens valiantly raged against unauthorised stage productions of his works, sometimes compromising by licensing his text to those producers willing to pay a few bob for his blessing. Often, though, he was totally defeated.

As for printed piracies, the law was supposedly on his side but proved disappointingly meek. In 1837, his publisher sued Edward Lloyd, publisher of *The Penny Pickwick*, which was 'written' by Thomas Peckett Prest. It was a book which trampled all over Dickens's intellectual property, but the judge declared it was a parody so far removed from the original that no reader would assume they were the same book. These knock-offs sold in their tens of thousands for a mere penny, often outselling the original text. The same had happened to Lord Byron some fifteen years earlier, forcing his publisher to release mega-cheap versions of his poems to stem the illegal tide.[12] This was a nuisance for the superstar poet, not least because his extravagant lifestyle saw him run up huge debts, so he needed the cash, but sometimes piracy was reassuring proof that everybody was talking about you, and Byron loved to be talked about. His ego may have been soothed, even if his wallet felt a little light.

Dickens was similarly ego-driven, but was even more obsessed with money, having experienced traumatic poverty in his childhood. He saw these knock-offs as both insults to his work and threats to his livelihood. Some of Dickens's most-hated 'piracies' were cheap clones with the occasional change of spelling – who could forget such classics as *Oliver Twiss* and *Nickelas Nickleberry* – while others, such as *Pickwick in America!*, were essentially illegal fan fiction that appropriated Dickens's beloved characters and continued their adventures in new scenarios. The obvious thing about fan fiction is that it's not usually more profitable than the original text,* and Dickens reacted with trademark outrage, barking in his so-called 'Nickleby Proclamation' that 'some dishonest dullards, resident in the by-streets and cellars of this town ... [publish] cheap and wretched imitations of our delectable Works'.

When he first toured America, in 1842, he found the situation to be even worse; writers were utterly unprotected from exploitation. But he returned home to some good news, learning of an update to British law that strengthened copyright beyond the life of the author. This stiffened his determination. In 1844, he sued his enemies once more, and this time he won. The defendants were a double act called Lee and Haddock† - who'd foolishly claimed their dodgy version of *A Christmas Carol* wasn't a parody, as had worked for *The Penny Pickwick,* but was instead an improvement on the original! It takes *cojones* to steal someone's work then proclaim you've made it better. Dickens presumably tap-danced with delight at his win, only for the dastardly duo to immediately file for bankruptcy. Dickens - who hated the legal system at the best of times - was forced to pay legal costs when he'd presumably been expecting compensation. This bitter victory was the last of his plagiarism adventures in the law courts, and you can probably see why.[13]

Pirates stole more than just creativity; they also hijacked an author's revenue. Why would someone pay full price for *Nicholas Nickleby* when *Nickelas Nickleberry* was only a penny? But this wasn't an experience solely limited to celebrity writers. Indeed, one of the criteria in my Chapter 3 checklist was that celebrity doesn't just mean getting rich; it's being famous enough for others to make money from a person's fame, often without permission.

Today, we see this in the gossip magazine industry, in which countless journalists, photographers, bloggers, and editors earn a living talking about famous people; they dissect their images, judge their bodies, explore the cracks in their relationships, and pit stars

---

* *Fifty Shades of Grey*, an erotic franchise that began as *Twilight* fan fiction, might be the exception to the rule.

† Not to be confused with the 1990s comedy duo Lee and Herring.

against each other in dramatic feuds. Often celebrities play along, giving tell-all interviews or arranging for paparazzi to 'secretly' snap them while they frolic on a beach. But compliance isn't essential, and the public pays for celebrity gossip regardless of how it's sourced. This parasitic commercialisation of fame is the bedrock of celebrity culture. Of course, most modern stars have very healthy bank accounts, but much of the cash bypasses them entirely. Most celebs are the product rather than the retailer.

We see this exploitation in the way the superstar actor David Garrick appeared as his celebrated character Abel Drugger on unauthorised tobacco cards and bookshop adverts in the mid-1700s.[14] One hundred years later, in 1888, the same was happening to the stars featured in the Duke's Cigarette Cards titled 'Histories of Poor Boys Who Have Become Rich, and Other Famous People', which featured collectible images of Tennyson, Edison, Barnum, Bernhardt, Carnegie, and Twain, among others.[15] There's no evidence to suggest these famous people gave permission to be depicted on commercialised collectibles.

In the 1760s, the industrial innovation of Josiah Wedgwood, Britain's premier potter, introduced cheap celebrity art to the middle classes. They could buy a Sarah Siddons chess set featuring her as the queen of the board, or maybe just a nice statue of her as Lady Macbeth for the mantelpiece.[16] Statuettes were also made of famous boxers, soldiers, actors, politicians (such as John Wilkes and later, in the nineteenth century, Richard Cobden), and even claimants to hereditary fortunes, such as the infamous Tichborne Claimant, who rose to bizarre notoriety in the 1860s when he said he was the Baronet of Tichborne, who'd allegedly drowned in a shipwreck.* Also available were pottery personifications of fancy continental celebs, such as Voltaire and Jean-Jacques Rousseau – the perfect gift for the aspiring Francophile in your life.

---

* He was an Australian butcher known as Thomas Chatto or Arthur Orton who claimed to be the missing heir to the baronetcy. Though found guilty of perjury, he became a cause célèbre and was hugely popular with the general public.

One of the biggest celebrities in late-eighteenth-century Paris was an American. As his nation's foreign ambassador, Benjamin Franklin found his celebrity amusingly surreal. As well as the paintings and engravings, there were also ceramic medallions made of his balding pate, and - as Antoine Lilti shows - Franklin popped up on snuffboxes, statues, cameos, rings, dishes, cups, and whatever else looked vaguely in need of a pudgy geriatric American. He wrote to his daughter about it in bemused bewilderment:

> These, with the pictures, busts, and prints (of which copies upon copies are spread everywhere) have made your father's face as well known as that of the moon, so that he durst not do any thing that would oblige him to run away, as his physiognomy would discover him wherever he should venture to show it. It is said by learned etymologists that the name Doll, for the images children play with, is derived from the word IDOL; from the number of dolls now made of him, he may be truly said in that sense, to be i-doll-ized in this country.'[17]

A similar befuddlement was expressed by W. G. Grace when, in the 1880s, he passed a teenage boy smoking a pipe that featured his famous bearded face carved into the clay bowl. The celebrated batsman clocked it with an amused double take, and the boy later recalled: 'On looking around, I saw him pulling his whiskers. With a shake of his head, he called me back, and asked me if he could look at the pipe. Proudly I handed it to him. He asked me how much it cost, and when I told him twopence, he said, "It cost more than that to get it as black as that." I smiled and he then asked me if I would sell it. I tried to tell him he could have it with pleasure, but before a word could come he had put 2s. 6d. in my hands and turned on his heels, laughing.'[18] It's an oddly charming vignette, but it must have been quite odd to see smoke puffing out of his own head.

Throughout the eighteenth and nineteenth centuries, celebrities'

images were used without their permission to sell products and promote other people's services. When the beautiful Cléo de Mérode
arrived in New York, her dancing proved rather disappointing in
its lack of Parisian kink, but she was nevertheless seized upon as a
brilliant sales engine: her biographer Michael D. Garval has found
adverts for Mérode underwear, belts, nightgowns, cigars, dolls,
and fake flowers, all of which exploited her name in the hope that
an association might entice customers.[19]

And it wasn't a solely European or North American phenomenon. Though the Indian film industry was slow to adopt the celebrity star system, and only developed a gossip industry for movie
stars in the 1950s, Kathryn Hansen has found that Marathi theatre
stars, such as Bal Gandharva - a man who played female parts due
to the ban on actresses - had his face appear on 'medicinal tonic,
soap, keychain, Gandharva cap, and toilet powder'.[20] Similarly, the
Indian film actress Leela Chitnis modelled for Lux soap in 1941.[21]
From the moment celebrity burst into life, stars were used to sell
stuff. But it wasn't until the late 1800s that most realised they could
get paid for their sponsorship work.

Greedy and needy

In the mid-1700s, British theatre witnessed an explosion in salaries
for celebrity performers, as cunning managers spotted the huge box
office appeal of special individuals. Though actresses were often
derided as sexual provocateurs, Felicity Nussbaum has shown that
many out-earned their male co-stars, while all the big-name actors
trounced the income of bestselling novelists, who earned sod all
by contrast (writing remains a poorly paid profession, I'm disappointed to report). Kitty Clive outperformed the much-admired
Charles Macklin in 1742-3; in 1747, Hannah Pritchard pocketed
an extra £200 over John Rich, while Sarah Siddons claimed £30
per night for a thirty-week run in the 1790s, and doubled that in
Manchester, putting her in the top bracket. Of course, by 1814 the
new superstar was Edmund Kean, whose miraculous debut, and

subsequent successes, saw him perform to around 35 per cent of all Londoners.* In return for his one-man rescue of the Drury Lane theatre, he picked up £50 per night.[22]

For three centuries, celebrities were often harnessed like donkeys to haul other people's products, but they also extracted generous incomes from the public's desire to devour their public personas and talents. This resulted in people from ordinary backgrounds being thrust into the big leagues of pseudo-aristocracy, where they flounced around in the fanciest of hats and drove the shiniest of carriages. But the money often ran out when their assets started to fade: a career built on wit and intellect might endure into old age, but beauty, youth, sex appeal, physical strength, and zeitgeist-surfing novelty are all temporary. Some of the most celebrated names of the long eighteenth century died in miserable poverty, including Emma Hamilton, Bill Richmond, Dorothy Jordan, Mary Robinson, and Beau Brummell. But when the going was good, it was great. Sometimes too great . . .

Farinelli's celebrity status as a musical Peter Pan ensured he shifted his benefit tickets; but historians have puzzled somewhat over its vast success compared to the disappointing sales of his opera company's other shows, which lost a ton of money.[23] Maybe he was a better singer than actor, so crowds thinned out once they'd heard the novelty of his voice? Maybe his benefit was lavishly rewarded because people wanted to be seen to be generous, as was the case with those virtue-signalling celebs who wrote into the *Telegraph* announcing their donation to W. G. Grace's benefit? Maybe Londoners were bored of him but didn't want to dissuade the next big European import from coming over? Whatever the reason, contemporary reports say Farinelli trousered something like £5,000 from performances, benefits, and gifts from wealthy donors. If true, that was a veritable fortune in the 1730s – something

---

* The Drury Lane theatre's accountant totted up 485,000 tickets sold that year. Quoted in David Worrall, *Celebrity, Performance, Reception: British Georgian Theatre as Social Assemblage* (Cambridge University Press, 2013).

like £10m today – but it hadn't been wall-to-wall success, night after night.

Despite the fact that it was probably a good time for him to leave, not everyone was delighted when Farinelli announced he was heading off for the sunnier climes of Paris and the Spanish royal court. The *Daily Post* crashed into his shins with a brutal, two-footed tackle:

> until the Winter Season and the Heaviness of our Purses invite him back again to London. But if our Brains were not as heavy as our Purses, such shameless Fellows would have no Business among us. Farinelli, what with his Salary, his Benefit Night, and the Presents made him by some of the wise People of this Nation, gets at least £5000 a Year in England, and yet he is not asham'd to run about like a Stroller from Kingdom to Kingdom, as if we did not give him sufficient Encouragement.[24]

This accusation of his being a fair-weather, fly-by-night money-grubber was harsh, but he wasn't the last star to be tarnished with the 'greedy' slur.

One of the strange dualities of celebrity is how financial success both confirms proof of genius – if we're all paying them so much, they must be good! – and is also a scourge with which to thrash them. Every time a footballer's salary is reported, we see furious people screaming that the money should go to nurses. Sadly, the public won't pay £50 a month to watch slow-motion replays of medical staff sticking an IV drip into lovely old Mildred from Aberdeen. Footballers command that ludicrous salary because that's the power of the marketplace and the value of our collective attention.

Between 1850 and 1852, Jenny Lind toured the USA, and her manager, P. T. Barnum, portrayed the 'Swedish Nightingale' as the sweetest, most Christian angel. But, behind the scenes, she was a fierce negotiator. By leveraging rival interest from other managers, she sparked a bidding war and squeezed Barnum like a satsuma until he offered a minimum fee of $1,000 per show, for 150 shows, plus first-class accommodation, dining expenses, and a travelling entourage of support staff.[25] And she demanded most of it up front, forcing Barnum to borrow heavily and risk everything. The extreme finances of this monster tour leaked to the press – presumably thanks to Barnum himself, who knew the promotional power of tabloid hubbub – and instigated a nationwide debate about whether a devout Christian, and a woman to boot, should earn this sort of money. Most newspaper columnists defended Lind, but presumably some Americans weren't so forgiving.

As we know, in 1882 Oscar Wilde followed Lind across the Atlantic. His tour was also a financial success, but he too encountered a probing culture of celebrity journalism that both hailed the exciting newcomer and challenged his temerity at daring to earn such sums. In an interview with a Rochester paper, Wilde defended himself against rumours repeated in other papers:[26]

'How much do you get a night?'

This was too much for Mr. Wilde. He pushed back his hair and threw his cigarette away. Finally he said:

'How much do your best lecturers get?'

'Some of them get $500 a night.'

'Well, I got $1,000 a night in Boston, and shall get the same here. Of course, in little cities I don't expect so much. But it is merely filling in the time . . . I am extremely impressed by the entire disregard of Americans for money-making . . .'

Here the reporter was so surprised that he dropped his pencil.

'. . . as shown by the remarks made by many of the western journals. They think it a strange and awful thing that I should want to make a few dollars by lecturing. Why, money-making is necessary for art. Money builds cities and makes them healthful. Money buys art and furnishes it an incentive. Is it strange that I should want to make money? And yet these newspapers cry out that I am making money!'

Not long after, the musical comedienne Anna Held countered rumours of her bankruptcy by arguing quite the opposite. Bankrupt?
Mais, non! She had plans of perhaps one day buying up 200 acres in
Quebec and opening a garden restaurant. Her notorious husband
and promoter, Florenz Ziegfeld, whom she kept at arm's length
from her chequebook - probably with good reason - warranted
barely a mention in this future fantasy. The money was clearly
hers, and hers alone.

While designed to curb gossip of her supposed money woes, the
assertion that she was actually swimming in filthy lucre produced a
scornful response in the press. Cartoons were printed of her squatting atop piles of money, while outraged journalists screeched in
bewilderment that a mediocre, skinny-hipped songstress could've
accrued such a windfall from the public's fervent adoration. She
was undeserving of her riches, presumably because, in their eyes,
she was undeserving of fame. The story had begun as a vicious in-
sinuation that she was broke, but ended up being about her vulgar
wealth. The follow-up to this media blitz was inevitable: hearing
that she was loaded, fans and strangers alike pestered her for charitable gifts, assuming she would bail them out of their personal dif-
ficulties.[27] Anna Held's money was never just her own. Somehow
it was considered a public resource.

Throughout celebrity's three-century story, the idea of the star
as communal property has lingered in the air like a pungent fart,
so it's no surprise that ordinary people assumed a celebrity might
be considered a sort of national ATM. Held was one of many stars
to receive begging and presumptuous letters; they also flooded
in through the heroic Grace Darling's letterbox, and, in the early
1800s, crammed the pigeonhole of France's great actor François-
Joseph Talma, who was inundated with requests not only to meet
fans in person, but also to assist them in legal battles, join them in
dodgy gambling rackets, or help them book places to stay in Paris,
as if he was some helpful travel agent.[28]

Among the most heartbreaking requests for celebrity generosity were those from children writing to Eleanor Roosevelt in the

1930s, begging her to buy them the Shirley Temple dolls their parents couldn't afford. Such was Temple's enormous popularity with kids - she was the most famous child in the world, and kids loved her for it - these young fans became desperate to own anything associated with the pint-size princess of the silver screen. The movie studio, realising that toddlers grow up fast, cottoned on to Shirley's limited shelf life as a marketing asset, and decided to throw her at everything: breakfast cereal, drinks, her own fashion range sold from the Sears catalogue, and the aforementioned dolls. These came in four sizes, the cheapest being only a couple of bucks, but their unaffordability was painfully felt by those kids too poor to scratch even that together. And so they turned to a political celebrity portrayed in the media as America's proxy mother.[29] Here's one of the letters, uncovered by the historian John F. Kasson:

Dear Mrs. Roosevelt,
   You have nieces and sons who were young and some still are wanted a thing very much but tried hard to get it and can't. I a girl from Chicago have tried so so hard to get five suscriptions [*sic*] to get a 22 inch Shirley Temple [doll] which the Daily Chicago Tribune is giving away. It is cheap for at 65 cents a month you get daily paper. You have millions of friends couldn't you please ask them to take for one year at 65 cents a month the Daily Chicago Tribune. I don't know how I'd ever thank you if you got them. I know one thing I'd pray with all my heart in Holy Mass and when receiving Holy Communion pray to God to bless you all. Please please do help me. Here is a picture of the Shirley Temple. If you do get them send them as soon as you can.
   Yours truly,
   [name redacted]

I've no idea if Mrs Roosevelt responded, but I love imagining her signing up to thousands of newspaper subscriptions and waking up to find the White House lawn being bombarded by a horde of bike-riding paperboys. Regardless of the outcome, it's the hidden economics lurking in this letter that I find fascinating. Here was an example of celebrity's commercialised interconnectedness: young fans unable to afford access to one heroic icon contacted another instead, but didn't ask Roosevelt to buy the dolls for them; they wanted the First Lady to acquire them through a sponsored advertorial deal negotiated between the toy manufacturers, movie studio, Temple's agent, and the *Chicago Tribune*. These kids were being sucked into a complex chain of business arrangements; their urge to acquire the doll probably felt like an act of undiluted intimacy with their celebrity favourite, but there was a profit-driven industry churning away in the background.

A *tour de farce*

In 1820, Edmund Kean embarked on an exciting adventure: he crossed the Atlantic to begin a tour of North America, following in the unstable footsteps of George Frederick Cooke - another shambling alcoholic - who'd done the same a decade beforehand. But Kean was even more famous than Cooke, and the Americans were ecstatic to receive him. Given what we know of Kean's spectacular flair for self-sabotage, you might be already stifling your giggles at the prospect of how he managed to bungle this opportunity. But his shows were triumphs (sorry!). The money poured in, he kept it together, and the American people were dazzled and charmed.

Hang on, let me just check my notes . . . Oops, sorry, yes, you were right. Then he got to Boston . . .

Kean was warned that Bostonians didn't go to the theatre in the summer off-season, but he scheduled performances anyway, expecting his stardom to have the attractive power of a giant magnet in a paperclip factory. No such luck. Night after night, Kean peeked out from behind the curtain to see an embarrassingly sparse audience. He claimed only twenty had bothered to show up for one particularly awful date. But the show must go on, right? Wrong.

Kean felt insulted, and – because no tickets had been sold – refused to perform until the managers forked out an extra $200 for his wounded reputation.[30]

Never the calmest of diplomats, he then published an open letter in the press, intending to defend his honour, but it came off sounding like a passive-aggressive whinge at Boston's lack of sophistication;[31] clearly, he was a genius who'd come all this way, and they didn't appreciate him enough. This went down like a kite made of anvils. Soon it escalated into a scandal, eagerly reported back in Britain, and the upshot was a very stern warning never to set foot in Boston again. Edmund Kean returned to Britain flush with cash, but somewhat deflated.

At home, things got worse. In 1825, while escaping his high-profile sex scandal mentioned in Chapter 5, he decided to try another US tour. Surely, he'd be welcomed back with open arms? He was the great Edmund Kean, and five years had passed! In New York, he was pelted with oranges. He again tried to apologise in the press, saying he'd go to Boston next.[32] As Kean took to the stage in November, the Bostonians rioted, with thousands of people tearing up the seats and smashing chandeliers. Incensed at his earlier insult, the mob broke their way into his dressing room, intent on doing him a violent mischief. Fortunately, he'd already been smuggled out of the theatre and was hiding at a theatre employee's house, so the enraged audience marched to this man's property, ready to beat the crap out of Kean. Luckily, the manager's wife said she was heavily pregnant, and this calmed things down. Edmund, meanwhile, cowered under a linen press in a back room.*[33]

Out on the road

The first British stage celebrities to tour America were both chaotic, charismatic addicts whose brilliance was offset by controversy. But while Kean's tours weren't exactly triumphs, they marked a key

---

* Seriously, someone make a movie about this guy. Please.

moment in the story of globalised celebrity. Previously, plenty of small-time acts had crossed the Atlantic to lead wandering lives as itinerant entertainers,[34] and Ann Hatton - the fame-chasing sister of Sarah Siddons - had found modest success with her opera, but Kean was perhaps the first huge star to step off the boat bathed in the golden light of reputation. Yet his tours came a full century after celebrity had first emerged: so why had it taken so long? Wasn't there money to be made in the 1700s?

The most obvious reason is that Britain and America had gone to war in 1776, and egos were still sore from the outcome. Secondly, American cities were tiny compared to London and Paris; when war broke out, New York's population was thirty times smaller than London's.[35] So the market was much less tempting. But geography also played a key role. Touring was physically and logistically arduous; it took months, and transport networks were less than comfortable. Benjamin Franklin had gone the opposite way to Europe a few decades before, but he was an ambassador on an official posting, and he wasn't trundling around France in a bumpy stagecoach.

Tours weren't a new concept. In eighteenth-century Europe, such luminaries as Farinelli, Rousseau, and Clara the Rhino had all displayed themselves in foreign territories thanks to the promotional power of the printing press. America, however, was massive. And there was a whacking great ocean in the way. Kean signed up to months at sea, and weeks spent commuting between cities in uncomfortable carriages. It was profitable but grimly deficient in glamour. His experience of the crossing would've been broadly similar to Ben Franklin's eight Atlantic voyages undertaken in his eventful life, with each one promising at least six weeks of being tossed by the waves, or even longer with unfriendly winds.

But by the 1840s technology was slowly smoothing the way. Ocean-going steamships could zip across the Atlantic in a mere two weeks, and that fell to just eight days by the 1860s. The rapid shrinking of those 3,000 miles now helped to foster a vibrant culture of transatlantic celebrity that made the USA a lucrative destination for Europe's finest, while Britain and Ireland warmly received famous Americans, most notably the anti-slavery campaigners Frederick Douglass (1845), Henry 'Box' Brown (who then lived in Britain for twenty-five years), and the bestselling novelist Harriet Beecher Stowe (1853).

America's vast internal geography had also hamstrung its own domestic celebrity culture. Things only started to open up in the mid-nineteenth century when the world welcomed the revolutionary triad of the telegraph machine, railway, and photography. Oh, and don't forget postal reforms; the invention of stamps and envelopes had an effect too, as did the escalation of industrialised news printing. But, even in the 1860s, many Americans lived in a nation of such sprawling size that different regions experienced their own local pop culture.[36]

While printed material was universally available, Broadway's premier live acts and opera companies were only just starting to play the big cities beyond the eastern seaboard. When a show had grown stale in New York, the coming of the railroad[37] now facilitated relocation to new cities where it was fresh and exciting. By the 1860s, so-called 'monster shows' packaged together multiple acts in travelling festivals, as entrepreneurs battled to outdo each other's publicity-baiting offerings.[38]

So, while steamships shortened the gap between Europe and America, rail transport supersized potential audiences. The thrilling speed of movement, and the ability to carry large cargo, allowed star performers to visit new provinces formerly out of reach – in 1898, Anna Held invested $22,000 on a luxury railway car, complete with kitchen, piano, dining room, staff sleeping quarters, and plush private bedroom, so she could avoid bedding down in bad hotels. It was this same carriage which was so famously burgled in 1906.[39] Perhaps she should have also invested in a guard dog, or borrowed a prowling cheetah from Sarah Bernhardt?

But railways also allowed huge stage productions to go out on the road (or, rather, down the tracks). Perhaps the most impressive example was Buffalo Bill's Wild West Show, which triumphantly toured America and Europe for years, despite the enormous challenge of moving the tents, costumes, horses, props, guns, and human cast. They got it down to a fine art, provided we ignore the occasional disaster. On the Mississippi, their steamboat sank in 1885 - they sued the shipping company for lost earnings and the death of many animals - and, in 1901, a train carrying the circus was hit by an oncoming freight train, causing the deaths of over 100 specially trained horses.[40]

It was in this bustling era of mass transit and mass communication that performers started to realise just how much money could be earned through transatlantic touring. Kean had stuffed his pockets with £6,000, which was a hefty payday for the 1820s,* but in 1880 Sarah Bernhardt did fifty American dates and the box office takings totalled 2,667,600 francs. If we use average wages as our metric, this box office triumph equated to the annual salary of 1,400 skilled labourers, which in 2019 lands us somewhere around $80m.† Much of that would've gone into her own pocket, presumably to pay for her menagerie of terrifying, carnivorous pets we heard about in Chapter 5. Indeed, her business manager described the tour as 'a businesswoman, on a business trip'.[41]

In 1894, Britain's beloved male impersonator, Vesta Tilley, was lured across the ocean by the vaudeville impresario Tony Pastor for a modest $300 per week. She proved a smash hit and eclipsed the other imported celebrity that year, Cléo de Mérode, so it wasn't surprising that Tilley kept being asked back. By 1912, the money on

---

* Perhaps about £6m in modern terms when measured against relative average wages. Jane Austen's fictional Mr Darcy was worth £10,000 a year, or £10m today.

† Calculating historical inflation is bafflingly unreliable - you get a huge range depending on whether you measure the value of goods, the size of the economy or the average wages of the time. At an exchange rate of five francs to the dollar, she earned $533,520 in 1880 prices. Adjusted for inflation, and compared to modern America's average earnings of $60k, it's now equivalent to $80m.

the table was $4,000 per week – or half a million bucks today* – but she declined the offer, as she didn't want to work Sundays.[42] It was a modest fee compared to Charles Dickens's second American tour of 1867. Dickens was alert to his failing health, and wanted to lay a gargantuan nest egg for his kids. He was aware of the tackiness of selling his art, and his best friend was aghast at the idea, but Dickens was able to justify it to himself: 'Securing for myself from day to day the means of an honourable subsistence, I would rather have the affectionate regard of my fellow men, than I would have heaps and mines of gold. But the two things do not seem to be incompatible.'

Dickens's massive American reading tour saw him narrate his own classic novels,[43] bringing fans closer to the author in both physical proximity and emotional depth. They witnessed his performance skills, heard his voice, and gazed upon his legendary beard as he recounted his celebrated stories. It was a powerful experience and thousands of fans queued overnight in the cold, and even bedded down on portable mattresses, to buy the expensive $2 tickets which were soon being hawked for much more. This caused its own scandal; was it not hypocritical for a writer famed for his attacks on poverty to be charging so much? Jenny Lind had survived the argument a decade earlier, but, clearly, she hadn't ended it.

Dickens's US extravaganza seemed rather crass to critics; he appeared to be overtly touting his fame as a product. Whereas his first tour had been motivated by curiosity (and his vengeful wrath at copyright infringers), this one looked and smelled like a money-making exercise. But he tried to give it an authentic quality too; as Malcolm Andrews shows,[44] Dickens commodified public friendship, but was genuine in his affections. He offered intimate access to his persona, his characters, and his physical being; he tried to connect emotionally with fans who responded to his writing style

---

* In terms of relative wages, $4,000 in 1912 would equate to about $490,000 per week today.

of chatty, beloved uncle. He'd wanted to be an actor as a teenager, and loved the gasps and tears extracted from his rapt audiences. Conscious of their desires for an emotive experience, he toured the theatres before each performance, roping off areas that had poor acoustics, so all of his fans could hear him clearly. He cared. But he also did it for the moolah.

We see this excitable bean-counting in his letters: 'Copperfield and Bob last night with great success. My present profit is over £1,000 per week!'; 'We have had a tremendous night. The largest house I have ever had since I first began. 2,300 people. Over £200 in money.'[45] Dickens even sometimes referred to his paying public as dehumanised wallets, with spectators simply representing box office takings: 'The room will not hold more than from eighty to ninety pounds.'[46] Dickens had always been obsessed with money. As a little boy his middle-class comfort had been upended into traumatic poverty by his dad's detention in debtors' jail. While the family was banged up, little Charlie was sent out to earn a measly living working in a boot polish factory, where he met a lad called Fagin. He was just twelve.[47] When literary fame later came knocking, and his family expanded to accommodate a wife, sister-in-law, and a cavalcade of kids, the pressure of being the family's sole breadwinner gnawed away at his psyche. Despite his reputation, and a gold-plated bank account, Dickens dreaded debt.

And so his 1867–8 British and American tour saw him performing the role of 'Mr Charles Dickens' literally to within an inch of his life. He wrote to his worried best friend and biographer John Forster: 'You have no idea how heavily the anxiety of it sits upon my soul. But the prize looks so large!' He was self-medicating with laudanum, sherry, and champagne to help him sleep, and eventually the exhaustion caught up with him. Several Midwestern appearances were cancelled, most controversially Chicago, which was still smarting from the time he'd snubbed them in his 1842 tour. They didn't take it well, but, when told of the outrage, Dickens sardonically replied: 'I would rather they go into fits than I did.' Even acknowledging his limitations, and calling off shows, he still took on too much. The tour guaranteed his family would never go broke, but it physically broke him. Dickens pushed his deteriorating body through a gruelling cycle of seventy-six public readings, in eighteen cities, so that he could scoop up £45,000 (about £30m today). It was to be a profitable self-sacrifice. He died two years later of sheer exhaustion, aged only fifty-eight.

Mr Ten Per Cent

For all his faults and vanities, Dickens was a hugely creative writer with the relentless drive of a worker ant pepped up on amphetamines. But he couldn't do it alone. Celebrity in the mid-1800s became an increasingly professionalised industry, and he was joined on tour by his rock'n'roll entourage. There was his valet, Henry Scott, in charge of the wardrobe department; George Allison was the lighting guy responsible for installing Dickens's gas-lamp rig in every theatre; there was the clerk, Mr Wild, and there were always one or two local boys hired to escort him around and guard his hotel room from frenzied fans and snooping journalists.

But the most important jobs of all - booking the venues, replying to fan mail, hectoring local journalists, and printing the posters - fell to his tour manager, George Dolby, who was savvy enough to anticipate the challenge ahead and consult the master of promotion, P. T. Barnum, to pick up some handy pointers. In the end, word of mouth proved the best promotional strategy. Dickens had acquired millions of fans over some thirty years, and he'd to fight off the autograph-hunters and stalkers in every new city. Dolby's job wasn't drumming up business, it was extracting maximum profit from every leg of the tour.[48] He turned out to be a natural and took his cut in return; a cool £2,888. It proved a most harmonious relationship.

Dickens wasn't the only celebrity to lean on practically minded support staff. Dolby followed up his Dickens gig by becoming Mark Twain's tour manager, but elsewhere there was an array of associated professionals - managers, publicity agents, bookers, promoters – to keep the show on the road, or drum up excitement before a celebrity waltzed into town in their finest shoes. One of the earliest celebrities to hire a tour manager was Franz Liszt, whose pan-European stardom was placed in the capable hands of Gaetano Belloni in 1841.

Belloni was in charge of bookings and finances, but he joined Liszt on the long slogs between tour dates, frequently sitting side by side with the fleet-fingered pianist while Liszt's bespoke car-riage – bought for 2,000 francs in 1840 – bounced along the roads, traversing rain and snow, and then rolled elegantly into the sophis-ticated cities of Europe. A luxurious carriage assured comfort and safety, but it also sprinkled Liszt in yet more shimmering glamour, allowing Belloni to make a meal of their arrivals by leaping out and opening Liszt's door with razzle-dazzle flair. It was a performative ritual akin to a modern bodyguard opening a limo door, or usher-ing a celebrity from their private jet.[49] Just as Clara the Rhino had been escorted by swordsmen, it turned Liszt's arrival into a public spectacle.

In the early 1900s, becoming a press agent became a lucrative career, as theatre and then cinema established themselves as nationwide industries. Perhaps surprisingly, it wasn't limited to middle-class dudes, and some of America's best-known theat-rical agents were female journalists who shimmied across from news reporting into the entertainment biz: Anna Marble became responsible for filling the New York Hippodrome's 5,200 seats, while Nellie Revell worked with many of the biggest Broadway and circus impresarios.[50] Rather than hidden operatives, weaving their manipulative magic from the murky shadows, Marble and Revell were often themselves discussed in newspapers or drawn in cartoons, and so acquired their own public reputations that needed managing. Revell even became known as 'the world's most famous invalid' after a debilitating spinal injury forced her to write her *Variety* magazine column from a hospital bed.

The circus required a lot of promotion, particularly when it travelled to a list of towns that had to be targeted separately. Buffalo

Bill worked hand in glove with his manager, Nate Salsbury, who organised the Wild West Show's scheduling and finances, but later in the century they also hired P. T. Barnum's protégé, James Bailey, who specialised in the logistics of moving massive circuses. The other vital cog in the machine was the press agent, Major Burke, whose job it was to think up publicity stunts (a picnic for local orphans!), invite celebrity guests (Queen Victoria!), and woo local journalists with the promise of spectacular entertainment for their readers (Horses! Guns! Buffalo!).[51]

We began this chapter with sporting celebrity, so allow me to mention one of the earliest, and most influential, sports agents – Christy Walsh. Having smuggled his way into Babe Ruth's hotel in 1921, disguised as a beer delivery boy (or maybe it was ice cubes; the stories come in a variety of flavours), Walsh propositioned the baseball superstar with a deal. Asked how much Ruth earned to write in the papers, the slugger said $5. Walsh promised to make it $500. They drank a beer to celebrate. Walsh soon boosted Ruth's brand profitability by hiring ghostwriters to produce articles in Ruth's name. In fact, Walsh invented the term *ghostwriter*.[52] These same scribes could also be relied upon to write positive praise in the papers, making sure to bury any potential scandals beneath tactical puffery.

With their assistance, Walsh set about mythologising Babe Ruth in the press, including setting up a bogus scientific investigation into why baseball's Most Valuable Player was physiologically superior to normal humans. But he also spotted how woeful Ruth was with money, and – noticing the vulture of career-ending injury swooping overhead – became determined to protect his client. Walsh signed Ruth up to pensions, annuities, moneymaking appearances, and tours, and also fined him $33,000 for financial carelessness, with the money going into an untouchable savings account. Indeed, the signing of the 'fine' cheque was published in the papers, as proof of Ruth's newfound fiscal responsibility – yes, even a rainy-day pension fund was turned into a photo op by this master of media manipulation.[53] Christy Walsh was more than an agent - he ran Ruth's life, later joking: 'I did everything but sleep with him.'[54] And it worked.[55]

In 1927, the *New York Tribune* declared: 'If there were any way of appraising the drawing power of the Babe I think that he would be shown to be the greatest moneymaker as an entertainer for all time.' It was an exaggeration, but a telling one. Babe Ruth was perhaps the first modern sports star to match the celebrity status of movie stars. Indeed, dubious reports claimed his life insurance policy was $5m, compared to Chaplin's $3m.[56] His involvement with a dynamic and far-sighted manager saw him scoop up $73,247 in 1927 from being a celebrity, while his generous baseball wages added a further $70,000. All in, 1927 hauled in the equivalent of $10m in modern money. And some of that dough came from product endorsement, with the *Wall Street Journal* declaring: 'He scores homers by allowing his name to be printed on boys' underwear, caps and shoes . . . He gathers in royalties from manufacturers of all kinds of soft drinks and holiday souvenirs.' There were also chocolate bars, notebooks, and cigarettes. Not bad for a guy who'd been getting $5 per article.[57]

Babe Ruth had been transformed from athlete into commercial brand, and corporations rushed to license his name for their products. I'll admit Babe Ruth underpants wasn't quite what I expected, but why not? He's sometimes been claimed as the first sports star to have done this commercial deal, but that's to forget England's own bat-wielding demigod.

I endorse this message

In 1891, the world's most famous cricketer - indeed, some might claim the world's most famous sporting celebrity - arrived in Adelaide. W. G. Grace had toured Australia before, in 1873-4, but it hadn't been a flawless visit; he'd ruffled feathers by shunning local media, and by ditching his professional teammates while he dined with the gentlemen amateurs and his new wife. But eighteen years on - now a much heftier, squidgier, boozier superstar - he was still one of the finest batsmen anywhere, even if his days of elite sprinting were now a wheezy impossibility. Plus, his fame was unrivalled. The tour was a risk, his fitness was in doubt, but there was no way he wasn't getting on that boat.

As the ship docked, crowds of gasping onlookers rushed aboard to shake him by the hand; they were drawn to his magnificent, silver-flecked beard that didn't so much quilt his face as hang off his ears and swing beneath his neck like a sloth dangling from a tree. Indeed, later he would be nicknamed 'the Beard', long before Steven Spielberg nabbed this hirsute honorific, and Grace's face fuzz was so iconic that fans would rush anyone who looked a bit like him, including a chap called Henry Warren who, many years later, stepped off a train and was immediately quizzed about cricketing statistics by a keen photographer. Grace saw the funny side, and gave Warren a signed photo.[58]

On that tour, Grace also became an ambassador for Goodfellow's Coca Water, a medicinal stimulant marketed as combating fever, alcoholic tremors, and vomiting.[59] Grace was secretly a big drinker who'd somehow been claimed as a teetotal champion by the temperance movement, so there was a dubious irony to this choice of product. But Goodfellow's were presumably delighted to have him aboard. He'd already been the face of a short-lived outdoor game called Stapleton!, which was killed by the rise of lawn tennis. In 1888, he'd more wisely taken up a role at W. H. Cook & Company, which was developing a 'Magic Bat' to sell to cricket-mad wannabes across the land. This was the perfect gig for him; the earliest example I've encountered of an athlete flogging sports equipment to a public willing to be seduced into thinking athletic glory is theirs for the taking if they just buy the right stuff.* The company could've made a fortune, but two years later, before the Magic Bat was even released, Grace cheerfully endorsed a rival company which sold a bat with an inbuilt spring for better balance.

---

* I own Adidas football boots named after Lionel Messi, and I'm 100 per cent sure it makes me a better footballer. Nobody on my team agrees.

As business geniuses go, I'm not sure W. G. Grace would've made it to week two of *The Apprentice*.

In 1895, having obviously enjoyed his medicinal drinks promotion, he crossed into the food industry and, almost inexplicably, became the face of Colman's mustard. As his biographer Richard Tomlinson points out,[60] there's no evidence he got paid for this. His problems with money, or keeping it, were considerable, so maybe he just forgot to ask, but it's also possible he squirrelled it away and we've just not found the receipt. W. G. Grace was very aware of his market value; he'd negotiated huge sums to tour overseas. Even if the finances are hazy, there's no doubting the power of the Colman's campaign. His reputation as the tall, broad, bushy-bearded goliath of cricket made him a brilliant image to stick on their posters. Mustard is a strong flavour, and so was Grace. He batted proudly on their tins and on their vibrant billboards with the tagline 'Colman's Mustard Heads the Field'.

The face of . . .

One final advertising deal to note: in 1902, Grace posed for photos with his son while playing Cricket, a Table Game, which was essentially Subbuteo for people who prefer sport to be played in cream-coloured pyjamas. It looks quite fun, and was very much on brand for him, but it flopped. Even one of Britain's foremost celebrities couldn't guarantee the success of a retail product. This brings us to an obvious question. Does celebrity advertising work? In recent decades, research by academics and corporate market-eers has consistently proven just how effective it can be. We're fascinated by famous people: we recognise them, trust them, fancy them, and aspire to be them. Their recommendations mean more, their glamour projects a resplendent glow onto whatever shiny gubbins they tell us to buy. They influence us.

So what's the secret to a successful marketing campaign involving a celeb?[61] Early research in the mid-twentieth century studied trustfulness and likeability, but - noticing how some endorsement campaigns were disasters, despite using well-liked stars – Grant McCracken argued for a 'Meaning Transfer' model[62] that suggested advertising works best when the meaning of the celebrity's brand fits with the product. Athletes selling car insurance makes less sense than athletes selling sports drinks; there needs to be a reason for them to be there. The best campaigns feel obvious, but plenty of ads ignore this advice, hoping we'll be wowed by positive associations with the tenuously connected star.*

It's worth mentioning too that, as well as transferring their celebrity allure to a product, the celeb can also transfer negative associations. When a beloved star has a catastrophic scandal, the spores of this insidious notoriety transfer onto the products they endorse, and corporations have to disinfect themselves to stop the black mould growing all over them. Celebrity giveth and celebrity taketh away.

Sponsored content(ment)

If celebrity is 300 years old, when did this formal coupling of capitalism and fame begin? Well, it's one of the defining features of *celebrity*, so the answer is obviously 'Immediately!' In the mid-1700s, one of London's leading actresses, Hannah Pritchard, ran her own clothing warehouse from Tavistock Street; she advertised the fashions by wearing them on stage, making her one of history's earliest celebs to launch their own clothing line.[63] We also see it in subtle places, such as when Casanova reported that, for three strange weeks, fashionable Parisians became weirdly obsessed with only buying their tobacco from a shop called La Civette because a glamorous duchess had been spotted shopping there.[64] She transferred her fame to the product, making their ordinary tobacco – the like of which was available in numerous shops – somehow more desirable because of its association with her.

---

* My all-time favourite head-scratcher was Mikhail Gorbachev advertising Pizza Hut!

In the mid-to-late nineteenth century, the most entrepreneurial celebrities began to use their fame to launch their own personal businesses. Mark Twain, who'd had notable money worries in the 1890s, trademarked his own branded whisky and tobacco in 1907;[65] Britain's favourite French chef, Alexis Soyer, sold personalised cookery books, utensils, and stoves in the 1840s-50s;[66] the bodybuilding sensation Eugen Sandow launched his own empire of fitness schools, magazine publications, medicinal ointments, therapeutic corsets, and a cocoa-flavoured health drink.[67] These were celebs whose established public profile allowed them to not just license their name to a commercial outfit, but actually to turn themselves into captains of industry. Or, at least, petty officers of industry. The risks, however, were considerable, and the product's success was contingent on their continued good name. Sandow's business empire imploded, not least because he was a German immigrant during the First World War, when that sort of thing was somewhat awkward. He should've changed his name to Windsor - it worked for the royal family.

The much more common route for celebrities in the late 1800s was sponsorship deals. Celebrities had always been used to sell other people's products, but by the end of the century the stars were actually starting to give permission. One of the earliest pioneers was, of course, P. T. Barnum: 'We had Jenny Lind gloves, Jenny Lind bonnets, Jenny Lind riding hats, Jenny Lind shawls, mantillas, robes, chairs, sofas, pianos - in fact, every thing was Jenny Lind!'[68] Among the biggest sellers were paper dolls crafted in her image, plus cigars and tobacco. Later in the century, Sarah Bernhardt did face cream, bicycles, and tea;[69] Anna Held licensed her name to petticoats;[70] the British actress Lillie Langtry endorsed Pears Soap, as did the hugely popular American preacher Henry Ward Beecher, whose advert cunningly used the phrase 'cleanliness is next to godliness',[71] which, in fairness, is a top-notch campaign slogan when you've hired America's most famously religious man.

By the early twentieth century, the British comedy superstar Dan Leno, who was king of the music hall, appeared on the box of G. P. Tea, and had his face carved into the spout of a collectible teapot;[72] the bob-haired Hollywood flapper Louise Brooks, who'd fought to keep her nudes from being published, became the face of Lux toilet soap and diamond solitaire engagement rings;[73] the baffling, bestselling modernist Gertrude Stein appeared in car adverts for Ford and was asked to promote cigarettes;[74] and Brenda Frazier - the tragic, high-society debutante - did soap and Studebaker cars, and accidentally pre-empted Homer Simpson by becoming the face of doughnuts when she was photographed dunking one.[75]

By the time Hollywood muscled its way in to become the biggest pop culture factory, celebrities were already long established as endorsers. Some products were everyday items stocked next to their cheaper rivals; adding the lustre of a celebrity face helped signal the excellence of a product in a sea of interchangeable others, just as Casanova's duchess had done with tobacco. You'll note from the above list that celebs were flogging soap, cigarettes, flour, tea, cosmetics, clothes - all frequent purchases for women, who were assumed to run the family household and were more likely to read celebrity magazines. So there was good logic in harnessing a star who appealed to this demographic. But these products were stuff people were buying anyway.

By contrast, some campaigns pushed a more aspirational message. Louise Brooks and Gertrude Stein were the face of once-in-a-lifetime luxury purchases: engagement rings and cars. This more prestigious line of advertising went beyond mere product sales. It also emulated the strategy of Hollywood PR departments, which worked in league with fan magazines to create an aspirational culture of celebrity glamour. This campaign marketed the movies themselves - encouraging punters to buy tickets to what looked like exciting stories starring beautiful people - but also charmed the public into following celebrity fashions. The products weren't the only thing on sale; so too was a lifestyle.

We see this in the vast archival trove of the UK Mass-Observation project conducted in the 1930s and 1940s by volunteers who answered questionnaires about their ordinary lives.

Using this source, Carol Dyhouse[76] has shown how the desire to be glamorous surged up the list of British women's priorities in the interwar years, and remained high even while Hitler's bombs fell around them. Inspired by movie stars, particularly mysterious American beauties, young British women rushed to buy lipsticks, hair-curling products, frocks, satin jammies, Joan Crawford-esque turbans and hats, and even fur coats and stoles. They did their hair like Ginger Rogers, Louise Brooks, and Lana Turner; they bought film magazines stuffed with adverts for clothes they'd seen in the latest movies, then went out to buy them in shops or get hold of the sewing patterns to make their own.

These young women reported being frustrated at their lack-lustre lives of near poverty and humdrum work; they longed for adventure, and pursued the aesthetic of screen sirens as a way to change how they felt about themselves. Swimming costumes had been clumpy, knitted sacks that buried the lady's figure in what was essentially a woollen bin bag, but the coming of stretchy Lastex in the 1930s meant young women could now swan around their local lido looking as if they were sunning themselves in Cannes; they also donned them in the growing number of beauty pageants. When war was declared in 1939, Mass-Observation tells us one Regent Street shop was flooded with 500 women trying to buy discounted furs and sables. Hitler's Luftwaffe lurked with malice, gas masks were hung around necks, rationing books advised the harshest of austerity, but looking a million dollars was still on some people's minds.

Back in the USA, Rita Hayworth wrote an article in 1946 asking her fans to join her at the dressing table. Charmingly, the subeditor even used glamour as a pun-tastic verb, swapping it with 'clamour' to create the headline: 'Every Woman Should Glamour for Attention'. Of course, clamour suggests a desperate scramble to be noticed, whereas traditional glamour was meant to be restrained, unruffled, unknowable beauty. Hayworth's contradiction was intentional, however. She said glamour was for all and it was a woman's duty to enthusiastically embrace it.[77]

We might think inviting a million copycats would rob Hollywood glamour of its rare power, but instead it strengthened the bond between fan and celebrity. Attainable glamour didn't make the actresses any less beautiful, but established them as trendsetters.[78] Stars became fashion gurus, proxies for cool older sisters or influential friends. Much like Eugen Sandow, who offered the chance to develop muscles like his own, the gorgeous Hollywood celebrities openly shared their secrets to looking great, inviting the ordinary public to clamber up the ladder and join them in their elevated echelon of hotness.

All considered, then, most celebrities profited from their fame, raking in cash from ticket sales, benefit performances, and sundry other income streams. But it was perhaps only in the last 150 years that they happily entered into ambassadorial arrangements, turning themselves into Trojan horses that snuck brand loyalty beyond our defences and into our gullible brains. Corporations exploit our celebrity fascination to lure us into buying breakfast cereal and laundry detergent, and the stars are handsomely rewarded for their service. But it wasn't so long ago that the stars were also themselves exploited. From the moment celebrity emerged in the first decade of the 1700s, famous people were used to sell all sorts of tat, for which they received no fee and gave no permission.

A lot has changed since then, not least thanks to modern copyright laws that defend their brand image, but twenty-first-century celebrity remains a hugely elaborate capitalist system in which big stars earn millions while the corporations rake in billions. It's certainly nice work if you can get it, but it's a parasitic system; celebs are whirring cogs in a much bigger machine. And that machine exists because of us. Celebrity capitalism functions because we're into it in a big way. Our passion is converted into hard cash. But the dynamic between stars and their fans isn't always harmonious, as the next chapter will reveal . . .

Chapter 8: The Fandom Menace?

Where everybody knows your name

There's a recurring trope in Hollywood's *Godzilla* movies whereby the gargantuan beast emerges from the sea and stomps into New York City, and everything goes to hell. People scream, journalists scramble to point their cameras, and everywhere the mighty lizard treads becomes the scene of noise, destruction, and chaos. This, of course, is movie fantasy. In reality, New Yorkers would probably be too busy yelling at taxi drivers to notice a giant lizard. But it's an image I enjoy, because when history's biggest international celebrities docked at New York's harbour, ready to launch into lucrative American tours, they too were met by battalions of scrambling photographers, and everywhere they stomped became a theatre of chaotic hubbub. The difference, of course, was people were running towards them, rather than away.

Dickens, Lind, Wilde, and Bernhardt were four such transatlantic titans of the 1800s, and there were plenty more.* However, I'd like to return to an old favourite. In 1934, New York played host to a new force of nature: not a terrifying, irradiated sea monster with flaming breath, but Gertrude Stein. After thirty years of Parisian living, and years of mockery, she was hailed as a literary phenomenon. And that meant something bizarre happened: everyone

---

* Alas, keeping this book svelte meant chopping out the story of the Austrian ballerina Fanny Elssler, who inspired *Elsslermania* in 1841 when she toured the USA, in a pre-Barnum coup orchestrated by the wonderfully named Chevalier Henry Wikoff. Elssler earned $1,000 per night, and even Congress was closed early when she visited Washington DC, so politicians could go and watch her perform.

recognised her. To us, this is hardly shocking; stars get recognised all the time. But the sensation of being known to strangers is itself intensely strange, and can have profound psychological effects. Stein made quite the impression, but New Yorkers also left quite the impression on her.

As we learned in Chapter 1, Gertrude Stein had already been a memorable name for decades, but now she became a notable face. Taxi drivers waved her across busy roads, fruit sellers offered up freebies, passers-by stopped to greet her, waiters asked for her autograph, shopgirls scurried across to say: 'How d'you do, Miss Stein?' She was incredibly famous, which made it all the funnier when, on the way up to meet her big-time US publisher, the only person not to recognise her was the elevator operator, who prodded the button for the employment agency on the third floor.[1] He'd thought Gertrude and her lover, Alice, were a pair of canteen cooks in need of a catering job, rather than former drinking buddies with Picasso.

Stein was pleasantly taken aback by it all: 'never could I have imagined the friendly, personal, simple, direct, considerate contact that I have with all of them. They all seem to know me and they all speak to me and I who am easily frightened by anything unexpected find the spontaneous, considerate contact with all and any New Yorker touching and pleasing and I am deeply moved and awfully happy about it.' But celebrity is an alienating experience, even more so when it happens with whiplash suddenness. When her name went up in lights on the Times Building, she felt an eerie jolt of uncertainty: 'Anybody saying how do you do to you and knowing your name may be upsetting but on the whole it is natural enough but to suddenly see your name is always upsetting. Of course it has happened to me pretty often and I like it to happen just as often but always it does give me a little shock of recognition and non-recognition.'

Stein was also perturbed by watching herself back on a big screen, having been filmed narrating her book for a newsreel organisation: 'when I saw myself . . . moving around and talking I did not like it particularly the talking, it gave me a very funny feeling and I did not like that funny feeling'.[2] Many of us recoil in confusion at hearing our voice played back - it sounds boomier inside our own echoey skulls - and, until the invention of camcorders and camera phones, very few of us ever saw ourselves the way others see us. It's no wonder Stein was perturbed. But perhaps that funny feeling didn't just come from the novelty of self-observation, but also from knowing she was public property. She belonged to strangers, though she was no stranger to them. They all knew her, because celebrity is an oddly lopsided dynamic. In this chapter, we'll race through some of the reasons behind why this happens, the power of fandom, and the occasionally alarming consequences when being famous makes a celebrity vulnerable to intrusive, or even dangerous, attention.

Intimate strangers

Like the proverbial tree toppling in the forest, *celebrity* needs an audience if it's to make a sound. A person can't be famous without a public who knows who they are. The theorist Chris Rojek suggests: 'celebrity = impact on public consciousness', which is a cheerfully succinct phrase for something so complex and extraordinary,[3] because becoming a star - or what Chaucer beautifully called being *stellified* - also effects change in the world. It creates an imbalanced relationship in which the public recognises the celebrity, and a committed fan can ferret around in a huge treasure chest of mental trivia - they know the celebrity's name, their favourite books, their past lovers, what tattoos they have, what physical and mental health issues they might have endured, and much more - but the celebrity knows literally nothing of the fan. Gertrude Stein was welcomed by millions who cheered her as if she was their kindly old aunt. But Stein couldn't put a name to any of the smiling faces.

This imbalance is known as a *parasocial relationship*.[4] It's the cognitive engine that, at its mildest, has us muttering: 'Hey, you look kinda familiar' to awkwardly shifting celebrities queuing in supermarkets. When the power is at its lowest setting, we're aware we know this person, but can't work out how: did we go to school with them? Did they buy a used car from us? Are they our friend's brother who we've seen in a Facebook photo album? However, at the most intense end of the spectrum, when the dial gets turned all the way up, we instead get parasocial adoration; this results in *erotomania*, otherwise known as believing our favourite popstar is cosmically destined to fall in love with us, wrote this ballad just for us, and 'ONE DAY WE'LL BE TOGETHER FOR EVER!!!!'

Such delusions of intimacy can occasionally graduate from innocent obsession to full-blown stalking. It's normal to adorn a bedroom with a celebrity's image; it's normal to have sexual fantasies about them; it's not normal to hide beneath their floorboards, and weave dolls from the pubes fished out of their bathroom plughole. Thankfully, despite the common trope of 'stalker fans', such extreme fandom is very rare. The vast majority of fans are not pathologically unwell, and are just enthusiasts who really like stuff. But to show the full gamut of celebrity experiences, I'll being sharing a few horror stories in this chapter that reveal the darker edges of obsessive fascination.

Celebrity parasocial dynamics* aren't only fuelled by molten fervour. Even when encountering a celeb for whom we're barely lukewarm, we may still find ourselves behaving oddly. Sometimes a person's fame perches on their shoulder like a brightly coloured parrot, squawking at us indecipherably until ordinary conversation becomes impossible. They seem famous, they act famous, so we freak out when we encounter them because, well, 'I don't know who this is, but they're probably important!' I've seen this happen when celebs were asked for a selfie by people who didn't even know who they were, simply because they saw other people do it. Celebrity is an elevated status, so perhaps these people just wanted

---

* I want to call it *parasocialism* but that sounds too much like Lenin jumping out of a plane.

to get close to privilege, to see what it feels like? But I suspect it's also a desire not to miss out. Meeting celebrities isn't something most of us do very often, so maybe it's like trying a weird new drink on holiday; they do it because when else would they get the chance?

Of course, when we *do* recognise a celebrity, that's when the hyperventilating might kick in, or going rigidly silent like a possum playing dead. The fact that celebrity can make us act so weirdly has inevitably led scholars to ponder its hidden motors. Why are humans so susceptible to its charms? Given *charisma*'s divine origins (if you recall, it meant grace gifted by God), some sociologists have wondered if celebrity is a glitzy substitute for religion, with glamorous stars role-playing as avatars for our primal instincts to worship stuff.[5] The pioneering French sociologist Emile Durkheim[6] argued in 1912 that sacred totems play a vital function in uniting individuals into strong communities through *communal effervescence*; it's what Chris Rojek neatly sums up as 'a state of popular excitement, frenzy, even ecstasy'.[7] This sounds like either a shamanic ritual or a drug-addled orgy, but the point is that maybe fans treat celebs as sacred totems, and so they collect relics - such as posters, autographs, concert tickets, etc. - as powerful tokens of divine contact.

Personally, I'm not totally convinced by the religion theory, not least because the objects of fandom aren't mutually exclusive: we're allowed to be massively into both *Star Wars* AND *Star Trek*, or Beyoncé AND Rihanna, whereas it would take a *really* lenient, pan-faith council of bishops, imams, rabbis, gurus, and priests to let us squeeze multiple faiths into a Choose-Your-Own-Adventure religion. Faith in the divine is supposed to be singular, ideologically resilient, and morally instructive; it's a lifelong commitment to a rule-based life. But celebrity obsession is often short-lived, messily contradictory, and - though celebrity culture helps us ask questions about ethical boundaries - not always coherent. Does celebrity even have a holy book? Maybe *Rolling Stone* magazine? Chris Hemsworth's Insta page? What would the commandments be: 'Thou Shalt Not Covet Kim Kardashian's Ass? Or Take My Name in Vanity Fair'?

Those are the reasons to be sceptical.[8] But there are also some clear parallels between religion and fandom: both help us make sense of the world, and bring individuals together in ecstatic communion. Scholars have noted that new fans talk of being 'converted' to their fandom, which hopefully alludes to a consensual baptism rather than a torturous Spanish Inquisition. Fandom is both a private practice (like prayer) and an assembled congregation performing rituals of observance (such as quoting lyrics or dialogue on fan websites). Both fans and theologians also expend great energy decoding ambiguous texts, with fans scouring celebrity social media looking for hints of shady feuds and secret love affairs, while exegetical scholars devote years to interpreting nuanced meaning in sacred chapter and verse.

We may also see a Christ-like trope of redemptive reincarnation in the way shamed celebs check themselves into rehab, write a blog post about their 'personal growth', give £50k to charity, and then rise anew, absolved of their sins. Sinning and atonement are the basis of Catholic confession, yet there seems to be a similar resetting ritual for controversial stars who get sacrificed – or 'cancelled' in internet slang – only to rise from the dead six months later with a new haircut.

So the religion thing isn't miles off, is it? But I think celebrity feels like religiosity because our culture is so deeply infused with the legacy of organised religions; there are so many pre-worn grooves into which fame's narrative needle smoothly slides. Our fascination with redemption and rebirth might simply be inherited cultural tropes rather than instinctual necessity to worship stuff hardwired into our biology. Or maybe it's just impractical to not allow celebrities back into our good books, because few stars can be interesting without being a bit dangerous. If we want to devour the drama, we have to accept they'll cross the line. Redemption is a necessary process for those whose primary purpose is entertaining transgression.

Of course, if you like your biology, and prefer your Big Theory-wielders to wear white lab coats and namecheck Darwin, you might enjoy the observations of primatologists that beta male macaques obsessively watch the behaviour of alpha males; they'll even trade delicious food for a better chance to observe them.[9] This has caused speculation that maybe we're just furless chimps, and our brains actually chug away on archaic software that makes us gawp at celebrities out of some instinctual urge to mirror our better-looking superiors. Evolutionary anthropologists, like Robin Dunbar, have argued that gossiping is how humans groom each other; when we chat about celebrities, we're basically just picking lice from our pal's fur. Such grooming apparently fosters trust between individuals and supports complex group hierarchies.[10] But are humans really just hairless, upright, shit-flinging, masturbatory apes? Actually, don't answer that . . .*

Let's assume Dunbar is correct and that humans take intense fascination in others, so as to suss out where we lie in the pecking order. Chimps watch dominant leaders whom they know personally; our early Stone Age ancestors might've curtain-twitched on their neighbours, but presumably none of them gave a hoot about those they'd never meet? Our brains are thus wired for in-group interactions of only a few hundred individuals, but we've been duped by the invention of printing, paintings, photography, film, television, the internet, etc. into thinking our massively complex society is much dinkier than it is.

Broadcasting technology simulates proximity. Our in-group is no longer 150 people sat around a campfire, it's tens of millions strong. But perhaps that gossiping instinct keeps trundling on, regardless, so we still natter about the scandalous and praiseworthy deeds of those we assume to be part of our tribe, even though they're thousands of miles away, and shop at much fancier places than us. Perhaps celebrities are foreigners who feel like neighbours?

The stuff that makes celebrities so exciting is what we talked

---

* In certain corners of Twitter, they are exactly this . . .

about in Chapter 3 - they're sexy, beautiful, talented, funny, annoying, and thrilling, and we'll pay cash to follow their entertaining high jinks - but I don't think we *worship* them. Instead, I think we just get used to watching them. They're not our friends; they're more like the cool kids two years ahead of us in high school, the ones having debauched parties, and exciting sex lives, while generally seeming to be impossibly cool, while we're still gangly, acne-ridden dweebs. The parasocial dynamic is an illusion of 'public intimacy' with those we can watch but not touch.[11] So, when we bump into a celebrity in a supermarket, we can be confused by their being out of context; we usually study them from afar, but suddenly we're within licking distance!*

If we're a big fan, that's when a secondary instinct kicks in: 'OH MY GOD! I LOVE THIS PERSON WITH THE INTENSITY OF A THOUSAND BURNING SUNS! I MUST TELL THEM OF MY LOVE!' Now comes the difficult challenge of playing it cool, and not embarrassing ourselves in the canned-foods aisle. The truth is that we're probably more likely to keep our emotions in check for a one-to-one interaction - you'd think getting up close would be more intense, but strangely it's when fans congregate together, to bask in celebrity adoration from a distance, that people lose their minds. That's when you get celebrity *mania*.

Fandemonium

On 1 December 1804, just a few hours before Napoleon Bonaparte crowned himself Emperor of France, the child prodigy Master Betty made his London stage debut. His enormous success in Ireland, Scotland, and northern England had laid the groundwork for a frenzied response, and things quickly turned ugly. The crowd was so vast, a 'strong detachment of guards' had to be drafted in to defend the theatre's box office, while extra security brusquely patrolled the inside.

---

* Please don't ever lick a celebrity, unless they ask you to. But, even then, don't.

On the second night, things got worse. Seething mobs surged to buy tickets; when these sold out, they smashed windows and ripped doors from their hinges. Inside the auditorium, a dispute over a private box resulted in two men drawing loaded pistols. Below them, in the stalls, people screamed and shoved in the desperate scramble for seats. Others had snuck in the night before and slept in prime position; they'd brought clubs with which to attack anyone trying to shift them. Meanwhile, outside, hundreds of ticketless fans rammed their bodies into the theatre, pulverising staircase banisters into splintered shards. Lord Byron reported that attending a Betty performance put him 'at the hazard of my life'.

You'd think the staircase snapping, and people waving guns around, would've been grounds for cancellation, but I guess that would've only incited the mob to greater violence. So Betty played on. By the end, thirty unconscious people had been carried out, either due to his theatrical brilliance or, more likely, because they were crushed against hysterical strangers and ran out of oxygen.* As Jeffrey Kahan puts it: '"Popular" does not begin to capture the fever Betty inspired. Embraced by royalty, caressed by dukes and duchesses, feted by poets, flattered by wits, panegyrized by painters and sculptors, wafted to morning rehearsals in coroneted carriages, attended by powdered lackeys, stuck up in printshop windows, coined into medallions, sliced into luncheon meats, assailed by admiring crowds, the collective phenomenon was so unfamiliar, unusual and irrational that British society had to create a new word for it – Bettymania.'[12]

As we know from Chapter 1, the Betty bubble soon popped. His fame was tied to Napoleon's coronation and the threat of French invasion, but also to his temporary youth. But the idea of celebrity mania wasn't new – there'd already been *Siddonsmania* – and it would return time and again. We've often been told that it was The Beatles or Elvis who'd first inspired such screaming fandemonium,

---

* I've been in heavy-metal mosh pits where it's a disappointing evening if you don't get a boot in the face, but this sounds way more intense.

but that's simply not true. In the 1840s, when Franz Liszt merely entered a busy room, it seemed, according to Hans Christian Andersen, 'as if an electric shock passed through it'.[13] As well as astonishing crowds with his incredible virtuosity, the sharp-featured, long-haired Liszt became a tantalising fantasy, embarking on affairs with society beauties, and working his way through a conveyor belt of starstruck ladies who queued outside his room in disguise.

In Berlin, a doctor called Adalbert Cohnfeld reported Liszt's fans treating the pianist with almost ecstatic reverence. They begged to kiss his hand, wore brooches and gloves branded with his image, poured the cold dregs of his half-slurped tea into their perfume bottles, and snatched up his abandoned cigar butts, retching from the heady dose of stale tobacco as they sucked what his sumptuous lips had sucked. The poet Heinrich Heine was baffled: 'how powerful, how shattering was his mere physical appearance'. He spotted noble ladies either passing out from delirium or squabbling over who got to take home his used handkerchief. Bewildered, Heine concluded Lisztomania was too outrageous to be real; it was surely a PR hoax orchestrated by some cunning manager?[14] Liszt was certainly a showman, but Heine was being naïve.

During their US tours, Jenny Lind, Charles Dickens,[15] and Oscar Wilde were also hounded by admirers chasing them from train, to hotel, to theatre, and back again. Some 20,000 people lined the streets to welcome Lind, and fights broke out among her fans over who would get her half-eaten peach or the shawl she dropped.[16] As for Wilde, he not only experienced being at the centre of the whirlwind, but got to witness someone else's storm. Upon arriving in Missouri, on 19 April 1882, Wilde wrote to a friend:

> outside my window about a quarter of a mile to the west there stands a little yellow house, with a green paling, and a crowd of people pulling it all down. It is the house of the great train-robber and murderer, Jesse James, who was shot by his pal last week, and the people are relic hunters . . . They sold his dust-bin and foot-scraper yesterday by public auction, his

door-knocker is to be offered for sale this afternoon, the reserve price being about the income of an English bishop . . .
his favourite chromo-lithograph was disposed of at a price
which in Europe only an authentic Titian can command.

Jesse James was a glamorous Wild West villain treated like a saint;
his ordinary stuff became 'relics' that acquired both symbolic
power and ludicrous monetary value, simply through association
with his dangerous brand. It was an irrational economy of celebrity
hyperinflation. His was a posthumous mania.[17] Of course, death
does powerful things to a celebrity, not least because the resource
becomes scarce - a dead celebrity produces no new entertainment,
so what they've already produced gains added value through scar-
city.[18] But there's also the emotional shock to consider, and this can
be easily exploited by those looking to make useful headlines.

In 1910, the movie actress Florence Lawrence was tragically killed
in a road accident. She'd been previously known as the 'Biograph
Girl', and then the 'IMP Girl' - in honour of the film studios who'd
hired her - but Lawrence was the first major star to be identified
after hundreds of fans had written begging letters to the studio,
demanding to know her name.* Her sudden death was understandably newsworthy, therefore, and must have been quite the shock
to her admirers. The biggest shock, of course, was for Florence
Lawrence, who had to read about her own death in the newspaper.† Historians now believe reports of her being run over were all
a big PR hoax orchestrated by her devious manager, Carl Laemmle,
who forcefully blamed rival studios for the humbug, before handily announcing Lawrence's miraculous revival just in time for the
release of her next movie. What a fortuitous coincidence!

---

* Early film stars were anonymous either because that gave the studio more
leverage in paying lower fees, or because theatre actors were embarrassed to be
slumming it in Hollywood and didn't want their names being associated with
the new lowbrow art form.

† This was quite common. Franz Liszt, Vesta Tilley, and Mark Twain all had the
odd experience of reading their own wrongly published obituaries.

Lawrence's fans went bananas. She was dispatched to St Louis to capitalise on the adoration, where she and another actor, King Baggot, were mobbed at Union Station by a heaving crowd that ripped the buttons from her dress. The crush was so intense, she had to be escorted out for her own safety, and was haunted by post-traumatic stress for years.[19] When death did come for her, aged just fifty-two, it found a broken, illness-ravaged woman who hadn't had a leading role for years. Her lonely suicide wasn't met with great media attention, and certainly no mania. Florence Lawrence died twice, but the public only cared about the first time.

Dead famous

Perhaps the most iconic Hollywood death of the silent era was that of the tango-dancing screen star Rudolph Valentino, the Italian heart-throb with the succulent lips, sleepy eyes, slicked-back hair, and thick eyebrows. Having conquered the box office playing a seductive Arab hottie in *The Sheik*, Valentino was heralded as an erotic icon whose sex appeal burned like a blowtorch. At the premiere of *The Son of the Sheik* – yes, Hollywood was already churning out lazy sequels even in the 1920s – he too was accosted by thousands of devoted fans and had to battle his way out of Times Square to avoid being trampled to death.[20] This caused a huge stir. Since 1916, people had joked about a new disease called 'filmitis', the symptoms of which turned people into gibbering, movie-loving morons either obsessed with film stars or desperate to become one.[21] Valentino's admirers regularly shrieked, wept uncontrollably, and passed out from excitement. To cynics, this was proof that female fans were hysterical, gullible fools, and not to be encouraged. You can probably guess what happened when Valentino unexpectedly died.

In 1926, the heart-throb collapsed with severe stomach pain. Surgery on perforated ulcers was successful, but he developed gastric infection and was then double-teamed by a surprise attack of lung inflammation. The doctors knew Valentino was doomed, but he wasn't told of his death sentence. And neither was the media, nor his loyal fanbase. They were presumably waiting for him to leap out of bed, grab a passing nurse, tango his way out of the hospital, mount a nearby stallion, and gallop off to the nearest movie set. The hospital switchboard was flooded with 2,000 calls each hour from fans eager to pass on their good wishes.[22] But his body failed, and the red-hot screen idol turned cold. Valentino's shock death caused a seismic outpouring of Valentino mania. Some refused to believe he'd been felled by such mundane illnesses, alleging accidental poisoning by a dodgy baldness cure, or even murder by a jealous husband who'd found him in bed with his wife.

It's claimed at least 50,000 people descended on his funeral, and women allegedly tore at their clothes in grief-stricken distress. Two days later, in London, a young starlet called Peggy Scott drank a fatal dose of poison and left a suicide note: 'I am only a little butterfly made for sunshine and I cannot stand loneliness and shadow. With his death, my last bit of courage has flown.' Press reports claimed they'd been lovers, but she may have been a fantasist. Rumours of many suicides did the rounds, but researchers have only found two more plausible attempts: a nineteen-year-old, and a young mother.[23]

At the time, fan suicides were deemed an extremely shocking new watershed - if *filmitis* hadn't been bad enough, suddenly it could be a terminal diagnosis! In truth, heartbroken fans making the ultimate gesture was an ancient tradition. According to Pliny the Elder, when a Roman charioteer named Felix died, a fan hurled himself onto his hero's funeral pyre to join him, though others said he'd merely fainted from the eye-watering pong of ritual incense.[24] Both versions are tragic, though the latter feels like it has real potential as a public health warning: 'Remember, kids, don't inhale!'

In the 1770s, male readers of Johann von Goethe's proto-Romantic tragedy *The Sorrows of Young Werther* had also been rumoured to enact copycat, cosplay suicides by dressing as Werther then shooting themselves in the head, in emulation of how he resolves the novel's doomed love triangle. Copies of the book were said to have been found on bodies, or mentioned in suicide notes, but Goethe's modern biographers dismiss such rumours as viral hoaxes. There's no doubting, however, that both the fictional Werther and the German author who'd created him became celebrity sensations across Europe, and the novel became a dangerous instrument of moral panic.[25] In truth, modern evidence shows vulnerable people are very susceptible to 'suicide contagion', and descriptive reports of suicidal methods - whether fake or not - can lead to widespread emulation. They were right to be alarmed.

At Valentino's funeral, the cliché is that the 50,000-plus people screeching at his death were obsessive fans, but many were most likely rubberneckers drawn to a public spectacle. There comes a tipping point when celebrity drama exerts its own gravity, and casual observers get sucked in. These mourners weren't all diehard fans, but nor were they mild-mannered observers. As Samantha Barbas describes it:

> The street in front of the funeral home, remarked observers, looked like a battlefield. Fans pressed against the windows, hoping to get a glimpse of the coffin; in the process, the glass shattered, and several onlookers were injured. When the funeral parlor at last opened its doors to the public, the crowd surged. 'The mass pushed forward a foot at a time, even shoving the horses along the sidewalk, so great was the pressure from behind,' said The New York Times. 'When the throng got too close to the doors . . . the police charged, breaking it up, pushing it back to the corners.' By the end of the day, over 100 men and women were seriously hurt; several were taken to the hospital with bruises and broken limbs.[26]

While Werther's hardcore fans were often presumed to have been sad young men - the floppy-fringed emo kids of the 1770s - Hollywood's equivalents were often described as hysterical females. In fact, there were plenty of blokes there too. But it's true that women were playing a disproportionate role in pop culture fandom as the century rolled on. In 1944, the NYPD was once again mobilised to face down another riot from uncontrollable fans. This time, it wasn't a movie star causing the commotion - though Hollywood had already cast him in small roles - but a crooner. His name was Frank Sinatra, and teenage girls were obsessed.

Sinatra had first risen to fame in 1942, when his youthful good looks and smooth voice had provoked a sensational response. He was undoubtedly beautiful, but he also offered something magical in a time of crisis - Japanese planes had bombed Pearl Harbor only months before, and millions of American men were mobilising for war. Much like Master Betty's Napoleon-bashing allure, Sinatra shone bright as a beacon of eroticised joy to teens surrounded by anxious family members and the blaring honk of patriotic propaganda.

In fairness, nobody saw it coming, least of all Sinatra, who recalled walking on stage and being blown away by the noise: 'The sound that greeted me was absolutely deafening. It was a tremendous roar. Five thousand kids, stamping, yelling, screaming, applauding. I was scared stiff.'[27] Never mind Elvis, Sinatra fever virtually invented the idea of the teenager, revealing a new demographic who felt things intensely and were willing to pay for strongly emotive experiences. His fans were known as 'bobby-soxers', and they were nothing if not committed.

Initially, the biggest problem was the several hundred fans who refused to leave theatres after Sinatra's shows. He and his band would play multiple all-day sets, to a constantly changing audience, but the eager superfans refused to budge. They'd stubbornly relish five or six performances in a row before eventually collapsing from hunger, thirst, and exhaustion. Or security would grow impatient and chuck them out. But on Columbus Day 1944, Sinatra returned to New York's Paramount Theatre, the scene of his first triumph, and things escalated dramatically. Only 3,500 tickets were available, but 10,000 fans queued to buy them. A further 20,000 proudly swarmed Times Square, chanting: 'We want Frankie!' in a defiant, energetic surge of youthful confidence. It all got out of hand. Ticket booths were destroyed, windows smashed, and 200 cops struggled to maintain order as the girls pursued access to the heart-melting hunk they dubbed Frank 'Swoonatra'.[28] It became known as the 'Columbus Day Riot', but unlike most riots it wasn't driven by anger; it was powered by celebrity desire.

At exactly the same time, the first swoon-worthy megastar of Indian cinema, Ashok Kumar, had just scored a box office smash with 1943's *Kismet*. He'd already appeared in several films alongside Devika Rani, perhaps the most prominent actress of the 1930s, but India's film industry hadn't yet created true movie stars – it boasted renowned actors, like Rani and Fearless Nadia, but no gossip industry was rubbing its thighs in voyeuristic delight at actors' private lives. Actors were known for their roles but not their personal mistakes and misdeeds. When Rani and Kumar parted, it was Kumar who broke through on his own, playing India's first cinematic antihero: a petty criminal who changes his ways. *Kismet*'s controversial themes saw it get a savage mauling from uptight social commentators, but audiences loved it. It was a box office sensation. Kumar was catapulted to enormous, unprecedented public attention; he was surrounded in the streets and barricaded inside his hotel by hordes of eager fans. If he wanted to go anywhere, police batons had to be swung at the adoring mob.[29] Movie mania had reached India with a bang, and Ashok Kumar became its first true star.

Screamagers

Despite decades of research, we still don't know exactly why fans, particularly young women, scream for their beloved idols. One theory is they coalesce into 'expressive crowds' as a way to release pent-up frustrations in a male-dominated society.[30] We might also mention the seductive magic of group-think, mass hysteria, and the swelling energy of the roaring crowd, all of which are used to explain football fans smashing up foreign pubs and singing disgusting, dehumanising songs about their hated rivals, who return to being colleagues and friends come Monday morning. Emotionally investing in a celebrity or sports team can be like joining a tribe. Indeed, the word 'fan' – being an abbreviation of fanatic – was first applied to noisy baseball lovers in 1887.[31] En masse, the individual vanishes into the mob; the rituals of belonging pull the person deeper into the mindset of 'us', which inevitably means anyone challenging the group is othered as 'them'.

But can we go even simpler? Perhaps it just feels great to share in something, and see our own passion reflected back by those around us? Surrendering to the pounding rhythm of a shared heartbeat can be a thrilling, life-affirming sensation. Seeing my favourite bands live is always more powerful than listening to them on headphones, even if the audio quality in the venue sounds like a billion angry wasps buzzing in a jam-jar full of nails.* The psychological terminology may be modern, but mass fandom really isn't.

A gyrating Elvis was sex on legs, but the idea of eroticised, impassioned allegiance to a famed individual predates celebrity; it's there in the way Romans sexualised charioteers and gladiators. As Juvenal joked in his *Satires*: 'And what were the youthful charms that captivated Eppia? What did she see to allow herself to be called "gladiator fodder"? . . . a wounded arm gave promise of a discharge, and there were various deformities in his face: a scar caused by the helmet, a huge boil upon his nose, a nasty septic dribble always trickling from his eye. But he was a gladiator! It is this that transforms these fellows into the most beautiful youths imaginable.'

That said, not all frenzied fandom was genuine. Sometimes, enthusiasm was a job for hired professionals.

Let me hear you make some noise!

In 1748, France's most industrious – but not yet most illustrious – writer mounted a new play in Paris. Voltaire was already renowned as a playwright, and was rather controversial as a philosophical writer, but he wasn't yet the iconic Enlightenment celebrity who'd

---

* As you can probably guess, I'm not really into smooth jazz . . .

end up banished to twenty-five years of Swiss exile, and only welcomed home to Paris at the very end of his life to join the literary pantheon. No, that was all yet to come, provided his new play went well. But earning success was going to be tricky because, annoyingly, Voltaire had made a powerful enemy in the shape of Prosper Jolyot de Crébillon, a rival writer who'd wangled the job of royal censor.

Theirs was the cattiest of feuds. Crébillon had tried to tank Voltaire's previous plays, so Voltaire retaliated by restaging Crébillon's play, *Sémiramis*, as his own, hoping to prove himself the better writer by improving on it. It was either a baller move or a petty provocation, like watching your enemy sing their favourite song at karaoke, waiting for them to sit down, staring them in the face, then getting up to sing it yourself. Incensed, Crébillon stuck his nose in wherever he could, hoping to sink *Sémiramis* from the outset. But Voltaire had a plan. He would fight fire with fire. He would cheat.

Arguably, Parisian theatre's most powerful person wasn't a playwright, though he wanted to be. No, he was instead master of the claque.* Jacques Rochette de La Morlière was a hired gun with a syndicate of professional applauders who were paid to cheer and clap at the right moments. La Morlière was a scoundrel and scandal magnet - think Casanova, but sleazier - but he excelled at faking audience responses. From 1747 to 1758, his choreographed gang of plants and patsies boosted and booed the plays of patrons and enemies, depending on who was footing the bill.[32] Voltaire had previously railed against claques, but now his moral outrage evaporated in a puff of wig powder as he handed out 400 tickets to professional clappers for the opening performance at Versailles. Crébillon tried to cram the theatre with his own booing cronies, but Voltaire had done enough. *Sémiramis* wasn't a decisive victory, his enemy still had plenty of admirers, but it set him on the road to international glory.[33]

---

* *Claque* means a slap or thwack in French.

Professional claquers were nothing new. In ancient Greece, the writer Menander lost playwriting competitions to Philemon,[34] who wowed the judges by packing the audiences with his cheering mates. Later on, Emperor Nero had an army of fawning goons to celebrate his poetry recitals and dubious Olympic achievements. If you recall, Heinrich Heine assumed that Lisztomania must've been a cynical sham. Though wrong, it was plausible; Liszt had spent time in Paris, the heartland of the claque, where a variety of fakery specialists awaited their cues from the chief: 'There were the commissaires, who memorized the better parts of the play and called their neighbours' attention to them; the *rieurs*, who laughed loudly during comedies; the *chatouilleurs* ("the ticklers"), who kept the audience in good humour; the *pleureuses*, women who wept during melodramas; and the *bisseurs*, who shouted for encores.'[35] From Paris, the idea of a primed audience spread to Vienna, Milan, New York, and, to a lesser extent, London. It became synonymous with opera, classical music, and theatre, and still continues today at the Russian Bolshoi Ballet company.[36]

You might be thinking: 'Oi, Greg! Doesn't this belong in the chapter about self-promotion gimmicks?' Maybe, but I mention it here because claques were professional equivalents to what fans had started to do for themselves; they cohered into powerful blocs, motivated by a desire to promote their favourites and scorch their enemies. Modern scholars divide these groups into three types: *defensive fans*, *toxic fans*, and *anti-fans*. The defensive ones are fiercely protective of their chosen thing; the toxic fans lash out against everyone, including their own kind and the thing they love if it disappoints them; and the anti-fans find pleasure in hate-watching things that others love.*

We think of fandom battles as modern, with spats between rival celebs spilling over into Twitter flame-wars between their loyal

---

* Most notably, some toxic fans of *Star Wars* sent abuse to actors in *The Phantom Menace* and *The Last Jedi*, and there was even a bizarre crowdfunding campaign to remake the latter film, which was deemed a betrayal by some.

acolytes, but it was already happening in the 1700s. The theatre historian Cheryl Wanko has uncovered several fan battles between supporters of early English actresses: highlights include Anne Oldfield vs Anne Bracegirdle, Anne Oldfield vs Jane Rogers, and Catherine Clive vs Susannah Cibber.

A letter in the *Daily Journal* of 6 December 1736 reported the impact of a fan-led claque that operated much like La Morlière's hooting and hollering plants, but without the payment: 'As thirty or forty Persons, pre-inclined and instructed, may outnoise three or four hundred impartial Auditors, a sufficient Number of Orders MAY be dispersed thro' the House, in such remote Corners, and different Parts, that what shall be demanded from so many distant Quarters, may look like the Sentiment of a Town.'

We might ask what the fans got out of this territorial pissing contest? Cheryl Wanko argues that championing a beloved star was an extension of fans' own identities: 'These groups gave the individual spectator a personal stake in the performer's success, thus also enabling the member's identity formation as camps defined themselves against each other.'[37] As with football fans, it became tribal; during the notorious 'Polly War',[38] being on Team Clive made it impossible to admire Susannah Cibber,* just as my fellow Spurs fans are raised to hate Arsenal fans, despite us sharing plenty in common.

If someone wanted to ruin a play, one weapon was the *catcall*; it was a small trumpet or whistle that produced a godawful, shrill parp, described by a journalist writing in the *Spectator* as 'the most harsh, unmusical sound that . . . ever wounded my ears'. It wasn't just tooted by fans wanting to belittle their enemies, but also by smirking wits and wannabe critics – the anti-fans – hoping their well-timed blast of aural terrorism might get a laugh, or turn the audience against the performer. Eighteenth-century playhouses

---

* In 1736, the so-called 'Polly War' broke out in the press when a theatre manager stripped Kitty Clive of her famous role of Polly in *The Beggar's Opera* and gave it to her rival, Susannah Cibber. Clive and her fans refused to accept this lying down.

were raucous hotbeds of shouting, food-chucking, booing, cheering, and physical violence. Celebrity actors often needed their fans to shout down the noisy abusers, but sometimes performers lost the entire audience, including their own supporters, and had to plead to get them back onside; or, in the case of the spectacularly arrogant Edmund Kean in Boston, had to throw down their wig and just leg it out the back door before the audience murdered them!

Dead keen on screen queens

The idea of a motivated fanbase was long established by the time Hollywood showed up, but early movie fans organised themselves into much bigger gangs. The first noticeable victory had been unmasking Florence Lawrence's identity, and fans soon became powerful players in the Hollywood game. Though the last chapter revealed how Hollywood glamour sold audiences an aspirational lifestyle – suggesting they were passive consumers of whatever they were given – actually, Samantha Barbas has argued that fans were also shaping what they were given.

By working almost as trade union representatives for their chosen star, fan groups were *boosters* who hectored studio bosses into offering better roles, better PR gimmicks, more flattering costumes, more attractive co-stars, and more sympathetic characters. They aggressively patrolled the media, leaping on journalistic errors and demanding corrections. They saw themselves as guardians of celebrity brand integrity. When a magazine proclaimed in 1948 that June Allyson was one of the worst-dressed women in Hollywood, her fan club responded with a letter of protest signed by 19,000 members. Fully unfurled, it came in at ninety feet in length.[39]

Because they were the ones buying the movie tickets, fan campaigns were often successful; studio moguls were attentive to audience feedback, and didn't just subtly tweak the image of existing stars, but radically rewrote their brand, or conjured up entirely new ones, inventing megastars from scratch in response to public desire. Samantha Barbas notes: 'In the 1930s, for example, when fans wrote to MGM demanding a tough-talking hero, the studio created a personality to fit the bill. Through careful casting and a skilful publicity campaign, Clark Gable, an undistinguished, unassuming stage actor, was transformed into a rugged, charming, and phenomenally popular star. Fans, to a great extent, actually created their idols.'[40] Clark Gable's macho image was pure confection - he had no interest in sports, hunting, or the great outdoors, but was often photographed looking like an overgrown boy scout, ready to build a fire, catch a fish, and maybe punch a bear if so needed.[41] Of course, he wasn't the only one to get an image makeover.

Hollywood PR, particularly in the 1920s-30s, invented heavily mythologised backstories, false romances, and alluring personality traits that bore little resemblance to the real actor. This tidal wave of bullshit was spread through fan magazines, which were independent publications with little actual independence; rather, they relied upon the studios to provide publicity materials, photographs, and star interviews. Such publications included *Photoplay*, *Modern Screen*, and *Silver Screen*, and they sold in huge quantities, but hardcore fans often learned not to trust them because they knew they were being manipulated.[42] However, by 1945 fan magazines were proving much less willing to roll over and have their tummies tickled by studio spin doctors, and, between 1948 and 1952, studio bosses repeatedly complained about their 'destructive' influence on the film industry's image.[43]

Signed, sealed, delivered, I'm yours

Historians' detective work may have unpicked the PR gimmicks, but the Hollywood bluster usually did the trick at the time. Despite the inauthenticity, Clark Gable's career skyrocketed once he'd embraced the surly beefcake persona, and his dubious credentials as outdoorsy athlete went largely unquestioned. But despite the success of the seductive mirage, film fans also wanted to know the real person behind the cynical smokescreen. As early as 1910, fans deluged Florence Lawrence with letters of startling intimacy: 'Dear Miss Flo, I know you will think I am bold – very bold – but I just can't help it. You see, I have seen you in so many moving pictures that it seems as though I should naturally speak to you if ever I met you on the street.' Another fan noted: 'I feel that I almost know you.'

Such fan mail reveals that audiences definitely fell for the artifice, yet were sophisticated enough to know it was a fiction. They wanted to hear from the actress, not the character. But they also wanted the gap between real life and *reel* life to allow only the merest sliver of daylight to shine through; fans desperately wanted Clark Gable to be the gruff huntsman they'd been sold, or they craved confirmation that Rita Hayworth was indeed the sultry vamp in satin negligee. They hoped that acting wasn't lying, just embellishment. Fans wanted to humanise stars, but they also hoped their fantasies would be authenticated.

The letters came in their thousands, and then in their millions. Before long, stars like Mary Pickford were hiring personal secretaries to wade through the postbags that piled up like sandbags in a battlefield trench, and the studios followed suit. In 1928, Hollywood's mailrooms were buried beneath a mountain of 32,250,000 messages, forcing studios to budget nearly $2m[44] to respond to them all with forged autographs and thank-you notes. In truth, by the 1930s various scandals had damaged the clean-cut fantasy. Both fans and stars now began to openly acknowledge the gulf between the star image and actors' private personalities. But it's not as if the studio PR teams packed up shop and went home; they still played the mood music in the background.[45]

Though Hollywood industrialised the idea of fan mail, it can't claim credit for the invention. Perhaps the most notable early recipient of barrowloads of fan letters was the megastar French writer and philosopher Jean-Jacques Rousseau, whose 1761 novel *Julie, or, The New Heloise* became an astonishing literary phenomenon. Rousseau received 'a multitude' of letters from thousands of devoted admirers who couldn't stop thinking about him. In a celebrated essay, the historian Robert Darnton focuses on one such fan named Jean Ranson who kept referring to Rousseau as 'our friend Jean-Jacques',[46] as if they played on the same five-a-side football team, while other devotees included a clockmaker, Jean Romilly, who wrote to his hero: 'I can no longer defer talking with you, it is almost two years now even three that I have wanted to tell you about all the idealized conversations I have with you because you should know that whether I'm sleeping or walking about, you are always present in my mind and I am only at ease in company when I can talk a little about you, either to those who love you or those who do not love you at all.'[47]

Being buffeted by a tsunami of adoration contributed to Rousseau's tumble into conspiratorial paranoia, to the point where he felt enraged when fans praised him or bought his image to hang on their wall. Other stars of the time also caused postmen to wheezily drag increasingly heavy sacks. David Garrick, Sarah Siddons, and France's great thespian François-Joseph Talma all received stacks of mail. But perhaps the most studied recipient of frenzied fan mail is Lord Byron, whose scandalously erotic poetry - published half a century after Rousseau seduced an entire continent - inspired an intense outbreak of fan fever that's made him the pouting poster boy for scholars of historical celebrity.*

Byromania - as his unfortunate wife, Annabella Milbanke, dubbed it - proved to be a powder keg of sexual power, and the poet with the luscious hair received an avalanche of love letters from female admirers, many of which he kept because, well, that's egotists for you. As had been the case with Rousseau, Byron's fans couldn't help but see their crush lurking inside his romantic characters, and so they sometimes addressed him as Childe Harold or the Corsair. And, as Corin Throsby has pointed out, the language in the letters is full of eyebrow-raising phraseology, with one writer

---

* Tom Mole, Corin Throsby and Ghislaine McDayter are the people to read if you'd like to know more. Check out the bibliography on my website for their works.

saying: 'she "sighs" for Byron, drawing attention to her "bosom" swelling with "wild tumults", referring to the "highest bliss" she would feel if she were Byron's "Valentine",' while another female correspondent gets hot and heavy with her description of what it felt like to read Byronic verse: '"Why, did my breast with rapture glow? / Thy talents to admire, / Why, as I read, my bosom felt? / Enthusiastic fire".'[48]

Such fan letters weren't just the Regency era's version of horny midnight sexts; they were playful explorations of fantasised intimacy, with several fans pledging to save him from his sins and lift him out of his melancholy. Byromania wasn't just about wanting to rip off his clothes; it was also about the soul. But, as Throsby notes, it was also fantasy - many of Byron's fans didn't actually want to meet him, they found the distance and pseudonymic playfulness deeply pleasurable. He was more fun as an idea than as a man.

The pleasure of being a fan

As a music fan, I've lost track of the number of times I've seen the singer from a headlining band gaze out across a surging festival crowd and make a heartfelt admission that this triumphal moment is what they'd dreamed of when *they* were the young fan looking up at their idol. For aspiring performers, fandom can be instructional; a young musician or actor might love a particular star as an inspirational role model, hoping they might one day grow up to collaborate with their hero as equals. But for most of us fandom isn't a stepping stone to a celebrity career; it's just a heightened sensation of loving something purely because it makes us happy, or inspires us to be confident in ourselves.

Yet, the received wisdom about fandom is almost entirely negative. For at least 200 years, fans have been condemned as glassy-eyed idiots whose brains turn to mush the moment they discover some new obsession. In 1822, the editor of a pirated version of Byron's poetry declared the poet to be 'bringing the minds of his readers into a state of vassalage or subjection', and he later decried 'the thoughtless, dazzled throng'. As Ghislaine McDayter notes, Byromania was seen as proof of the mob's easy manipulation; the fear was, it might start with an innocent craving for romantic poetry but would surely end in full-blown revolution![49]

Celebrity fandom was believed to be dangerously irrational, because it was passive consumption. Such snobbery was only challenged in the 1990s by the pioneering fandom scholar Henry Jenkins, who argued that fans are capable of creativity and critical thinking, and often take great pleasure in 'poaching' the original text and turning it into a playground, giving rise to things like fan fiction and eroticised slash fiction.*[50] Jenkins's corrective was important, though he might have pushed back a little too hard; Sharon Marcus cautions that most fans really do like what they're given,[51] and don't spend their days typing out alternative endings to TV shows, or homoerotic what-if scenarios where characters furiously screw each other instead of solving the murder case.

One of the most obvious indications that Byron's fans weren't empty-headed numpties is the way his poetry was used in 'commonplacing' scrapbooks. These had been around since the late medieval era, but in the Romantic era Byron was probably the most beloved and most quoted writer in Britain, and his works were often filleted by fans into personally curated collections of best bits. These scrapbooks could then be shown to friends and visitors, as what some scholars have called an early form of social media, and the focus on individual lines of meaningful text proves that fans were expert analysists, able to make editorial judgements about which sections to celebrate and which to cut, rather than just blinking fools who found everything equally amazing.[52]

Thousands of people thrilled at the very mention of Lord Byron, but the dangerous poet was also something of a fan too. I don't mean of himself – though it's perhaps not a stretch to argue his

---

* Fan fiction is when a fan extends a pre-existing story, using the same cast of characters. Slash fiction is when that new fan-written version queers the narrative by introducing a homosexual relationship between male characters. Femmeslash is the same but for lesbian romance.

favourite person was the fella in the mirror – but I mean it in the sense of liking other celebrities. When his mother-in-law died, he was delighted to be able to sign his letters as Noel Byron, or N. B., which were the same initials as his political hero, Napoleon Bonaparte.[53] He also kept his own commonplace books, got excited by watching Edmund Kean perform on stage, cheered for his faves in the boxing ring, and had long been a devotee of Rousseau's heart-twanging Romanticism.

Indeed, when Byron romped his way across Europe, joined by fellow Romantics Percy and Mary Shelley, they went on an impassioned sightseeing tour of the locations in *Julie, or, The New Heloise*, and places where Rousseau had stayed. This mobile fandom became an important episode in the history of celebrity tourism, and it soon became popular to visit the sites associated with the glorious dead, not least when Byron's own fans followed in his footsteps and discovered Rousseau through Byron's journey, in the same way Kanye West introduced young hip-hop fans to Paul McCartney.*

To visit the authentic sites where beloved characters emoted, or where great authors created their masterpieces, was a kick that allowed the tourist to imagine themselves as the object of their obsession; it was a sort of celebrity karaoke experience. This trend for *necro-tourism* had lurched into gear in the mid-1700s, when various luminaries – including two future American presidents, Thomas Jefferson and John Adams – rocked up at Stratford-upon-Avon in England to bask in the genius of Shakespeare. They visited his house, were guided around the town, and were probably offered dodgy souvenirs supposedly made from Shakespeare's favourite mulberry tree, which must have been bloody massive to supply all those gullible sightseers.

While David Garrick had helped transform Shakespeare into

---

* Amusingly, some Twitter users thought Kanye had 'discovered' McCartney as if he was some new, unsigned artist rather than one of the greatest songwriters of all time.

England's national poet, Scotland's bard was Robert Burns and his birthplace was also transformed into a public site of pilgrimage, as was the lavish Abbotsford castle built by the superstar Scottish novelist Sir Walter Scott, who died in 1832. Meanwhile, Yorkshire's most famous literary family, the Brontës, died tragically young but, by the 1890s, their unassuming home of Haworth Parsonage was a shrine to 10,000 visitors per year. One enthused American was so obsessed with trying to preserve the authentic experience that he bought the original window from Charlotte's room so he could make photo frames from the glass that she'd once gazed through.[54]

Previously, celebrity fans and culture vultures had been happy visiting official memorials, with London's Westminster Abbey playing host to various literary heroes in Poets' Corner. But in the 1800s these seemingly lost their appeal and it became fashionable to visit famous people's actual graves or homes; the public wanted to get near to the authentic celebrity, because it proved a profoundly powerful experience.[55] The great American writer Washington Irving visited Shakespeare's tomb in 1820 and later wrote: 'I trod the sounding pavement, there was something intense and thrilling in the idea, that, in very truth, the remains of Shakespeare were mouldering beneath my feet. It was a very long time before I could prevail upon myself to leave.'

But if visiting the world of dead celebs became a lucrative tourism industry, you won't be surprised to discover living stars were also up for grabs. The dead may have lost their privacy, but at least they didn't have to live with gawping fans sticking their heads through the window.

Public property

In 1873, *Lippincott's Magazine* reported a quaint story about Alfred, Lord Tennyson, who was poet laureate and one of the most famous men in Victorian Britain. According to a visiting friend, who'd popped down to see Tennyson at his Farringford house on the Isle of Wight, the great man with the great beard was a highly strung host. While out walking in the countryside, he would prick up his ears and shout: 'Come! Let's walk on - I hear tourists!' Unsure, the companion would wait a moment, then reassuringly point out: 'Oh no, see! There's nothing in sight but a flock of sheep!'[56] This, apparently, happened a few times. It's an amusing vignette devoid of jeopardy, and it would make for a jolly comedy sketch, with Tennyson becoming increasingly terrified of rabbits, leaves, and then household objects. But if we look more closely the laughter starts to fade.

After years in the public eye, Tennyson had become hyper-vigilant to threats, like an ex-soldier who flinches every time a car backfires. Nobody was trying to kill him - quite the opposite, in fact - but a London life of endless double-take glances, elbow nudges, excited jostling, and shouts of acclaim had forced him to flee the capital in 1853, and he'd found the Isle of Wight to be a tranquil haven. But, as Paraic Finnerty has shown, Tennyson's huge fame inevitably turned the nearby village of Freshwater into a tourist attraction, and soon travel guides were regaling excited tourists with how best to intercept the poetical rockstar on his night-time walks.

Having picked Farringford as a quiet idyll, by the late 1860s Tennyson found it had become 'a literary shrine' attracting a surge of goggling celebrity-hunters, from all over the world. The American writer M. D. Conway described his fellow countrymen as being like hunters stalking their prey with their rifle-like cameras: 'I knew I was near the much-hunted poet by seeing one of his natural enemies ... the muzzle of his fatal instrument was already prepared and pointed to a spot where the famous man loves to walk ... But, alas for the solitude he came to seek at Farringford! He startles a curious eye lurking in every bush, and doesn't know when he returns from his walk how many copies of him have been snatched by the remorseless nitrate.'[57] The Tennysons rather snobbishly dubbed these bush-lurking, camera-wielding celebrity-hunters as 'Cockneys'. Eventually, the attention became too much, so they fled Farringford and moved to an isolated house on the Surrey–Sussex border.[58]

Meanwhile, another talismanic British icon was the nursing pioneer Florence Nightingale, who loathed being famous. Due to her chronic illness, which rendered her bedridden for years, she didn't have to deal with the awkward everyday encounters with admirers, but she still had to encounter her distinctive name being appropriated by the excitable public. Indeed, one of the most unsettling consequences of fame was reading newspaper obituaries for dead kids named Florence in her honour, a sadly common occurrence in an era when so many children perished before the age of five. Her celebrity also impinged upon her father, William Nightingale, who wrote that his daughter's rise made him 'tremble for my own name'; seeing it appear in the press was 'simply an abomination', and he shunned public contact with admirers. Inevitably, as with Tennyson's property, the family homes were soon visited by trespassers eager to see where the Nightingales lived. It caused much consternation.[59]

Being a celebrity is excitingly glamorous when it's all champagne-soaked parties, luxury hotels, gorgeous homes, fast cars, and cool friends. But there are twenty-four hours in every day, and the fun stuff only fills a few of them. For the remaining hours, celebs are just people with ordinary problems, but they don't get to keep office hours, like doctors or university lecturers, outside of which we aren't allowed to bug them. Celebrities are always famous, and therefore always under scrutiny. And that can be a somewhat miserable existence.

In 1862, the *Sixpenny Magazine* published a short essay called 'Celebrity: Its Pains and Penalties'[60] which compared celebrity to slavery, with the public being 'the most tyrannical of masters'. Obviously, slavery is much, much worse – and in this book we've encountered Sara Baartman, Frederick Douglass, and Bill Richmond, who knew the difference first hand – but the essay's argument certainly tarnished the idea of fame being round-the-clock fun: 'Being a "lion" means you no longer belong to yourself; your person, your gestures, your words, your name have become public property,' the article argued.

Many historical stars would've recognised these words, as would the celebrities of today. If Tennyson was Britain's most beloved poet, America was dead keen on Henry Wadsworth Longfellow – another wearer of magnificent facial fuzz – but, whereas Tennyson hid himself from public advances, Longfellow was strangely open-hearted towards uninvited visitors. Having been tragically widowed when his wife's frock caught fire in 1861 (his face was badly burned in trying to extinguish her, hence the bushy beard to mask the scars), the poet found his home a regular visiting spot for well-wishers and fans, and he responded by keeping a box of pre-signed autographs on the mantelpiece, and sometimes even inviting people in for dinner.[61] However, there was also a 'crazy woman'[62] who arrived with all her baggage and declared she was his wife. The police had to be called to remove her. There's always one . . .

Tennyson and Longfellow were literary lions – celebrity intellectuals – but the animal analogy was doubly fitting, because celebrity status can feel like being cooped up in a zoo. These big beasts are powerful and glorious, but they're trapped behind bars while the public stares at them from afar, or shouts provocations to do something photogenic while they're trying to sleep. In 1837, a young Charles Dickens wrote an amusing sketch about being invited to a dinner party where a great lion would be among the guests, and he found plenty of ways to make the obvious jokes; he described endeavouring to get 'a full view of the interesting animal', talked about a metaphorical 'keeper' who mingles among the crowd making sure to praise the lion, and then jokingly referenced putting one's head in the lion's jaws. He also had fun invoking the notion of performing monkeys, bears, and elephants, before noting that bipedal lions in top hats are much more susceptible to flattery than the snarling ones you see in zoos.[63] It's a quaintly satirical piece about how celebrity is essentially a circus performance. But the irony was that the man making the jokes was himself soon to become not just a lion, but King of the Jungle.

In the piece, Dickens plays the role of observer, watching from afar, and never actually speaks to the lion. It's a surveillance mission. Similarly, other celebrities spoke of being stared at as if they were exotic animals. France's illustrious writer Voltaire grumpily shouted at some English visitors who'd arrived at his house without a formal introduction, and had proceeded to gawp a little too obviously: 'Well, gentlemen, you now see me, and did you take me to be a wild beast or a Monster that was fit only to be stared at, as a show?'[64] This might have been a reference to Clara the Rhino, our unlikely celebrity from an earlier chapter, or it might just have been a generic rant. Either way, an elderly Voltaire felt objectified by these strangers.

Meanwhile, another human spectacle was Sarah Siddons, whose memoirs recount: 'My door was soon beset by various persons quite unknown to me, whose curiosity was on the alert to see the new Actress, some [of] whom actually forced thier [sic] way into my Drawing-room in spite of remonstrance or opposition.' One older lady barged in uninvited, declaring her doctor wouldn't let her see a play so she'd decided to come and stare at the actress in her private dressing room instead. It's perhaps unsurprising that Siddons became reticent about going to parties and public concerts: 'It has pleased God to place me in a situation of great publicity but my natural disposition inclines me to privacy and retirement.'[65] Whether that was her natural introversion, or a wise coping mechanism, is up for debate.

Siddons's trendsetting contemporary, Mary 'Perdita' Robinson, was famed for her public displays of extravagant fashion, and had no qualms in racing around London in her fancy carriage while wearing sumptuous haute couture; we can hardly describe her as a shrinking violet, but her constant ability to draw a crowd wasn't always fun. She wrote in her memoirs: 'I scarcely ventured to enter a shop without experiencing the greatest inconvenience. Many hours I have waited till the crowd disperse, which surrounded my carriage, in my expectation of quitting the shop.'[66]

In truth, this might have been something of the self-promotional brag, but it's certainly plausible her fame became a hindrance. A century later, Cléo de Mérode lamented that her *cartes de visite* were sold at newsstands and railway stations: 'If I ventured a few steps in the street, young girls would rush to buy these cards, and run after me, asking me to autograph them. This became such an obsession that often I gave up on going out, and preferred to stay shut away in my hotel room.'[67]

In 1853, the American novelist Harriet Beecher Stowe arrived in England, having published a smash hit called *Uncle Tom's Cabin*. As Michael Newbury puts it:

> Upon her ship's arrival, Stowe was surprised to find hordes of spectators 'very much determined to look'; Stowe wanted to attend a particular church service in London, 'but dared not for fear of being recognized'; upon her entrance into one hall, Stowe felt the terror of a near stampede as one woman was almost trampled to death; finally, when it came to addressing her admirers, Stowe, retreating firmly into the conventions of domestic privacy, called exclusively upon her husband, Calvin, to speak for her. Calvin, in turn, described the mob as ever more grasping, intrusive and demanding: 'I am tired to death of the life I lead here. All that was anticipated by the newspapers, & ten times more, has befallen us. From the lowest peasant to the highest noble, [my] wife is constantly beset, & I for her sake, so that we have not a moment's quiet.'[68]

By the 1930s, the young debutante Brenda Frazier was similarly mobbed by strangers waving autograph books; in 1939, during an Easter parade, she was surrounded by 200 New Yorkers and had to be rescued by police. Like Sarah Siddons, 160 years before her, Frazier had also received an unwanted visitation from a woman shouting, 'I've just got to look at you!'[69] when she was undressing in a changing room.

Meanwhile, in LA, the glitziest Hollywood stars found themselves pursued across the city by devoted fans and savvy operators.

As Samantha Barbas tells it: 'One fan, Herbert Strock, boasted to *Modern Screen* magazine that he had devised "ingenious methods to get at the stars . . . Learning that Miss Jean Harlow was having lunch in a popular Hollywood restaurant, I gathered together a group of autograph collectors and induced them to stand in front of the eating place," he explained. Strock was particularly proud of his ability to spot and follow celebrities' vehicles: he had spent so much time star-watching that he had memorized "the license numbers, makes and types of automobiles owned by the various stars."'[70]

Such detailed knowledge of celebrity geography soon fuelled the rise of professional tour companies that bussed fans around the city, showing them where major stars lived and partied. Most movie stars were less than keen on being pointed at by coachloads of strangers, but an article in the *Washington Herald* noted that the chances of actually spotting a celeb were pretty slim, and eleven out of twelve fans who visited Hollywood failed to meet their favourite star. Some of the tourists stubbornly refused to leave the city, however, occasionally forcing civic authorities to put an urgent call into the movie studio requesting an emergency handshake to get rid of the lingering nuisance.[71] This was forceful behaviour by the fans, but they got what they wanted by using the legal levers of PR and good old-fashioned making a fuss. In some ways, I admire their plucky persistence.

That said, I certainly don't endorse the invasive chicanery used by other, more desperate movie fans. In 1932, Jean Harlow was unwell, and resting up at home, when two devotees snuck into her house disguised as nurses. Obviously, that's pretty creepy. In 1934, Harlow this time found herself pursued around the studio lot by an obsessive fan, John Stoneburg, who was promptly arrested once she'd raised the alarm. That's just plain scary. Three years later, Jeanette MacDonald - the star of many musicals - married Gene Raymond, only to find the church lawn bestrewn with 1,500 fans who'd somehow learned the location of the wedding. That's just intrusive.

When the Hollywood golden couple Mary Pickford and Doug-las Fairbanks embarked on their honeymoon in 1920, they were unable to leave their hotels. When they got to England, Pickford relates: 'Douglas and I were swept up by mobs of fans till I could neither eat nor sleep, let alone drink in the historic sights. Our first stop was the Ritz in London. Outside our window we saw them, thousands and thousands of them, waiting day and night in the streets below, for a glimpse of us.'[72] None of these stories ended tragically, but they were all unpleasant in their own way. And they certainly weren't the worst.

Crossing the line

On 17 February 1816, a beautiful young actress called Frances Maria Kelly was performing on stage at London's Drury Lane when a man in the sixth row stood up, pulled out a pistol, aimed it at her, and fired. Luckily, the bullet whizzed past her body and slammed into the scenery. Before he could reload, the crowd bundled him to the floor, and he was dragged off to the local magistrate. What had Miss Kelly done to deserve such violence? The would-be as-sassin, a young man named George Barnet, testified that she knew exactly why he'd done it. But Kelly was clueless. They'd never met before, but then she pulled out two recent angry letters, the first of which outlined Barnet's deadly logic of duelling with the woman he desired:

> Years ago I was your admirer; but always met with disap-pointment. Coquetry indulged you; although always ob-tained at the expense of others; without vanity to myself, I think my good intentions towards you have been more trifled than any of my cotemporaries [sic]. My claim to your person is therefore greater which determines me to demand your hand, or in other words to make you my wife. You will either consent to this, or accept my challenge. I will attend you at any hour you please, on Wednesday, or before. I have

witnessed your dexterity of firing a gun; but suppose a pistol
will better suit you, as being much lighter.

As the historian Ruth Scobie recounts,[73] this is a story drawn from
celebrity's dark recesses. Barnet was a young professional who'd
sadly fallen into a mentally unstable condition, and his long-held
crush on a famous actress had gradually warped into violent erotomania – a delusion that this stranger was in love with him, and
should therefore be his wife. Scobie notes that Kelly had perhaps
ignored the first letter because she was used to such things; did
actresses often get such alarmingly weird demands? It's certainly
a plausible speculation. After all, those in the public eye might
expect to encounter at least a few fans who don't know where the
line is.

In 1940, a twelve-year-old Shirley Temple (though studio PR
claimed she was younger, to elongate her cutesy career) was doing
radio promotion when a woman stood up in the theatre and
pointed a gun at her. Luckily, two law enforcement agents leapt
into action and disarmed her. While George Barnet had been motivated by misfiring adoration, this would-be assassin hungered for
tragic vengeance. Her baby had died at the same time as Temple
had supposedly been born, and she felt her child's life had been
snatched away to bring Temple into the world. It's a bleakly poetic
metaphor that the studio's PR lie, designed to keep Shirley artificially young, nearly caused her to stop ageing entirely.

We all know the worst-case horror stories of celebrities slain
by psychologically unstable people: Andy Warhol and Monica
Seles survived to tell the horrible tale, but John Lennon, the heavy-
metal guitarist Dimebag Darrell, and YouTube singing star Christina Grimmie were among those tragically murdered. In reality,
most historical celebrities probably coasted through their careers
without ever being seriously endangered, but many would've
felt moments of fearful discomfort as the public encroached into
their private space, crushing them in an avalanche of adoration, or
grasping for uninvited access to their famous bodies.

Cléo de Mérode was allegedly grabbed and kissed in the street by a labourer named Gaspardin who'd fallen in love with her photo. The newspaper reports might be inaccurate, but they claimed: 'Cleo's companion began caning her assailant, but Gaspardin promptly knocked him down. Before the assembled passers-by knew what it was all about the dirty, muscular fellow had again enfolded the frail dancer and was kissing her lips repeatedly and frantically, despite her cries and her efforts to avoid him.'[74]

We might also look at the obsessive superfans who pursued the British music hall star Lydia Thompson, who was famed in the UK and USA for her blonde hair. One of them, Emma Waite, was merely a kind-natured young black woman who desperately wanted to be Thompson's maid, and spent most of her income on pursuing an intense Thompson fandom. Her story isn't alarming, though it is perhaps eye-opening. However, Holly Gale Millette has also discovered the story of 'A cross-dressing female who first observed [Thompson] in New York [and who] followed her as far as Chicago before she was eventually apprehended . . . There was also a male who, believing her to be the spirit of his dead wife, approached her more than fourteen times and broke into her hotel room thrice in New Orleans.'[75]

We've already heard about Longfellow's unwanted visitor declaring herself to be his wife, but such confusions weren't unheard of. Thompson's contemporary on the circuit was the much-admired Vesta Tilley, who performed songs as male characters. In Liverpool, Tilley was followed around by a mentally unwell man who was adamant they were married. He'd linger mute at the stage door every night, jiggling his cardboard sandwich board which declared 'Vesta Tilley Is My Wife'. He also paraded it up and down Liverpool city centre. One night, one of Tilley's waggish friends beckoned him to meet the celebrity in the bar. By now Tilley had removed her wig, makeup, and male costume, and looked like an elegant lady instead of a cheeky chappie. The friend made the formal introductions, to which the man shouted: 'That person Vesta Tilley? Whom are you trying to fool? Do you think I don't know my own wife!' It's rather intriguing he only saw her as wife material when she was wearing trousers.

Earlier, we met Shirley Temple's pushy mother, who ignored her tiny daughter's complaints about the icy punishment chamber on the set of her *Baby Burlesks*. But spare a thought for the Temple family, including Shirley's young siblings and her father, George, because they all found themselves living as round-the-clock guardians to a global phenomenon. Immediately, upon her debut success, it became apparent they'd have to move house. Not only was Shirley surrounded in public by screaming hordes, who rushed forward to touch her bouncing curls, but soon their Santa Monica home became a tourist hotspot, with her father saying: 'People came swarming down here like a cloud of locusts.'

Off went the Temples to a Beverly Hills mansion, to live behind a sturdy shield of high fence, electric gates, and broad-chested, pistol-carrying bodyguard who escorted Shirley at all times. The doors were alarmed, a camera monitored her bedroom, and the police had a direct link to the house. These weren't to deter star-seekers in tour buses, as annoying as they were, but to protect her from the much graver threat – kidnappers and extortionists.[76]

In 1927, the handsome young pilot Charles Lindbergh flew his way into the record books, and into the American psyche, as a glamorous aviation pioneer. Having flown from New York to Paris, emerging as a victorious underdog, he became a national icon of boyish derring-do. But he'd never wanted to be famous, and recoiled in disgust at the way his reputation was manipulated by an intrusive press. Sometimes he fought back in petty ways, such as flinging mud at gathered journalists, but mostly he just hid himself away and scowled.[77]

Fleeing from infuriating public scrutiny, he moved his wife and baby son to a fancy farmhouse in New Jersey. But one night in March 1932, tragedy struck. Their toddler, also called Charles, was snatched from the nursery and a ransom note for $50,000 left on the windowsill. An enormous manhunt was launched; even the mafia offered to help, including Al Capone, and huge resources were thrown at finding 'Little Lindy'. Thousands of leads were chased by the FBI and local authorities. Many more ransom letters came, and the demand grew. It was paid in full. But the Lindbergh Baby didn't return to his nursery. Tragically, the boy's body was found in the woods near the house. He'd been smashed over the head, half buried, and left to the animals.

It was a horrific story, but it also incited a media superstorm. Suspects were numerous; a nanny within the household panicked when the finger was pointed at her. She killed herself despite already having been exonerated. A man called Dr John Condon somehow inveigled himself into being the intermediary between family and kidnapper, but in flamboyantly building his part also ended up looking suspicious. Many fraudsters tried to exploit the situation. In the end, a German immigrant called Richard Hauptmann was charged, but protested his innocence all the way to his execution. Nobody's quite sure who did it, but it was a media sensation heralded as the new 'trial of the century' (after the one involving Evelyn Nesbit).

The Lindbergh Baby's brutal fate became a national trauma that turned Charles Lindbergh's heroic aviation fame into morbid notoriety. As the years went on, Lindbergh became a vociferous campaigner for American isolation from the Second World War, and was branded a Nazi sympathiser for his fascination with Hitler's regime. History hasn't judged him kindly. But the fact that such a famous man had been the victim of so horrific a crime sent shockwaves through the celebrity world. Startled, other stars bought kidnapping insurance policies and tightened domestic security, and when Shirley Temple joined their ranks as the youngest, and perhaps biggest, star in the celebrity firmament, the threat to her became imminently real.

Two years after her breakthrough, in May 1936, her father received a letter in the post - it instructed him to airdrop $25,000 over a farm in Nebraska, or 'Shirley will encounter dire results'. Three months later, the would-be extortionist was arrested on his family farm. He was only sixteen, and protested he'd done it on a whim after watching a movie with a kidnapping plotline; he'd never intended any violence. Shirley's dad went out and bought a gun anyway. Being the most famous child in the world made Shirley Temple adorable, but it also made her vulnerable. George Temple wasn't taking any risks.

The glamour of sacrifice

Fandom has been unfairly ridiculed for two centuries, but being a fan is often a positive, productive experience; and it's hard to imagine celebrity culture without the screaming enthusiasm of the public. Would celebrity be so vibrantly energetic if we all just half-heartedly shrugged our way through the latest edition of the *Hollywood Inquirer*? I doubt it. But such passion can transform celebrity status into a gilded cage. Sometimes those we adore are trapped by our love, and either retreat into their fortified mansions, fearful of being hounded, or start to develop complex psychological symptoms.

The scorching heat of public fascination is something that few stars are mentally resilient enough to cope with, and it's no wonder that so many celebrities tumble into drug and alcohol addictions. Fame is a surreal existence that inflates the ego, then shatters it with a sledgehammer when the fans get bored, or turn their backs on former heroes. Florence Lawrence was mobbed in the street, but died unloved and miserable; Fatty Arbuckle was a beloved comedian destroyed by scandal and abandoned by his fans; Oscar Wilde, the dandy aesthete who wooed America and earned huge sums, died in shameful Parisian exile after being punished by the state for gross indecency.

Some stars get off lightly, and some are just built of stronger stuff, but nobody entirely escapes the pressure, particularly when we also revel in hating celebs as much as in cheering them on. Though fandom is a celebratory movement that builds and sustains careers, offering celebrities the chance to accrue great wealth and perhaps even flourishing career satisfaction, fandom is also a sturdy pillar in a celebrity infrastructure which, on its bad days, burns through stars like human fossil fuel, caring not a jot for their emotional well-being or the acrid smog their bones produce.*

Centuries ago, children of the Inca civilisation in Peru were honoured with a diet of lavish food, drugs, and booze before being led up to the sacred mountain. There they were killed in religious sacrifices for the benefit of wider society. It was a glorious, useful death, but it was still a death. Might celebrity be a little similar sometimes? If so, most of us are complicit in the sacrifice. Whether we're hardcore *defensive fans*, hate-watching *anti-fans*, or just vaguely bored consumers happy for the shiny distractions, we most likely play some part in that complex three-way relationship between celebrities, audiences, and the media. When Princess Diana was chased to her death by speeding paparazzi, her brother's angry eulogy announced the press had blood on their hands. But the paparazzi don't operate in a vacuum, they work for us. They're our dealers, and we're hooked on their supply.

So despite the horrified moralising that followed Diana's death, and a brief détente from the chastised tabloids, plenty more celebrities have since been damaged because of our thirst for human novelty. Being famous can be fun, exciting, lucrative, and glorious. It's not always tragic, or even harmful. Most fans are great. These are important things to stress. But, for some celebrities, fame can also be a contract with the Devil in which the sinister small print only reveals itself once the signature has dried. And it's been that way for many, many years.

---

* If you don't believe me, Joey Berlin's book *Toxic Fame: Celebrities Speak on Stardom* (Visible Ink Press, 1996) features 500 pages of interview excerpts, listing all the ways that being famous can properly mess you up. It's quite the sobering read.

Epilogue: Famous for Fifteen Minutes

Anyone can be president

When Donald Trump was elected president of the United States in 2016 – and once the world had retrieved its jaw from the floor – a joke began to do the rounds: 'Obama showed that anyone can be president. Trump shows that *anyone* can be president.' For many, Trump fell way below the quality threshold for 'Leader of the Free World'. He was unworthy in character, capacity, and conduct; a mendaciously dangerous liar who enabled the worst, most bigoted fringes of society while declaring war on the abstract concept of truth. How people voted for him, while claiming to be good Christians, baffles me. But what I can say with confidence is that Donald Trump arrived as a celebrity candidate, and that's how the media chose to cover him.

Celebrity is part of the entertainment industry, but so is scandalous notoriety, meaning Trump's behaviour shed its moral gravity and instead became a soap opera. It didn't matter that he was despicable, he was TV ratings gold; Trump was an event, a human story of relentless headline-grabbing controversy. His bizarre and shocking rants began to acquire their own dramatic arc. Instead of the usual media cycle of 'blunder, backtrack, apology, resignation', Trump just ploughed on with his insensitive, inflammatory ineptitude, never apologising and never accepting his unfitness for office.

Like Nero at the Olympics, he changed the rules to suit his strengths. He'd served his media apprenticeship on *The Apprentice*, a reality show where the loudest provocateurs hogged the screen, so that's the role he decided to play. The cameras were always trained on Trump; even his empty rostrum was eagerly monitored on live news, every rambling speech breathlessly covered as if it were announcing some impending alien invasion. He got airtime like no other candidate in history, an estimated $5bn worth of free exposure.[1]

Exposure should have exposed him. But celebrity is a powerful force. That a controversial TV star - one famous for firing people from a job they didn't even have - could become president revealed how easily news journalism could be hijacked by the entertainment industry. Or was it vice versa? Trump made money for the news networks, and became a celebrity president for a celebrity era. If we look back at some of the previous White House incumbents, we can certainly argue that JFK was movie star hot; Ronald Reagan had been an actor; Bill Clinton oozed charisma; Barack Obama was elevated as a transformative hero - they'd all possessed a certain glamorous fame - but they were also renowned politicians. All had held public office before sitting down at the Resolute Desk. They weren't true celebrities, and, even if you think they were, they weren't *only* celebrities.

Trump, by contrast, barely understood politics at all. His Twitter feuds with basketball stars, or North Korea's supreme leader, weren't part of some master strategy. There was no end goal in sight. Instead, he lived by Andy Warhol's credo, 'Don't pay attention to what they write about you. Just measure it in inches.' Trump cared not for consequences, only limelight. It was performative narcissism by a man woefully unprepared for the job. And that loops us back to that opening joke, '*anyone* can be president'. It's a punchline that apes Daniel Boorstin's frustrated refrain that a celebrity is 'someone known for his well-knownness'; it's the notion that fame - once earned through ability - has been neutered into meaningless, unearned notoriety.

Boorstin's critique was published in 1962[2] and was a powerful challenge to a post-war culture which, in his eyes, had allowed advertising, celebrity, commerce, spin, manufactured opinion, and publicity stunts to transform America into a bewildering desert of illusory mirages. Celebrities were 'human-pseudo events', their artificial fame unrelated to merit or worthiness; pop culture was a handmaiden to manipulative forces trying to sell an American dream that promised to fulfil every desire, so long as people kept buying the latest model. Boorstin warned the reader: 'We risk being the first people in history to have been able to make their illusions so vivid, so persuasive, so "realistic", that they can live in them.' His ideas have certainly been influential, but it's not Boorstin who gets namechecked in debates about celebrity culture. Instead, we invariably turn to the predictions of a pop artist with weird hair.

Famous for fifteen minutes?

In 1968, Andy Warhol prophesised: 'In the future, everyone will be world-famous for fifteen minutes.' Ironically, this quote is now itself famous, though it's often misquoted; the 'world fame' bit usually gets sliced off. But what did Warhol really mean? Was he being literal? Some academic chin-strokers have argued he was predicting a future where the flattening of social hierarchies, and the triumph of his Pop Art aesthetic, would make everything of equal value; everyone would be famous because nobody would be more deserving of fame than anyone else. Warhol later said something similar about Studio 54 (his favourite nightclub), noting that everyone boogying there was a star, meaning none of them were. But 'world-famous for fifteen minutes' probably wasn't intended to be so philosophically nuanced.

It's more likely that Warhol was just piggybacking on the artist Larry Rivers, who, in 1967, said: 'Everybody will be famous.'[3] Rivers, however, wasn't talking about the global population, or a thrilling future of aesthetic equality; he was commenting on the pace of change in the 1960s New York art world. The community was seemingly bursting with innovative creativity and art lovers were trying to keep up with all the emergent styles. It felt to Rivers like an explosion of constant, exhausting novelty. Call me a cynic, but I read 'everybody will be famous' not as gnomic prophecy but as eye-rolling sarcasm. It's an ironic exaggeration, an extrapolation of exponential growth based on a few extra hipsters showboating their way around New York's coolest galleries while wearing sunglasses indoors.

Indeed, when *Time* quoted Warhol in October 1968, it was in this same specifically artistic context: 'Whole new schools of painting seem to charge through the art scene with the speed of an express train, causing Pop Artist Andy Warhol to predict the day "when everyone will be famous for fifteen minutes."' He didn't mean *everybody*, did he? Soon after, a scathing book attacking contemporary art quoted Warhol again,[4] but by now he was saying: 'There's going to be a day when no one will be famous for more than a week. Then everyone will have a chance to be famous.' A few months later, Warhol's work was displayed in Sweden and that's when his famous quote reached prominence: 'In the future, everyone will be world-famous for fifteen minutes.' Only quarter of an hour, Andy? What if we need the toilet when the paparazzi come knocking!? Thankfully, in 1969, the *New Republic* printed a tweaked update stating Warhol meant 'for at least fifteen minutes'. Phew! I'm not sure my bladder could've held out otherwise . . .

For such a memorable line, Warhol really took his time to nail it down. Was he just trolling us with grandiose soundbites? Maybe he liked the concept but couldn't settle on the detail? A quote from 1979 suggests he was happy to muck about with it: 'I'm bored with that line. I never use it anymore. My new line is, "In fifteen minutes everybody will be famous."'[5] This was him cheekily referencing a journalist who'd accidentally mangled the quote. But perhaps his playfulness masked genuine sincerity. Did Warhol foresee the impending internet, with its game-changing democratising power? Did he really think universal celebrity was lurking around the next corner? I doubt it. But he knew things were changing. And he had a front-row seat at the birth of reality TV.

In 1973, a fateful year for telly addicts, PBS broadcast *The American Family*, a ground-breaking observational documentary about the Loud family from California, who were to become the first reality TV stars. The standout 'personality' was Lance Loud, a flamboyant young man who was openly gay and seemingly enjoying life, something which transformed him into a hotly discussed public figure. He was mocked, criticised, admired, and championed. Undaunted, Lance seemed to grasp his newfound fame with confident purpose, making it clear that his TV persona was semi-fictional.* The TV version of Lance Loud wasn't real; he was a construct of manipulative editing. The reality TV blueprint was there from the outset.

More extraordinary, however, was the coincidental fact that Lance had previously been Andy Warhol's penfriend. As a teen, the young fan had dyed his hair silver in Warholian adoration and had enthusiastically written to his idol. The artist had written back, and they'd graduated to chatting on the phone. The communication was cut off when Warhol was shot and nearly killed in 1968, an attack that shocked him into becoming a recluse. But when Lance suddenly appeared on TV, and then became a burgeoning gay icon, they reconnected as adults. Admittedly, this was some five years after Warhol's famous prediction, but perhaps he felt a little vindicated? Someone he knew had received their 'fifteen minutes of fame'.

Warhol's logic does stand up (even if he played with his prediction so much that we question his sincerity). In our hyperconnected age of social media, it's possible that anyone could get famous. The avenues to notoriety are now so numerous, and the daily churn of gossip so immense, that all of us might yet become briefly known to millions of strangers. It might be for committing a terrible crime, or for hilariously falling over on camera, or for saving a child from a burning building, or for swearing accidentally when being interviewed on the news, or for giving a hilariously stupid answer on a TV quiz show.

---

* In a TV interview with Dick Cavett, Lance Loud claimed the editing made him seem 'obnoxious', and that he didn't really enjoy watching the show, but he was glad he'd done it.

Talent might be utterly irrelevant. But I quibble strongly with Warhol's 'everyone will be famous'. It's absurd to think every person on the planet - nearly 8 billion humans! - will experience a metamorphosis so extreme, and so short, as to make a mayfly's life seem epic by comparison. We can't all be famous. Celebrity needs a paying audience. We can't all hang around in a circle, bedecked in sunglasses and designer jeans, paying each other to be our fans like some absurdist version of the *Reservoir Dogs* standoff.

Barriers to entry

Since the arrival of Lance Loud, the idea that anyone *could* be launched into the celebrity stratosphere has understandably intensified, and the barriers to entry perhaps seem to be lowering. Boorstin's acolytes allege that celebrity no longer requires any qualifications; that anyone can become famous. Firstly, it's wrong to assume there were always more obstacles or quality filters in previous eras. Celebrity has long been a vehicle for astonishing social mobility, often recruiting its revolving cast of shiny hopefuls from the ordinary masses. Jump in your time machine, punch 1680 into the display, and you'd see a proto-celeb like Nell Gwyn - a barely literate actress, born into poverty, and possibly in proximity to prostitution - become famed for her stage performances and her seduction of the king. Transport yourself to the early 1900s and you'd see Charlie Chaplin become the most famous actor on the planet, despite spending his childhood in genuine London poverty.

Of course, *celebrity* isn't always low-status either - Lord Byron was born with a silver spoon in his mouth, even if said spoon was removed by his drunkard dad who pawned it then did a runner, abandoning his family to meagre accommodation because the family pile was in tumbledown disrepair. But, without question, celebrity culture has often elevated the lowliest to the upper echelons of privilege. Anyone could be a celebrity because, in many ways, that's sort of the point of celebrity. It's a form of class-skipping prestige, a parallel aristocracy drawn from below and powered by human spectacle; the roots of this surprising mobility can even be unearthed as far back as the ancient world, where gladiators and charioteers escaped their shackles to hobnob with the rich and powerful, or even to marry emperors.

But surely there's a difference between then and now? Indeed, there is. The bandwidth has increased. Many more celebrity careers can be maintained today than was possible in the past. In 1709, the year of Henry Sacheverell's speech, the famous satirist Jonathan Swift conceived of his 'Chamber of Fame', a sort of precursor to what we now call Halls of Fame, but he found space for only 132 worthies. Here's how he described the layout of the room:

> there are to be three tables, but of different lengths; the first is to contain exactly twelve persons; the second, twenty; and the third, a hundred. This is reckoned to be the full number of those who have any competent share of fame. At the first of these tables are to be placed, in their order, the twelve most famous persons in the world, not with regard to the things they are famous for, but according to the degree of their fame, whether in valour, wit, or learning. Thus, if a scholar be more famous than a soldier, he is to sit above him. Neither must any preference be given to virtue, if the person be not equally famous. When the first table is filled, the next in renown must be seated at the second, and so on in like manner to the number of twenty . . .[6]

One hundred and thirty-two celebrities in total? Oh, Mr Swift, you adorable thing! There are now way more movie stars crammed into a single room at the Oscars, let alone adding up all the stars of television, music, sport, publishing, etc.

But TV stars, film stars, popstars, and sports stars simply didn't exist in the eighteenth century. The first three of those categories are blindingly obvious to us, but sporting celebrity might feel like a strange omission. There were a few well-known athletes back in the Georgian era, but sports lacked their vital infrastructure and rules. Cricket was a popular pastime, but rugby didn't officially get going until the 1840s, baseball wasn't popular until the 1850s, tennis had to wait until the 1870s, and American football diverged from rugby in the 1880s.

My own beloved football (soccer) team, Tottenham Hotspur Football Club, was born twenty-four hours after Thomas Edison opened his first electrical power plant in Manhattan, in 1882. Organised sport is very modern. And the sharing of its joyous highs and lows was so much harder until radio and television came along. Even sports journalism only got up and running in the early 1800s, mostly for horseracing and boxing, and only became widely read in the late 1800s. All considered, then, sporting celebrity is either 2,000 years old, if you count the ancient charioteers, or barely 200 years old. And I'd rather argue for the latter.

As for music stars, they existed in the eighteenth, nineteenth, and early twentieth centuries – initially in opera, and then later in variety, music hall, and jazz – but pop music is a mid-twentieth-century innovation built on the technological platforms of the phonograph, radio, and jukebox. Pop requires both recording and reproduction technology. Until music could be recorded, live performance was everything. If someone lived out in the sticks, or even if they were a city-slicker but their favourite singer was an Italian castrato breezing into town on a whirlwind tour, they might've heard them perform only once in a lifetime. Famous songs were much more available than famous singers. Between 1900 and 1910, at least 100 different songs sold a million copies in America[7] – but as printed sheet music, not audio. Until the phonograph got a stranglehold on the market, just after the First World War, home entertainment involved bashing the tune out on your own piano, with your family and dog singing/howling along in accompaniment.

It's no surprise that *celebrity* has often been decried as a modern phenomenon because people were looking in the wrong place for historical precedents. It's not that *celebrity* is new, it's that film stars, sport stars, and popstars are new; their heritage is patchy because structural, technological, and sociological obstacles determined what sorts of career were possible. The earliest celebrity in this book is a furious clergyman with a poodle perm, which I don't think anyone was hunting for.

Under the influencer

As we canter to the end of this book, let me briefly turn from the past towards the present (and maybe the future). All around us, a whole new revolution is happening online, where social media *influencers* are redefining fame once more. The digital landscape has incubated a novel form of pseudo-celebrity, particularly one beloved by younger audiences, where the qualifications for success are often being able to exhibit nothing more than chirpy, chatty normalness – a constant stream of 'Hi, guys! Me again . . .' videos about going to the shops and eating a frozen yoghurt. There are also the eSports online gaming stars, the pouting models, the ab-encrusted fitness vloggers, the jokers who create viral memes and prank videos for their legions of fans.[8]

I've watched them with intrigue while writing this book, but I don't classify these online personalities as celebrities. Social media influencers can have massive followings, but their cultural impact tends to be small and their presence in the world is tightly focused, often limited to digital platforms. Of course, their income model isn't so dissimilar to celebrity; they too get rich by doing advertising endorsements. Indeed, in 2018, *The Atlantic* magazine[9] reported wannabe influencers were advertising products for free, without having contacted the brand. Their logic was 'fake it till you make it'; do unpaid adverts to convince fans they're officially sponsored, because that's the metric for online success, and fans want to follow successful people. Once enough fans click 'subscribe', the corporations should hopefully offer real sponsorship money to reach this sneakily assembled captive audience.

How do *influencers* differ from *celebrities*? A celebrity is someone who features in mainstream media, and might be expected to pop up on the radio, on TV, in newspapers, in magazines, in cinemas, on social media, in shop advertising, etc. They don't have to be famous to both your grannie and your milkman, but they might appear in the *Daily Mail*'s 'sidebar of shame' or be a question in a pub quiz. That's not to say YouTube stars can't successfully cross over, because it does happen. In 2017 I started to receive a lot of amusing tweets about how I look a little bit like Joe 'The Body Coach' Wicks, an über-buff diet and exercise guru with a cheeky-chappy persona. I'd never heard of him, but he'd managed to grow his online audience so much that book publishers and TV producers decided to pounce. This inevitably brought him into the eyeline of my Twitter followers, who thought it would be funny (it was funny) to photoshop my head onto his ludicrously toned body.*

Through his newfound media platforms, Wicks suddenly became familiar to a large audience of general consumers; cultural omnivores who daily feast on a variety of media. And, as soon as the bandwagon had developed sufficient momentum, the standard media protocol was enacted: tabloids began printing paparazzi photos of him walking in the street, looking dapper at red carpet events, and kissing his glamorous model girlfriend. He was no longer just a kale-munching, squat-busting internet bloke with a niche audience; he'd been transformed into a celebrity health guru, but also into a celebrity people wanted to know about. His face now appeared in front of those who didn't know who he was, but - through that continued media exposure - they began to recognise him.

This, for me, is the key distinction between celebrity and influencer. A celebrity is often in our eyeline, regardless of whether we give a damn. Obviously, there are celebs we love, and whose activities we deliberately seek out, but a lot of the time we're not being devoted fans so much as passive audiences exposed to a vast media tapestry of celebrity images. And yet, thanks to that exposure, we

---

* Doing the reverse, and popping his head on my scrawny torso, would be deeply depressing for all involved.

may still think of these people as being famous and might be able to identify a photo of them. Their image lives in the wider world. By contrast, influencers are sustained by a direct relationship with fans who deliberately opt in to following them.[10] Every follower gives tacit consent to the interaction, and may feel intense parasocial feelings for this online star, but the rest of us may have no idea the star even exists. The influencer doesn't live in the wider world, they live in a corner – admittedly, it might be a massive, diamond-encrusted corner – of the internet.

However, there are obvious similarities too. Once established as being famous, celebrities increasingly use social media to circumvent journalists and go direct to their fans. This doesn't stop the media covering them, or feasting on their social media posts as gossip fuel – so it isn't evidence of a withering away of celebrity culture – but it is moving a little closer to the tacit opt-in relationship of influencers and their followers. There are also similarities in how both groups sell access to their lives; celebrities allow magazine photographers into their homes and weddings, doing big-money deals for tasteful coverage of rites of passage and glamorous occasions, while YouTubers monetise intimate ordinariness through embedded adverts that tinkle away for three seconds before we get to gaze at their bedrooms.

Celebrity and influencer may yet fuse completely, forcing a redefining of celebrity's meaning. Indeed, several scholars have already dubbed internet influencers 'microcelebrities', a term defined by Theresa Senft as meaning 'a new style of online performance that involves people "amping up" their popularity over the Web using technologies like video, blogs and social networking sites'.[11] I've focused this book on the history of celebrity, but its future may produce some radical surprises. By the time a robot historian comes to judge this book (hello, future robot historian!), it might do so with the same tutting disappointment that I reserve for Daniel Boorstin; perhaps all celebrity culture will one day be opt-in, web-based, and fundamentally different to what has gone before. Or perhaps we'll all be microcelebrities, as Warhol predicted. Time will tell.

But I don't believe we're all destined for fifteen minutes of fame, or a world filled by 8 billion influencers. And I'm pretty relieved about that. My attitude to celebrity used to be ambivalent, but, the more I read, the more I think celebrity sounds like a lucrative, but existentially grim, purgatory that I'd hate to endure. I'm lucky to have a rewarding career as a public historian, but sometimes it involves appearing on TV. As someone recovering from crippling body image issues, I find this part of my job hard. Seeing myself on screen makes me feel nauseous, and it's doubly harrowing seeing viewers' comments on Twitter, as they discuss my body, hair, voice, choice of clothes, and the way I gesticulate wildly when I get excited. Even when people are complimentary, I squirm.

I'm not a celebrity. But I've had a couple of weird experiences in which my involvement in a popular TV show resulted in me getting an unsettling glimpse of what happens when fans go too far. I once had to involve the police. If we're really all due fifteen minutes of fame, I hope that I've had mine already, because - besides the usual caveats of war, disease, and the deaths of my loved ones - I can't think of anything worse. But, of course, on a wider scale, celebrity isn't going away. It's one of the most powerful forces in global culture, and its significance as a barometer of morality, taste, and opinion will continue to dominate our lives, just as it shaped public attitudes and popular culture in the past.

The story of how celebrity built our world is complex and has resisted standard patterns of linear progression; this book gave me so many headaches over the past four years. But, if I've done my job properly, next time you see a celebrity superstar, hopefully your brain will briefly flash up a mental image of Doctor Henry Sacheverell, and you'll remember that the gorgeous stars at the Oscars really aren't so different from a bellowing clergyman in a stupid wig. Well, okay, they're a bit different ... but you know what I mean.

Acknowledgements

This book has taken four years to produce, and has coincided almost exactly with four relentless years of heartbreaking infertility for me and my wife, Kate. Without doubt, my greatest debt is to Kate, whose courageous resilience - as we battled through multiple miscarriages and six rounds of brutal IVF - has inspired me in ways I never thought possible. Without her love, I'd be nothing, and this book would never have been finished. More importantly, without Kate's bravery, we never would have got our rainbow after the storm, our daughter Esmé, born four days before I finished editing this sentence.

That I got to write this book in the first place is thanks to the far-sighted wisdom of Bea Hemming, whose instant confidence in the idea gave me a real boost, particularly when I then realised the daunting scale of the challenge ahead. When Bea was offered an exciting new opportunity, I landed in the wonderful care of Holly Harley, whose limitless kindness and encouragement - despite my habit of sending despairing Twitter messages at 3 a.m. - was remarkably unwavering. Holly did nearly four years in the trenches with me, and guided me through writing most of the chapters. I would have been a gibbering wreck without her regular, uplifting pep talks.

A few months before I finished writing, Holly was offered a great new role at another company. This meant *Dead Famous* has been delivered unto you, dear reader, by the excellent Jenny Lord, who heroically rode to the rescue to not only shepherd my sprawling thoughts into a cogent book, but also to save you from a lot of bad jokes written when I was sleep-deprived. Count yourself lucky to have dodged those bullets. Jenny then handed me onto the splendid Maddy Price, who oversaw publication and marketing. Of course, supporting Jenny and Maddy in this vital process were Jo Whitford and Mark Handsley, whose diligent attention to detail neutralised my sloppy mistakes and extensive orthographic crimes. Mark also made sure my references were vaguely intelligible which was quite the job, I can assure you.

It's rare for an author to benefit from the combined talents of five superb editors (I suppose it's the only advantage of taking ages to finish) but, to the heroic quintet of Bea, Holly, Jenny, Jo, and Maddy, I must also add my brilliant agent, Donald Winchester, who not only gave great advice on structuring the book but has patiently endured my long phone calls and rambling emails for six years, and yet he remains eternally charming and unflappable.

Writing can feel rather lonely at times; it's easy to see it as a two-way grudge match between the author and the blank page, but - in actual fact - publishing a book takes an army of talented pro-fessionals boasting a wide array of skills. Hopefully you'll notice the many people listed in the credits - without them, these words would never have reached you. I'm enormously grateful to all of them for their hard work and enthusiasm, but special mention must go to Cathy Dunn for tracking down the wonderful images of celebrities you can see in the book, and to the designer of the book's cover, Loulou Clark, who was extraordinarily patient in putting up with my hare-brained ideas and infuriating insistence on running Twitter polls for reader feedback. I love the cover, and I'm so excited to see it debut in all the fanciest of bookshops.

Researching this book was the biggest challenge of my career, and involved devouring over a thousand sources, in the form of books, journal articles, academic theses, blogs, lectures, fan mag-azines, and old newspapers in the hunt for juicy stories and nu-anced understanding. I simply can't do justice to the sheer range of fascinating work I've encountered, produced by thousands of scholars and popular biographers who dedicated millions of hours to trying to better understand the past. I owe everything to their extraordinary scholarship, which is summarised in 1.4 million words of notes on my laptop, the vast majority of which couldn't fit into the final manuscript, no matter how much I tried.

My trawling through their work was meant to be a solitary process, but there were two short spells, somewhere around the first and third miscarriages, where my brain frazzled and all I wanted to do was be with my wife. For those few weeks, progress was only maintained thanks to the efforts of some very clever young researchers, who kindly notarised big piles of books I sent them, or helped me track down elusive PhD theses, all while juggling their own busy careers. My sincerest thanks go to Zenia Duell, Holly Nielsen, Henri Ward, Lydia Murtezaoglu, and Kirsty Walsh for their invaluable assistance and exemplary attention to detail.

As I embarked on this project, I was lucky enough to be able to call upon a fantastic team of experts to help me begin to navigate the vastness of historical popular culture. I'm indebted to: Dr Hannah Greig, Dr Nicola Phillips, and Dr Ruth Scobie for their early advice on eighteenth-century theatre; Dr Simon Morgan for his guidance on definitions of historical celebrity; Prof. Sarah Churchwell and Dr Anne Margaret Daniel for their F. Scott Fitzgerald expertise; Dr Anna Maria Barry for her knowledge of opera; Dr Hannah-Rose Murray for all things Frederick Douglass; Dr Emily Bowles for helping me find my way with Dickens; Dr Nicola Vinovrški for sharing her thesis about Casanova; Dr Ruth Penfold-Mounce for her thoughts on posthumous celebrity; Dr Penny C. S. Andrews for a crash course in Fandom Theory; Dr Sunny Singh, Prof. Rosie Thomas, and Dr Katherine Butler Schofield for their help on exploring celebrity in pre-1950s India; and Prof. Llewelyn Morgan, Prof. Sarah Bond, Dr Kate Cook, and Susie Dent for their linguistics brilliance, both ancient and medieval.

Once the book was nearly complete, I was privileged to receive incredible support from a host of generous scholars who read the unedited manuscript and offered vital feedback and corrections. This roster of historical titans comprises Dr Hannah Greig, Prof. Kate Williams, Dr Ruth Scobie, Prof. Llewelyn Morgan, Dr Bob

Nicholson, Dr Anna Senkiw, Dr Simon Morgan, Dr Penny C. S. Andrews, Dr Sadiah Qureshi, and Dr Michell Chresfield. Every one of them took time out from their busy schedules to make this book better, and I'm so grateful.

And, throughout these past four difficult years, I've been extremely lucky to have a wonderful support network getting me and Kate through the dark days. To our ever-loving family, our steadfast friends, our generous colleagues who supported us when we faltered, to my fabulous agents at Knight Ayton and Watson, Little, and to the many, many lovely people on Twitter who've cheered me up when I'd lost all hope – to you all, I offer a massive, Clara-the-Rhino-sized 'Thank you!'

With love,

Greg

September 2019

Credits

Weidenfeld & Nicolson would like to thank everyone who worked on the publication of *Dead Famous* in the UK.

Editorial
Jenny Lord
Holly Harley
Jo Whitford
Maddy Price

Copy-editor
Mark Handsley

Proofreader
Lorraine Jerram

Audio
Paul Stark
Amber Bates

Design
Loulou Clark
Joanna Ridley

Production
Hannah Cox

Marketing
Cait Davies

Publicity
Virginia Woolstencroft

Sales
Jen Wilson
Laura Fletcher
Esther Waters

Rights
Susan Howe
Krystyna Kujawinska
Jessica Purdue
Richard King
Louise Henderson

Finance
Jennifer Muchan
Jasdip Nandra
Elizabeth Beaumont
Afeera Ahmend
Sue Baker

Operations
Jo Jacobs
Sharon Willis

Recommended Reading for Curious Readers

There wasn't room for both references and a bibliography, so please go to www.gregjenner.com to see the latter.

But, if you're curious to know more about some of the subjects mentioned in *Dead Famous*, here's a thematic selection of books I'm happy to recommend. I've put an asterisk beside those that are written for a popular audience. The others are more scholarly, and might use academic language sometimes, but nothing in this list is too challenging for the adventurous reader. Enjoy!

Celebrity Theory

Edward Berenson and Eva Giloi (eds.), *Constructing Charisma: Celebrity, Fame, and Power in Nineteenth-Century Europe* (Berghahn Books, 2010)

* Joe Berlin (ed.), *Toxic Fame: Celebrities Speak on Stardom* (Visible Ink, 1996)

Daniel Boorstin, *The Image: A Guide to Pseudo-Events in America* (Atheneum, 1980)

Leo Braudy, *The Frenzy of Renown: Fame and Its History* (Vintage, 1997)

David Cannadine, 'The Context, Performance and Meaning of Ritual: The British Monarchy and the "Invention of Tradition", c.1820–1977', in Eric Hobsbawm and Terence Ranger (eds.), *The Invention of Tradition* (Cambridge University Press, 1983)

* Carol Dyhouse, *Glamour: Women, History, Feminism* (Zed Books, 2011)

Joshua Gamson, *Claims to Fame: Celebrity in Contemporary America* (University of California Press, Berkeley, 1994)

* Fred Inglis, *A Short History of Celebrity* (Princeton University Press, 2010)

H. J. Jackson, *Those Who Write for Immortality: Romantic Reputations and the Dream of Lasting Fame* (Yale, 2015)

*   Antoine Lilti (trans. Lynn Jeffress), *The Invention of Celebrity: 1750–1850* (Polity, 2017)

P. David Marshall, *Celebrity and Power: Fame in Contemporary Culture* (University of Minnesota Press, 1997)

*   John Potts, *A History of Charisma* (Palgrave Macmillan, 2009)

Joseph Roach, *It* (University of Michigan Press, 2007)

Chris Rojek, *Celebrity* (Reaktion, 2004)

Jerome C. Young, *The Age of Charisma* (Cambridge University Press, 2017)

Fandom Theory

Melissa A. Click (ed.), *Anti-Fandom: Dislike and Hate in the Digital Age* (New York University Press, 2019)

Mark Duffett, *Understanding Fandom: An Introduction to the Study of Media Fan Culture* (Bloomsbury Academic, 2013)

Henry Jenkins, *Textual Poachers: Television Fans & Participatory Culture* (Routledge, 1992)

Corin Throsby, 'Byron, Commonplacing and Early Fan Culture', in Tom Mole (ed.), *Romanticism and Celebrity Culture, 1750–1850* (Cambridge University Press, 2009)

Ancient Fame

*   Mary Beard, *The Roman Triumph* (Harvard University Press, 2007)

Alan Cameron, *Porphyrius the Charioteer* (Oxford University Press, 1973)

Isabel Davis and Catherine Nall (eds.), *Chaucer and Fame: Reputation and Reception* (D. S. Brewer, 2015)

Hazel Dodge, *Spectacle in the Roman World* (Bristol Classical Press, 2011)

*   Robert Garland, *Roman Celebrity* (Duckworth, 2006)

Gianni Guastella, *Word of Mouth: Fama and Its Personifications in Art and Literature from Ancient Rome to the Middle Ages* (Oxford University Press, 2017)

Philip Hardie, *Rumour and Renown: Representations of Fama in Western Literature* (Cambridge University Press, 2012)

*   Maria Wyke, *Caesar: A Life in Western Culture* (Granta, 2007)

Eighteenth-Century Celebs

*   Alfred Owen Aldridge, *Voltaire and the Century of Light* (Princeton University Press, 2015)

Donna T. Andrew and Randall McGowen, *The Perreaus and Mrs. Rudd: Forgery and Betrayal in Eighteenth-Century London* (University of California Press, 2001)

* Robyn Asleson et al., *A Passion for Performance: Sarah Siddons and Her Portraitists* (Getty Publications, 1999)

* Helen Barry, *The Castrato and His Wife* (Oxford University Press, 2011)

* Ian Campbell Ross, *Laurence Sterne: A Life* (Oxford University Press, 2001)

* Ron Chernow, *Washington: A Life* (Penguin, 2011)

* Quintin Colville (ed.), *Emma Hamilton: Seduction & Celebrity* (Thames & Hudson, 2018)

* Leo Damrosch, *Jean-Jacques Rousseau: Restless Genius* (Mariner Books, 2007)

Laura Engel, *Fashioning Celebrity: Eighteenth-Century British Actresses and Strategies for Image Making* (Ohio State University Press, 2011)

* John Ferling, *The Ascent of George Washington: The Hidden Political Genius of an American Icon* (Bloomsbury, 2009)

* Michelle Hetherington (ed.), *Cook & Omai: The Cult of the South Seas* (National Library of Australia, 2001)

* Ian Kelly, *Mr Foote's Other Leg: Comedy, Tragedy and Murder in Georgian London* (Picador, 2012)

Matthew J. Kinservik, *Sex, Scandal, and Celebrity in Late Eighteenth-Century England* (Palgrave Macmillan, 2007)

Heather McPherson, *Art & Celebrity in the Age of Reynolds and Siddons* (Pennsylvania State University Press, 2017)

Felicity Nussbaum, *Rival Queens: Actresses, Performance, and the Eighteenth-Century British Theatre* (University of Pennsylvania Press, 2010)

* Glynis Ridley, *Clara's Grand Tour* (Atlantic, 2004)

Leslie Ritchie, *David Garrick and the Mediation of Celebrity* (Cambridge University Press, 2019)

* James Sharpe, *Dick Turpin: The Myth of the English Highwayman* (Profile, 2005)

* Doug Stewart, *The Boy Who Would Be Shakespeare: A Tale of Forgery and Folly* (Da Capo Press, 2010)

* Caroline Weber, *Queen of Fashion: What Marie Antoinette Wore to the Revolution* (Aurum, 2007)

* Kate Williams, *England's Mistress: The Infamous Life of Emma Hamilton* (Arrow, 2006)

Nineteenth-Century Celebs

Malcolm Andrews, *Charles Dickens and His Performing Selves: Dickens and the Public Readings* (Oxford University Press, 1997)

* Barry Anthony, *The King's Jester: The Life of Dan Leno, Victorian Comic Genius* (IB Tauris, 2010)

* Debby Applegate, *The Most Famous Man in America: The Biography of Henry Ward Beecher* (Doubleday, 2006)

* Mark Bostridge, *Florence Nightingale: The Woman and Her Legend* (Penguin, 2008)

Charlotte Boyce et al., *Victorian Celebrity Culture and Tennyson's Circle* (Palgrave Macmillan, 2013)

Daniel Cavicchi, *Listening and Longing: Music Lovers in the Age of Barnum* (Wesleyan University Press, 2011)

* Ruth Cowen, *Relish: The Extraordinary Life of Alexis Soyer, Victorian Celebrity Chef* (Weidenfeld & Nicolson, 2007)

Clifton Crais and Pamela Scully, *Sara Baartman and the Hottentot Venus: A Ghost Story and a Biography* (Princeton University Press, 2008)

* Hugh Cunningham, *Grace Darling: Victorian Heroine* (Hambledon, 2007)

* Raymund Fitzsimons, *Edmund Kean: Fire from Heaven* (Dial Press, 1976)

Michael D. Garval, *Cléo de Mérode and the Rise of Modern Celebrity Culture* (Ashgate, 2012)

* Eve Golden, *Anna Held and the Birth of Ziegfeld's Broadway* (University of Kentucky Press, 2000)

* Robert Gottlieb, *Sarah: The Life of Sarah Bernhardt* (Yale University Press, 2010)

* Claire Harman, *Charlotte Brontë: A Life* (Penguin, 2015)

* Oliver Hilmes (trans. Stewart Spencer), *Franz Liszt: Musician, Celebrity, Superstar* (Yale University Press, 2016)

Matthew Hofer and Gary Scharnhorst (eds.), *Oscar Wilde in America: The Interviews* (University of Illinois Press, 2010)

* Michael T. Isenberg, *John L. Sullivan and His America* (Illini Books, 1994)

* Jeffrey Kahan, *Bettymania and the Birth of Celebrity Culture* (Lehigh University Press, 2010)

* Jeffrey Kahan, *The Cult of Kean* (Routledge, 2018)

Christine Kenyon Jones (ed.), *Byron: The Image of the Poet* (University of Delaware Press, 2008)

* Christopher Klein, *Strong Boy: The Life and Times of John L. Sullivan, America's First Sports Hero* (Lyons Press, 2013)

Ghislaine McDayter, *Byromania and the Birth of Celebrity Culture* (State University of New York Press, 2009)

* Lynn McDonald, *Mary Seacole: The Making of the Myth* (Iguana, 2014)

* Larry McMurty, *The Colonel and Little Missie: Buffalo Bill, Annie Oakley, and the Beginnings of Superstardom in America* (Simon & Schuster, 2006)

* Sara Maitland, *Vesta Tilley* (Virago, 1987)

* Sharon Marcus, *The Drama of Celebrity* (Princeton University Press, 2019)

Mary O'Connell, *Byron and John Murray: A Poet and His Publisher* (Oxford University Press, 2015)

Stanley Plumly, *Posthumous Keats: A Personal Biography* (W. W. Norton & Company, 2008)

* Simon Rae, *W. G. Grace: A Life* (Faber, 1998)

* Lucy Riall, *Garibaldi: Invention of a Hero* (Yale University Press, 2008)

* A. H. Saxon, *P. T. Barnum: The Legend and the Man* (Columbia University Press, 1989)

* Mary Seacole, *The Wonderful Adventures of Mrs Seacole in Many Lands* (1857)

Renée M. Sentilles, *Performing Menken: Adah Isaacs Menken and the Birth of American Celebrity* (Cambridge University Press, 2004)

* John Stauffer et al., *Picturing Frederick Douglass: An Illustrated Biography of the Nineteenth Century's Most Photographed American* (Liveright, 2015)

* Richard Tomlinson, *Amazing Grace: The Man Who Was W. G.* (Little, Brown, 2015)

* Vesta Tilley, *Recollections of Vesta Tilley* (Hutchinson, 1934)

Clara Tuite, *Lord Byron and Scandalous Celebrity* (Cambridge University Press, 2015)

* Alan Walker, *Franz Liszt: The Virtuoso Years, 1811-1847* (Cornell University Press, 1983)

* David Waller, *The Perfect Man: The Muscular Life and Times of Eugen Sandow, Victorian Strongman* (Victorian Secrets, 2011)

* Mary Warner Blanchard, *Oscar Wilde's America: Counterculture in the Gilded Age* (Yale University Press, 1998)

* Luke G. Williams, *Richmond Unchained: The Biography of the World's First Black Sporting Superstar* (Amberley, 2015)

Twentieth-Century Celebs

* David S. Brown, *Paradise Lost: A Life of F. Scott Fitzgerald* (Belknap Press, 2017)

* Kelly R. Brown, *Florence Lawrence, the Biograph Girl: America's First Movie Star* (McFarland, 2007)

* Gioia Diliberto, *Debutante: The Story of Brenda Frazier* (Alfred A. Knopf, 1987)

* Marybeth Hamilton, *The Queen of Camp: Mae West, Sex and Popular Culture* (HarperCollins, 1996)

* John F. Kasson, *The Little Girl Who Fought the Great Depression: Shirley Temple and 1930s America* (W. W. Norton & Company, 2014)

* Barbara Leaming, *If This Was Happiness: A Biography of Rita Hayworth* (Viking, 1990)

* Jane Leavy, *The Big Fella: Babe Ruth and the World He Created* (Harper-Luxe, 2018)

Karen Leick, *Gertrude Stein and the Making of an American Celebrity* (Routledge, 2009)

Adrienne L. McLean, *Being Rita Hayworth: Labor, Identity, and Hollywood Stardom* (Rutgers University Press, 2004)

Neepa Majumdar, *Wanted: Cultured Ladies Only! Female Stardom and Cinema in India, 1930-1950s* (University of Illinois Press, 2009)

* Barry Paris, *Louise Brooks: A Biography* (University of Minnesota Press, 1990)

* Deborah Paul (ed.), *Tragic Beauty: The Lost 1914 Memoirs of Evelyn Nesbit* (Lulu, 2006)

* D. J. Taylor, *Bright Young People: The Rise and Fall of a Generation 1918-1940* (Vintage, 2008)

* Paula Uruburu, *American Eve: Evelyn Newsbit, Stanford White, the Birth of the 'It' Girl, and the Crime of the Century* (Riverhead Books, 2008)

* Mae West, *Goodness Had Nothing to Do with It: The Autobiography* (W. H. Allen, 1960)

The Hollywood Fame Machine

* Samantha Barbas, 'Movie Crazy: Stars, Fans and the Cult of Celebrity, 1910-1950', PhD thesis (University of California, Berkeley, 2000)

* Scott Eyman, *The Speed of Sound: Hollywood and the Talkie Revolution 1926-1930* (Simon & Schuster, 1997)

* Jennifer Frost, *Hedda Hopper's Hollywood: Celebrity Gossip and American Conservatism* (New York University Press, 2011)

* Tom Kemper, *Hidden Talent: The Emergence of Hollywood Agents* (University of California Press, 2010)
* Adrienne L. McLean (ed.), *Glamour in a Golden Age: Movie Stars of the 1930s* (Rutgers University Press, 2011)
* Anne-Helen Peterson, *Scandals of Classic Hollywood: Sex, Deviance, and Drama from the Golden Age of American Cinema* (Plume, 2014)

Journalism and Gossip

* Neal Gabler, *Walter Winchell: Gossip, Power and the Culture of Celebrity* (Alfred A. Knopf, 1994)
  Kate Jackson, *George Newnes and the New Journalism in Britain 1880–1910: Culture and Profit* (Ashgate, 2001)
  David Vincent, *Privacy: A Short History* (Polity Press, 2016)
  Joel H. Wiener, *The Americanization of the British Press, 1830–1914: Speed in the Age of Transatlantic Journalism* (Palgrave Macmillan, 2011)

Other Themes

* Scott Bonn, *Why We Love Serial Killers: The Curious Appeal of the World's Most Savage Murderers* (Skyhorse, 2014)
  Michael Dobson, *The Making of the National Poet: Shakespeare, Adaptation and Authorship, 1660–1769* (Clarendon, 1992)
  Nadja Durbach, *Spectacle of Deformity: Freak Shows and Modern British Culture* (University of California Press, 2010)
  Paul Fryer (ed.), *Women in the Arts in the Belle Epoque: Essays on Influential Artists, Writers and Performers* (MacFarland, 2012)
  V. A. C. Gatrell, *The Hanging Tree: Execution and the English People, 1770–1868* (Oxford University Press, 1996)
  Ruth Penfold-Mounce, *Death, the Dead and Popular Culture* (Emerald Publishing, 2018)
* David Schmid, *Natural Born Celebrities: Serial Killers in American Culture* (University of Chicago Press, 2005)
  Jacob Smith, *The Thrillmakers: Celebrity, Masculinity, and Stunt Performance* (University of California Press, 2012)
  Marlene Tromp (ed.), *Victorian Freaks: The Social Context of Freaks in Britain* (Ohio University Press, 2008)
  Nicola J. Watson, *The Literary Tourist* (Palgrave Macmillan, 2006)

References

Introduction
1 Storm Gloor, 'Just How Long Is Your Fifteen Minutes? An Empirical Analysis of Artists' Time on the Popular Charts', *Journal of the Music & Entertainment Industry Educators Association*, vol. 11, no. 1 (2011).

1: Getting Discovered
1 Barry Cornwall, *The Life of Edmund Kean* (3rd edn, 2 vols., 1847; BiblioLife).

2 Chris Rojek, *Celebrity* (Reaktion, 2004).

3 Author unknown, 'Recollections of Kean', in *The New Monthly Magazine and Literary Journal*, vol. 2 (1834).

4 *Morning Chronicle* (27 January 1814).

5 I've used various sources for Kean's life: 'Kean, Edmund (1787-1833)', in Robert Crowcroft and John Cannon (eds.), *The Oxford Companion to British History* (2nd edn; Oxford University Press, 2015); Peter Thompson, 'Kean, Edmund (1787-1833)', in *The Oxford Dictionary of National Biography* (Oxford University Press, 2004); Barry Cornwall, *The Life of Edmund Kean* (3rd edn, 2 vols., 1847; BiblioLife); Raymund Fitzsimons, *Edmund Kean: Fire from Heaven* (Dial, 1976); Thomas Colley Grattan, 'My Acquaintance with the Late Mr. Kean', in *The New Monthly Magazine and Literary Journal*, vol. 3 (1833); Alfred L. Nelson and Gilbert B. Cross (eds.), *Drury Lane Journal: Selections from James Winston's Diaries, 1819-1827* (The Society for Theatre Research, 1974). Also I'm grateful to David Worrall's analysis in *Celebrity, Performance, Reception: British Georgian Theatre as Social Assemblage* (Cambridge University Press, 2013).

6 James Monaco, 'Celebration', in *Celebrity: The Media as Image Makers* (Dell, 1978).

7 Ovid, *Metamorphoses*, Book 15.

8 Robert A. Gurval, 'Caesar's Comet: The Politics and Poetics of an Augustan Myth', *Memoirs of the American Academy in Rome*, vol. 42 (1997).

9 Clara Tuite, *Lord Byron and Scandalous Celebrity* (Cambridge University Press, 2015).

10 Jeffrey Kahan, *Bettymania and the Birth of Celebrity Culture* (Lehigh University Press, 2010).

11 See Judith Plotz, *Romanticism and the Vocation of Childhood* (Palgrave, 2001), for more on the political power of childhood in the early 1800s.

12 For a study of modern backlashes and the pleasure of hate-watching, see Melissa A. Click (ed.), *Anti-Fandom: Dislike and Hate in the Digital Age* (New York University Press, 2019).

13 John F. Kasson, *The Little Girl Who Fought the Great Depression: Shirley Temple and 1930s America* (W. W. Norton & Company, 2014).

14 Temple told this story on Terry Wogan's chat show in the UK.

15 Shirley Temple, 'My Life and Times: The Autobiography of Shirley Temple, Part 1', *Pictorial Review*, August 1935.

16 Geoffrey Bond, 'Byron Memorabilia', in Christine Kenyon Jones (ed.), *Byron: The Image of the Poet* (University of Delaware Press, 2008).

17 Mary O'Connell, *Byron and John Murray: A Poet and His Publisher* (Oxford University Press, 2015).

18 Thomas Moore, *The Works of Lord Byron: With His Letters and Journals, and His Life*, vol. II (14 vols., John Murray, 1832).

19 Mary O'Connell, 'Byron and Albemarle Street', in Peter Cochran (ed.), *Byron in London* (Cambridge Scholars, 2008).

20 Mabel Dodge, 'Speculations, or Post-Impressionism in Prose', in *Arts & Decoration*, March 1913.

21 Karen Leick, *Gertrude Stein and the Making of an American Celebrity* (Routledge, 2009).

22 Gertrude Stein and Carl Van Vechten, *The Letters of Gertrude Stein and Carl Van Vechten, 1913–1946* (Columbia University Press, 2013).

23 For a good discussion on how highbrow modernists and lowbrow celebrity mingled in the 1930s, see Timothy W. Galow, *Writing Celebrity: Stein, Fitzgerald, and the Modern(ist) Art of Self-Fashioning* (Palgrave Macmillan, 2011).

24 Loren Glass, *Authors Inc.: Literary Celebrity in the Modern United States, 1880–1980* (New York University Press, 2004).

25 Bryce Conrad, 'Gertrude Stein in the American Marketplace', *Journal of Modern Literature,* vol. 19, no. 2 (Autumn 1995), pp. 215–33.

26 'The Infant Lyra', *The European Magazine, and London Review,* vol. 87 (1825).

27 See this page on the British Library website to read the letter: http://blogs.bl.uk/music/2018/05/mozartinlondon.html.

28 Ilias Chrissochoidis, 'London Mozartiana: Wolfgang's Disputed Age & Early Performances of Allegri's *Miserere*', *Musical Times* (Summer 2010).

29 For more on Liszt, see Oliver Hilmes, *Franz Liszt: Musician, Celebrity, Superstar*, trans. Stewart Spencer (Yale University Press, 2016); and also Alan Walker, *Franz Liszt: The Virtuoso Years, 1811-1847* (Cornell University Press, 1983).

30 Robert Shaughnessy, 'Siddons [née Kemble], Sarah: (1755-1831)', *The Oxford Dictionary of National Biography* (Oxford University Press, 2004), https://doi.org/10.1093/ref:odnb/25516.

31 See Jan McDonald, 'Acting and the Austere Joys of Motherhood: Sarah Siddons Performs Maternity', in Jane Milling and Martin Banham (eds.), *Extraordinary Actors: Essays on Popular Performers, Studies in Honour of Peter Thompson* (University of Exeter Press, 2004); also look at Robin Asleson, 'She Is Tragedy Personified: Crafting the Siddons Legend in Art and Life', in Robyn Asleson, Shelley Bennett and Mark Leonard, and Shearer West, *A Passion for Performance: Sarah Siddons and Her Portraitists* (Getty, 1999).

32 Julie Peakman has several books in this area, see: *Lascivious Bodies: A Sexual History of the Eighteenth Century* (Atlantic, 2004); *Whore Biographies, 1700-1825* (8 vols., Routledge, 2006-7); *Sexual Perversions, 1670-1890* (Palgrave Macmillan, 2009).

33 Lisa O'Connell, 'Authorship and Libertine Celebrity: Harriette Wilson's Regency Memoirs', in Peter Cryle and Lisa O'Connell (eds.), *Libertine Enlightenment: Sex, Liberty and Licence in the Eighteenth Century* (Palgrave Macmillan, 2003).

2: Fame Thrust upon Them

1 This quote from Cholly Knickerbocker's gossip column is taken from Gioia Diliberto's biography, *Debutante: The Story of Brenda Frazier*. She says she found it in the *New York Journal-American* in 1936, but the newspaper only acquired this name in 1937, after a merger, so it was likely published in the *New York American* in 1936.

2 All this is found in Gioia Diliberto, *Debutante: The Story of Brenda Frazier* (Alfred A. Knopf, 1987).

3 James Monaco, 'Celebration', in *Celebrity: The Media as Image Makers* (Dell, 1978).

4 Taylor Lorenz, 'Rising Instagram Stars are Posting Fake Sponsored

Content: "It's street cred - the more sponsors you have, the more credibility you have"', *The Atlantic* (18 December 2018).

5 See various studies by Patricia M. Greenfield and Yalda T. Uhls.

6 For more on Grace Darling's rescue and celebrity, I recommend Hugh Cunningham, *Grace Darling: Victorian Heroine* (Hambledon, 2007).

7 Edmund Burke, *A Philosophical Enquiry into the Origin of Our Ideas of the Sublime and Beautiful* (1757).

8 Mark Bostridge, *Florence Nightingale: The Woman and Her Legend* (Penguin Books, 2008).

9 Lynn McDonald, 'Mary Seacole and Claims of Evidence Based Practice and Global Influence', *Nursing Open*, vol. 3, issue 1 (2015).

10 'Mother of the Regiment', *The Argus* (Australian newspaper; 4 November 1857).

11 Lynn McDonald, 'Mary Seacole and Claims of Evidence Based Practice and Global Influence', *Nursing Open*, vol. 3, issue 1 (2015).

12 Corry Staring-Derks, Jeroen Staring and Elizabeth N. Anionwu, 'Mary Seacole: Global Nurse Extraordinaire', *Journal of Advanced Nursing* (November 2014).

13 My thanks to Dr Bob Nicholson of Edge Hill University for suggesting this quotation.

14 The most enjoyable rummage through the current psychological literature is Dean Burnett's amusing primer *The Idiot Brain: A Neuroscientist Explains What Your Head Is Really Up To* (Guardian Faber, 2016).

15 Laurie Langbauer, 'Leigh Hunt and *Juvenilia*', *Keats-Shelley Journal*, vol. 60 (2011).

16 Melissa A. Click (ed.), *Anti-Fandom: Dislike and Hate in the Digital Age* (New York University Press, 2019).

17 Geoffrey Holmes, *The Trial of Doctor Sacheverell* (Eyre Methuen, 1973).

18 Brian Cowan, 'Doctor Sacheverell and the Politics of Celebrity in Post-Revolutionary Britain', in Emrys D. Jones and Victoria Joule (eds.), *Intimacy and Celebrity in Eighteenth-Century Literary Culture* (Palgrave Macmillan, 2018).

19 Antoine Lilti, *The Invention of Celebrity: 1750-1850*, trans. Lynn Jeffress (Polity, 2017).

20 More of the hullaballoo can be found in Ron Chernow, *Washington: A Life* (Penguin Books, 2011).

21 John Ferling, *The Ascent of George Washington: The Hidden Political Genius of an American Icon* (Bloomsbury, 2009).

22 Barry Schwartz, *George Washington: The Making of an American Symbol* (Macmillan, 1987).

23 Gary Alan Fine, *Difficult Reputations: Collective Memories of the Evil, Inept and Controversial* (University of Chicago Press, 2001).

24 Ibid.

25 See Graham Dawson, *Soldier Heroes: British Adventure, Empire and the Imagining of Masculinities* (Routledge, 1994).

26 See the essays by Quintin Colville, Hannah Greig and Margarette Lincoln in the excellent book, edited by Quintin Colville and Kate Williams, *Emma Hamilton: Seduction & Celebrity* (Thames & Hudson, 2018).

27 For an excellent and accessible biography of Emma, see Kate Williams, *England's Mistress: The Infamous Life of Emma Hamilton* (Arrow, 2006).

28 Alex Kidson, *George Romney: A Complete Catalogue of His Paintings* (Yale University Press, 2015).

29 David Nasaw, *Going Out: The Rise and Fall of Public Amusements* (Harvard University Press, 1999).

30 Marybeth Hamilton, *The Queen of Camp: Mae West, Sex and Popular Culture* (HarperCollins, 1996).

31 For more, see Deborah Paul (ed.), *Tragic Beauty: The Lost 1914 Memoirs of Evelyn Nesbit* (Lulu, 2006).

32 *The History of the Remarkable Life and Death of John Sheppard* (1724); *A Narrative of the Robberies, Escapes, &c. of John Sheppard*, 8th edn (1724).

33 Maximillian Novak, 'Daniel Defoe and "Applebee's Original Weekly Journal": An Attempt at Re-Attribution', *Eighteenth-Century Studies*, vol. 45, no. 4 (Summer 2012).

34 Matthew Buckley, 'Sensations of Celebrity: "Jack Sheppard" and the Mass Audience', *Victorian Studies*, vol. 44, no. 3 (Spring 2002).

35 David Brandon, *Stand and Deliver: A History of Highway Robbery* (Sutton, 2010).

36 Erin Mackie, *Rakes, Highwaymen, and Pirates: The Making of the Modern Gentleman in the Eighteenth Century* (Johns Hopkins University Press, 2014).

37 V. A. C. Gatrell, *The Hanging Tree: Execution and the English People, 1770–1868* (Oxford University Press, 1996).

38 Jeffrey Jerome Cohen (ed.), *Monster Theory: Reading Culture* (University of Minnesota Press, 1996).

39 See E. P. Thompson et al., *Albion's Fatal Tree: Crime and Society in Eighteenth-Century England* (Random House, 1976).

40 Andrea McKenzie, 'The Real Macheath: Social Satire, Appropriation, and Eighteenth-Century Criminal Biography', *Huntington Library Quarterly*, vol. 69, no. 4 (December 2006).

41 Lilti, *Invention of Celebrity*.

42 Benedict Anderson, *Imagined Communities: Reflections on the Origin and Spread of Nationalism* (rev. edn, Verso, 2006).

43 Donna T. Andrew and Randall McGowen, *The Perreaus and Mrs. Rudd: Forgery and Betrayal in Eighteenth-Century London* (University of California Press, 2001).

44 *The Diabo-Lady: Or, A Match in Hell. A Poem,* published by Fielding and Walker, 1777 - the author was likely William Combe.

45 Gordon Turnbull, 'Criminal Biographer: Boswell and Margaret Caroline Rudd', *Studies in English Literature, 1500–1900*, vol. 26, no. 3, *Restoration and Eighteenth Century* (Summer 1986).

46 Max Gluckman, *Rituals of Rebellion in South-East Africa* (Manchester University Press, 1954).

47 David Schmid, *Natural Born Celebrities: Serial Killers in American Culture* (University of Chicago Press, 2005).

48 Emile Durkheim, *The Rules of Sociological Method* (original publication in French, 1895) by Steven Lukes (ed.), trans. W. D. Halls (The Free Press, 1982).

49 Scott Bonn, *Why We Love Serial Killers: The Curious Appeal of the World's Most Savage Murderers* (Skyhorse, 2014).

50 See Karen Halttunen, *Murder Most Foul: The Killer and the American Gothic Imagination* (Harvard University Press, 2000).

51 For more, see Schmid, *Natural Born Celebrities*.

52 Hallie Rubenhold, *The Five: The Untold Lives of the Women Killed by Jack the Ripper* (Doubleday, 2019).

3: What the Hell Is a Celebrity, Anyway?

1 See Tom Mole (ed.), *Romanticism and Celebrity Culture, 1750–1850*, editor's introduction (Cambridge University Press, 2009).

2 This etymology is widely reported in many texts, but I found this database of contested 'keywords' useful: http://keywords.pitt.edu/keywords_defined/celebrity.html.

3 Malcolm Muggeridge, *Muggeridge through the Microphone* (BBC, 1967).

4 Daniel Boorstin, *The Image: A Guide to Pseudo-Events in America* ([1962] Atheneum, reissued 1980).

5 Fred Inglis, *A Short History of Celebrity* (Princeton University Press, 2010).

6 For a quick summary of this idea, see the opening chapter of H. J. Jackson, *Those Who Write for Immortality: Romantic Reputations and the Dream of Lasting Fame* (Yale University Press, 2015).

7 Richard Salmon, 'The Physiognomy of the Lion: Encountering Literary Celebrity in the Nineteenth Century', in Mole (ed.), *Romanticism and Celebrity Culture*.

8 Samantha Barbas, 'Movie Crazy: Stars, Fans and the Cult of Celebrity, 1910-1950', PhD thesis (University of California, Berkeley, 2000).

9 Nicola Vinovrški, 'Casanova's Celebrity: A Case Study of Well-Knownness in 18th-Century Europe', PhD thesis (University of Queensland, 2015).

10 Elizabeth Edwards, '"Local and Contemporary": Reception, Community and the Poetry of Ann Julia Hatton ("Ann of Swansea")', *Women's Writing*, vol. 24 (2017).

11 Judith Pascoe, 'Ann Hatton's Celebrity Pursuits', in Mole (ed.), *Romanticism and Celebrity Culture*.

12 David Higgins, 'Celebrity, Politics and the Rhetoric of Genius', in Mole (ed.), *Romanticism and Celebrity Culture*.

13 Graeme Turner, *Understanding Celebrity* (SAGE, 2004).

14 Neal Gabler, *Toward a New Definition of Celebrity*, https://learcenter.org/pdf/Gabler.pdf.

15 Stacy A. Rozek, '"The First Daughter of the Land:" Alice Roosevelt as Presidential Celebrity, 1902-1906', *Presidential Studies Quarterly*, vol. 19, no. 1, part I (Winter 1989).

16 Anne-Helen Peterson, *Scandals of Classic Hollywood: Sex, Deviance, and Drama from the Golden Age of American Cinema* (Plume, 2014).

17 S. Gundle and C. T. Castelli, *The Glamour System* (Palgrave Macmillan, 2006).

18 Ruth Bierry, 'The New "Shady Dames" of the Screen', *Photoplay*, vol. 42, no. 3 (August 1932).

19 Hilary Lynn, 'What Is This Thing Called "X"?', *Photoplay* (April 1933).

20 Patricia Fara, *Fatal Attraction: Magnetic Mysteries of the Enlightenment* (Icon Books, 2005).

21 See Jerome C. Young, *The Age of Charisma* (Cambridge University Press, 2017), for an excellent overview.

22 See the BBC documentary *David Bowie: Five Years*, directed by Francis Whately, 2013.

23 Tom Mole, *Byron's Romantic Celebrity: Industrial Culture and the Hermeneutic of Intimacy* (Palgrave Macmillan, 2007).

24 Simon Morgan, 'Celebrity: Academic "Pseudo-Event" or a Useful Concept for Historians?', *Cultural and Social History*, vol. 8, no. 1 (2011).

25 Turner, *Understanding Celebrity*.

26 P. David Marshall, *Celebrity and Power: Fame in Contemporary Culture* (University of Minnesota Press, 1997).

27 Brian Cowan, *News, Biography, and Eighteenth-Century Celebrity* (Oxford Handbooks Online, 2016).

28 See Inglis, *A Short History of Celebrity*.

29 Jürgen Habermas, *The Structural Transformation of the Public Sphere* (John Wiley & Sons, 1962).

30 Stella Tillyard's essay 'Celebrity in 18th Century London', *History Today* (June 2005), is available online and is a great summary.

31 Julia Novak, '"Rais'd from a Dunghill, to a King's Embrace": Restoration Verse Satires on Nell Gwyn as Life Writing', *Life Writing*, vol. 13, no. 4 (2016).

32 Elaine McGirr, 'Nell Gwyn's Breasts and Colley Cibber's Shirts: Celebrity Actors and Their Famous "Parts"', in Emrys D. Jones and Victoria Joule (eds.), *Intimacy and Celebrity in Eighteenth-Century Literary Culture* (Palgrave Macmillan, 2018).

33 James Loxley, Anna Groundwater and Julie Sanders (eds.), *Ben Jonson's Walk to Scotland: An Annotated Edition of the Foot Voyage* (Cambridge University Press, 2015).

34 Jennifer R. Holl, 'Stars Indeed: The Celebrity Culture of Shakespeare's London', PhD dissertation, City University of New York (UMI Dissertations Publishing, 2013).

35 For an argument in favour of medieval religious celebrity, read Aviad Kleinberg's article 'Are Saints Celebrities?', *Cultural and Social History*, vol. 8, issue 3 (2011).

36 Leo Braudy, *The Frenzy of Renown: Fame and Its History* (Vintage, 1997).

37 Robert Garland, *Celebrity in Antiquity: From Media Tarts to Tabloid Queens* (Bloomsbury, 2006).

38 There's more on the dark side of charioteer fame in Parshia Lee-Stecum, 'Dangerous Reputations: Charioteers and Magic in Fourth-Century Rome', *Greece and Rome*, vol. 53, issue 2 (October 2006).

39 G. S. Aldrete, 'Material Evidence for Roman Spectacle and Sport', in Paul Christesen and Donald G. Kyle (eds.), *A Companion to Sport and Spectacle in Greek and Roman Antiquity* (Wiley–Blackwell, 2014).

40 For more on Porphyrius, see Alan Cameron, *Porphyrius the Charioteer* (Oxford University Press, 1973).

41 See Maria Wyke's very readable book *Caesar: A Life in Western Culture* (Granta, 2007) for an enjoyable study of how Caesar's reputation evolved after his death.

42 Mary Beard, *The Roman Triumph* (Harvard University Press, 2007).

43 Social theorist Chris Rojek argues that modern celebs also have two bodies: one biological and one perpetually frozen in media imagery. See Chris Rojek, 'The Two Bodies of Achieved Celebrity', in Robert van Krieken & Nicola Vinovrški (eds.) *Historical Social Research 32 - Celebrity's Histories: Case Studies & Critical Perspectives* (2019).

44 This was most famously articulated in Ernst H. Kantorowicz, *The King's Two Bodies: A Study in Medieval Political Theology* (reprinted by Princeton University Press, 2016).

45 Edward Berenson and Eva Giloi (eds.), *Constructing Charisma: Celebrity, Fame, and Power in Nineteenth-Century Europe* (Berghahn Books, 2010).

46 David Cannadine, 'The Context, Performance and Meaning of Ritual: The British Monarchy and the "Invention of Tradition", c.1820-1977', in Eric Hobsbawm and Terence Ranger (eds.), *The Invention of Tradition* (Cambridge University Press, 1983).

47 Eva Giloi, '"So Writes the Hand That Swings the Sword": Autograph Hunting and Royal Charisma in the German Empire, 1861-1888', in Berenson and Giloi (eds.), *Constructing Charisma*.

48 Edward Owens, 'All the World Loves a Lover: Monarchy, Mass Media and the 1934 Royal Wedding of Prince George and Princess Marina', *The English Historical Review*, vol. 133, issue 562 (June 2018).

49 For more on her clothing and jewels, see Caroline Weber, *Queen of Fashion: What Marie-Antoinette Wore to the Revolution* (Aurum, 2007).

50 There's a great analysis of this descent into celebrity indignity in Antoine Lilti, *The Invention of Celebrity: 1750-1850*, trans. Lynn Jeffress (Polity, 2017).

51 For more, see Philip Hardie, *Rumour and Renown: Representations of Fama in Western Literature* (Cambridge University Press, 2012).

52 Gianni Guastella, *Word of Mouth: Fama and Its Personifications in Art and Literature from Ancient Rome to the Middle Ages* (Oxford University Press, 2017).

53 Marcus Tullius Cicero, *De Officiis*, 2.44.

54 I'm grateful to Dr Kate Cook of Manchester University for her guidance here. She mentioned a handful of plays, most notably *Helen* by Euripides,

but noted to me that δύσκλεια is not commonly found in literary texts.

55 My thanks to Prof. Llewelyn Morgan at Brasenose College, University of Oxford, and Prof. Sarah Bond at the University of Iowa for their advice on this. See Sarah Bond, 'Altering Infamy: Status, Violence, and Civic Exclusion in Late Antiquity', *Classical Antiquity*, vol. 33, issue 1 (2014).

56 Thanks to the lexicographer Susie Dent for this information. *Infamy*, first used in 1380, seems to have derived from the Old French *infamie*, which itself came from the Latin *infamia*. *Notorious* comes from the Latin *notus*, meaning known or recognised.

57 For more, see Albert Borowitz, *Terrorism for Self-Glorification: The Herostratos Syndrome* (Kent State University Press, 2005).

58 Guastella, *Word of Mouth*.

59 Vinovrški, *Casanova's Celebrity*.

4: Image Is Everything

1 Julia H. Fawcett, 'Creating Character in "Chiaro Oscuro": Sterne's Celebrity, Cibber's Apology, and the Life of "Tristram Shandy"', *The Eighteenth Century*, vol. 53, no. 2 (Summer 2012).

2 Colley Cibber, *A Letter From Mr Cibber to Mr Pope* (G. Ewing, 1742).

3 Laurence Sterne, in *Letters of the Late Rev. Mr. Laurence Sterne to His Most Intimate Friends: With a Fragment in the Manner of Rabelais, to which are Prefixed Memoirs of His Life and Family*, vol. 1 (1776).

4 Ian Campbell Ross, *Laurence Sterne: A Life* (Oxford University Press, 2001).

5 Bradford Mudge, '"Enchanting Witchery": Sir Joshua Reynolds's Portrait of Kitty Fisher as Cleopatra', *Eighteenth-Century Life*, vol. 40, no. 1 (January 2016).

6 Laura J. Rosenthal, *Infamous Commerce: Prostitution in Eighteenth-Century British Literature and Culture* (Cornell University Press, 2006).

7 Marcia Pointon, 'The Lives of Kitty Fisher', *British Journal for Eighteenth-Century Studies*, vol. 27, issue 1 (March 2004).

8 Ibid.

9 Mudge, '"Enchanting Witchery"'.

10 Caroline Turner, 'Images of Mai', in Michelle Hetherington (ed.), *Cook & Omai: The Cult of the South Seas* (National Library of Australia, 2001).

11 For a detailed assessment of Omai's time in Britain, see Richard Connaughton, *Omai: The Prince Who Never Was* (Timewell, 2005).

12 William Van Lennep (ed.), *The Reminiscences of Sarah Kemble Siddons, 1773-1785* (Widener Library, 1942).

13 This story is referenced in Robyn Asleson, Shelley Bennett and Mark Leonard, and Shearer West, *A Passion for Performance: Sarah Siddons and Her Portraitists* (Getty, 1999). Their reference is as follows: '*Whitley, Artists and Their Friends, 2: 5*, cites Mrs. Gilbert Stuart Newton's letter of 1833 regarding a visit to Thomas Campbell. Campbell asked for Samuel Rogers's recollection of his visit to Reynolds's studio. His letter was published in *Scribner's Monthly*, c.1885'.

14 Van Lennep (ed.), *The Reminiscences of Sarah Kemble Siddons.*

15 William Hazlitt, 'On Sitting for One's Picture' (1823).

16 See Tom Mole's essay in Christine Kenyon Jones (ed.), *Byron: The Image of the Poet* (University of Delaware Press, 2008).

17 Laura Engel, *Fashioning Celebrity: Eighteenth-Century British Actresses and Strategies for Image Making* (Ohio State University Press, 2011).

18 Shweta Sachdeva, 'In Search of the Tawa'if in History: Courtesans, Nautch Girls and Celebrity Entertainers in India (1720s–1920s)', PhD thesis (SOAS, 2008).

19 Felicity Nussbaum, *Rival Queens: Actresses, Performance, and the Eighteenth-Century British Theatre* (University of Pennsylvania Press, 2010).

20 Anne Oldfield's fame had turned into celebrity by the time she died in 1730, and there was great public fascination when the contents of her house were auctioned off. See Claudine van Hensbergen, 'Anne Oldfield's Domestic Interiors: Auctions, Material Culture and Celebrity', in Emrys D. Jones and Victoria Joule (eds.), *Intimacy and Celebrity in Eighteenth-Century Literary Culture* (Palgrave Macmillan, 2018).

21 Source quoted in Engel, *Fashioning Celebrity.*

22 Michael Gamer and Terry F. Robinson, 'Mary Robinson and the Dramatic Art of the Comeback', *Studies in Romanticism*, vol. 48, no. 2 (Summer 2009).

23 Eve Golden, *Anna Held and the Birth of Ziegfeld's Broadway* (University of Kentucky Press, 2000).

24 Philip Edward Baruth (ed.), *Introducing Charlotte Charke: Actress, Author, Enigma* (University of Illinois Press, 1998); for a nuanced discussion, see Julia H. Fawcett, *Spectacular Disappearances: Celebrity and Privacy, 1696–1801* (University of Michigan Press, 2016).

25 Georgina Lock and David Worrall, 'Cross-Dressed Performance at the Theatrical Margins: Hannah Snell, the Manual Exercise, and the New Wells Spa Theater, 1750', *Huntington Library Quarterly*, vol. 77, no. 1 (Spring 2014).

26 Lucy Riall, *Garibaldi: Invention of a Hero* (Yale University Press, 2008).

27 Annelise K. Madsen, 'Dressing the Part: Mark Twain's White Suit, Copyright Reform, and the Camera', *The Journal of American Culture*, vol. 32, issue 1 (March 2009).

28 Larry McMurty, *The Colonel and Little Missie: Buffalo Bill, Annie Oakley, and the Beginnings of Superstardom in America* (Simon & Schuster, 2006); see also Robert W. Rydell and Rob Kroes, *Buffalo Bill in Bologna: The Americanization of the World, 1869-1922* (University of Chicago Press, 2005).

29 'Letter from George Colman to David Garrick dated Paris, July 27th 1766', in James Boaden (ed.), *The Private Correspondence of David Garrick with the Most Celebrated Persons of His Time: Volume 1: Now First Published from the Originals, and Illustrated with Notes, and a New Biographical Memoir of Garrick* (Cambridge University Press, 2013).

30 Heather McPherson, 'Garrickomania: Art, Celebrity and the Imaging of Garrick' (Folger Shakespeare Library Online).

31 Ruth Scobie, 'David Garrick's Wigless Celebrity', a 2016 lecture for TORCH (The Oxford Research Centre in the Humanities, University of Oxford), http://Torch.Ox.Ac.Uk/David-Garricks-Wigless-Garrick.

32 Jane Moody, 'Stolen Identities: Character, Mimicry, and the Invention of Samuel Foote', in Mary Luckhurst and Jane Moody (eds.), *Theatre and Celebrity in Britain, 1660-2000* (Palgrave Macmillan, 2005); see also Ian Kelly, *Mr Foote's Other Leg: Comedy, Tragedy and Murder in Georgian London* (Picador, 2012).

33 Heather McPherson, *Art & Celebrity in the Age of Reynolds and Siddons* (Pennsylvania State University Press, 2017).

34 Peter Benes, *For a Short Time Only: Itinerants and the Resurgence of Popular Culture in Early America* (University of Massachusetts Press, 2016).

35 Jason Goldsmith, 'Celebrity and the Spectacle of Nation', in Tom Mole (ed.), *Romanticism and Celebrity Culture, 1750-1850* (Cambridge University Press 2009).

36 See Sacheverell's entry on the National Portrait Gallery website.

37 All this detail is taken from Antoine Lilti, *The Invention of Celebrity: 1750-1850*, trans. Lynn Jeffress (Polity, 2017).

38 Patricia Anderson, *The Printed Image and the Transformation of Popular Culture: 1790-1860* (Clarendon Press, 1991).

39 David E. Sumner, *The Magazine Century: American Magazines Since 1900* (Peter Lang, 2010).

40 Harold Holzer, Gabor S. Boritt and Mark E. Neely Jr, *The Lincoln Image:*

Abraham Lincoln and the Popular Print (University of Illinois Press, 2005).

41 John Stauffer, Zoe Tronn and Celeste-Marie Bernier, *Picturing Frederick Douglass: An Illustrated Biography of the Nineteenth Century's Most Photographed American* (Liveright, 2015).

42 Hannah-Rose Murray, 'A "Negro Hercules": Frederick Douglass' Celebrity in Britain', *Celebrity Studies*, vol. 7, issue 2 (2016).

43 Quoted in Douglass's newspaper, *The North Star*, on 7 April 1849.

44 Michael Newbury, 'Eaten Alive: Slavery and Celebrity in Antebellum America', *ELH*, vol. 61, no. 1 (Spring 1994).

45 Annie Rudd, 'Victorians Living in Public: Cartes de Visite as 19th-Century Social Media', *Photography and Culture*, vol. 9, issue 3 (November 2016).

46 Rachel Teukolsky, 'Cartomania: Sensation, Celebrity, and the Democratized Portrait', *Victorian Studies*, vol. 57, no. 3 (Spring 2015).

47 'Lady Beggars', *Vanity Fair* (February 1862).

48 Rudd, 'Victorians Living in Public'.

49 For much more detail, see Mary Warner Blanchard, *Oscar Wilde's America: Counterculture in the Gilded Age* (Yale University Press, 1998).

50 Matthew Hofer and Gary Scharnhorst (eds.), *Oscar Wilde in America: The Interviews* (University of Illinois Press, 2010).

51 See Daniel A. Novak, 'Sexuality in the Age of Technological Reproducibility: Oscar Wilde, Photography, and Identity', in Joseph Bristow (ed.), *Oscar Wilde and Modern Culture* (Ohio University Press, 2009).

52 For a short but detailed look at the trial, I recommend Viv Gardner, 'Gertie Millar and the Rules for Actresses and Vicars' Wives', in Jane Milling and Martin Banham (eds.), *Extraordinary Actors: Essays on Popular Performers, Studies in Honour of Peter Thomson* (University of Exeter Press, 2004).

53 You can read Foley's apology online at Google Books in 1904's *British Journal of Dental Science and Prosthetics*, vol. 47.

54 Brooks's career nosedived after she went to Germany, but critics rediscovered her in later decades and she's now an iconic figure in early cinema, not just for her hair but also for her subtle, natural acting style. I really enjoyed Barry Paris, *Louise Brooks: A Biography* (University of Minnesota Press, 1990).

55 Marysa Demoor, *Marketing the Author: Authorial Personae, Narrative Selves and Self-Fashioning, 1880–1930* (Palgrave Macmillan, 2004).

56 Robert Gunn, '"How I Look": Fanny Fern and the Strategy of Pseudonymity', *Legacy*, vol. 27, no. 1 (2010).

57 Mark Twain, *The Autobiography of Mark Twain, Volume 3: The Complete and Authoritative Edition* (University of California, 2015).

58 Ann R. Hawkins and Maura Ives (eds.), *Women Writers and the Artifacts of Celebrity in the Long Nineteenth Century* (Ashgate, 2012).

59 Lizzie White, 'Commodifying the Self: Portraits of the Artist in the Novels of Marie Corelli', in Hawkins and Ives (eds.), *Women Writers and the Artifacts of Celebrity*.

60 Whitney Arnold, 'Rousseau and Reformulating Celebrity', *The Eighteenth Century*, vol. 55, no. 1 (Spring 2014).

61 Lilti, *Invention of Celebrity*.

5: The Art of Self-Promotion

1 Michael Keevak, *The Pretended Asian: George Psalmanazar's Eighteenth-Century Formosan Hoax* (Wayne State University Press, 2004).

2 Jack Lynch, *Deception and Detection in Eighteenth-Century Britain* (Ashgate, 2008).

3 Lisa Forman Cody, *Birthing the Nation: Sex, Science, and the Conception of Eighteenth-Century Britons* (Oxford University Press, 2005).

4 *Daily Telegraph* (14 January 1796).

5 William-Henry Ireland, *A Full and Explanatory Account of the Shakespearean Forgery by myself the writer William Henry Ireland* (1796).

6 For more on the story, see Doug Stewart's entertaining book *The Boy Who Would Be Shakespeare: A Tale of Forgery and Folly* (Da Capo, 2010).

7 A.H. Saxon, *P. T. Barnum: The Legend and the Man* (Columbia University Press, 1989).

8 T. H. Clarke, *The Rhinoceros from Dürer to Stubbs: 1515–1799* (Sotheby's, 1986).

9 For more on Clara's incredible story, I recommend Glynis Ridley, *Clara's Grand Tour* (Atlantic, 2004).

10 David Higgins, 'Celebrity, Politics and the Rhetoric of Genius', in Tom Mole (ed.), *Romanticism and Celebrity Culture, 1750–1850* (Cambridge University Press, 2009).

11 H. J. Jackson, *Those Who Write for Immortality: Romantic Reputations and the Dream of Lasting Fame* (Yale University Press, 2015).

12 Ibid.

13 William Hazlitt, 'On the Living Poets' (1818).

14 Robert Montgomery, *The Puffiad* (1830).

15 Leigh Hunt, *Lord Byron and Some of His Contemporaries* (H. Colburn, 1828).

16 Alison Moore, 'The Spectacular Anus of Joseph Pujol: Recovering the Pétomane's Unique Historic Context', *French Cultural Studies*, vol. 24, no. 1 (February 2013).

17 This story is quoted by Eve Golden, *Anna Held and the Birth of Ziegfeld's Broadway* (University of Kentucky Press, 2000); she says it is from the *New York Journal* in October 1897, but she doesn't give an exact date.

18 *The Evening Journal* (1896), quoted in Golden, *Anna Held and the Birth of Ziegfeld's Broadway*.

19 Jacob Smith, *The Thrill Makers: Celebrity, Masculinity and Stunt Performance* (University of California Press, 2012).

20 Golden, *Anna Held and the Birth of Ziegfeld's Broadway*.

21 Ibid.

22 Matilda Alice Powles de Frece, *Recollections of Vesta Tilley* (Hutchinson, 1934).

23 Daniel Cavicchi, *Listening and Longing: Music Lovers in the Age of Barnum* (Wesleyan University Press, 2011).

24 Robert Gottlieb, *Sarah: The Life of Sarah Bernhardt* (Yale University Press, 2010).

25 Sharon Marcus, *The Drama of Celebrity* (Princeton University Press, 2019).

26 Elizabeth Silverthorne, *Sarah Bernhardt* (Chelsea House, 2004).

27 Mary Louise Roberts, 'Rethinking Female Celebrity: The Eccentric Star of Nineteenth-Century France', in Edward Berenson and Eva Giloi (eds.), *Constructing Charisma: Celebrity, Fame, and Power in Nineteenth-Century Europe* (Berghahn Books, 2010).

28 Raymund Fitzsimons, *Edmund Kean: Fire from Heaven* (Dial, 1976).

29 Percy Bysshe Shelley, *Letters: Shelley in Italy* (Clarendon Press, 1964).

30 Sos Eltis, 'Private Lives and Public Spaces: Reputation, Celebrity and the Late-Victorian Actress', in Mary Luckhurst and Jane Moody (eds.), *Theatre and Celebrity in Britain, 1660–2000* (Palgrave Macmillan, 2005).

31 Gottlieb, *Sarah: The Life of Sarah Bernhardt*.

32 Kimberly Snyder Manganelli, *Transatlantic Spectacles of Race: The Tragic Mulatta and the Tragic Muse* (Rutgers University Press, 2012).

33 Anne-Helen Peterson, *Scandals of Classic Hollywood: Sex, Deviance, and Drama from the Golden Age of American Cinema* (Plume, 2014).

34 Michael Williams, '"Gilbo Garbage" or "The Champion Lovemakers of Two Nations": Uncoupling Greta Garbo and John Gilbert', in Shelly Cobb and Neil Ewen (eds.), *First Comes Love: Power Couples, Celebrity Kinship and Cultural Politics* (Bloomsbury Academic, 2015).

35 Sarah Churchwell, '"The Most Envied Couple in America in 1921": Making the Social Register in the Scrapbooks of F. Scott and Zelda Fitzgerald', in Cobb and Ewen (eds.), *First Comes Love*; see also Ruth Prigozy, 'Scott, Zelda, and the Culture of Celebrity', in Ruth Prigozy (ed.), *The Cambridge Companion to F. Scott Fitzgerald* (Cambridge University Press, 2002).

36 Antoine Lilti, *The Invention of Celebrity: 1750–1850*, trans. Lynn Jeffress (Polity, 2017).

37 Fitzsimons, *Edmund Kean*.

38 Laura Engel, *Fashioning Celebrity: Eighteenth-Century British Actresses and Strategies for Image Making* (Ohio State University Press, 2011).

39 Paul Goring, 'Theatrical Riots and Conspiracies in London and Edinburgh: Charles Macklin, James Fennell and the Rights of Actors and Audiences', *The Review of English Studies*, vol. 67, issue 278 (1 February 2016).

40 Lawrence W. Levine, *Highbrow/Lowbrow: The Emergence of Cultural Hierarchy in America* (Harvard University Press, 1988).

41 Jeffrey Kahan, *The Cult of Kean* (Routledge, 2018).

42 George Cruikshank, *The Theatrical Atlas* (7 May 1814), https://www.metmuseum.org/art/collection/search/389121.

43 Fitzsimons, *Edmund Kean*.

44 This is in his introduction to *This Must Be the Place: Memoirs of Montparnasse by Jimmie 'the Barman' Charters*; it's quoted in Lyle Larsen, *Stein and Hemingway: The Story of a Turbulent Friendship* (McFarland, 2014).

45 Caroline De Costa, *The Diva and Doctor God: Letters from Sarah Bernhardt to Doctor Samuel Pozzi* (Xlibris, 2010); see also Gottlieb, *Sarah: The Life of Sarah Bernhardt*.

46 Gottlieb, *Sarah: The Life of Sarah Bernhardt*.

47 Amy Fine Collins, 'The Powerful Rivalry of Hedda Hopper and Louella Parsons', *Vanity Fair* (April 1997).

48 Jennifer Frost, *Hedda Hopper's Hollywood: Celebrity Gossip and American Conservatism* (New York University Press, 2011).

49 Leslie Ritchie, *David Garrick and the Mediation of Celebrity* (Cambridge University Press, 2019).

50 Michael Harris, *London Newspapers in the Age of Walpole: A Study of the Origins of the Modern English Press* (London Associated Presses, 1987).

51 As ever, see Lilti's excellent *Invention of Celebrity*.

52 Stella Tillyard, 'Celebrity in 18th-Century London', *History Today*, vol. 55, issue 6 (June 2005), http://www.historytoday.com/stella-tillyard/celebrity-18th-century-london.

53 Joel H. Wiener, *The Americanization of the British Press, 1830-1914: Speed in the Age of Transatlantic Journalism* (Palgrave Macmillan, 2011).

54 Kate Jackson, *George Newnes and the New Journalism in Britain, 1880-1910: Culture and Profit* (Ashgate, 2001).

55 Ann K. McClellan, 'Tit-Bits, New Journalism, and Early Sherlock Holmes Fandom', *Journal of Transformative Works*, vol. 23 (2017).

56 Wiener, *Americanization of the British Press*.

57 Charlotte Boyce, Paraic Finnerty and Anne-Marie Millim, *Victorian Celebrity Culture and Tennyson's Circle* (Palgrave Macmillan, 2013).

58 Richard Salmon, 'Signs of Intimacy: The Literary Celebrity in the "Age of Interviewing"', *Victorian Literature and Culture*, vol. 25, no. 1 (1997).

59 Neal Gabler, *Walter Winchell: Gossip, Power and the Culture of Celebrity* (Alfred A. Knopf, 1994).

60 Gioia Diliberto, *Debutante: The Story of Brenda Frazier* (Alfred A. Knopf, 1987).

61 Kerrie Holloway, 'The Bright Young People of the Late 1920s: How the Great War's Armistice Influenced Those Too Young to Fight', *Journal of European Studies*, vol. 45, no. 4 (October 2015).

62 I recommend D. J. Taylor's book *Bright Young People: The Rise and Fall of a Generation 1918-1940* (Vintage, 2008) as a great overview.

6: Bodies of Opinion

1 Irene Gammel, *Looking for Anne: How Lucy Maud Montgomery Dreamed Up a Literary Classic* (Key Porter Books, 2008).

2 Sue Morgan, '"Wild Oats or Acorns?" Social Purity, Sexual Politics and the Response of the Late Victorian Church', *Journal of Religious History*, vol. 31, issue 2 (June 2007).

3 Paula Uruburu, *American Eve: Evelyn Nesbit, Stanford White, the Birth of the 'It' Girl, and the Crime of the Century* (Riverhead Books, 2008).

4 Deborah Paul (ed.), *Tragic Beauty: The Lost 1914 Memoirs of Evelyn Nesbit* (Lulu, 2006).

5 Ali Gray, 'Is a Woman's Idea of the Perfect Body Really That Much Different Than a Man's?', *Marie Claire* (11 April 2014).

6 Shearer West, 'Siddons, Celebrity and Regality: Portraiture and the Body of the Ageing Actress', in Mary Luckhurst and Jane Moody (eds.), *Theatre and Celebrity in Britain, 1660-2000* (Palgrave Macmillan, 2005).

7 Quintin Colville and Kate Williams (eds.), *Emma Hamilton: Seduction and Celebrity* (Thames & Hudson, 2018).

8 Robert Gottlieb, *Sarah: The Life of Sarah Bernhardt* (Yale University Press, 2010).

9 David Monod, 'The Eyes of Anna Held: Sex and Sight in the Progressive Era', *The Journal of the Gilded Age and Progressive Era*, vol. 10, issue 3 (June 2011). For more on her, see Eve Golden's very readable *Anna Held and the Birth of Ziegfeld's Broadway* (University of Kentucky Press, 2000).

10 Michael D. Garval, *Cléo de Mérode and the Rise of Modern Celebrity Culture* (Ashgate, 2012).

11 'Dandy Dogs', *Atlanta Constitution* (8 November 1896).

12 Robert N. Keely, *Paris and All the World Besides* (Howard Myers, 1930).

13 D. Garval, *Cléo de Mérode and the Rise of Modern Celebrity Culture.*

14 'First Picture of Cleo's Ears', *New York Journal* (14 September 1897).

15 *Tacoma Daily News* (20 October 1897).

16 'CLEO A FLAT FAILURE', *Los Angeles Times* (10 October 1897).

17 Matthew Hofer and Gary Scharnhorst (eds.), *Oscar Wilde in America: The Interviews* (University of Illinois Press, 2010).

18 Mary Warner Blanchard, *Oscar Wilde's America: Counterculture in the Gilded Age* (Yale University Press, 1998); and Hofer and Scharnhorst (eds.), *Oscar Wilde in America.*

19 'Veronica Lake Is Paramount's Bid for Year's Best Glamor Starlet', *Life* magazine (3 March 1941).

20 *Life* magazine (24 November 1941).

21 Patricia A. Suchy, 'Lake Effects', *CineAction*, no. 56 (June 2001).

22 For a well-written biography, see Barbara Leaming, *If This Was Happiness: A Biography of Rita Hayworth* (Viking, 1990).

23 Her biographer Barbara Leaming writes that Hayworth confided in Orson Welles, her husband, about the abusive and exploitative relationship.

24 'What It Takes to Be a Hollywood Husband! "Mr. Rita Hayworth" Tells', *Screenland* (1940).

25 Larry Carr, *Four Fabulous Faces: The Evolution and Metamorphosis of Garbo, Swanson, Crawford and Dietrich* (Penguin Books, 1978).

26 It's fairly theoretical at times, but don't be put off by the academic phraseology - it's a fascinating study: Adrienne L. McLean, *Being Rita Hayworth: Labor, Identity, and Hollywood Stardom* (Rutgers University Press, 2004).

27 For more on Fearless Nadia (what a name!) please see Rosie Thomas, *Bombay Before Bollywood: Film City Fantasies* (State University of New York Press, 2013), and Neepa Majumdar, *Wanted: Cultured Ladies Only! Female Stardom and Cinema in India, 1930–1950s* (University of Illinois Press, 2009).

28 The most detailed analysis of what we do and don't know is Clifton Crais and Pamela Scully, *Sara Baartman and the Hottentot Venus: A Ghost Story and a Biography* (Princeton University Press, 2008), but you might also enjoy Rachel Holmes, *The Hottentot Venus: The Life and Death of Saartjie Baartman: Born 1789 - Buried 2002* (Bloomsbury, 2008).

29 Jocelyn Harris, *Satire, Celebrity, and Politics in Jane Austen* (Bucknell University Press, 2017).

30 Ibid.

31 'Mrs Mathews', *Memoirs of Charles Mathews, Comedian*, vol. IV (Richard Bentley, 1839).

32 Robert Bogdan, *Freak Show: Presenting Human Oddities for Amusement and Profit* (University of Chicago, 1990).

33 There's loads on this subject, but a decent starting place is Marlene Tromp (ed.), *Victorian Freaks: The Social Context of Freaks in Britain* (Ohio University Press, 2008).

34 Nadja Durbach, *Spectacle of Deformity: Freak Shows and Modern British Culture* (University of California Press, 2010).

35 Brian Rejack, 'Daniel Lambert's Figure: Embodying Romantic Periodical Texts', *Nineteenth-Century Contexts*, vol. 38, issue 1 (2016).

36 Joyce L. Huff, 'The Dissemination, Fragmentation, and Reinvention of the Legend of Daniel Lambert, King of Fat Men', in Tromp (ed.), *Victorian Freaks*.

37 Max Olesker, 'The Rise and Rise of the Spornosexual', *Esquire* (January 2015).

38 Thomas Cation Duncan, *How to Be Plump, or, Talks on Physiological Feeding* (Duncan Brothers, 1878).

39 As quoted in John Mariani, *America Eats Out* (William Morrow and Co., 1991).

40 For a wider assessment of this period of cultural anxiety, when women and gay men threatened gender orthodoxy, see Elaine Showalter, *Sexual Anarchy: Gender and Culture at the Fin de Siècle* (Little, Brown, 1992).

41 Dominic G. Morais, 'Branding Iron: Eugen Sandow's "Modern" Marketing Strategies, 1887-1925', *Journal of Sport History*, vol. 40, no. 2 (Summer 2013).

42 This is a lively read, though a couple of sports historians have criticised elements of the research: David Waller, *The Perfect Man: The Muscular Life and Times of Eugen Sandow, Victorian Strongman* (Victorian Secrets, 2011). For a more critical study, try David Chapman, *Sandow the Magnificent:*

Eugen Sandow and the Beginnings of Modern Bodybuilding (University of Illinois Press, 1994).

43 Waller, *Perfect Man*.

44 For an interesting analysis of changing attitudes to fatness, see Alan J. Bilton, 'Nobody Loves a Fat Man: Fatty Arbuckle and Conspicuous Consumption in Nineteen Twenties America', *American Studies,* vol. 57, no. 1 (2012).

7: Show Me the Money!

1 Peter T. Struck, 'Greatest of All Time: Lifestyles of the Rich and Famous Roman Athletes', *Lapham's Quarterly* (August 2010).

2 For all things Roman sport, check David Potter, *The Victor's Crown* (Quercus, 2011); see also G. S. Aldrete, 'Material Evidence for Roman Spectacle and Sport', in Paul Christesen and Donald G. Kyle (eds.), *A Companion to Sport and Spectacle in Greek and Roman Antiquity* (Wiley-Blackwell, 2014); see also Sinclair Bell, 'Roman Chariot Racing: Charioteers, Factions, Spectators', in Christesen and Kyle (eds.), *Companion to Sport and Spectacle*; and see also Hazel Dodge, *Spectacle in the Roman World* (Bloomsbury, 2011).

3 I never got to write the biography. I've instead gone down the route of trying to get it made as a TV drama, but thankfully Luke G. Williams did a fine job with his excellent *Richmond Unchained: The Biography of the World's First Black Sporting Superstar* (Amberley, 2015).

4 Michael T. Isenberg, *John L. Sullivan and His America* (Illini Books, 1994).

5 Christopher Klein, *Strong Boy: The Life and Times of John L. Sullivan, America's First Sports Hero* (Lyons Press, 2013).

6 Richard Tomlinson, *Amazing Grace: The Man Who Was W. G.* (Little, Brown, 2015).

7 'Death of Richmond, the Celebrated Boxer', *Morning Post* (2 January 1830).

8 Helen Barry, *The Castrato and His Wife* (Oxford University Press, 2011).

9 *The Daily Advertiser* (15 March 1735).

10 Felicity Nussbaum, *Rival Queens: Actresses, Performance, and the Eighteenth-Century British Theatre* (University of Pennsylvania Press, 2010).

11 Ibid.

12 Clara Tuite, *Lord Byron and Scandalous Celebrity* (Cambridge University Press, 2015).

13 Anne Humpherys, 'Victorian Stage Adaptations and Novel Appropriations', in Sally Ledger and Holly Furneaux (eds.), *Charles Dickens in Context*

(Cambridge University Press, 2011); see also Paul Schlicke, 'Dickens and the Pirates: The Case of the Odd Fellow', *Dickensian*, vol. 100 (Winter 2004).

14 Heather McPherson, 'Garrickomania: Art, Celebrity and the Imaging of Garrick' (Folger Shakespeare Library Online).

15 You can see them at Duke University's Digital Library, https://idn. duke.edu/ark:/87924/r37p8tq26. Digital Collection: W. Duke, Sons & Co. Advertising Materials, 1880-1910: Card Series: N79 Histories of Poor Boys Who Have Become Rich and Other Famous People, W. Duke, Sons & Co., 1888.

16 Felicity Nussbaum, 'Actresses and the Economics of Celebrity, 1700-1800', in Mary Luckhurst and Jane Moody (eds.), *Theatre and Celebrity in Britain, 1660-2000* (Palgrave Macmillan, 2005).

17 Antoine Lilti, *The Invention of Celebrity: 1750-1850*, trans. Lynn Jeffress (Polity, 2017).

18 Tomlinson, *Amazing Grace*.

19 Michael D. Garval, *Cléo de Mérode and the Rise of Modern Celebrity Culture* (Ashgate, 2012).

20 Hansen's work is mentioned in a wider history of Indian film, Neepa Majumdar, *Wanted: Cultured Ladies Only! Female Stardom and Cinema in India, 1930-1950s* (University of Illinois Press, 2009).

21 Gupta Ruchi, *Advertising Principles and Practice* (S. Chand, 2012).

22 Raymund Fitzsimons, *Edmund Kean: Fire from Heaven* (Dial, 1976).

23 For all things Farinelli, see this trio of articles: Judith Milhouse and Robert D. Hume, 'Construing and Misconstruing Farinelli in London', *Journal for Eighteenth-Century Studies*, vol. 28, issue 3 (December 2005); Xavier Cervantes, '"Let 'Em Deck the Verses with Farinelli's Name": Farinelli as a Satirical Trope in English Poetry and Verse of the 1730s', *Journal for Eighteenth-Century Studies*, vol. 28, issue 3 (December 2005); Berta Joncus, 'One God, So Many Farinellis: Mythologizing the Star Castrato', *Journal for Eighteenth-Century Studies*, vol. 28, issue 3 (December 2005).

24 *Daily Post* (7 July 1737).

25 A. H. Saxon, *P. T. Barnum: The Legend and the Man* (Columbia University Press, 1989).

26 'A Man of Culture Rare', *Rochester Democrat and Chronicle* (8 February 1882).

27 Eve Golden, *Anna Held and the Birth of Ziegfeld's Broadway* (University of Kentucky Press, 2000).

28 Lilti, *Invention of Celebrity*.

29 Quoted from John F. Kasson, *The Little Girl Who Fought the Great Depression: Shirley Temple and 1930s America* (W. W. Norton & Company, 2014); see also Kathryn Fuller-Seeley, 'Shirley Temple: Making Dreams Come True', in Adrienne L. McLean (ed.), *Glamour in a Golden Age: Movie Stars of the 1930s* (Rutgers University Press, 2011).

30 The story was reported in the *Sheffield Independent* back in the UK, in July 1821.

31 The letter was reprinted in London in the *Public Ledger and Daily Advertiser* (13 July 1821).

32 Reported in the *Fife Herald* (15 December 1825).

33 Joseph Fitzgerald Molloy, *The Life and Adventures of Edmund Kean: Tragedian, 1787-1833* (Downey & Co., 1897).

34 Peter Benes, *For a Short Time Only: Itinerants and the Resurgence of Popular Culture in Early America* (University of Massachusetts Press, 2016).

35 In 1776, New York's population was about 25,000 compared to London's 750,000. In 1700, it was barely 5,000! - we know this thanks to the work of the historical demographer Robert V. Wells.

36 See Daniel Cavicchi, *Listening and Longing: Music Lovers in the Age of Barnum* (Wesleyan University Press, 2011).

37 Robert C. Toll's book *The Entertainment Machine: American Show Business in the Twentieth Century* gives a potted history of how film, comedy, radio, theatre, and television came to dominate American pop culture. He looks at the economics and logistics of showbiz, and how technology came to conquer geography.

38 Cavicchi, *Listening and Longing*.

39 Golden, *Anna Held and the Birth of Ziegfeld's Broadway*.

40 Robert W. Rydell and Rob Kroes, *Buffalo Bill in Bologna: The Americanization of the World, 1869-1922* (University of Chicago Press, 2005).

41 Robert Gottlieb, *Sarah: The Life of Sarah Bernhardt* (Yale University Press, 2010).

42 Anthony Slide, *The Encyclopedia of Vaudeville* (University of Mississippi Press, 2012).

43 Whitney Helms, 'Performing Authorship in the Celebrity Sphere: Dickens and the Reading Tours', *Papers on Language & Literature*, vol. 50, no. 2 (Spring 2014).

44 Malcolm Andrews, *Charles Dickens and His Performing Selves: Dickens and the Public Readings* (Oxford University Press, 1997).

45 Madeline House and Graham Storey (eds.), *The Letters of Charles Dickens*, vols. 6 and 11 (Clarendon Press, 1999).

46 Ibid.

47 John Forster, *The Life of Charles Dickens* (Chapman and Hall, 1872).

48 Jillian Martin, 'Making It in America: How Charles Dickens and His Cunning Manager George Dolby Made Millions from a Performance Tour of the United States, 1867-1868', PhD thesis (Georgia State University Press, 2014).

49 Oliver Hilmes, *Franz Liszt: Musician, Celebrity, Superstar*, trans. Stewart Spencer (Yale University Press, 2016).

50 Marlis Schweitzer, 'Singing Her Own Song: Writing the Female Press Agent Back into History', *Journal of American Drama and Theatre*, vol. 20, no. 2 (Spring 2008).

51 Larry McMurty, *The Colonel and Little Missie: Buffalo Bill, Annie Oakley, and the Beginnings of Superstardom in America* (Simon & Schuster, 2006).

52 Alva Johnston, 'The Ghosting Business', *New Yorker* (23 November 1935).

53 Kal Wagenheim, *Babe Ruth: His Life and Legend* (Open Road, 2014).

54 Christy Walsh, *Adios to Ghosts* (Zinskith, 1937).

55 I ran out of space in this chapter, but, for a fascinating history of how movie agents came to exist in the 1920s, see Tom Kemper, *Hidden Talent: The Emergence of Hollywood Agents* (University of California Press, 2010).

56 Jane Leavy, *The Big Fella: Babe Ruth and the World He Created* (Harper, 2018).

57 Wagenheim, *Babe Ruth: His Life and Legend*.

58 Simon Rae, *W. G. Grace: A Life* (Faber, 1998).

59 Tomlinson, *Amazing Grace*.

60 Ibid.

61 For a general overview of the themes here, see Barry King, *Taking Fame to Market: On the Pre-History and Post-History of Hollywood Stardom* (Palgrave Macmillan, 2015).

62 Varsha Jain and Subhadip Roy, 'Understanding Meaning Transfer in Celebrity Endorsements: A Qualitative Exploration', *Qualitative Market Research: An International Journal*, vol. 19, no. 3 (June 2016).

63 Daniel O'Quinn, *The Cambridge Companion to British Theatre, 1730-1830* (Cambridge University Press, 2007).

64 Nicola Vinovrs˘ki, 'Casanova's Celebrity: A Case Study of Well-Knownness in 18th-Century Europe', PhD thesis (University of Queensland, 2015).

65 Louis J. Budd, 'Mark Twain as an American Icon', in Forrest G.

Robinson (ed.), *The Cambridge Companion to Mark Twain* (Cambridge University Press, 2006).

66 Ruth Cowen, *Relish: The Extraordinary Life of Alexis Soyer, Victorian Celebrity Chef* (Weidenfeld & Nicolson, 2007).

67 Dominic G. Morais, 'Branding Iron: Eugen Sandow's "Modern" Marketing Strategies, 1887-1925', *Journal of Sport History*, vol. 40, no. 2 (Summer 2013).

68 P. T. Barnum, *Barnum's Own Story: The Autobiography of P. T. Barnum* (Dover, reissued 2017).

69 Gottlieb, *Sarah: The Life of Sarah Bernhardt*.

70 Golden, *Anna Held and the Birth of Ziegfeld's Broadway*.

71 Paul Fryer (ed.), *Women in the Arts in the Belle Epoque: Essays on Influential Artists, Writers and Performers* (MacFarland, 2012).

72 Barry Anthony, *The King's Jester: The Life of Dan Leno, Victorian Comic Genius* (IB Tauris, 2010).

73 Barry Paris, *Louise Brooks: A Biography* (University of Minnesota Press, 1990).

74 Karen Leick, *Gertrude Stein and the Making of an American Celebrity* (Routledge, 2009).

75 Gioia Diliberto, *Debutante: The Story of Brenda Frazier* (Alfred A. Knopf, 1987).

76 Carol Dyhouse, *Glamour: Women, History, Feminism* (Zed, 2011).

77 'Every Woman Should Glamour for Attention', *Film Review Annual* (MacDonald and Co., 1946).

78 McLean (ed.), *Glamour in a Golden Age*.

8: The Fandom Menace?

1 See the following: Karen Leick, *Gertrude Stein and the Making of an American Celebrity* (Routledge, 2009); Gertrude Stein, *The Autobiography of Alice B. Toklas* (The Bodley Head, 1933); Gertrude Stein, *Everybody's Autobiography* (Random House, 1937); Bryce Conrad, 'Gertrude Stein in the American Marketplace', *Journal of Modern Literature*, vol. 19, no. 2 (Autumn 1995); Linda Wagner-Martin, *'Favored Strangers': Gertrude Stein and Her Family* (Rutgers University Press, 1995); Kirk Curnutt, 'Inside and Outside: Gertrude Stein on Identity, Celebrity, and Authenticity,' *Journal of Modern Literature*, vol. 23, no. 2 (Winter 1999-2000); Donald Gallup (ed.), *The Flowers of Friendship: Letters Written to Gertrude Stein* (Alfred A. Knopf, 1953).

2 Stein, *Everybody's Autobiography*.

3 Chris Rojek, *Celebrity* (Reaktion, 2004).

4 Jayson L. Dibble, Tilo Hartmann, and Sarah F. Rosaen, 'Parasocial Interaction and Parasocial Relationship: Conceptual Clarification and a Critical Assessment of Measures', *Human Communication Research*, vol. 42, issue 1 (January 2016).

5 Murray Milner Jr, 'Is Celebrity a New Kind of Status System?' (in *Symposium: Celebrity in America Today*), *Society*, vol. 47, issue 5 (September 2010).

6 Emile Durkheim, *The Elementary Forms of Religious Life* (1912).

7 Rojek, *Celebrity*.

8 For a more eloquent challenge to celebrity as a religious concept, see Nathalie Heinrich's article, 'Limits of Religious Analogy: The Example of Celebrity', in *Social Sciences* 3(1), 2014.

9 S. V. Shepherd, R. O. Deaner, and M. L. Platt, 'Social Status Gates Social Attention in Rhesus Macaques', *Current Biology*, vol. 16, no. 4 (2006).

10 Robin Dunbar, *Grooming, Gossip and the Evolution of Language* (Harvard University Press, 1996).

11 Joseph Roach, 'Public Intimacy: The Prior History of "It"', in Mary Luckhurst and Jane Moody (eds.), *Theatre and Celebrity in Britain, 1660–2000* (Palgrave Macmillan, 2005).

12 Jeffrey Kahan, *Bettymania and the Birth of Celebrity Culture* (Lehigh University Press, 2010).

13 Anna Harwell Celenza, *Hans Christian Andersen and Music: The Nightingale Revealed* (Routledge, 2017).

14 See Oliver Hilmes, *Franz Liszt: Musician, Celebrity, Superstar*, trans. Stewart Spencer (Yale University Press, 2016); and also Alan Walker, *Franz Liszt: The Virtuoso Years, 1811–1847* (Cornell University Press, 1983).

15 G. W. Putnam, 'Four Months with Charles Dickens', *The Atlantic* (October 1870).

16 A. H. Saxon, *P. T. Barnum: The Legend and the Man* (Columbia University Press, 1989).

17 Mary Warner Blanchard, *Oscar Wilde's America: Counterculture in the Gilded Age* (Yale University Press, 1998); and Joseph Bristow (ed.), *Oscar Wilde and Modern Culture* (Ohio University Press, 2009).

18 Ruth Penfold-Mounce, *Death, the Dead and Popular Culture* (Emerald Publishing, 2018).

19 Kelly R. Brown, *Florence Lawrence, the Biograph Girl: America's First Movie Star* (McFarland, 2007).

20 Allan R. Ellenberger, *The Valentino Mystique: The Death and Afterlife of the Silent Film Idol* (McFarland & Co., 2005).

21 Anna Steese Richardson, '"Filmitis": the Modern Malady - Its Symptoms and Its Cure', *McClure's Magazine* (January 1916).

22 A quote from *Variety* magazine's 1926 obituary, referenced in Elizabeth Guider, 'Showbiz Swooned over Valentino's Demise', *Variety*, vol. 400, issue 5 (19-25 September 2005).

23 Anne-Helen Peterson, *Scandals of Classic Hollywood: Sex, Deviance, and Drama from the Golden Age of American Cinema* (Plume, 2014).

24 Pliny, *Natural History*, 7.186.

25 Frank Furedi, 'The Media's First Moral Panic', *History Today*, vol. 65, issue 11 (November 2015).

26 Samantha Barbas, 'Movie Crazy: Stars, Fans, and the Cult of Celebrity, 1910-1950', PhD thesis (University of California, Berkeley, 2000).

27 Peter Townsend, *Pearl Harbor Jazz: Changes in Popular Music in the Early 1940s* (University of Mississippi Press, 2009).

28 Robert C. Toll, *The Entertainment Machine: American Show Business in the Twentieth Century* (Oxford University Press, 1982).

29 'The Writings of Saadathasan Manto', *Journal of South Asian Literature*, vol. 20, no. 2 (Summer/Fall 1985).

30 Chris Richards, 'Beatlemaniacs, Beliebers, Directioners - Why Do They Scream?', *Washington Post* (26 July 2014).

31 David Shulman, 'On the Early Use of Fan in Baseball', *American Speech*, vol. 71, no. 3 (Autumn 1996).

32 Thomas M. Kavanagh, *Enlightened Pleasures: Eighteenth-Century France and the New Epicureanism* (Yale University Press, 2010).

33 Alfred Owen Aldridge, *Voltaire and the Century of Light* (Princeton University Press, 2015).

34 Michael Fontaine and Adele C. Scafuro (eds.), *The Oxford Handbook of Greek and Roman Comedy* (Oxford University Press, 2014).

35 'The Claque', *Encyclopaedia Britannica Online* 1998.

36 'Wild Applause, Secretly Choreographed', *New York Times* (4 August 2013).

37 Cheryl Wanko, 'Patron or Patronised?: "Fans" and the Eighteenth-Century English Stage', in Tom Mole (ed.), *Romanticism and Celebrity Culture, 1750-1850* (Cambridge University Press, 2009).

38 Berta Joncus, '"In Wit Superior, as in Fighting": Kitty Clive and the Conquest of a Rival Queen', *Huntington Library Quarterly*, vol. 74, no. 1 (March 2011).

39 Barbas, 'Movie Crazy'.

40 Ibid.

41 See Christine Becker, 'Clark Gable: The King of Hollywood', in Adrienne L. McLean (ed.), *Glamour in a Golden Age: Movie Stars of the 1930s* (Rutgers University Press, 2010).

42 Anthony Slide, *Inside the Hollywood Fan Magazine: A History of Star Makers, Fabricators, and Gossip Mongers* (University of Mississippi Press, 2010).

43 Mary Desjardins, '"Fan Magazine Trouble": The AMPP, Studio Publicity Directors, and the Hollywood Press, 1945-1952', *Film History*, vol. 26, no. 3 (2014).

44 Ibid.

45 For more on this, see Joshua Gamson's classic book *Claims to Fame: Celebrity in Contemporary America* (University of California Press, Berkeley, 1994).

46 Robert Darnton, 'Readers Respond to Rousseau: The Fabrication of Romantic Sensitivity', in *The Great Cat Massacre and Other Episodes in French Cultural History* (Viking, 1984).

47 Quoted in Antoine Lilti, *The Invention of Celebrity: 1750-1850*, trans. Lynn Jeffress (Polity, 2017).

48 Corin Throsby, 'Flirting With Fame: Byron's Anonymous Female Fans', *Byron Journal*, vol. 32, issue 2 (2004).

49 Ghislaine McDayter, *Byromania and the Birth of Celebrity Culture* (State University of New York Press, 2009).

50 Henry Jenkins, *Textual Poachers: Television Fans & Participatory Culture* (Routledge, 1992).

51 Sharon Marcus, *The Drama of Celebrity* (Princeton University Press, 2019).

52 Corin Throsby, 'Byron, Commonplacing and Early Fan Culture', in Mole (ed.), *Romanticism and Celebrity Culture*.

53 Peter Cochran, *The Burning of Byron's Memoirs: New and Unpublished Essays and Papers* (Cambridge Scholars, 2014).

54 Claire Harman, *Charlotte Brontë: A Life* (Penguin Books, 2015).

55 Nicola J. Watson, *The Literary Tourist* (Palgrave Macmillan, 2006).

56 *Lippincott's Magazine of Popular Literature and Science*, vol. 12, no. 32 (November 1873).

57 *Harper's New Monthly Magazine*, vol. 40 (1870).

58 For more on Tennyson and his famous friends, I recommend Charlotte Boyce, Paraic Finnerty and Anne-Marie Millim, *Victorian Celebrity Culture and Tennyson's Circle* (Palgrave Macmillan, 2013).

59 Mark Bostridge, *Florence Nightingale: The Woman and Her Legend* (Penguin Books, 2008).

60 'Celebrity: Its Pains and Penalties', *Sixpenny Magazine*, vol. 3, no. 11 (May 1862).

61 David Haven Blake, 'When Readers Become Fans: Nineteenth-Century American Poetry as a Fan Activity', *American Studies*, vol. 52, no. 1 (2012).

62 The quotation is from Longfellow's son, Ernest.

63 Timothy Spurgin, '"Notoriety Is the Thing": Modern Celebrity and Early Dickens', *Dickens Studies Annual*, vol. 45 (2014).

64 Quoted by Charles Burney, *London Magazine*, vol. xl (1770).

65 James Boaden, *Memoirs of Mrs. Siddons: Interspersed with Anecdotes of Authors and Actors* (1826).

66 *Memoirs of the Late Mrs. Robinson*, vol. II (R. Phillips, 1801).

67 Cléo de Mérode, *Le Ballet de ma vie* [The Ballet of My Life] (Editions Pierre Horay, 1955).

68 Michael Newbury, 'Eaten Alive: Slavery and Celebrity in Antebellum America', *ELH*, vol. 61, no. 1 (Spring 1994).

69 Gioia Diliberto, *Debutante: The Story of Brenda Frazier* (Alfred A. Knopf, 1987).

70 Barbas, *Movie Crazy*.

71 Ibid.

72 Quoted in Jib Fowles, *Starstruck: Celebrity Performers and the American Public* (Smithsonian, 1992).

73 Ruth Scobie, an academic blog, 'George Barnet, Miss Kelly, and Celebrity Obsession' (25 September 2014), https://oxfordcelebrity network.wordpress.com/2014/09/25/george-barnet-miss-kelly-and-celebrity-obsession/.

74 Michael D. Garval, *Cléo de Mérode and the Rise of Modern Celebrity Culture* (Ashgate, 2012).

75 Holly Gale Millette, '"Mad about the Blonde": Lydia Thompson's Transatlantic Celebrity and Fandom', *Comparative American Studies: An International Journal*, vol. 14, no. 1 (2016).

76 For more on these stories, see: John F. Kasson, *The Little Girl Who Fought the Great Depression: Shirley Temple and 1930s America* (W. W. Norton & Company, 2014); and Kathryn Fuller-Seeley, 'Shirley Temple: Making Dreams Come True', in Adrienne L. McLean (ed.), *Glamour in a Golden Age: Movie Stars of the 1930s* (Rutgers University Press, 2010).

77 Charles A. Ponce de Leon, 'The Man Nobody Knows: Charles A. Lindbergh and the Culture of Celebrity', *Prospects: An Annual of American Cultural Studies*, vol. 21 (October 1996).

Epilogue: Famous for Fifteen Minutes

1 Mary Harris, 'A Media Post-Mortem on the 2016 Presidential Election', *Media Quant* (14 November 2016), http://www.mediaquant.net/2016/11/a-media-post-mortem-on-the-2016-presidential-election/.

2 Daniel Boorstin, *The Image: A Guide to Pseudo-Events in America* ([1962] Atheneum, reissued 1980).

3 This quote can be found in George Rickey, *Constructivism: Origins and Evolution* (G. Brazillier, 1967).

4 Alan Levy, *The Culture Vultures: or, Whatever Became of the Emperor's New Clothes?* (Putham, 1968).

5 *Andy Warhol's Exposures, Photographs by Andy Warhol,* Text by Andy Warhol with Bob Colacello, Section: Studio 54, Page 48, Grosset & Dunlap: A Filmways Company, New York. (Verified on paper), 1979

6 Jonathan Swift, *The Works of the Rev. Jonathan Swift*, vol. 5, in *Tatler*, no. 67 (1709).

7 Robert C. Toll, *The Entertainment Machine: American Show Business in the Twentieth Century* (Oxford University Press, 1982).

8 I recommend the 2018 feature-length documentary *The American Meme* as an eye-opening primer on all this.

9 Taylor Lorenz, 'Rising Instagram Stars Are Posting Fake Sponsored Content: "It's Street Cred - The More Sponsors You Have, The More Credibility You Have"', *The Atlantic* (18 December 2018).

10 Alice Marwick defines it as 'a state of being famous to a niche group of people'; see A. E. Marwick, *Status Update: Celebrity, Publicity, & Branding in the Social Media Age* (Yale University Press, 2013).

11 Theresa Senft, *Camgirls: Celebrity & Community in the Age of Social Networks* (Peter Lang, 2008).

Index